Contact with Extraterrestrial Intelligence and Human Law

Studies in International Criminal Law

VOLUME 5

The titles published in this series are listed at *brill.com/sicl*

Contact with Extraterrestrial Intelligence and Human Law

The Applicability of Rules of War and Human Rights

By

Michael Bohlander

BRILL | NIJHOFF

LEIDEN | BOSTON

Cover illustration: Untitled watercolour, 2011, Edward Matwijkiw (1937–2012), reproduced with kind permission of the family.

Library of Congress Cataloging-in-Publication Data

Names: Bohlander, Michael, editor.
Title: Contact with extraterrestrial intelligence and human law : the applicability of rules of war and human rights / by Michael Bohlander.
Description: Leiden ; Boston : Brill | Nijhoff, 2023. | Series: Studies in international criminal law, 2666-903X ; vol. 5 | Includes bibliographical references and index. | Summary: "It is statistically unlikely that humans are the only intelligent species in the universe. Nothing about the others will be known until contact is made beyond a radio signal from space that merely tells us they existed when it was sent. That contact may occur tomorrow, in a hundred years, or never. If it does it will be a high-risk scenario for humanity. It may be peaceful or hostile. Relying on alien altruism and benign intentions is wishful thinking. We need to begin identifying as a planetary species, and develop a global consensus on how to respond in either scenario"– Provided by publisher.
Identifiers: LCCN 2023024078 (print) | LCCN 2023024079 (ebook) | ISBN 9789004677692 (hardback) | ISBN 9789004677708 (ebook)
Subjects: LCSH: Space law. | Search for Extraterrestrial Intelligence (Study group : U.S.) | Life on other planets. | Extraterrestrial beings. | Human-alien encounters. | Interstellar communication. | Space warfare. | War (International law) | International law and human rights.
Classification: LCC KZD1145 .C66 2023 (print) | LCC KZD1145 (ebook) | DDC 341.4/7–dc23/eng/20230601
LC record available at https://lccn.loc.gov/2023024078
LC ebook record available at https://lccn.loc.gov/2023024079

Typeface for the Latin, Greek, and Cyrillic scripts: "Brill". See and download: brill.com/brill-typeface.

ISSN 2666-903X
ISBN 978-90-04-67769-2 (hardback)
ISBN 978-90-04-67770-8 (e-book)

This book is printed on acid-free paper and produced in a sustainable manner.

For Laura

Children are a gift from God

Psalm 127:3

Contents

Foreword XI
Preface XIII
List of Figures XV
Abbreviations XVI

1 **Introduction** 1
1 An Initial Caveat: the UFO/UAP Debate – the Elephant in the Room 1
2 Structure of the Book 8

2 **The Scientific SETI Environment** 13
1 Introduction 13
1.1 *The Drake Equation and the Fermi Paradox* 15
1.1.1 Drake Equation 16
1.1.2 Fermi Paradox 18
2 Anthropocentrism and -morphism 21
3 SETI Approaches and the Nature of Contact 25
4 Astrobiology 34

3 **Social Science Aspects of SETI** 37
1 Gauging the Risk and Impact of First Contact on Global Society 37
1.1 *The Rio and San Marino Scales* 39
1.2 *IAASETI Declarations of Principles* 41
1.3 *Excursion: IAASETI and Its Attitude to Research into UAP* 43
1.4 *The DISC Quotient – Linking Impact and Linguistics* 45
2 Exolinguistics 45
3 Exosociology, Exophilosophy and Exotheology 49
4 The Metalaw Debate – Premature Speculation and Proper Use of Legal Considerations 52
5 Conclusion 66

4 **Science Fiction and (First) Contact Scenarios** 67
1 Science Fiction Literature 67
2 Types of First Contact 72
2.1 *The Hercules Text* 72
2.2 The *Rama* Cycle – *Rama I and II* 72
2.3 The *Tripods* Tetralogy and the *Forge of God* 76
2.3.1 *The Tripods* 77

2.3.2 *The Forge of God* 80
2.4 *The Mote in God's Eye* 82
2.5 The *Three-Body Problem* as an Example of the Risk Inherent in METI 85
3 Interspecies Comprehension and Communication 89
3.1 *Rama III* and *IV* 90
3.2 *Semiosis* 92
3.3 *Children of Time* and *Children of Ruin* 94
4 Interspecies Armed Conflict 96
4.1 *Ender's Game* 96
4.2 *The Forever War, Starship Troopers, Old Man's War Trilogy,* and *Anvil of Stars* 98
5 Conclusion 105

5 Hostile Contact and Current International and Domestic Law 107
1 Introduction 107
2 Liability of Humans 110
2.1 *International Criminal Law* 110
2.1.1 Overview of Core Crimes 112
2.1.2 Individual Problems 116
2.2 *Domestic Law* 133
3 Liability of ETI 134
3.1 *Jurisdiction* 134
3.2 Nullum Crimen *Principle* 136
4 Conclusion 136

6 Preparing for Hostile Contact 139
1 Introduction 139
2 Weapons Technology 144
3 Strategy and Tactics 147
3.1 *Weapons Development and Deep Space Strategy* 148
3.2 *The Strategic Parameters of Deep Space Warfare* 150
3.2.1 Distances, Speeds, and Celestial Mechanics 151
3.2.2 Psychological Aspects 156
4 Conclusion: an End to the Idea of a Peaceful Use of Outer Space? 158

7 Legal Prolegomena of Peaceful Relationships with ETI 161
1 Introduction 161
2 Joining the "Galactic Club" – a Future Theory of Humans' Rights Protection in Interstellar Civilisation Networks? 163

2.1 *Overview of Possible Factors Affecting Human Rights Guarantees* 170
2.1.1 Network Regulation Density 170
2.1.2 Rights Hierarchies and Enforcement Mechanisms 171
2.2 *Individual Rights* 174
2.2.1 Preamble 176
2.2.2 Recognition as a Person before the Law 177
2.2.3 Self-determination, Political Activity 178
2.2.4 Equality and Minority Rights 179
2.2.5 Right to Life, Ban on Cruel and Degrading Treatment, Torture and Slavery 180
2.2.6 Due Process Rights, Right to Liberty 181
2.2.7 Freedom of Movement 182
2.2.8 Privacy, Freedom of Religion and Expression, Assembly and Association 182
2.2.9 Family and Personal Status; Child Rights 184
2.2.10 Restrictions on Exercise of Rights 184
3 Conclusion 185

8 Conclusion and Outlook 188

Epilogue 192

Annexes 197
Bibliography 209
Index 241

Foreword

> We shall not cease from exploration, and the end of all our exploring will be to arrive where we started and know the place for the first time.
>
> T. S. ELIOT

The search for extra-terrestrial (ET) life is probably one of the most multidisciplinary endeavours humankind has ever undertaken. Finding any evidence of alien life will be one of the most significant discoveries we will ever make, and we can only speculate on the profound impact contact with an intelligent ET civilisation will have on us, knowing that we are not alone in the Universe.

If this search has taught us anything over recent decades, it is that we must first look at ourselves to understand what makes us human, so that we can contemplate intelligent life on (and from) other worlds and how we should conduct ourselves in a contact situation. Are we to approach the very thing we are so keen to discover, potentially with fear, mistrust or even hostility, without considering plans for our actions? Indeed, we have a duty to ourselves and our planet to ensure our security. Examining our own history, with its many first encounters, conflicts, diplomatic meetings and negotiated solutions, may offer us the knowledge and guidance necessary for making such plans.

Admittedly, ET life may stretch or even go beyond our powers of imagination, and the behavioural conventions of another civilisation may well be at odds with our own, so we must keep an open mind about what might be out there. We are reaching out into the unknown: our unknowns may be known or unknown, but we need to start somewhere. Furthermore, our technology for searching is only just beginning to allow us to appreciate the expanse of our Universe and the wonders that potentially lie out there: the first discovery of an exoplanet was, in fact, made only 30 years ago. The existence of Homo Sapiens on this planet has been a mere blink in time's cosmic 'eye' and our journey of discovery has only just begun. We do not know where it will take us or when it will answer our questions. Nevertheless, for many of us it is a journey we are compelled to undertake.

Imagine, if you will, that we discover the existence of another intelligent lifeform on another planet, around a not-too-distant star in our galaxy. There are, of course, many other possible scenarios, from single-cell organisms in our own solar system to advanced life thousands of light years away or further.

What will we do? What can we do? Should we compromise Humanity's (often hard-fought-for and fragile) moral compass, so that we can join the Galactic Club? What research has been, or is being, undertaken to prepare us for such an event?

Through the lens of contact with ET (or evidence thereof), Prof. Michael Bohlander expertly takes us through examples of our current scientific thinking, our methodologies for dealing with such an event, and our imaginative speculations over what might ensue. He explores some of the key research areas we have thus far investigated, the potential contribution of science fiction – how often have elements depicted in this genre (or what we would have once considered magic) become science fact – and the protocols and legal apparatus we already have in place that may prove useful.

It would indeed be an awful waste of space if we were the only intelligent lifeforms in the Universe. It would also be an awful waste of our abilities of enquiry and communication if we did not prepare for the event that we are so driven towards and hopeful for. It is, therefore, important that we look at where we are and where we should be, and understand how we can bridge the gap between these two points. This book takes us through such a thought-provoking journey. Buckle up.

Dr John Elliott
Chair, UK SETI Research Network
Member, IAA SETI Permanent Committee

Preface

I confess that I like Science Fiction – experience shows that many researchers engaged in the search for extraterrestrial intelligence (SETI) have found inspiration in its challenge of what often passes for intellectual orthodoxy, not unlike Paul Feyerabend's credo "*Against Method*". The idea for this book began when I was reading the second volume of Liu Cixin's *Three-Body-Problem* trilogy, *The Dark Forest*. Until then, SETI was something that had always casually interested me as something that I as a non-scientist could never really be part of. However, together with books such as Orson Scott Card's *Ender's Game*, Liu Cixin's work raised the question of how Earth would and should defend itself, if it even could, in the face of a hostile encounter with an alien civilisation. Would we extend them the same minimum civility as the interhuman laws of war dictate – at least on paper? Or would we reach for the ultimate indiscriminate weapon in our arsenal as a first choice to ensure the free survival of the human species? What would this in turn mean for our own understanding of humanitarian law? This aggressive scenario was then extended to encompass problems arising from a peaceful encounter – namely, what if the terms and conditions for joining an interstellar network of civilisations were of a nature that they would violate fundamental ethical and legal values which humans had fought for over centuries? What would we be willing to trade? These questions are obviously on the face of it highly speculative, yet at the very latest since the now openly declared official global interest in the UFO/UAP phenomenon since the 2020s, a topic previously – like SETI as a whole – shunned by most academics for fear of reputational and career damage, establishing actual contact may no longer be the domain of astronomers, and the above questions may become relevant sooner than imagined. If any of these phenomena were indeed shown not to be of this Earth, or at least not manmade, we would seriously have to reassess whether we still are the dominant species on this planet.

SETI was and still is a learning curve for me as a lawyer and this book is partly meant to aid other lawyers in understanding its basics, but also to help scientists comprehend that what they do can have legal ramifications beyond the relatively simple matter of regulating signal detection protocols. On my journey I have been supported by eminent experts in the field, first and foremost by Dr John Elliott, longstanding member of the IAASETI Permanent Committee and Chair of the UK SETI Research Network. He was also kind enough to review an earlier version of this book and to grace it with a foreword. Among the many others who have lent their assistance or engaged in joint endeavours, I wish to mention (in alphabetical order) Dr Andreas Anton – especially for reading the full manuscript and writing the epilogue –, Dr Ulrike Bohlmann, Professor Kathryn Denning, Dr Martin Dominik, Daniel Gerritzen – for reading the entire manuscript and providing comments – and Professor Hakan Kayal. The usual disclaimer applies. I am grateful to Mr Nickolas Tan (Durham LLB Class of 2023) for his support in preparing the manuscript. Thanks are also due to Durham Law School for its generous research leave policy that allowed me to draft most of the manuscript while on leave from teaching and administrative duties.

Chapters 3 and 7 contain slightly modified versions of material that was previously published in article form as "Metalaw – What is it good for?" in 188 *Acta Astronautica* (2021) 400–404, and "Joining the 'Galactic Club': What Price Admission? – A hypothetical case study of the impact of human rights on a future accession of humanity to interstellar civilisation networks" in 132 *Futures* (2021) 102801, both reproduced with kind permission of Elsevier. I would like to thank Mr Leslie Tennen, member of the IAA SETI Permanent Committee, for arranging permission to use the IAASETI materials, and Dr Andrew Siemion, Director of the SETI Institute at Berkely, for permission to use the 2015 METI Statement.

All webpages cited were last accessed on 20 February 2023.

The book is dedicated to our daughter Laura.

Michael Bohlander
Durham, February 2023

Figures

1 Forms of contact, impact and response 9
2 NEAR Shoemaker | 433 Eros anomaly 33
3 Rio scale calculator categories – lowest impact factors at the bottom of each category 40
4 Orbital plane of the solar system 151

Abbreviations

AC	Appeals Chamber
AI	Artificial Intelligence
ASEAN	Association of Southeast Asian Nations
AU	Astronomical Unit
CAH	Crimes Against Humanity
CDF	Colonial Defense Forces
CETI	Communicating with Extraterrestrial Intelligence
CIA	Central Intelligence Agency
CU	Colonial Union
DISC	Decipherment Impact of a Signal's Content
DNA	Deoxyribonucleic Acid
ECHR	European Convention on Human Rights
ECREE	"Extraordinary claims require extraordinary evidence"
ECtHR	European Court of Human Rights
EoC	Elements of Crimes
ESA	European Space Agency
ET	Extraterrestrial
ETC	Extraterrestrial Civilisation
ETH	Extraterrestrial Hypothesis
ETI	Extraterrestrial Intelligence
EU	European Union
FTL	Faster-Than-Light
GG	*Grundgesetz* (Basic Law)
GPS	Global Positioning System
HRA	Human Rights Act 1998
IAA	International Academy of Astronautics
IAASETI	IAA SETI Permanent Committee
ICC	International Criminal Court
ICCPR	International Covenant on Civil and Political Rights
ICCS	Statute of the International Criminal Court
ICJ	International Court of Justice
ICL	International Criminal Law
ICTR	International Criminal Tribunal for Rwanda
ICTY	International Criminal Tribunal for the Former Yugoslavia
IDH	Interdimensional Hypothesis
IEO	Inner-Earth-Objects
IHL	International Humanitarian Law

ISS	International Space Station
LGBTQ	Lesbian, Gay, Bisexual, Transgender and Queer
LINCOS	Lingua Cosmica
LSST	Large Synoptic Survey Telescope
MAD	Mutually Assured Destruction
METI	Messaging to ETI
MILAMOS	Manual on International Law Applicable to Military Uses of Outer Space
NASA	National Aeronautics and Space Administration
NEO	Near-Earth-Objects
OST	Outer Space Treaty
POW	Prisoner of War
ROSCOSMOS	Russian State Space Corporation (*Государственная корпорация по космической деятельности*)
SETA	Search for Extraterrestrial Artefacts
SETI	Search for Extraterrestrial Intelligence
SF	Science Fiction
SPD	Space Policy Directive
TC	Trial Chamber
UAP	Unidentified Aerial/Anomalous Phenomenon
UDHR	Universal Declaration of Human Rights
UFO	Unidentified Flying Object
UK	United Kingdom
UN	United Nations
UNOOSA	United Nations Office for Outer Space Affairs
UNSC	United Nations Security Council
USS	United States Ship
USSF	United States Space Force
WW I	World War I
WW II	World War II
ZPO	*Zivilprozessordnung* (Code of Civil Procedure)

CHAPTER 1

Introduction

It is statistically rather unlikely that humans are the only intelligent and space-faring species in the known universe, yet we can know nothing about the species identity of other civilisations until and unless contact is made beyond a mere signal from afar that tells us nothing more than that and where they existed when it was sent. Their civilisation models, their culture, morals and customs are more likely to be (very) different to ours than not, if human diversity is anything to go by. We need to be prepared as best as possible as one of probably many cosmic species for the first encounter and be in a grounded position to represent, and if necessary – and possible – defend, our values and ethical parameters. For that, we need to acquire our own cosmic species consciousness and act accordingly. Relying on alien altruism and benign intentions is wishful thinking. That is the fundamental premise of this book.

We may, however, never discover any sign of another extraterrestrial civilisation due to the sheer interstellar distances and the problems of the Einsteinian lightspeed barrier to which indigenous human propulsion technology will in all likelihood not find a remedy anytime soon. We may do so tomorrow by receiving a signal from outer space, finding a non-human artefact in our solar system, or even an active spacecraft of some sort appearing in Earth orbit. We may already have done so, for example, with the famous "Wow! Signal" received in 1977.

1 An Initial Caveat: the UFO/UAP Debate – the Elephant in the Room

We may ourselves, however, have been discovered by extraterrestrial intelligences (ETI) who may already be infiltrating Earth's airspace and oceans as so-called Unidentified Aerial/Anomalous Phenomena, or UAP, many of which were previously called UFOs. This is a caveat that requires some careful explanation before we continue with the investigation that this book is actually about. If some are to be believed, we may have had a non-human presence on Earth for decades or centuries, possibly even millennia, and that presence may not have originated in outer space at all, if "outer space" is understood merely in a non-quantum sense: If there are indeed multiple parallel universes,[1] or

1 See Tom Siegfried, *The Number of the Heavens – A History of the Multiverse and the Quest to Understand the Cosmos* (Harvard University Press, Cambridge, 2019).

 | DOI:10.1163/9789004677708_002

anything from ten to 26 dimensions of spacetime as the different versions of string theory, for example, appear to postulate,[2] is it so outlandish to think that a highly advanced species may also have found a way of traversing whatever boundaries and obstacles may lie between them? For current human science and technology, there is not much of a difference between accepting that and believing in the anti-Einsteinian blasphemy of the feasibility of faster-than-light (FTL) travel. Others even wonder whether it is not a question of our definition of reality and our powers of perceiving said reality in the first place. Jacques Vallée expressed the following view in the context of the UFO phenomenon:

> As an alternative to the extraterrestrial hypothesis, I propose to regard the UFO phenomenon as a physical manifestation of a form of consciousness that is alien to humans but is able to co-exist with us on the earth. When the object we call a UFO is visible to us in the reality of everyday life, I think it constitutes both a physical entity with mass, inertia, volume and energy, and a window toward another mode of reality. [...] Purists will point out that this form of consciousness might very well be extraterrestrial. Indeed, if reality is no longer restricted to three axes of space and one axis of time, the Visitors could be from anywhere and any time. [...] We do not know how much of the event is generated by an external phenomenon and how much is supplied by the human mind. We should acknowledge this complexity.[3]

Whatever the real state of affairs will turn out to be, and there may possibly be multiple explanations for different or indeed the same phenomena after all, once contact with a non-human intelligence is established, confirmed beyond doubt and communicated to the world, that world of humanity will change irrevocably and existentially, and especially so if humanity is found to be inferior to, and at the mercy of, that intelligence, and again more so if that intelligence is unmasked as being hostile to humans. As Pröschold[4] has argued, there is a strong case to believe that the persistent aversion, for example, of the vast majority of scientists to engage in research about what used to be called

2 Joseph Polchinski. *String Theory Vol. 1: An Introduction to the Bosonic String* (CUP, New York, 1998); *id. String Theory Vol. 2: Superstring Theory and Beyond* (CUP, New York, 1998); Barton Zwiebach, *A First Course in String Theory* (CUP, Cambridge, 2009).

3 Jacques Vallée. 1990. *Confrontations – A Scientist's Search for Alien Contact* (Anomalist Books, San Antonio, 1990), pp. 145, 151.

4 Bernhard M. Pröschold, *Ausserirdische – Das grosse Tabu unseres Zeitalters*. 2nd ed. (Selbstverlag, 2013),p. 16.

UFOs and is now called UAPs has to do with a primal human fear of being powerless in the face of entities who for all practical intents and purposes will have appeared as gods, angels or demons to our ancestors, and whose powers we now, of course, regard through the lens of advanced science – yet the *de facto* position of helplessness may not have changed equally dramatically. A radio or optical signal detected by astronomers and traced to originate from a constellation tens of thousands of light years away from Earth is much less threatening than countenancing the idea of a powerful non-human intelligence closer to home – the assumption being that it is likely to be a message from the distant past of the civilisation that sent it and which may since have become extinct, and in any event that there will not be a chance of a two-way conversation in real time.

There is, however, no epistemological or methodological justification for this narrow approach to evidence. Carl Sagan's (in-)famous and flawed ECREE rule ("extraordinary claims require extraordinary evidence") for direct contact research has done a lot of lasting damage in this context. It has in effect restricted the concept of evidence to data that can be measured, recorded and ideally reproduced by instrumental observation assemblies. Past – and thus not repeatable – human narratives about contact are largely ignored as incredible, unreliable, or explained away. All that despite the fact that for hundreds of years judges all over the world have sent defendants to their deaths or to prison on the basis of mere witness evidence, sometimes – as often in cases of rape – possibly on the testimony of a single person.[5] Natural scientists in their vast majority obviously have not in any manner been exposed to, or trained in, the art of forensic decision-making, where it is human persuasion that leads to drastic decisions impacting on people's lives in serious ways. The unspoken hubris of many natural scientists about the superiority of their allegedly objective tools and methods over those of the social sciences is ultimately misplaced, because they also proceed from certain pre-conceived premises which they then seek – and often manage – to verify or falsify, yet what may seem to be scientific truth today may be consigned to the trial-and-error scrapheap of history tomorrow.[6] Human error is a factor in any intellectual discipline. Be

5 This point is also emphasised by Ross Coulthart, *In Plain Sight – An investigation into UFOs and impossible science* (Harper Collins, Sydney, 2021) p. 14.

6 For example, as far as the already mentioned string theory is concerned, its verification by instrumental observation – Heisenberg's uncertainty principle and observer effect even permitting – is still outstanding; currently it is no more than an admittedly highly sophisticated intellectual construct, which is, however, not accepted throughout the scientific community even as a viable theory. See for a brief explanation Dean

that as it may, it will be a rare natural scientist who would want to apply her strict scientific method to legal disputes when it is her word against another's – she will want to be *believed* and have somebody else make real-world decisions based on that belief, like the many people who provided testimony over the years about a contact experience, not all of which can simply be discarded as mistaken or fabricated.[7] However, engaging with such ideas as an academic in any discipline has been and still is seen by many as liable to wreck careers, something which Harvard Chief Astronomer Avi Loeb has explained – and complained about – at length in his book "*Extraterrestrial*", published in 2020,[8] in which he also put forward his view that the interstellar object called 'Oumuamua, which traversed our solar system in 2017 and displayed a trajectory and qualities not easily reconciled with a natural object such as an asteroid, may very well have been an alien artefact – which quickly exposed him to raised collegial eyebrows himself. While conventional methods of the search for ETI (SETI)[9] such as radio or optical astronomy have seemed to be making headway in recent years as far as acceptance in the scientific community is concerned, the line is still drawn by most when it comes to UAP/UFOs. The globally influential IAA SETI Permanent Committee (IAASETI),[10] for example, has so far declined to amend its Terms of Reference[11] to include research into UAP, even after an internal debate among members took place, triggered by an innocent email query by the author with the then Chair Claudio Maccone in 2021[12] about the historical reasons for the strict aversion to UAP research. That was admittedly before the 2022 Congressional hearing on UAP, yet some of the instances on which that hearing was based had been public record for some time, among them the well-documented and -analysed USS Nimitz incident of

---

Simonton. Heisenberg effect, in Neil J Salkind (ed.) *Encyclopedia of research design* (SAGE Publications, Thousand Oaks, 2010), pp. 564–567.

7 See on that debate Susan A Clancy, *Abducted: How People Come to Believe They Were Kidnapped by Aliens* (Harvard University Press, Cambridge, 2005); Andrea Pritchard et al. (eds.) *Alien Discussions: Proceedings of the Abduction Study Conference at MIT* (North Cambridge Press, Cambridge, 1994); C.D.B. Bryan, *Close Encounters of The Fourth Kind: Alien Abduction, UFOs, and the Conference at MIT* (Knopf, New York, 1995).

8 Avi Loeb, *Extraterrestrial: The First Sign of Intelligent Life Beyond Earth* (Houghton Mifflin Harcourt, Boston/New York, 2021).

9 See for an overview of the vast literature as of 2016 at Stéphane Dumas, *Catalogue of SETI Publications*, 2016, www.academia.edu/14895760/Catalogue_of_SETI_Publications.

10 IAA SETI Permanent Committee – https://iaaseti.org/en/.

11 "These terms of reference exclude any consideration of UFO phenomena". – https://iaaseti.org/en/terms-reference/. This was still the state of affairs on 20 February 2023, when the webpage was last accessed.

12 See on this in more detail Chapter 3, at 1.3.

2004.[13] In May 2022, it transpired that even NASA was now cooperating with the Pentagon's UAP research.[14] That might give the IAA – and others – pause to reconsider their stance.[15]

Nonetheless, the book addresses the issues around SETI based on the traditional – and so far as scientific evidence in the public domain is concerned still prevailing – assumption that contact has not yet been made and that the true nature of the reported UAP as extraterrestrial or not has not yet been fully verified. This book does not proceed from any other premise. Yet, it argues that serious research into UAP must be possible and that this field of enquiry cannot and must not be excluded from rigorous SETI scholarship. Its reflections about search methods, contact scenarios, communication problems, interstellar travel, defence strategy etc. as well as the ultimate overall question about how humanity should prepare naturally stand in an uneasy tension with the possibility that those UAP might turn out to be of extraterrestrial, or perhaps more generally non-human, origin any day. That tension remains, and it remains unresolved. It needs to be acknowledged and to be embraced until science can provide certainty or the archives of the world's militaries and governments are opened, should they already contain knowledge about the true nature of UAPs.

---

13 Robert Powell et al. *A Forensic Analysis of Navy Carrier Strike Group Eleven's Encounter with an Anomalous Aerial Vehicle,* Scientific Coalition for UAP Studies, www.explorescu.org/post/2004-uss-nimitz-strike-navy-group-incident-report, 2019.

14 See for an overview of the recent developments the partially declassified version of the Report by the Director of National Intelligence. 2021. (U) Preliminary Assessment Unidentified Aerial Phenomena, https://documents2.theblackvault.com/documents/odni/DEOM-2021-00006.pdf; for the US congressional hearing: https://youtu.be/aSDweUbGBow; for NASA Unidentified Aerial Phenomena Independent Study: https://science.nasa.gov/uap; for ROSKOSMOS: Andreas Müller, Auch Russlands Raumfahrt-Chef äußert sich über außerirdisches Leben und UFOs, 2021.

www.grenzwissenschaft-aktuell.de/russlands-raumfahrt-chef-rogozin-aeussert-sich-ueber-ausserirdisches-leben-und-ufos20220613/ (in German); for Canada: Natural Resources Ministry. Letter to MP Larry Maguire, 2022, www.larrymaguire.com/_files/ugd/ba2ab2_878aa8c5de7749bbb4196435c156271c.pdf; On the holdings of over 12,000 pages of related records in the George W. Bush Presidential Library, see Greenewald, John, Letter from George W. Bush Presidential Library. https://twitter.com/blackvaultcom/status/1534242020906045441/photo/1; on the holdings of the Obama equivalent see id., Letter from Barack Obama Presidential Library, 2022, https://twitter.com/blackvaultcom/status/1502019931382059016.

15 For a description and analysis of the UFO sightings in Germany and how they were treated over the decades until the 2020s, see Andreas Müller, *Deutschlands UFO-Akten – Über den politischen Umgang mit dem UFO-Phänomen in Deutschland* (Books on Demand, Norderstedt, 2021).

The "behaviour" and capabilities displayed by UAP according to some reports serve as an indication that whoever made them is in possession of scientific knowledge and technology far more advanced than those available to humanity at this time, at least as far as public knowledge is concerned. However, in the context of this book's aim, a particularly disquieting finding based on a number of reports about these UAPs or UFOs may be that there has – again at least as far as is publicly known or verifiable – never been an attempt by any UFO to communicate with any human craft or vessel or to react to human communication attempts. Instead, the reports might seem to support the assumption that they display at the very least what one could call in anthropomorphic terms an attitude of supreme indifference. Moreover, the reasons for their alleged presence and activities remain so far entirely unknown. The abduction reports, as far as they can be believed,[16] and in particular those about strange and often painful invasive procedures, or in some cases even alleged sexual acts, performed on abductees, raise the question – and with it cause for prudent reluctance as far as their trustworthiness is concerned – what reasonable motivation could be behind them.[17] In a few cases, UFOs' behaviour is reported to have endangered human aircraft and pilots, for example, due to near-collision incidents caused by the unexpectedly erratic flight manoeuvres and trajectories of some UAP. In some of the earlier serious UFO literature, there have been reports about seemingly reckless or even intentional harm being caused to humans and animals.[18] There have been accounts at least since WW I of instances when UFOs had allegedly been fired upon (or even shot down) by human aircraft, ground anti-aircraft fire, or naval ships, and which had in some cases fired back or reacted in other ways which disabled the human aircraft or vessel, again allegedly in some cases resulting in the injury,

16 Interestingly, as Jacques Vallée pointed out, these abduction stories were already a staple topic of early SF writing from 1880 to 1945, see Jacques Vallée, *Confrontations – A Scientist's Search for Alien Contact* (Anomalist Books, San Antonio/Carlottesville, 1990), p. 179. He referred to the research by Bertrand Méheust, *Science-Fiction et Soucoupes Volantes – Une réalité mytho-physique,* revised ed. (Terre de Brume, Rennes, 1978).

17 Surely an advanced intelligent species could simply use their equivalent of anaesthetics or non-invasive medical imaging equipment. What could they possibly still learn about the human physiology and anatomy that they do not know yet after all those previous cases of reported abductions – unless we really are, as Carl Sagan aptly put it, being "visited by a different extraterrestrial civilization every second Tuesday". – Carl Sagan, Cosmos: A Personal Voyage. PBS broadcast, 1980.

18 Jacques Vallée, *Confrontations – A Scientist's Search for Alien Contact* (Anomalist Books, San Antonio/Charlottesville, 1990) 220–230.

death, or even outright disappearance of humans involved.[19] There has, however, as far as can be seen, never been an incident reported when UFOs showed any sign of altruistic behaviour towards humans, unless one wanted to include the non-retaliation to attacks by humans.[20] Due to the pervasive impact of military and other governmental restrictions on access to information or its reporting – which in the USA can exclude even the President[21] from those who have a "need to know" – as well as the concerns about the reliability and degree of corroboration of individual encounter narratives even by trained military personnel, the evidence base is often contentious, to say the least.

Why is all this relevant, if the book does not take a definitive stand on UFOs? Because it means that if they are indeed at some stage found to be of non-human or extraterrestrial origin, humanity thus has so far no reason to believe that they would be invariably benign in an altruistic sense, or that any other ETI would be in the future. It could also mean that what little evidence there is so far would not seem to support the urban myth that any ETI capable of interstellar expansion will be so morally advanced that they will by definition be altruistic to other species. There certainly is so far no evidence of UFOs' adherence to a Prime Directive[22] akin to that of the Star Trek universe – quite the opposite. The state of affairs thus remains rather confusing, because as Jacques Vallée has rightly argued, "if the aliens were simply 'hostile' in the first-order sense of the word, they could have taken over our planet a long time ago".[23] Having addressed this particular elephant in the room, we now turn to an overview of the book's topics.

---

19 See Jacques Vallée, *supra* note 18, pp. 120 and 127. For a historical overview of allegedly full-scale hostile military encounters with alien craft since WW I, see the reports collected in Frank Joseph, *Military Encounters with Extraterrestrials – The Real War of the Worlds* (Bear & Company, Rochester, 2018).

20 See, for example, Leslie Kean, *UFOs – Generals, Pilots, and Government Officials go on the Record* (Three Rivers Press, New York, 2010). 82–98.

21 There is a need to be "read onto" so-called "Special Access Programs" (SAPs), some of which are so restricted that only a small number of people on a "Special Access Programs Oversight Committee" have access to the information about the programme: There are officially "unacknowledged" programmes where any democratic oversight worthy of the name is removed entirely, so-called "Waived Unacknowledged SAPs". – See Ross Coulthart, *In Plain Sight – An investigation into UFOs and impossible science* (Harper Collins, Sydney, 2021), pp. 112–113; 117; 150; 158–172; 266–271.

22 As Arkady and Boris Strugatsky had already shown in their 1964 novel *Hard to be a God*, even the benevolent application of a prime directive can lead to difficult questions of situational ethics. – Arkady Strugatsky and Boris Strugatsky, *Hard to be a God* (Gollancz, London, 2015), 37–38.

23 His research, however, still led him to the disconcerting observation in 1990 that while during early, "innocent" days, any negative effects from contact with aliens were considered

2 Structure of the Book

Leaving the as yet imponderable nature of UAP aside, any traditional treatment of SETI-related aspects is bound to face a large number of interlinking individual factors which have been summarised in Figure 1 – however, without any claim of being exhaustive.

This book cannot discuss all of them in equal detail. Some of the factors in particular require intricate scientific knowledge of physics, astronomy etc. which the author does not possess. To the extent that it was necessary to do so, some aspects of natural science have been addressed, supported by generous advice of colleagues who are experts in the fields, and further reading supplied for those wishing to delve into the matter more deeply. However, all factors ultimately fall into the three major categories of forms of contact, impact and response. It is possible to hypothesise about those and their major structural subdivisions even as a non-scientist, especially as the aim of the book is not to add to the scientific discussion. The author's experience of the SETI debate to date has shown that there is a lack of mutual understanding between what one might call the scientific and the normative disciplines. To give a blunt example, most academic lawyers (as a sub-species of social scientists) and certainly legal practitioners in general still do not understand the science of SETI and hence cannot understand why it should be necessary for law to engage with it. Vice-versa, most SETI scientists may have at best a marginal comprehension of the legal issues arising from SETI, and more to the point, from the after all intended endgame of contact being made, especially direct contact. This book endeavours to provide that baseline of mutual understanding of the SETI environment and the legal issues that will fall to be determined for the scenario of contact. It chooses to address the extremely speculative hypotheticals of hostile contact on the one hand and the accession to an interstellar network of civilisations, or "Galactic Club", on the other, as stress tests for fundamental human ethical and legal values in the areas of the law of armed conflict and as a corollary, international criminal law, as well as human rights law.

Chapter 2 deals with the fundamentals of the scientific SETI environment. After a general overview we will be considering staple items such as the Drake Equation and the Fermi Paradox, and look at the problems of anthropocentrism and -morphism and how they can impact on search premises and patterns, as well as SETI approaches and the nature of contact, and finally the

accidental, "[t]hese days of innocence and rationalisation are gone; the witnesses [...] were deliberately zapped by a superb, advanced technology that did not care whether its effects were lethal or not". *Supra* note 18, pp. 139, 229.

I. Forms of contact

1. Distant (outside solar system)

1.1. Signal detection
1.2. Forms of signals
1.2.1. Messages (directed/undirected)
1.2.2. Artefacts (see 2. below)
1.3. Means of decipherment
1.4. Signal verification
1.5. Information updates

2. Proximity (within solar system | non-Earth arrival)

2.1. Passing/stationary spacecraft/probe
2.1.1. Manned/unmanned/sentient machine
2.1.2. Communication possible/impossible
2.2. Derelict artefact (including structures)
2.2.1. With biological life forms
2.2.2. Without biological life forms

3. Earth Arrival

3.1. Covert
3.2. Overt
3.3. Type of arrival
3.3.1. Single small spacecraft (reconnaissance etc.)
3.3.2. Mothership
3.3.3. Fleet
3.3.4. Other means of transportation
3.3.5. Derelict (see 2.2.1 and 2.2.2)
3.3.5.1. Ancient derelict discovery
3.3.5.2. Current derelict arrival (crash, salvage etc.)
3.3. Biologicals or sentient machines
3.4. Landing/non-landing (orbit)

4. Type of contact

4.1. Communication/no communication
4.2. ETI attitude towards humans/Earth
4.2.1. Benign
4.2.2. Hostile
4.2.3. Indifferent
4.2.4. Unknown
4.3. Transient/permanent contact

II. Forms of impact

1. Immediate public response to dissemination

1.1. Panic
1.2. Welcoming
1.3. Hostile

2. Wider societal repercussions

2.1. Theology
2.2. Philosophy
2.3. Anthropology
2.4. Politics
2.5. Science exchange
2.6. Legal issues

3. Nature of impact

3.1. Mutually controlled by consensus
3.2. Unilaterally controlled by ETI -benign/hostile
3.2.1. Tutelage
3.2.2. Subjugation
3.2.3. Annihilation

III. Forms of response

1. Ex ante responses/risk assessment

1.1. SETI (passive/active)
1.2. Unified discovery protocols
1.3. Unified post-detection (PD) protocols
1.3.1. Regarding public dissemination
1.3.2. Regarding impact risk containment
1.3.3. Regarding coordination of response under 2
1.3.4. Legal issues (status of ETI, derelicts etc. in human law, PD jurisdiction [civilian/military] etc.)

2. Ex post responses (depending on I.1.4. and II.3.)

2.1. Reaction time
2.1.1. Communication attempts
2.1.2. Preparing welcome of ETI
2.1.2. Defence preparation
2.2. No reaction time
2.2.1. Cooperation
2.2.2. Acquiescence
2.2.3. Defence
2.3. Creating framework for future humanETI relations

FIGURE 1 Forms of contact, impact and response

general field of astrobiology. This should provide a sufficient grounding for readers who are new to the field of SETI. Those already well-versed in the SETI science may choose to skip that chapter.

Chapter 3 will address the social science aspects of SETI. As already alluded to above, there is a need for gauging the risk and impact of first contact on global society, according to the nature of the contact. In this context, we will study the so-called Rio and San Marino Scales which were modelled on earlier earthquake scales, the IAA SETI Declarations of Principles, and Baxter and Elliott's DISC quotient as a competitor model to the above scales which links the degree of impact to the linguistic question of the progress of signal decipherment. Related to the latter, we shall query what the field of exolinguistics can contribute to the decipherment effort and whether and how a message for which there will very likely be no equivalent to a Rosetta Stone can ever hope to be understood by humans. The risk management after a contact event will have to encompass not only possible technological disruption but also the wider societal ramifications, which is the subject, among others, of the disciplines of exosociology, exophilosophy and exotheology. In the confluence of law and philosophy in particular, we will study the concept of a cosmic metalaw and ask whether it is premature speculation and what the proper use of legal considerations should be at this time.

Chapter 4 will then take an in-depth look at the undisputed first source of motivation for many who have found a heart for SETI: Science Fiction. After an overview of the literature genre and its impact on SETI thinking, the chapter will first address literary examples around the types of first contact, followed by the major problem of how to achieve interspecies comprehension and communication. Finally, we arrive at one of the main themes of this book, interspecies armed conflict and the link to ways to achieve conflict avoidance.

Chapter 5 takes up the final topic from the previous chapter and interrogates in-depth the potential problems arising from hostile contact for the underlying principles of humanity's current inter-human international and domestic law through the lens of international and domestic criminal law, and whether and how it can be applied to an interspecies conflict. After an overview, we will first look at the liability of humans under international criminal law through a detailed examination of the critical elements of the four core crimes, i.e., genocide, crimes against humanity, war crimes and aggression, the latter at the example of the potential consequences of space exploration for – not necessarily sapient – species on other planets that humans might one day visit. A brief excursion to domestic law is followed by an examination of the potential liability of ETI, in particular by a look at whether Earth's courts would have jurisdiction over ETI and how the traditional *nullum crimen* or legality principle ("no crime without prior law") would function in this context.

Moving on from law to action, Chapter 6 will ask how we can or should prepare for hostile contact, what the current state of preparedness is, and what the future challenges are. Again, an overview will introduce the chapter topic, which will be further dissected through the lenses of current weapons technology, followed by a look at strategy and tactics, in particular issues surrounding the interface between weapons development and deep space strategy. The strategic parameters of deep space warfare, especially distances, speeds, and celestial mechanics we turn to next, and round off with a look at psychological factors and their relationship to operating in a deep space combat theatre.

Turning to the hope that there might be potential for conflict avoidance, Chapter 7 will address some legal prolegomena of how peaceful relationships with ETI might be reached and shaped, and take another look at the possibility of a concept such as the "Prime Directive" and other examples of whether the manner in which humans have more or less successfully attempted to avoid armed conflict, such as the United Nations, may be transposed to the interspecies environment. The chapter will take a particularly close look at the speculative accession to a "Galactic Club", through the analytical lens of current international human rights law as a global indicator of what our shared moral values are, and ask the question what humanity would be willing to trade in order to get access, for example, to technology which would end the problems of global food and energy scarcity or climate change. The chapter will, however, not deal with the equally vexing question of whether extraterrestrial intelligent life-forms should be given protection on Earth by an analogous application of human rights – that must remain for another time.[24] Suffice it to say at this point, that the argument in that respect might borrow heavily from the discussion about the equal application of the concept of crimes against humanity in Chapter 5.

Chapter 8 will provide a brief overall conclusion and outlook.

The book ends with an Annex of the most relevant documents cited in the discussion.

These ruminations can obviously only serve to provide highlights on the more fundamental questions they seek to elucidate. Most of these questions are still awaiting a definitive answer based on evidence which the majority of humans – and especially their political and military leaders – would be willing to accept as a sufficient basis for serious action, resulting in the allocation of

24 See also Chapter 7, note 70.

significant and sustained funding. The book's purpose, however, is nonetheless to instil the insight that humanity cannot afford to wait much longer before it has to address all eventualities around the conundrum of contact with an alien species in a pro-active manner. We all hope that if and when contact should happen, it will be peaceful and usher in a new era of humanity's journey on the path to take its place among its neighbours in the cosmos. Until then, the old Latin proverb applies: "*Si vis pacem, para bellum*".

CHAPTER 2

The Scientific SETI Environment

1 Introduction

As mentioned in the introduction, there is no denying that to engage with SETI research as an academic of any discipline, probably even among astronomers, still entails the risk of being assigned to the lunatic fringe[1] and thrown together in the same pot with UFOlogists and "alien hunters". Social science has made some advances into the field in recent years but in the general public perception, the "hard" SETI research is still mostly connected with the various disciplines of natural science. It stands to reason that the vast majority of lawyers and legal academics will have only a fleeting familiarity with the topic at best, and if so then more likely than not largely through SF literature and films.

Space law,[2] as a sub-category of public – and increasingly also private or commercial – international law, has become a serious and respected mainstream discipline ever since humanity properly entered the Space Age in the 1950s.[3] However, it only deals with a number of aspects of human activity in space; it is not – so far at least – concerned with principles such as the famous "Prime Directive" of the Star Trek franchise etc., i.e., not with interspecies relations in the sense of a "cosmic metalaw" (on which see in more detail Chapter 3). It already contains some rules that might be brought to bear on scenarios of contact with alien life in the wider sense, for example, through the discovery of microorganisms on a different planet or moon and the resultant danger of contamination of the biosphere on that celestial body and on Earth

1 On this general point, see recently the critique by Adam Dowd, Strategic Ignorance and the Search for Extraterrestrial Intelligence: Critiquing the Discursive Segregation of UFOs from Scientific Inquiry, 16 *Astropolitics* (2018) 75–95.

2 For an overview, including national space laws, see UN Office for Outer Space Affairs – www.unoosa.org/oosa/en/ourwork/spacelaw/index.html.

3 However, already in 1948, famous SF author Olaf Stapledon gave an address to the British Interplanetary Society on the way humanity might adapt itself to space exploration and colonisation of other worlds, in which he imagined genetic modification of humans to suit the conditions on other planets, for example, higher gravity; see Olaf Stapledon, Interplanetary Man, 7 *Journal of the British Interplanetary Society,* (1948), 213–233. On a modern extension of some of these thoughts, see Daniel Deudney, *Dark skies: space expansionism, planetary geopolitics, and the ends of humanity* (OUP, Oxford, 2020) and the related book review by John W Traphagan, *Space Policy* (2021) 55.

 DOI:10.1163/9789004677708_003

by bringing back samples of those organisms. The latter problem area is dealt with under the heading of "planetary protection",[4] a concept different from that of "planetary defence",[5] i.e., the effort only of protecting *Earth* from the impact of comets, asteroids etc., commonly divided into Near-Earth-Objects (NEO)[6] or the so-called Inner Earth Objects (IEO), i. e. those existing within Earth's entire orbit around the sun. Yet, the rules are worded broadly enough to

4 On the issue of planetary protection, see for more detail Gerhard Kminek, Jean-Louis Fellous et al., The International Planetary Protection Handbook, An online-only supplement, *Space Research Today* (2019), www.sciencedirect.com/journal/space-research-today/vol/205/suppl/S; Michael Meltzer, *When biospheres collide: a history of NASA's planetary protection programs*, 2011 – www.nasa.gov/connect/ebooks/when_biospheres_collide_detail.html; Bergit Uhran et al., Updating Planetary Protection Considerations and Policies for Mars Sample Return, 49 *Space Policy* (2019) 101322; Monica Vidaurri et al., Absolute Prioritization of Planetary Protection, Safety, and Avoiding Imperialism in All Future Science Missions: A Policy Perspective, 51 *Space Policy* (2020) 101345; John D. Rummela and D. E (Betsy) Pugel, Planetary protection technologies for planetary science instruments, spacecraft, and missions: Report of the NASA Planetary Protection Technology Definition Team (PPTDT), 23 *Life Sciences in Space Research* 2019, 60–68.

5 See only the 2013 special issue of *Acta Astronautica* for an overview of the diverse topics discussed in the planetary defence debate: Ian Carnelli, Editorial, Planetary Defence Conference 2011, Bucharest, Romania, 90 *Acta Astronautica* (2013), 1–2; A.W. Harris et al., The European Union funded NEOShield project: A global approach to near-Earth object impact threat mitigation, *ibid.*, 80–84; Bong Wie, Hypervelocity nuclear interceptors for asteroid disruption, *ibid*, 146–155; Denis A. Usikov, Information and Communication Technologies (ICT) as keys to the enhancement of public awareness about potential earth impacts, *ibid.* 173–179; Megan Bruck Syal et al., Limits on the use of nuclear explosives for asteroid deflection, *ibid.*, 103–111; Brian Kaplinger et al., Nuclear fragmentation/dispersion modelling and simulation of hazardous near-Earth objects, *ibid.*, 156–164; Jan Thimo Grundmann et al., Probes to the inferior planets – A new dawn for NEO and IEO detection technology demonstration from heliocentric orbits interior to the earth's? *ibid.* 129–145; John P McVey and Nahum Melamed, Survey of potentially hazardous object threat negation campaign options, *ibid.*, 22–32; Ross Findlay and Olaf Eßmann, A space-based mission to characterize the IEO population, *ibid.*, 33–40; Detlef Koschny et al., Asteroid observations at the Optical Ground Station in 2010 – Lessons learnt, *ibid.,* 49–55; Cyrus Foster et al., Mission concepts and operations for asteroid mitigation, involving multiple gravity tractors, *ibid.*, 112–118; Patrick Michel, Physical properties of Near-Earth Objects that inform mitigation, *ibid.*, 6–13; Claudio Bombardelli et al., The ion beam shepherd: A new concept for asteroid deflection, *ibid.*, 98–102; Alison Gibbings et al., Experimental analysis of laser ablated plumes for asteroid deflection and exploitation, *ibid.*, 85–97; Donald K Yeomansand Alan B Chamberlin, Comparing the Earth impact flux from comets and near-Earth asteroids, *ibid.*, 3–5.

6 See the definition by UNOOSA: "A near-Earth object is an asteroid or comet which passes close to the Earth's orbit. In technical terms, a NEO is considered to have a trajectory which brings it within 1.3 astronomical units of the Sun and hence within 0.3 astronomical units, or approximately 45 million kilometres, of the Earth's orbit". – www.unoosa.org/oosa/en/ourwork/topics/neos/index.html. For a wider overview of UNOOSA documents on NEO see *ibid.*

be applied in theory to the discovery, for example, of an alien artefact or even to contact with ETI.

The intricacies of the rules of space law are known only to a rather close – albeit growing – community of specialists because the general perception still appears to be that their field of practical application is so narrow that it does not merit being included, for example, into even the optional modules of the average undergraduate law degree or even post-graduate master programme syllabi. Before we can deal with them, we must therefore set out the main aspects of the non-legal discussion around SETI, in other words, describe the facts and ideas which will inform any further debate around the legal impact of SETI. This chapter will – with the necessary brevity – introduce the main conceptual avenues of current scientific SETI studies[7] for the non-specialist but cannot cover the entire range and history of the highly diverse approaches that have developed since the initial period.[8]

1.1 *The Drake Equation and the Fermi Paradox*

We will begin by addressing the perennial fundamental questions of "Is anyone out there?"[9] and "Where is everybody?",[10] i.e., the

---

7 On issues of terminology, see Iván Almár, SETI terminology: Do we interpret SETI terms correctly? 68 Acta *Astronautica* (2011) 351–357.

8 For more detail see See Michael A.G. Michaud, C*ontact with Alien Civilizations – Our Hopes and Fears about Encountering Extraterrestrials* (Copernicus Books, New York, 2010 – hereafter: Michaud), pp. 25–53; Michael Schetsche and Andreas Anton, Die *Gesellschaft der Außerirdischen – Einführung in die Exosoziologie* (Springer, Wiesbaden, 2019 – hereafter: Schetsche/Anton), pp. 73–92; Florence Raulin Cerceau and Bénédicte Bilodeau, A comparison between the 19th century early proposals and the 20th–21st centuries realized projects intended to contact other planets, 78 *Acta Astronautica* (2012) 72–79; Michael Gross. Listen out for life, 25 *Current Biology* (2015) 1151–1153; John Billingham, SETI: The Nasa Years, in Douglas Vakoch (ed.), *Archaeology, anthropology, and interstellar communication* (NASA History Series, 2013), pp. 1–22, www.nasa.gov/connect/ebooks/archaeology_anthropology_and_interstellar_communication.html; Stephen J Garber, A Political History of NASA's SETI Program, *ibid.*, pp. 23–48; Asif A. Siddiqi,. *Beyond Earth – A Chronicle of Deep Space Exploration, 1958–2016*. 2nd ed. (NASA, Washington, 2018) www.nasa.gov/connect/ebooks/beyond_earth_detail.html; Kenneth I Kellermann, et al. Is Anyone Out There? in Kenneth I Kellermann, et al., *Open Skies – The National Radio Astronomy Observatory and Its Impact on US Radio Astronomy* (Springer, New York, 2020), pp. 229–260; Ronald D Ekeres et al., *SETI 2020: A Roadmap for the Search for Extraterrestrial Intelligence* (SETI PR, San Jose, 2002).

9 Frank Drake and Dava Sobel, *Is Anyone Out There? The Scientific Search for Extraterrestrial Intelligence* (Delacorte Press, New York, 1992).

10 See Stephen Webb, *If the Universe Is Teeming with Aliens ... WHERE IS EVERYBODY?: Seventy-Five Solutions to the Fermi Paradox and the Problem of Extraterrestrial Life*, 2nd ed., (Springer, New York, 2015).

tension[11] between the statistical predictions of the existence of a veritable multitude of extraterrestrial civilisations flowing from the Drake Equation, and the incongruent absence so far, of any evidence of the existence of even one of them, i.e., the so-called Fermi Paradox.[12]

1.1.1 Drake Equation

At the Green Bank Conference on Extraterrestrial Intelligent Life held on 1 and 2 November 1961, Frank Drake, one of the founding fathers of modern SETI research, presented his famous equation[13] "which would shape subsequent SETI investigations for the next half century. [It] estimated the number of communicative civilizations in the Galaxy by accounting for factors necessary for intelligent life to develop [such as] the number of stars with habitable planets [...], the fraction of those planets that develop life, and most important, but also most uncertain, the mean lifetime of a technical, communicative civilization":[14]

$$N = R_* f_p n_e f_l f_i f_c L$$

In this equation, the individual factors mean the following:

N = number of communicative civilizations in the Galaxy

R_* = mean rate of star formation over galactic history

f_p = fraction of stars with planetary systems

n_e = number of planets per planetary system with conditions ecologically suitable for the origin and evolution of life

f_l = fraction of suitable planets on which life originates and evolves to more complex forms

f_i = fraction of life-bearing planets with intelligence possessed of manipulative capabilities

11 For an attempt at a joint analysis of both see Nikos Prantzos, A joint analysis of the Drake equation and the Fermi paradox, 12 *International Journal of Astrobiology* (2013) 246–253.

12 See recently Carl L DeVito, On the Meaning of Fermi's paradox, 106 *Futures* (2019) 21–23; Milan M Ćirković, *The Great Silence: Science and Philosophy of Fermi's Paradox* (OUP, Oxford, 2018); Duncan H. Forgan, A numerical testbed for hypotheses of extraterrestrial life and intelligence, 8 *International Journal of Astrobiology* (2009) 121–131; Nikos Prantzos, *ibid.*

13 He looked back on the moment in Frank Drake, Reflections on the Equation, 12 *International Journal of Astrobiology* (2013) 173–176; see also Mark J Burchell, W(h)ither the Drake equation? 5 *International Journal of Astrobiology* (2006) 243–250.

14 Kenneth I Kellermann et al., *supra* note 8.

f_c = fraction of planets with intelligence that develops a technological phase during which there is the capability for and interest in interstellar communication

L = mean lifetime of a technological civilization.[15]

Now as then, the mathematical values of all individual factors to the Equation are ultimately speculative. While some argue that the recent and increasing discoveries of large numbers of exoplanets confirm that the values for the first six factors could at this time optimistically be estimated at anywhere between 0.1 to 1, the factor L remains in essence the most uncertain because apart from the human species' example, there are no data available as yet.[16] Even extrapolations from the findings of recent astronomical research can lead to wildly varying results, although the first three parameters may be narrowed down to a certain degree based on those findings. Nevertheless, N in our own Galaxy may vary between one (including humanity) or zero (not taking into account humanity) and several millions, with Frank Drake, for example, having estimated a number of 10,000.[17] However, the Drake Equation is in the end not a tool for determining N with any reasonable degree of mathematical accuracy, but more of a conceptual lens through which to approach the question of whether we can at least express educated guesses at degrees of likelihood that SETI is not a lost cause to begin with. That said, Michael Schetsche and Andreas Anton, for example, using a range of different degrees of optimism for the individual factors of the Drake Equation, have calculated a range for N from $N = 0$ to $N = 468{,}750$ for the Milky Way, and based on what they call a "defensible assumption" with a conservative factor of 20,000 years for L, arrive at $N = 56.3$ for our galaxy.[18] Despite the fact that even this number is, of course, speculative, it has a rather more realistic ring to it given the billions of stars suspected to be accompanied by exoplanets in the Milky Way alone.

15 Kenneth I Kellerman, *ibid.*; see also John G Sotos, Biotechnology and the lifetime of technical civilizations, 18 *International Journal of Astrobiology* (2019) 445–454; John-Oliver Engler and Henrik von Wehrden, 'Where is everybody?' An empirical appraisal of occurrence, prevalence and sustainability of technological species in the Universe, 18 *International Journal of Astrobiology* (2019) 495–501.

16 *Supra* note 14.

17 As recalled by Seth Shostak, *Sharing the Universe – Perspectives on Extraterrestrial Life.* (Berkeley Hills Books, Albany, 1998) p. 183 (hereafter Shostak, Sharing): "Without doubt, determining N is still more sorcery than science". See also the references in Schetsche/Anton, pp. 45–67.

18 Schetsche/Anton, pp. 66–67.

1.1.2 Fermi Paradox

Once we accept the possibility inherent in such – however crude – statistical approximations of a sizeable number of extraterrestrial civilisations which can only increase dramatically if we remember that there are, according to current estimates, anywhere between 100 billion to one trillion galaxies in the known universe, we must countenance the potential existence of millions of other civilisations, a proportion of which may have advanced as far as or even further than humanity.[19] If we discount the narratives of past direct contact on or near Earth and only refer to the traditional SETI approach, the question becomes unavoidable of why we have not heard from them.

The most prominent scientist, apart from, for example, Konstantin Tsiolkovskii, to have pondered this question in some detail in the 20th century and to have ultimately given it his name[20] was the Italian physicist Enrico Fermi. He argued that any technologically advanced civilisation will at some stage of its development begin to colonise space and hence Earth should have been colonised or at least visited by alien beings, if intelligent life had developed somewhere in the universe[21] prior to life on Earth, and we should be able to find evidence for their presence, for example, through artefacts. Given that we have not found any, they cannot have been here and hence they do not exist.[22] There are quite a number of attempts at explaining this apparent contradiction[23] but one central objection to Fermi's argument is the realisation

19 *Ibid.*, pp. 67–68.

20 The essence of the paradox had already been addressed earlier by the equally famous space exploration theorist Konstantin Tsiolkovskij. See Michaud, pp. 164–165.

21 On the general question of the development of intelligent life based on the acceleration of the Universe and the consequences for the Fermi Paradox, see Frank J Tipler, Intelligent life in cosmology, 2 *International Journal of Astrobiology* (2003) 141–148.

22 Schetsche/Anton, pp. 68–69.

23 Tsiolkovskii himself had already been of the view that the paradox was not really necessarily a paradox because advanced alien civilisations may not wish to contact Earth due to humanity's low level of civilisational development and the grave risk arising from premature contact – in a sense humanity is put on a galactic no-go reservation. John Ball in 1973 expanded on this view by qualifying Earth as a "wildlife sanctuary" or even a zoo, hence the term "zoo hypothesis"; see John Ball, The Zoo Hypothesis, 19 *Icarus* (1973) 347–349. ETI may be able to monitor Earth but may simply not wish to be detected themselves. See Michaud, pp. 164–165 and on the general debate in more detail at 165–189, with an excellent bullet point overview of the different arguments and counterarguments at pp. 180–189. See also Duncan H Forgan, Spatio-temporal constraints on the zoo hypothesis, and the breakdown of total hegemony, 10 *International Journal of Astrobiology* (2011) 341–347; *id.*, The Galactic Club or Galactic Cliques? Exploring the limits of interstellar hegemony and the Zoo Hypothesis, 16 *International Journal of Astrobiology* (2017) 349–354. – As we will especially see in the following sections on SETI approaches and the SF treatments of the topic, there is also the possibility that advanced intelligent civilisations

that after decades of SETI research, humanity's active search for ETI to-date is still anything but comprehensive. It is also based on an anthropocentric view of motives of potential alien civilisations for the colonisation of space surrounding their home world – such as overpopulation, scarce resources etc.[24] It is thus fair to say that Fermi's argument and similar ones were and still are at the very least based on insufficient data. In the words of Michaud:

> We do not know enough to definitively answer the questions that are at the heart of the paradox. Our searches may someday resolve the issue. Just one detection of an extraterrestrial technology, and the paradox collapses.[25]

In this context, it appears apposite to mention, *colorandi causa*, one controversial incident, which could have already provided this one detection but has ultimately remained inconclusive, yet it has not been disproved as a potentially artificial signal, either:[26] The (in-)famous "Wow!" signal from 1977.[27] The signal has its name from the following event: US astrophysicist Jerry Ehman was performing a routine check of the signal printouts at the Big Ear radio telescope at Ohio State University on 15 August 1977. The signal received from 23:16 hrs for 72 seconds surprised him so much, that he wrote the word "Wow!" next to the signal printout. The signal was anomalous in several ways:

- It was clearly distinguishable against the usual cosmic background noise.
- Its frequency was very close to that of the neutral hydrogen line (1420 MHz), a hyper-fine transition line in a neutral, i.e., not electrically charged hydrogen atom transitioning between the different spin states (parallel or anti-parallel) of its proton and electrons. It had been postulated very early on as an ideal starting point for signal searches because hydrogen gas, which emits static noise at that frequency, exists throughout the galaxy and had therefore already been used previously in radio astronomy, so the assumption was that ETI would have realised that sending a signal at that frequency would be recognised as a transmission on a "hailing frequency" on a "universal channel"[28]

---

are hiding their existence on purpose to avoid detection by potentially hostile galactic neighbours.

24 Michaud, pp. 165–189.

25 Michaud, p. 189.

26 Schetsche/Anton, p. 79.

27 An image of the Wow!-signal printout can be found at https://de.wikipedia.org/wiki/Wow!-Signal#/media/Datei:Wow_signal.jpg.

28 Shostak, Sharing, pp. 151–152.

by other advanced civilisations capable of detecting that frequency as an indication of an at least equal stage of development.[29]

- The signal was received for 72 seconds, which was the exact time the Big Ear radio telescope took to turn out of the signal's vector range by the Earth's rotation, which made it highly likely that the signal was of interstellar origin and not caused by something like a plane or a satellite etc., moving much faster and at a much closer distance relative to the telescope.[30]

It thus fulfilled almost all criteria for an artificial signal from afar.[31] The problem was, however, that the signal reception was a unique event and could not be replicated since. It was thus not accepted as scientifically legitimate in the SETI community.[32] The technology available at Big Ear at the time was not sophisticated enough, either, to determine whether the signal contained any kind of message hidden, for example, in a modulation. Later attempts at a "natural" explanation or a debunking of the signal related to asteroids, satellites, radio or TV transmissions etc. have, however, not produced a convincing result, either.[33] A less well-known example of a candidate signal is the strong laser signal received by Ragbir Bhathal in December 2008[34] from star cluster 47 Tucanae, which led him to write on the printout "Is it ET?". Other strong signals such as the 2001 Lorimer fast radio burst detection (and later occasions) at the 1420 MHz frequency gave rise to hopes of having received a candidate signal.[35] In any event, Fermi's Paradox is intellectually not a sufficiently resilient

29 See on the relevance and choice of the hydrogen line in particular Claudio Maccone, SETI and the IAA SETI Permanent Committee: Past, Present and Possible Future, in Patricia M Stearns and Leslie Tennen (eds.), *Private Law, Public Law, Metalaw and Public Policy in Space*, (Springer, New York, 2016) p. 146, and Patricia, M Stearns and Leslie Tennen, SETI, Metalaw, and Social Media, *ibid.* p. 161. On a more recent proposal for optical frequencies, see Shin-ya Narusawa et al., Which colors would extraterrestrial civilizations use to transmit signals?: The "magic wavelengths" for optical SETI, 60 *New Astronomy* (2018) 61–64, and on alternative frequencies Kenath Arun et al. Alternative standard frequencies for interstellar communication, 18 *International Journal of Astrobiology* (2017) 209–210.

30 Schetsche/Anton, p. 77.

31 For a recent attempt to locate a probable source, see Alberto Caballero, An approximation to determine the source of the WOW! Signal, 23 *International Journal of Astrobiology* (2022) 129–136.

32 Shostak, Sharing, pp. 166–167.

33 Schetsche/Anton, pp. 78–79 with references. See also Ed Wheeler, The 'Wow' Signal, Drake Equation and Exoplanet Considerations, 67 *JBIS* (2014) 412–417, who argues that the uniqueness may have been intended.

34 The graphic of the "Is it ETI?" printout is available online at Bhathal, Ragbir, Signals From Space, 2017, www.thelivingmoon.com/43ancients/02files/SETI_LASER_like_Signal_Dis covered.html.

35 Daniel Gerritzen, *Erstkontakt* (Kosmos, Stuttgart, 2016) pp. 90–94.

proposition to justify ceasing and desisting from SETI research *a priori* and *in limine*. The scientific burden of proof is on those who (categorically) deny the existence of ETI, which in philosophical or legal terms equals to a typically highly difficult proof of a negative – in this case a negative of literally astronomical proportions. Or, as Webb correctly put it, "[s]ome would argue that until we can rule out that possibility, there is no Fermi Paradox".[36]

2 Anthropocentrism and -morphism

As we can already deduce from the debate around the conceptual foundations of Fermi's Paradox, i.e., the alleged potential motivations of ETI for space colonisation, the inevitably inherent anthropocentrism and -morphism[37] of the entire debate and its epistemological consequences for all SETI research must be highlighted and analysed. The simple fact of the matter is that any conjectures made by humans about the physical nature and appearance (if any), motives and intellectual processes guiding the behaviour of ETI, are tainted by the limitations of human imagination[38] and our own intellectual and emotional DNA.[39]

---

36 Stephen Webb, *If the Universe Is Teeming with Aliens – Where is Everybody? – Fifty Solutions to the Fermi Paradox and the Problem of Extraterrestrial Life* (Copernicus Books, New York, 2002) p. 42.

37 For an application of Darwinism on speculation about the evolution of ETI on other planets, see Samuel R Levin and Thomas W Scott, Darwin's aliens, 18 *International Journal of Astrobiology* (2019) 1–9; Marcelo Gleiser, From cosmos to intelligent life: the four ages of astrobiology, 11 *International Journal of Astrobiology* (2012) 345–350; J. Chela-Flores, Testing evolutionary convergence on Europa, 2 *International Journal of Astrobiology* (2003) 307–312.

38 See on the involuntary conceptual imprinting of human characteristics on ETI, J.L. Petit, Communication with aliens, as an opening of the horizon of a scientific Humanity – A philosopher's reflections, 12 *International Journal of Astrobiology* (2013) 263–270.

39 See for more detail Andreas Anton and Michael Schetsche, Anthropozentrische Transterrestrik. Zur Kritik naturwissenschaftlich orientierter SETI-Programme, 15 *Zeitschrift für Anomalistik* (2015) 21–46; Ulrike M Bohlmann and Moritz J F Bürger, Anthropomorphism in the search for extra-terrestrial intelligence – The limits of cognition? 143 *Acta Astronautica* (2018) 163–168; Steven J. Dick, Anthropology and the Search for Extraterrestrial Intelligence: An Historical View, 22 (2) *Anthropology Today* (2006) 3–7; Milan M Ćirković, Post-postbiological evolution? 99 Futures (2018) 28–35; Niklas Alexander Döbler, The Concept of Developmental Relativity: Thoughts on the Technological Synchrony of Interstellar Civilizations, 54 *Space Policy* (2020) 101391; Steven J Dick and Mark L Lupisella (eds.) *Cosmos and Culture: Cultural Evolution in a Cosmic Context* (NASA, Washington, 2009) www.nasa.gov/connect/ebooks/hist_culture_cosmos_detail.html;

In terms of modern Science Fiction TV or film series, which is as good an indicator as anything of human imagination at its wildest, this can be shown by naming but two, albeit prominent, examples: Where *Star Wars* at least tries to use body shapes that are not based on an essentially perpendicular legs-torso-arms-head design,[40] *Star Trek* even in its more modern different iterations fails consistently and its alien species – unless they are the equivalent of terrestrial animals – are typically humanoid, if not outright human,[41] in appearance and seem to be distinguishable visually only by a variety of cranial bone or cartilage ridges, pointed ears or skin colour patterns reminiscent of some of Earth's tribal scar traditions. "Evil" aliens[42] are often given an insectoid or reptilian skin or body shape, clearly reflecting and utilising archetypal human phobiae.[43]

Apart from implied human premises about the necessary existence of certain technological "hardware"[44] developments, two major fields of controversy lie in what Schetsche and Anton call "contact optimism" (*Kontaktoptimismus*) and "communication optimism" (*Kommunikationsoptimismus*).[45] By this they

---

E.R. Taylor, If technological intelligent extraterrestrials exist, what biological traits are de rigueur?, 17 *Life Sciences in Space Research* (2018) 15–22; Douglas A. Vakoch (ed.). *Archaeology, anthropology, and interstellar communication.* (NASA, Washington, 2013) www.nasa.gov/connect/ebooks/archaeology_anthropology_and_interstellar_communication.html.

40 Yet even so, the arch-villain of the planet Tatooine, Jabba the Hutt, is in essence merely an oversized slug with arms and a humanoid face, and who meets his end by strangulation in the same general body region below the mouth where the human windpipe would be located.

41 Suffice it to say that ETI might take issue with being described as belonging to a sub-species category defined by human physical characteristics – this has been referenced in some modern SF narratives.

42 A famous exception in Arthur C. Clarke's 1953 novel, *Childhood's End*, which was broadcast by the Syfy Channel as a three-part TV series in 2015, is the character Karellen, the chief of the alien "Overlords" and "Supervisor for Earth", under whose overall benevolent tutelage humanity is unknowingly being readied for merging with the "Overmind", a mysterious collective entity travelling the Universe seeking to consume individual(ist) species into its collective whole. After many years of hiding from the sight of the humans in his spaceship, Karellen is ultimately revealed to the world as having horns, hooves, leathery wings and a tail, i.e., as the very picture humanity has in some religions or storytelling traditions nurtured over centuries for the shape of the Devil or of demons.

43 For an overview of the human visual and conceptual imagination of aliens over time see Ron Miller, *Aliens – Past, Present and Future* (Watkins, London, 2017). For a thorough analysis of the depiction of ETI particularly in film media see Mario Springnagel, *Die Darstellung von außerirdischer Intelligenz im Film* (*Extraterrestrial Intelligence in the Movies*) (Unpublished PhD thesis, 2017) – https://othes.univie.ac.at/49475/.

44 See the list of relevant sub-categories in Schetsche/Anton, p. 80.

45 Schetsche/Anton, pp. 80–81.

mean the assumption that any intelligent advanced civilisation will want to engage in communication and seek contact with other civilisations in the way humans would imagine it, not least in the sense that they would be in a position to encode their messages in a way that other, literally "alien" civilisations would be in a position to decode them. As we will see below when addressing exolinguistics, this assumption is fraught with massive difficulties, especially when the task is moving from detecting a recurrent signal pattern and classifying it as artificial and having generic elements also found in terrestrial language construction, to understanding the substance of any message possibly contained in this pattern, leave alone any moral or emotional meaning, if the ETI in question has morals or emotions as humans would understand them in the first place. This problem also resurfaces as a major issue in the context of the debate about a cosmic "metalaw" allegedly shared by all intelligent and moral[46] species, which is highly relevant to the second aim of this book, i.e., the preparation of a unified legal human response framework for potential (hostile) contact and discussed in more detail below.

The concern about anthropocentrism applies equally to phenomena such as the often adduced "*lingua franca*" of cross-cultural communication, i.e., mathematics, encapsulated in models such as the allegedly self-explaining "Lingua Cosmica" (LINCOS) originally developed by Hans Freudenthal[47] in 1960 and today advocated, for example, by Alexander Ollongren.[48] The emerging field of ethnomathematics makes the assumption doubtful that there is only one kind of mathematics on Earth, and that ETI will use the same approach to mathematical logic as the astronomers on (the Western hemisphere of) Earth.[49] How much more likely will the potential for a major discrepancy between alien and human mathematics be, if there is such a bandwidth among human

---

46 Even this qualifier is subtly anthropocentric as it implies that intelligence always goes hand-in-hand with the development of an ethical outlook of some sort on the world, and more often than not the development of some idea of philosophy or ideology; see, for example, Mark Lupisella, *Cosmological Theories of Value – Science, Philosophy and Meaning in Cosmic Evolution* (Springer, New York, 2020).

47 Hans Freudenthal, Logica als methode en als onderwerp, 35 *Euclides* (1960) 241–255; *id.* *Lincos – Design of a Language for Cosmic Intercourse, Part 1* (North-Holland Publishing Co., Amsterdam, 1960).

48 See Alexander Ollongren, *Astrolinguistics: Design of a Linguistic System for Interstellar Communication Based on Logic* (Springer, New York, 2012); *id.*, On the signature of LINCOS. 67 *Acta Astronautica* (2010) 1440–1442; *id.*, Large-size message construction for ETI: Inductive self-interpretation in LINCOS, 68 *Acta Astronautica* 68 (2011) 539–543; *id.*, Recursivity in Lingua Cosmica, 68 Acta Astronautica (2011) 544–548.

49 See for an introduction Marcia Ascher, *Ethnomathematics – A Multicultural View of Mathematical Ideas* (Chapman and Hall/CRC, London, 1994).

approaches already? There are also concerns, expressed, for example, by Paul Watzlawick,[50] about the theoretical possibility of a self-explanatory system based on Kurt Gödel's Incompleteness Theorems[51] which suggest that no system can completely explain itself without reference to an external framework.

These are just a few examples of how difficult, if not impossible, it is for humans – or any species which has not yet had contact or intelligently communicated with an "other" totally alien to itself – to imagine and speculate about the "maximally alien", as Schetsche and Anton[52] call it, in this case with the term "alien" retaining its original meaning as an embodiment of (ultimate) strangeness. As Vossenkuhl points out, strangeness is, of course, a mutually relational concept – yet awareness of one's own and of the other's strangeness is no epistemological guarantee of the ability to understand, let alone to be able to adopt, the stranger's self-perception:

> We encounter here a variant of the problem of the psychologically alien: What gives us the right to assume that the other feels and thinks about any random number of things and events as we do; and what gives us the right to assume that our understanding of the alien other is identical with its own self-understanding?[53]

The realisation of a barrier between one's own and an "other's" perception of self and of the extraneous world already applies for contacts between humans from different cultural, religious, societal, ethnic or gender backgrounds. Münkler and Ladwig consequently call the confrontation with a non-human other a "borderline case of definitive incomprehensibility",[54] something "at the very end of the spectrum of familiarity".[55] Georg Simmel expressed it as follows: "The inhabitants of Sirius are not in the strict sense alien to us […] [,] they do not exist for us at all, they are beyond near and far".[56] Hence, humanity

50 Paul Watzlawick, *Wie wirklich ist die Wirklichkeit?* (Piper, Munich, 2012) pp. 192–193.

51 Kurt Gödel, Über formal unentscheidbare Sätze der Principia Mathematica und verwandter Systeme, 38 *Monatshefte für Mathematik und Physik* (1938) 173–174.

52 Schetsche/Anton, p. 16 (Translation by the author).

53 Wilhelm Vossenkuhl, Jenseits des Vertrauten und Fremden, in Odo Marquard (ed.) *Einheit und Vielfalt* (Meiner, Hamburg, 1990) p. 109 (Translation by the author).

54 Herfried Münkler und Bernd Ladwig, Dimensionen der Fremdheit, in Herfried Münkler (ed.) *Furcht und Faszination – Facetten der Fremdheit* (Akademie, Berlin, 1997), pp. 11–43 (Translation by the author).

55 Schetsche/Anton, p. 15 (Translation by the author).

56 Georg Simmel *Soziologie: Untersuchungen über die Formen der Vergesellschaftung*, 4th ed. (Duncker & Humblot, Berlin, 1958) p. 509 (Translation by the author).

is currently left with the reflection of how to prepare for contact with the "maximally alien", without being able to assume any similarity between both sides in any respect.

3 SETI Approaches and the Nature of Contact

The question of the potential nature of contact has so far largely determined the mode of the search – which has been entirely unsuccessful so far if one looks only at the astronomy aspect: Traditionally, SETI had been mostly the domain of astronomers[57] and astrophysicists, and contact with ETI was mostly understood to be made by receiving a message from afar, picked up by radio antennae,[58] optical cameras etc. A lot of thinking over the years[59] has therefore gone into how to confirm distant signal detection as a type of first contact, always bearing in mind that while the signal may be artificial[60] in nature and origin, it may nonetheless be random at the same time in that it does not have to be directed at anyone in particular (for example, the distress beacon of a long derelict spacecraft), least of all humans, and given the vast interstellar distances may already be hundreds or thousands of years old at the time of reception on Earth, with the consequence that the civilisation sending it may already have become extinct. Considering (past) direct contact as a possibility,[61]

57 See, for example, Jill Tarter et al., The first SETI observations with the Allen telescope array, 68 *Acta Astronautica* (2011) 340–346.

58 On the classification of messages, see Alexander Zaitsev, Classification of interstellar radio messages, 78 *Acta Astronautica* (2012) 16–19.

59 See on the manifold premises even more sophisticated modern attempts at so-called "intelligent targeting" must postulate in order to justify certain statistical expectations, Philip Lubin, The search for directed intelligence, 1 *REACH Reviews in Human Space Exploration* (2016) 20–45.

60 See, in particular for the question of "technosignatures", i.e., technological signatures which permit the inference of an advanced intelligence capable of technologically shaping its environment, NASA and the Search for Technosignatures – A Report from NASA Technosignatures Workshop, 2018, https://arxiv.org/ftp/arxiv/papers/1812/1812.08681.pdf.; and more recently Jacob Haqq-Misraet al., Searching for technosignatures in exoplanetary systems with current and future missions, 198 *Acta Astronautica* (2022) 194 –207.

61 Schetsche and Anton rather scathingly query the basic assumption in a broad section of the mainstream SETI community, and which they say is still holding sway over much of the scientific as well as the public debate, that we will never directly encounter ETI because of the "vast and insuperable interstellar distances in the universe", which no civilisation will be able or willing to traverse, and call it "one of the most serious misapprehensions" in SETI history. They raise the epistemological and socio-psychological concern that this may be the case because "only aliens placed at a sheer insurmountable distance allow us untroubled sleep" (translation by the author) and pose the radical

as we already saw, inevitably means dealing with things such as "foo fighters",[62] UFOs,[63] Area 51,[64] crop circles,[65] the Roswell incident[66] and alien abductions,[67] and triggers Shostak's[68] famous "giggle factor" among established scientists.[69] This is the case regardless of whether direct contact narratives follow the mainstream extraterrestrial hypothesis (ETH), i.e., visitors from the stars, causing immediate friction with the traditional thinking behind the Fermi Paradox,[70] or the even more speculative interdimensional hypothesis (IDH),

---

ensuing question of whether some of the protagonists might subconsciously not be more interested in preventing contact than in facilitating it. – Schetsche/Anton, p. 90 at fn. 12.

62 Report by the so-called Robertson Panel: Report of scientific advisory panel on unidentified flying objects convened by office of scientific intelligence, 1953, www.cufon.org/cufon/robert.htm.

63 See the NSA UFO Documents Index at https://www.nsa.gov/Helpful-Links/NSA-FOIA/Frequently-Requested-Information/Unidentified-Flying-Objects-UFOs/ and the disappointingly brief and superficial 9-page public version of the report by the Office of the Director of National Intelligence (ODNI), Preliminary Assessment: Unidentified Aerial Phenomena, of 25 June 2021, www.dni.gov/files/ODNI/documents/assessments/Prelimary-Assessment-UAP-20210625.pdf.

64 Overview at www.britannica.com/place/Area-51, 2021.

65 Richard Taylor, Coming soon to a field near you, *Physics World* (2011) 1–4; and in German Werner Anderhub and Andreas Müller, *Phänomen Kornkreise: Forschung zwischen Volksüberlieferung, Grenz-und Naturwissenschaft* (AT Verlag, Baden/Munich, 2005).

66 See R Weaver and J McAndrew, *The Roswell Report: Fact Versus Fiction in the New Mexico Desert*, 1995, https://web.archive.org/web/20130216035900/ http://www.afhso.af.mil/shared/media/document/AFD-101201-038.pdf.

67 For a critical view see Susan A. Clancy, *Abducted: How People Come to Believe They Were Kidnapped by Aliens* (Harvard University Press, Cambridge, 2005). A major seminal study was conducted by Andrea Pritchard al (eds.), *Alien Discussions: Proceedings of the Abduction Study Conference at MIT* (North Cambridge Press, Cambridge, 1994) and the report about the MIT conference by C. D. B. Bryan, *Close Encounters of The Fourth Kind: Alien Abduction, UFO s, and the Conference at MIT* (Knopf, New York, 1995).

68 Seth Shostak, SETI and the Media, in R.P Norris and F.H. Stootman (eds.) *Bioastronomy 2002: Life Among the Stars – IAU Symposium,* (Astronomical Society of the Pacific, San Francisco, 2004) p 541.

69 On a critique of this attitude from a research strategy point of view, see Adam Dodds, Strategic Ignorance and the Search for Extraterrestrial Intelligence: Critiquing the Discursive Segregation of UFOs from Scientific Inquiry, 16 *Astropolitics* (2018) 75–79.

70 Despite the fact that serious and moreover sceptical research has been conducted in this field and has failed to discredit every incident of direct contact reports; see, for example, Leslie Kean, 2010. *UFO s – Generals, Pilots and Government Officials Go on the Record* (Three Rivers Press, New York, 2010); on Leslie Kean's campaign for proper recognition and investigation of the UAP/UFO phenomenon see Soo Youn, The woman who forced the US government to take UFOs seriously – www.theguardian.com/world/2021/jun/14/leslie-kean-ufo-reporter-us-government-report. See further Michaud, pp. 143–161; Schetsche/Anton, pp. 253–276.

which claims that alien visitations on Earth are made (also) by beings from (an)other dimension(s), an approach that conceptually rather elegantly sidesteps the whole premise of the Fermi Paradox and the physical problems of interstellar travel but does, of course, require an even greater leap of faith from the beholder.[71] Clearly, these two options do not mutually exclude each other.

SETI has so far been mostly a "listening" exercise in the broader sense, i.e., using passive methods of observation, but active SETI (also called METI – Messaging to ETI, or CETI – Communicating with ETI) by sending messages into space also has had a large following, not least since the so-called "Arecibo Message"[72] sent by Frank Drake in the direction of the star cluster M13 in 1974.[73] On 4 February 2008, NASA itself beamed the Beatles song "Across the Universe" into space in the direction of the North Star, where it will arrive 431 years after transmission.[74] Active SETI by its very nature carries the risk of alerting potentially hostile and technologically superior ETI to humanity's presence and has thus been controversial.[75] In essence, METI is an activity

71 A well-known and founding representative of this idea was seen in the seminal book by the French former astronomer Jacques Vallée, *Passport to Magonia – From Folklore to Flying Saucers* (Daily Grail Publishing, Brisbane, 1969 – cited here after the 2014 edition) and the joint work by J Allen Hynek and Jacques Vallée (eds.), *The Edge of Reality: A Progress Report on Unidentified Flying Objects* (Henry Regnery, Chicago, 1975); Jacques Vallée, *Messengers of Deception: UFO Contacts and Cults* (Bantam Books, New York, 1980); *id.* 1988. *"Alien Contact Trilogy": Dimensions – A Casebook of Alien Contact* (Anomalist Boks, San Antonio/Charlottesville, 1988); *id. Confrontations – A Scientist's Search for Alien Contact* (Anomalist Books, Antonio/Charlottesville, 1990); *id., Revelations – Alien Contact and Human Deception* (Anomalist Books, Antonio/Charlottesville, 1991/2008). He summarised the development from the early times of the research environment in 2014 in *The Invisible College – What a Group of Scientists Has Discovered About UFO Influences on the Human Race* (Anomalist Books, San Antonio/Charlottesville, 2014). A recent reprisal of some of his ideas is found in the more popular science volume by Anthony Peake, *The Hidden Universe – An investigation into non-human intelligences* (Watkins, London, 2019).

72 Michaud, p. 50; Frank Drake, The search for extra-terrestrial intelligence, 369 *Phil. Trans. R. Soc. A* (2011) 633–643; Christopher P McKay, The search for life in our Solar System and the implications for science and society, 369 *Phil. Trans. R. Soc. A* (2011) 594–606.

73 For a description of the message construction and the content of the message, see http://www.naic.edu/challenge/about-message.html.

74 NASA Beams Beatles' 'Across the Universe' Into Space, 2008. www.nasa.gov/topics/universe/features/across_universe.html.

75 Michaud, pp. 49–53; 241–247; Douglas A Vakoch, Responsibility, capability, and Active SETI: Policy, law, ethics, and communication with extraterrestrial intelligence, 68 *Acta Astronautica* (2011) 512–519.; Kelly C Smith, METI or REGRETTI: Ethics, Risk, and Alien Contact, in Kelly C Smith and Carlos Mariscal (eds.) *Social and Conceptual Issues in Astrobiology* (OUP, Oxford, 2020) pp. 209–238; Kathryn Denning, Unpacking the great transmission debate, 67 *Acta Astronautica* (2010) 1399–1405; Adam Korbitz, Toward understanding the active SETI debate: Insights from risk communication and perception,

with the self-professed aim of bringing about a situation which humanity will be unable to control.

In 2015, a number of members of the SETI community, including tycoon Elon Musk – a man who, on 6 February 2018, after all sent a Tesla car into space as a payload on the maiden flight of his Falcon Heavy rocket and admitted that "[i]t's kind of silly and fun", [but] conceded [that] "silly and fun things are important"[76] – issued a "METI Statement"[77] calling for a "worldwide scientific, political and humanitarian discussion [to] occur before any message is sent". However, none of the great proponents of METI, such as Frank Drake, Carl Sagan (who both together also designed the plaques on the Pioneer 10 and 11 probes) or Douglas Vakoch, joined it. Recent research by Trueblood and Hatfield has moreover shown that at least in the UK people are weary of any decision-making processes that involve a referendum, a clear result of the 2016 Brexit referendum and the ensuing political chaos resulting in repeated general elections within a short time. Of those in favour of a referendum model, however, 56% were in favour of making contact, and only 13% were opposed to

---

105 *Acta Astronautica* (2014) 517–520; John W Traphagan, Cargo Cults and the Ethics of Active SETI, 46 *Space Policy* (2018) 18-22; Paolo Musso, The problem of active SETI: An overview, 78 *Acta Astronautica* (2012) 43–54; Alan Penny, Transmitting (and listening) may be good (or bad), 78 *Acta Astronautica* (2012) 69–71; Jacob Haqq-Misra et al., The benefits and harm of transmitting into space. 29 *Space Policy* (2013) 40-48; Karim Jebaria and Niklas Olsson-Yaouzis, A Game of Stars: Active SETI, radical translation and the Hobbesian trap, 101 *Futures* (2018) 46–54; Seth Shostak, Are transmissions to space dangerous?, 12 *International Journal of Astrobiology* (2013) 17–20. On the developing cultural signal diversity debate see Paul E Quast, A profile of humanity: the cultural signature of Earth's inhabitants beyond the atmosphere, 20 *International Journal of Astrobiology* (2021) 94–214; Harold P. de Vladar, The game of active search for extra-terrestrial intelligence: breaking the 'Great Silence', 12 *International Journal of Astrobiology* (2013) 53–62.

76 Jeol Gunter, Elon Musk: The man who sent his sports car into space, 2018, www.bbc.com/news/science-environment-42992143. One may be forgiven for generally qualifying Mr Musk's actions and ideas as at times somewhat erratic, yet fun and silliness are certainly no motives that allow for a sustainable and principled approach to such questions as SETI, not least given the "lunatic fringe" reputation SETI still enjoys among large parts of society. There are even fan pages where people can track the progress of the car, a Tesla Roadster "manned" by a dummy astronaut called "Starman", by the second; see Ben Pearson, Where is Starman? Track Elon Musk's Tesla Roadster in Space! www.whereisroadster.com/.

77 Regarding Messaging to Extraterrestrial Intelligence (METI)/Active Searches for Extraterrestrial Intelligence (Active SETI), https://setiathome.berkeley.edu/meti_statement_0.html, 2016.

it.[78] Nonetheless, what David Brin said, in an episode of CNN's Larry King Show of 30 April 2010, needs mentioning:

> It's these narrow beams that are being sent out from taxpayer-paid observatories like Arecibo and Evpatoria in Ukraine that are causing the fuss. Without consulting the taxpayers, without consulting the governments, without consulting fellow scientists at all in other disciplines. These people have taken upon themselves to act on their assumptions that aliens are universally altruistic. And it's not so much the beamed messages that we object to, those of us who've been dissenting lately. But rather the arrogance of not talking to anybody else on this planet before assuming they have the right to do this.[79]

Keith Cooper has also urged caution based on the anticipated time lag between message and response and argued in favour of a slower pace with more preparatory observation, not least because of the possibly delayed consequences of a rushed course of action:

> METI researchers should not feel that they are missing out on much – if other civilisations are so far away that we would not receive a reply in our lifetimes, then there really should be no rush to transmit on behalf of our descendants, who might not be too happy that we were presumptuous enough to do so.[80]

In this context, Stephen Hawking's warning from the Discovery Channel series "Into the Universe with Stephen Hawking"[81] puts an additional question mark over METI:

78 Peter Hatfield and Leah Trueblood, SETI and democracy, 190 *Acta Astronautica* (2021) 596–603. Their research even made it into the general media with an article in The Guardian of 10 September 2019: See Ian Sample, If aliens call, do not hold a referendum on what to do next, say Britons – www.theguardian.com/science/2019/sep/10/aliens-call-vote-referendum-britons.

79 From the transcript at CNN Larry King Live, Stephen Hawking's Warning on Space Aliens. 2010, http://transcripts.cnn.com/TRANSCRIPTS/1004/30/lkl.01.html. Critically also Daniel Gerritzen. *Erstkontakt* (Kosmos, Stuttgart, 2010) p. 297.

80 Keith Cooper, *The Contact Paradox – Challenging our Assumptions in the Search for Extraterrestrial Intelligence* (Bloomsbury Sigma/London, 2019) p. 317.

81 Series 1, Episode 1: Aliens, 2010, www.imdb.com/title/tt1658579/?ref_=ttep_ep1.

> We only have to look at ourselves to see how intelligent life might develop into something we wouldn't want to meet.[82]

If one accepts the premise that an unknown number of ETI have been visiting regions of space outside their home region for a long time, then it would seem reasonable to expect the existence of artefacts, such as (derelict) spacecraft, simple debris, or installations on planets or larger asteroids etc., but depending on their state of technological advancement also astronomical mega-structures such as the so-called "Dyson Spheres"[83] or "Dyson Ships",[84] i.e., self-contained and technologically engineered stationary (quasi-)planetary or mobile colony habitats, and they themselves may be the object of search efforts,[85] resulting in the movement of Search for Extraterrestrial Artefacts (SETA).[86] In the latter context, none less than former Harvard chief astronomer Avi Loeb, for example, is of the – highly controversial – view that there are good reasons to assume that the anomalous object discovered traversing our solar system in 2017 and given the name *'Oumuamua* was a piece of (possibly derelict) alien

82 Cited in a BBC overview of Hawking's most memorable quotes, at Paul Rincon, Stephen Hawking's warnings: What he predicted for the future, 2018 – www.bbc.com/news/science-environment-43408961.

83 Milan M Ćirković, Astroengineering, Dysonian SETI, and naturalism: A new Catch-22, 152 *Acta Astronautica* (2018) 289–298. Some even recommend focussing on Dyson Sphere-type artefacts as proper targets for astronomic SETI research; see Massimo Teodorani, A strategic "viewfinder" for SETI research, 105 *Acta Astronautica* (2014) 512–516.

84 Massimo Teodorani, Search for high-proper motion objects with infrared excess. 105 *Acta Astronautica* (2014) 547–552.

85 R. Weinberger and H. Hartl have, for example, tentatively announced the view based on searching for optical messages of such constructions that no ETI within 10,000–20,000 light years from Earth has chosen to reveal its existence through such objects. – R Weinberger, and H Hartl, A search for `frozen optical messages' from extraterrestrial civilizations, 1 *International Journal of Astrobiology* (2002) 71–73.

86 See, for example, Seth Shostak, ETI: the argument for artefact searches, 19 *International Journal of Astrobiology* (2020) 456–461; P C W Davies and R V Wagner, Searching for alien artifacts on the moon, 89 *Acta Astronautica* (2013) 261–265; Schetsche/Anton, pp. 93–106; Richard A Carrigan Jr,, Is interstellar archaeology possible? 78 *Acta Astronautica* (2012) 121–126; Morris Jones, 2015. Reconsidering macro-artefacts in SETI searches, 116 *Acta Astronautica* (2015) 161–165; Duncan H Forgan and Martin Elvis, Extrasolar asteroid mining as forensic evidence for extraterrestrial intelligence, 10 *International Journal of Astrobiology* (2011) 307–313. For a new version of the Drake Equation including a SETA approach, see James Benford, A Drake Equation for Alien Artefacts, 21 *Astrobiology* (2021) 757–763.

technology of interstellar[87] origin.[88] Another relatively recent example from

---

87 On a study of possible ways to reach Oumuamua and other interstellar objects (ISOs) via nuclear thermal rockets see Adam Hibberd and Andreas M Hein, Project Lyra: Catching 1I/'Oumuamua–Using Nuclear Thermal Rockets, 179 *Acta Astronautica* (2021) 594–603.

88 He has explained his arguments in his book Avi Loeb, *Extraterrestrial: The First Sign of Intelligent Life Beyond Earth* (Houghton Mifflin Harcourt, New York, 2021). Loeb is also highly critical of the conservatism displayed by the traditional scientific establishment, which considers SETI research as damaging to a scientist's career prospects, stating that SETI "has never been more than an oddity to the vast majority of scientists; to them, it is a subject worthy of, at best, glancing interest and at worst, outright derision. Few of repute have dedicated their careers to advancing the field, and even at its zenith, in the 1970s, only about a hundred scholars were publicly associated with the SETI Institute. For more speculative fields of mathematical gymnastics are known to attract bigger communities of physicists [...] [T]he explicit and implicit encouraging of conservative science is both depressing and concerning, given the extent of anomalies the universe still contains. While it is not obvious to me why extraordinary claims require extraordinary evidence (evidence is evidence, no?), I do believe that extraordinary conservatism keeps us extraordinarily ignorant. Put differently, the field doesn't need more cautious detectives". – at pp. 90 and 101–102. The latter reference is to Carl Sagan's famous dictum from a TV broadcast on PBS in 1980 that "extraordinary claims require extraordinary evidence", often given the acronym "ECREE", which has been used in particular to discredit accounts of UFO sightings, abductions etc. The full quote is: "Extraordinary claims require extraordinary evidence. ... For all I know, we may be visited by a different extraterrestrial civilization every second Tuesday, but there's no support for this appealing idea. The extraordinary claims are not supported by extraordinary evidence". – Carl Sagan, Cosmos: A Personal Voyage, PBS broadcast, December 14, 1980. As Deming has convincingly shown, the ECREE rule is ill-conceived in principle and its disparaging use in the practice just described misguided; see David Deming, Do Extraordinary Claims Require Extraordinary Evidence? 44 Philosophia (2016) 1319–1331. Criticism is also due from the point of general (forensic) witness psychology, a topic in the context of ECREE that still awaits a fuller treatment. In the same critical vein as Loeb, see Sean McMahon, Sean, Do Extraordinary Claims Require Extraordinary Evidence? – The Proper Role of Sagan's Dictum in Astrobiology, in Kelly C Smith and Carlos Mariscal (eds.) *Social and Conceptual Issues in Astrobiology* (OUP, Oxford, 2020) pp. 126–127: "There are many social factors, not considered here, which may incline a scientist to a posture of hard-headed immovability; it is probably better for one's career to be known as a trenchant skeptic than as a credulous dupe. But the cautious scientific skepticism appropriate to such a young field with such profound subject matter should not be allowed to spill over into reactionary 'pseudo-skepticism.' We should follow the evidence where it leads (guided by rational modes of inquiry), not impose double standards. In particular, there is no good reason to think that the detection of extraterrestrial life should require extraordinary evidence. It would be a shame if the astrobiological community failed to recognize one of the most "wow!-extraordinary" discoveries in the history of science out of a misguided belief that such claims are somehow automatically unacceptable". – See further on 'Oumuamua G.R. Harp et al., Radio SETI observations of the interstellar object 'OUMUAMUA, 155 *Acta Astronautica* (2019) 51–54 and erratum at Acta 167 Astronautica, 483; Christopher Cowie,

the year 2000 is the currently still unexplained anomaly – rectangular and 45 m across in size – photographed by the NEAR Shoemaker probe during its mission to 433 Eros (see Figure 2).[89]

Major coordinated SETI activities of the astronomy type remain[90] popular: A number of mostly privately funded[91] SETI projects set in motion in 2015 are the Breakthrough Initiatives,[92] i.e., the traditionally passive Breakthrough Listen[93] and Breakthrough Watch,[94] the message development endeavour of Breakthrough Message,[95] and the more active Breakthrough Starshot[96] which

---

The 'Oumuamua Controversy: A Philosophical Perspective, 5 *Nature Astronomy* (2021) 526–527.

89 The View from Low Orbit, NASA Photo https://nssdc.gsfc.nasa.gov/planetary/image/near_20000501.jpg. The image printed here has been rotated by 90°. The picture caption provided by NASA at https://nssdc.gsfc.nasa.gov/planetary/mission/near/near_eros_3.html reads: "The View from Low Orbit – This image of Eros, taken from the NEAR Shoemaker spacecraft on May 1, 2000, is among the first to be returned from 'low orbit'. Between May and August, the spacecraft will orbit at altitudes near 50 kilometers (31 miles) or less. This will be the prime period of activity for some of the spacecraft's science instruments. The X-ray / gamma-ray spectrometer will build up maps of chemical abundances, while the laser rangefinder measures the shape of Eros to within meters (a few feet). At the same time the magnetometer will watch for indications of Eros' magnetic field and the near-infrared spectrometer will map rock types. The imager will take pictures of the entire surface of Eros that capture features as small as 4 meters (13 feet) across. This particular image, taken from an orbital altitude of 53 kilometers (33 miles), shows a scene about 1.8 kilometers (1.1 miles) across. Numerous craters and boulders as small as 8 meters (26 feet) across dot the landscape. *The large, rectangular boulder at the upper right is 45 meters (148 feet) across.*" (Image 0132577092) [Emphasis added]. NEAR Shoemaker soft-landed on 433Eros in early 2001; see http://spaceartefacts.com/human-objects-on-asteroid-433-eros . Obviously, it could not have photographed itself from orbit so that it can be excluded that the anomaly is NEAR Shoemaker itself. At a size of 45 m across, it is also far too large to be the probe itself. – A freedom of information request by German science journalist Daniel Gerritzen with JPL for higher-resolution photos met with the reply that NASA did not have any better footage of the anomaly. – Email by Daniel Gerritzen to the German ETI Research Network of 3 January 2021 (on file with the author).

90 Michael A. Garrett, SETI reloaded: Next generation radio telescopes, transients and cognitive computing, 113 *Acta Astronautica* (2015) 8–12.

91 The prohibitive cost of large-scale SETI projects has resulted in innovative funding proposals; see Jacob Haqq-Misra, Funding the Search for Extraterrestrial Intelligence with a Lottery Bond, 51 *Space Policy* (2020) 101230.

92 See https://breakthroughinitiatives.org/.

93 See https://breakthroughinitiatives.org/initiative/1; Pete S Worden et al., Breakthrough Listen – A new search for life in the universe, 139 Acta Astronautica (2017) 98–101.

94 See https://breakthroughinitiatives.org/initiative/4.

95 See https://breakthroughinitiatives.org/initiative/2.

96 See https://breakthroughinitiatives.org/initiative/3.

FIGURE 2
NEAR Shoemaker | 433 Eros anomaly
Enlarged and enhanced segment from upper right original image quadrant
SOURCE: HTTPS://NSSDC.GSFC.NASA.GOV/PLANETARY/IMAGE/NEAR_20000501.JPG

envisages using Earth-based-laser-propelled[97] miniature probes attached to light sails in order to reach and survey planets and star systems outside our own solar system within time frames that are capable of reaching speeds so that travel to the destination and relaying data do not necessarily exceed the regular life span of individual humans as would be the case if existing conventional chemical propulsion systems were used. A final future project is Breakthrough Enceladus proposed together with NASA,[98] to send an astrobiological probe to Saturn's moon Enceladus.

Hakan Kayal has recently proposed a move to a more inclusive approach he calls HYPER-SETI, which is based on the assumption that there may be a wealth of communication already happening in outer space but at a level of technological development that humanity is still unable to reproduce or interact with. He posits that although we are not necessarily capable of picking up the signal as such, we may be able to detect anomalies the chosen form of communication leaves in the observable universe and that detection of patterns may be an indicator of an artificial origin.[99]

97 For the previous NASA Breakthrough Propulsion Physics Programme begun in 1996 and studying "the ultimate breakthroughs in space transportation: propulsion that requires no propellant mass, propulsion that attains the maximum transit speeds physically possible, and breakthrough methods of energy production to power such devices. Topics of interest include experiments and theories regarding the coupling of gravity and electromagnetism, vacuum fluctuation energy, warp drives and worm-holes, and superluminal quantum effects", see NASA Breakthrough Propulsion Physics Program, 2013, https://ntrs.nasa.gov/citations/19980201240.

98 See NASA and Breakthrough Starshot Foundation LLC Under Space Act Umbrella Agreement, 2018, www.nasa.gov/saa/domestic/26617_2017_Annex1_Brkthru_Encel_FullyExecuted.pdf.

99 Hakan Kayal, HYPER-SETI – A New Way of Searching for Extraterrestrial Intelligence. – https://www.uni-wuerzburg.de/fileadmin/ifex/2019/IAC-19_A4_1_13_x48686_full_paper.pdf. – Paper given at the 70th International Astronautical Congress (IAC), Washington D.C., United States, 21-25 October 2019.

4 Astrobiology

Astrobiology,[100] (previously) also called exobiology by some,[101] was defined by NASA, to name but one example, as

> the study of the origin, evolution, distribution, and future of life in the universe. This multidisciplinary field encompasses the search for habitable environments in our Solar System and habitable planets outside our Solar System, the search for evidence of prebiotic chemistry and life on Mars and other bodies in our Solar System, laboratory and field research into the origins and early evolution of life on Earth, and studies of the potential for life to adapt to challenges on Earth and in space. [102]

Today, the NASA definition seems to have been shortened to "[a]strobiology is the study of the origin, evolution, and distribution of life in the universe".[103] NASA has in principle been embedding astrobiological aspects in the planning of all of its missions for some decades.[104] However, it would be inaccurate to confine the wider academic field of astrobiology today to the "biology" part. As a rising number of publications show, astrobiology

100 The invention of that term in 1953 is ascribed to Russian astronomer Gavriil Tikhov; see Charles S Cockell, 'Astrobiology' and the ethics of new science, 26 *Interdisciplinary Science Reviews* (2001) 90–96; Manasvi Lingam and Abraham Loeb, What's in a name: the etymology of astrobiology, 19 *International Journal of Astrobiology* (2020) 379–385.

101 The term "exobiology" was coined in the late 1950s by Nobel Prize winner Joshua Lederberg, and referred "to the study of life's origins on Earth and the development of instruments and methods to search for signs of life on other celestial bodies"; Steven J Dick and James E Strick, *The Living Universe: NASA and the Development of Astrobiology* (Rutgers University Press, New Brunswick, 2004) p. 29. See also Audra J Wolfe, Germs in Space: Joshua Lederberg, Exobiology, and the Public Imagination, 1958–1964, 93 *Isis* (2004) 183–205. – The term "bioastronomy" has also been used; see, for example, R P Norris and F H Stootman (eds.). 2004. *Bioastronomy 2002: Life Among the Stars – IAU Symposium,* (Astronomical Society of the Pacific, San Francisco, 2004).

102 See NASA About Astrobiology, https://astrobiology.nasa.gov/about/. For a popular science introduction see Marc Kaufman, A History of Astrobiology, NASA, 2022, https://astrobiology.nasa.gov/about/history-of-astrobiology/. A more academic description is given by Steven J. Dick, Astrobiology and Society: An Overview, in Kelly C Smith and Carlos Mariscal (eds.) *Social and Conceptual Issues in Astrobiology* (OUP, Oxford, 2020) pp. 9–20.

103 See Marc Kaufman, Life, Here and Beyond, NASA, 2022, https://astrobiology.nasa.gov/about/.

104 It currently has analysis groups on the following topics: Outer Planets Assessment Group (OPAG); Mars Exploration Program Analysis Group (MEPAG); Exoplanet Exploration Program Analysis Group (ExoPAG); Lunar Exploration Analysis Group (LEAG); Small

has moved into an interdisciplinary mode of research that makes it for all intents and purposes nigh indistinguishable from the general conceptual envelope and the individual facets of SETI research, the only major difference being that astrobiology is not interested in *intelligent* life only, but also considers the existence of, and contact with, any life-forms[105] such as microbes, plants etc. and the consequences for, for example, exohabitat contamination and planetary protection caused by (human) space exploration and resource exploitation. For example, Cambridge University Press alone has been running a series called "Cambridge Astrobiology" since 2006 that has so far dealt with astrobiology-related issues such as planet formation,[106] planetary systems,[107] bio-chemistry and fine-tuning,[108] philosophical, ethical and theological perspectives,[109] so-called "astrobiological analogs" used to approximate hypothetical projections of conditions on other planets with similar habitats on Earth,[110] evolution theory,[111] the Drake Equation,[112] discovery and societal impact,[113] the Fermi Paradox,[114] and a universal theory of life.[115] Its competitor Oxford University Press recently published an edited collection on social and conceptual issues in astrobiology,[116] which includes sections on philosophy, ethical issues, and social and legal issues.[117] For our purposes, there is thus no need to dwell on further conceptual differences

---

Bodies Assessment Group (SBAG) and the Venus Exploration Analysis Group (VEXAG) – see Analysis Groups, NASA, 2022, https://astrobiology.nasa.gov/analysis-groups/.

105 For an overview of the discussion regarding a definition of "life", see N Irwin Louis and Dirk Schulze-Makuch, The Astrobiology of Alien Worlds: Known and Unknown Forms of Life, 6 (9) *Universe* (2020) 130.

106 Hubert Klahr and Wolfgang Brandner (eds.), 2006. *Planet Formation: Theory, Observations, and Experiments* (CUP, Cambridge, 2006).

107 Ralph Pudritz et al (eds.), *Planetary Systems and the Origins of Life* (CUP, Cambridge, 2007).

108 John D Barrow et al. (eds.), *Fitness of the Cosmos for Life* (CUP, Cambridge, 2016).

109 Constance M Bertka (ed.), *Exploring the Origin, Extent, and Future of Life* (CUP, Cambridge, 2010); Milan M Ćirković, *The Astrobiological Landscape* (CUP, Cambridge, 2012).

110 Peter D Doran et al. (eds.), *Life in Antarctic Deserts and other Cold Dry Environments* (CUP, Cambridge, 2010).

111 Muriel Gargaud et al. (eds.), *Origins and Evolution of Life* (CUP, Cambridge, 2011).

112 Douglas A. Vakoch and Matthew F Dowd (eds.) *The Drake Equation* (CUP, Cambridge, 2015).

113 Steven J. Dick, *Astrobiology, Discovery, and Societal Impact* (CUP, Cambridge, 2018).

114 Duncan H Forgan, *Solving Fermi's Paradox* (CUP, Cambridge, 2019).

115 Carol E Cleland, *The Quest for a Universal Theory of Life* (CUP, Cambridge, 2019).

116 Kelly C Smith and Carlos Mariscal (eds.), *Social and Conceptual Issues in Astrobiology* (OUP, Oxford, 2020).

117 It shall suffice here to mention that OUP naturally has had its own comprehensive astrobiology publication programme for some time. – See https://global.oup.com/academic/search?q=Astrobiology&cc=de&lang=en.

other than bearing in mind that astrobiology does not require looking at the "I" in ETI mentioned above.

While SETI still appears to be dominated by sciences such as astronomy, physics, biology etc., there has been a rise in interest in the social sciences for some time. To these we turn in the next chapter.

CHAPTER 3

Social Science Aspects of SETI

1 Gauging the Risk and Impact of First Contact on Global Society

If one accepts, for argument's sake, the possibility of human contact with ETI, it becomes immediately clear that the consequences of contact for human society (and of its becoming public) will be massive, much more so than the "mere" discovery of non-sentient microbes on Mars – which in and of itself would already put paid to any contention from certain interested quarters that life only developed on Earth. There would, for example, be serious ramifications into the field of theology for almost all human religions. The impact of such a discovery would also depend on the kind of contact: Finding microbes – but nothing else – on Mars, as we just said, would most likely pale in comparison to the detection of a radio signal from afar. That would be much more significant but probably be felt by most people to pose no immediate and direct threat due to the interstellar distances involved – and to a certain degree probably even regardless of whether an actual message could be deciphered from the signal pattern or not. Things would, however, get much more dramatic if a derelict space craft or another technological artefact as possibly already present on 433 Eros or observed in the case of the object 'Oumuamua were to be discovered or confirmed to exist in our solar system. Finally, public awareness of an active alien spaceship or probe arriving in our solar system, in Earth's orbit or even landing on Earth would most likely cause pandemonium, especially if the craft was crewed by biological[1] life forms. There would be acute challenges to global and local risk and disaster management. Given that a merely passive signal detection could already have such consequences, how wise is it to advertise our existence by engaging in active SETI and sending signals into space whose potential recipients and their characteristics, capabilities and intentions we know nothing about?[2] Are METI scientists, as Fred Hoyle wrote in The Black Cloud, "a small group of desperate men, who to gratify insatiable ambitions

1 Whether carbon-based or not.

2 See, for example David Brin, A Contrarian Perspective on Altruism: The Dangers of First Contact, IAASETI Permanent Committee website, 2002, http://resources.iaaseti.org/brin.pdf.

 | DOI:10.1163/9789004677708_004

had allied themselves with the thing in the sky, men who were guilty of treason against the entire human species"?[3]

The wider scientific and SETI community have for some time engaged in considering the different parameters of various contact scenarios and the criteria for determining their impact, as well as the guidelines for managing and containing the expected risks and impact.[4] We shall take a brief look at some of

3 Fred Hoyle, *The Black Cloud.* (William Heinemann Ltd, Portsmouth, 1957 – cited after the Penguin edition, 1960) p. 199 – The background to this sentence is that the scientists working at a secret facility in the UK and in contact with the ETI of the Cloud warn it of an impending missile strike with hundreds of hydrogen warheads sent by the US and the USSR, also to assure it that they had no hand in the attack. The Cloud ETI accepts their explanation and then re-directs the missiles roughly back along their trajectory so that they hit the countries which fired them, leading to massive loss of human life and the scientists becoming "marked men". *Ibid.*, pp. 196–199.

4 See, for example, for an overview of the disciplines and considerations involved, Gordon M Gartrelle, Unknown caller: can we effectively manage the announcement of discovery of extraterrestrial life?, 14 *International Journal of Astrobiology* (2015) 577–587; Mark Neal, Preparing for extraterrestrial contact, 16 *Risk Management* (2014) 63–87; Thomas Moynihan, Existential risk and human extinction: An intellectual history, 116 *Futures* (2020) 102495; Alexey Turchin and David Denkenberger, Global catastrophic and existential risks communication scale, 102 Futures (2018) 27–38; Allen E. Goodman, Diplomatic and political problems affecting the formulation and implementation of an international protocol for activities following the detection of a signal from extraterrestrial intelligence, 21 *Acta Astronautica* (1990) 103-108; *id.*, Diplomacy and the search of extraterrestrial intelligence (SETI), 21 Acta Astronautica (1990) 137-141; Karim Jebaria and Niklas Olsson-Yaouzis, A Game of Stars: Active SETI, radical translation and the Hobbesian trap, 101 *Futures* (2018) 46–54; Janne M Korhonen, MAD with aliens? Interstellar deterrence and its implications, 86 *Acta Astronautica* (2013) 201–210; Joao Pedro de Magalhaes, A direct communication proposal to test the Zoo Hypothesis, 38 *Space Policy* (2016) 22–26; James D Millera, and D Felton, The Fermi paradox, Bayes' rule, and existential risk management, 86 *Futures* (2017) 44–57; Gabriel G de la Torre, Toward a new cosmic consciousness: Psychoeducational aspects of contact with extraterrestrial civilizations, 94 *Acta Astronautica* (2014) 577–583; Douglas A Vakoch et al., What should we say to extraterrestrial intelligence?: An analysis of responses to "Earth Speaks", 86 *Acta Astronautica* (2013) 136–148; Seth D Baum, The far future argument for confronting catastrophic threats to humanity: Practical significance and alternatives, 72 *Futures* (2015) 86–96; Joseph Voros, On a morphology of contact scenario space, *Technological Forecasting & Social Change* (2018) 126–137; Ivan Almár and Margaret S Race, Discovery of extra-terrestrial life: assessment by scales of its importance and associated risks, 369 *Phil. Trans. R. Soc. A* (2011) 679–692; Martin Dominik and John C Zarnecki, The detection of extra-terrestrial life and the consequences for science and society, 369 *Phil. Trans. R. Soc. A* (2011) 499–507; Albert A Harrison, Fear, pandemonium, equanimity and delight: human responses to extra-terrestrial life, 369 *Phil. Trans. R. Soc. A* (2011) 656–668; *id.*, Proximity, System Level, and Human Response to Extraterrestrial Life, in: Workshop on the societal implications of astrobiology – Final Report, Ames Research Center, November 16–17, 1999, in NASA, *Workshop on the societal implications of Astrobiology*, 1999, p. 56, www.astrosociology.org/library/pdf/nasa-workshop-report-societal-implications-of-astrobiology.pdf.; Simon Conway Morris, Predicting what extra-terrestrials will be

the prevailing models[5] and then turn to the most concrete[6] and quasi-official existing manifestations of preparing for contact, and the public dissemination of the news about it – the IAA Declarations of Principles.

1.1 *The Rio and San Marino Scales*

The common idea behind these scales was the creation of an instrument of prediction analogous to the Richter Scale for earthquakes. They are, in a sense, adaptations of the earlier Torino Scale,[7] published in 1997, which was drafted to predict the impact risk of NEOs[8] such as asteroids and comets, and thus has a space-related origin but no link to the impact of detection of ETI. The Rio Scale, so called because the idea was first put forward at the 29th review meeting of the SETI Committee at the 51st IAA Congress in Rio de Janeiro, in October 2000. was accepted in 2002.[9] The IAASETI Permanent Committee (IAASETI) describes the purpose as follows:

> Nearly everyone is familiar with the Richter Scale [...]. Can we similarly quantify the importance of a candidate SETI signal? The Rio Scale is an attempt to do just that. It is an ordinal scale between zero and ten, used to quantify the impact of any public announcement regarding evidence of extraterrestrial intelligence.[10]

like: and preparing for the worst, 369 *Phil. Trans. R. Soc. A* (2011) 555–571; Mazlan Othman, Supra-Earth affairs, 369 *Phil. Trans. R. Soc. A* (2011) 693–699; Ted Peters, The implications of the discovery of extra-terrestrial life for religion, 369 *Phil. Trans. R. Soc. A* (2011) 644–655; Christopher P Mackay, The search for life in our Solar System and the implications for science and society, 369 *Phil. Trans. R. Soc. A* (2011) 594–606.

5 For a compact overview of the development of the efforts at establishing agreed procedures around signal detection, see Michael A.G. Michaud, Contact with Alien Civilizations – Our Hopes and Fears about Encountering Extraterrestrials (Copernicus Books, New York, 2010), (hereafter: Michaud) pp. 25 -53, 358–374.

6 However, the award for most concrete effort may probably have to go to William M Kramer and Charles W Bahmer, *Fire Officer's Guide to Disaster Control, 2nd ed.* (Pennwell, Tulsa, 1992) who dedicate the book's entire Chapter 13 to the topic of "enemy attack and UFO potential", at pp. 439–473 (A copy was obtained by the author courtesy of Mr Rex Heisdorffer, Assistant Chief, Newton Fire Department, Iowa).

7 See https://cneos.jpl.nasa.gov/sentry/torino_scale.html.

8 See for a modern incarnation the NASA funded Jet Propulsion Laboratory's Center for NEO Studies (CNEOS), at https://cneos.jpl.nasa.gov/.

9 See for this and the following https://iaaseti.org/en/rio-scale/ with a number of links and references for further reading at the bottom of the page.

10 IAA SETI Permanent Committee, Introduction to Rio Scale Calculator, 2005, https://iaaseti.org/en/rio-scale/.

Class of Phenomenon

- Earth-specific message, or an ET artifact, capable of contact, or a physical encounter
- Omnidirectional message with decipherable information, or a functioning ET artifact or space probe
- Earth-specific beacon to draw our attention, or an ET artifact with a message to mankind
- Omnidirectional beacon designed to draw attention, or an ET artifact with a message of a general character
- Leakage radiation, without possible interpretation, or an ET artifact the purpose of which is understandable
- traces of astroengineering, or any indication of technological activity by an extant orextinct civilization at any distance, or an ET artifact, the purpose of which is unknown

Type of Discovery

- SETI/SETA observation; steady phenomenon verifiable by repeated observation or investigation
- Non-SETI/SETA observation; steady phenomenon verifiable by repeated observation or investigation
- SETI/SETA observation; transient phenomenon that has been verified but never repeated
- Non-SETI/SETA observation; transient phenomenon that is reliable but never repeated
- From archival data; a posteriori discovery without possibility of verification

Apparent Distance

- Within the solar system
- Within a distance which allows communication (at lightspeed) within a human lifetime
- Within the Galaxy
- Extragalactic

Credibility of Report:

- Absolutely reliable, without any doubt
- Very probable, with verification already carried out
- Possible, but should be verified before taken seriously
- Very uncertain, but worthy of verification efforts
- Obviously fake or fraudulent

FIGURE 3 Rio scale calculator categories – lowest impact factors at the bottom of each category
SOURCE: HTTPS://IAASETI.ORG/EN/RIO-SCALE-CALCULATOR/

There is an online "Rio Scale Calculator" which allows the calculation of the impact factor depending on the type of contact scenario and provides a good summary of the factors the scale is looking for (see Figure 3):[11]

11 IAA SETI Permanent Committee, Rio Scale Calculator, 2005, https://iaaseti.org/en/rio-scale-calculator/. – See Duncan H Forgan et al., Rio 2.0: revising the Rio scale for SETI detections, 17 *International Journal of Astrobiology* (2019) 336–344. On a critical deconstruction with the conclusion that it should not be used to inform the media or the public, see John W Traphagan, Deconstructing the Rio Scale: problems of subjectivity and generalization, 18 *International Journal of Astrobiology* (2019) 463–467, with a rebuttal by Duncan H Forgan et al., Rebuttal to: 'Deconstructing the Rio Scale: problems of subjectivity and generalization', 18 *International Journal of Astrobiology* (2019) 492–493.

A similar scale exists for quantifying the potential impact of active SETI transmissions, the San Marino Scale of 2005,[12] also with its own online calculator.[13] They both contain a range of differing degrees of impact intensity resulting from any combination of factors which are, however, not in any way a mathematical expression of the expected risk and impact, or of the actions to be taken – nor can they be. In essence, all they can say is that the closer to home and the more direct and unequivocally established the contact, the greater the societal upheaval and the ensuing complexity of the challenges for global risk and disaster management to be expected.[14] This is all the more problematic given that it is unclear at best, whether any government has made any preparations for such a contingency – in effect, however, only those nations with major military and spacefaring capacities would probably be in a position to do so. There are certainly no such efforts recorded on a global co-ordinated level.

1.2 *IAASETI Declarations of Principles*[15]

In 1998, the IAA adopted the "Declaration of Principles Concerning Activities Following the Detection of Extraterrestrial Intelligence", also called the "SETI Protocol I". In it, the members of the IAA committed themselves to a series of principles which were meant to govern the post-detection period and to ensure that extraordinary claims were not made without proper prior vetting. They oblige the researchers to self-verify any potential discovery and seek independent verification by third parties prior to announcement to the public, and also inform their national authorities (Principles 1 and 2). They should also inform observers in a number of international institutions (Principle 3). Confirmed discoveries should be promptly disseminated through scientific

12 IAA SETI Permanent Committee, The San Marino Scale, 2008, https://iaaseti.org/en/san-marino-scale/, also with further reading at the bottom of the page.

13 The link from the IAASETI page to the calculator page <http://avsport.org/IAA/smicalc.htm> was, however, still broken at the time of writing. The author had previously queried this with the IAASETI Committee webmaster on 5 and 6 March 2021 but the link was not repaired nor was an explanation given other than that the broken link had nothing to do with IAASETI. – Email correspondence between the author and Matt Lebofsky of 5 and 6 March 2021 (on file).

14 Harrison, for example, had also proposed criteria for a matrix along those lines, see Albert A Harrison, Fear, pandemonium, equanimity and delight: human responses to extra terrestrial life, 369 *Phil. Trans. R. Soc. A* (2011) 656–668; *Id.*, Proximity, System Level, and Human Response to Extraterrestrial Life, in: Workshop on the societal implications of astrobiology – Final Report, Ames Research Center, November 16–17, 1999; in NASA, *Workshop on the societal implications of Astrobiology*, 1999, p. 56, www.astrosociology.org/library/pdf/nasa-workshop-report-societal-implications-of-astrobiology.pdf.

15 The full text of the referenced following documents is reproduced in Annex A.

and public media and data freely shared with the international science community; the discovery should be confirmed and monitored, and data should be stored and made available, too (Principles 4, 5 and 6). If the detection is through electromagnetic signals, international protection of the relevant frequencies should be sought (Principle 7). No response to the signal should be made before international consultations have taken place (Principle 8). The procedures for detection shall, finally, be continuously monitored by a group of experts (Principle 9).

In 2010, the SETI Permanent Study Group of the International Academy of Astronautics at its annual meeting in Prague, drafted and adopted the "Declaration of Principles Concerning the Conduct of the Search for Extraterrestrial Intelligence", also sometimes called "SETI Protocol II". The purpose of the new document was "to declare our commitment to conduct this search in a scientifically valid and transparent manner and to establish uniform procedures for the announcement of a confirmed SETI detection". It broadly revisits the principles of Protocol I and aims for a closer alignment with the United Nations in particular in the process of dissemination of a discovery and especially the decision of whether and how to send a response. Like Protocol I, however, the neuralgic point is that informing the public is the decision – and actually the duty – of the researcher, without waiting for authorisation from any (democratically elected) political body. Unlike Protocol I, the 2010 Declaration was never adopted by the full IAA.

Finally, in 1995, the SETI Committee of the IAA had already proposed a "Draft Declaration of Principles Concerning Sending Communications with Extraterrestrial Intelligence", the so-called "Reply Protocols", which in essence aims to make the sending of any message dependent on prior international consultation, stating in Principle 8 that "[n]o communication to extraterrestrial intelligence should be sent by any State until appropriate international consultations have taken place [and that] States should not cooperate with attempts to communicate with extraterrestrial intelligence that do not conform to the principles of this Declaration". However, given that this particular horse had already bolted with the 1974 Arecibo Message by Frank Drake and the famous pictograms of the Pioneer 10 and 11 probes designed by Carl Sagan and Frank Drake[16] which were actually *advertising* the precise position of Earth in the solar system so that ETI could find it, the sincerity of the intention in the Reply Protocols was somewhat questionable, as indeed is no. 8 of Protocol I. The Reply Protocols have not been adopted, either. In sum, it seems fair to

16 See, for example, the image at Robert Nemiroff and Jerry Bonnell, Astronomy Picture of the Day, 1996, https://apod.nasa.gov/apod/ap960630.html.

say that there is no agreed,[17] let alone legally binding, procedure for either the search for ETI nor the required action in the case of (signal) detection.

1.3 *Excursion: IAASETI and Its Attitude to Research into UAP*

The IAASETI approach, despite the inclusion in its terms of reference of the words "or other evidence" in any event only really seems to cover the alternative of a signal from afar, because nobody appears to have been seriously looking for anything else so far and UFO phenomena – which could on the face of it include a large part of SETA research – are, for example, explicitly and apodictically removed from the scientific focus in the IAASETI Terms of Reference:[18] "These terms of reference currently[19] exclude any consideration

---

17 But see the comment by an ESA staff member referenced below in the section on Metalaw, that ESA would in practice abide by the IAASETI Protocol(s).

18 See IAA SETI Permanent Committee, Terms of Reference – https://iaaseti.org/en/terms-reference/.

19 The author queried this by email of 3 April 2021 with Claudio Maccone, the then Chair of the IAASETI Permanent Committee, which consisted mainly of this text: *"I was forwarded your recent email on the next IAASETI congress, which contained a line that said 3 papers were rejected because they dealt with UFO s and that this was 'unacceptable to astronomers'. I am aware that the IAASETI terms of reference (categorically) exclude UFO-related research. Given that Seth Shostak advised in his 2002 paper on "SETI and the Media" to adopt a more nuanced approach, I have been bemused by this exclusionary attitude from the beginning, not least because the seemingly accepted discipline of SETA deals with issues that are/can be largely identical. Moreover, if I see correctly, not all IAASETI members are astronomers. I have been unable to find any information about when and why IAASETI decided to go down that route, and if there are any minutes of meetings/proceedings etc. that would shed light on the issue. John Elliott was not aware of any and a request to the Co-Vice Chair remains unanswered. It may not be IAASETI's intention but from a purely research-ethics-related and collegial point of view, the exclusion obviously has the effect of disparaging the work of serious UFO researchers (in fact employing Shostak's extraneous "giggle factor" within the wider SETI community) and of blotting out a field where more tangible evidence might possibly exist, which is after all the gist of SETA research. I see no material difference whether an artefact – whether derelict or operative, manned or unmanned – is found on Earth or on the Moon. In a way, if taken literally, the current terms of reference would preclude any research – and publication or presentation – about an alien spacecraft that landed in broad daylight on the Piazza Navona and left again after its crew got some excellent Italian ice cream from one of the local gelaterias – if you pardon the humorous example. I would be grateful if you could enlighten me about the origin and proper meaning of the IAASETI terms of reference and why even serious, and above all rigorous, UFO research seems to be discounted as non-scientific. The saying about the baby and the bath water comes to mind".* – Eventually a "tiger team" was set up within the Committee to discuss the relationship to UFO research in more depth. The author is not a member of the Committee and hence unaware whether a new position has been reached and whether unanimously or not, although the lack of a change of the terms of reference on the IAASETI webpage would

of UFO phenomena".[20] By way of a brief legal detour, it seems appropriate to express a degree of puzzlement with this approach. After all, Article V(3) of the Treaty on Principles Governing the Activities of States in the Exploration and Use of Outer Space, including the Moon and Other Celestial Bodies (Outer Space Treaty),[21] states:

> States Parties to the Treaty shall immediately inform the other States Parties to the Treaty or the Secretary-General of the United Nations *of any phenomena they discover in outer space, including the Moon and other celestial bodies,* which could constitute a danger to the life or health of astronauts. [Emphasis added.]

This is repeated almost verbatim in Article 5(3) of the Agreement Governing the Activities of States on the Moon and Other Celestial Bodies (Moon Agreement).[22] Article 13 of the Moon Agreement adds:

> A State Party which learns of the crash landing, forced landing or other unintended landing on the Moon *of a space object, or its component parts, that were not launched by it*, shall promptly inform the launching State Party and the Secretary-General of the United Nations.

While it may be fair to say that the drafters of these instruments may not necessarily have primarily had extraterrestrial space objects in mind, the wording of the articles easily allows their inclusion. *A minore ad maius*, it would moreover seem rather odd if there was to be no obligation to inform the UN about the detection of a non-human craft. In any event, the attitude of IAASETI blots out the ramifications which these international agreements should at least in practice have for the question of whether one can with good reasons simply

---

seem to suggest a negative answer to that question. – Email correspondence with Claudio Maccone of 3 April 2021 and ensuing email trail on which the author was still copied in until the debate was moved to the internal forum (all on file with the author).

20 However, Seth Shostak, while fully aware of the historically proven potential of the "UFO scene" for tainting the "serious" SETI science effort, acknowledged as early as 2002 that the approach should be on a case-by-case basis, following proper scientific method. – Seth Shostak, SETI and the Media, in R P Norris and F H Stootman (eds.) *Bioastronomy 2002: Life Among the Stars– IAU Symposium,* (Astronomical Society of the Pacific, San Francisco, 2004) pp. 540–541.

21 See Annex B.I. – We shall leave aside the discussion about whether and to what extent the treaty is binding or actually being adhered to by the spacefaring nations.

22 See Annex B.II.

exclude research into UAP, especially if there may be practical and cogent reasons to have as much information to hand as possible. Again, with the new development around official UAP research since 2021, IAASETI would be well-advised to reconsider its stance.

1.4 *The DISC Quotient – Linking Impact and Linguistics*

John Elliott and Stephen Baxter[23] have presented their own version[24] of an impact scale along the lines of the Rio Scale, the so-called DISC quotient model (DISC = Decipherment Impact of a Signal's Content), i.e., "a numerical method to characterise the significance of the receipt of a complex and potentially decipherable signal from extraterrestrial intelligence [...]. The purpose of the scale is to facilitate the public communication of work on any such claimed signal, as such work proceeds, and to assist in its discussion and interpretation".[25] In other words, significance of impact is set in relation to the degree of signal decipherability and the amount of data discovered, from the likely rapid identification of potential information-carrying structures and their "syntax" – for example, is it a message or an image – to deeper levels of structural understanding and semantic content. This evaluation could change with the influx of new decipherment information, leading to amended impact levels over time. It is thus not a static model. While it would take too long for our purposes to analyse the approach in detail, it leads us on to our next issue, that of linguistic communication hurdles.

2 Exolinguistics

As already addressed above, the question of detecting a transmission pattern and determining it to be an artificial signal, and hence evidence of an advanced, technologically mature civilisation, is an entirely different thing from understanding the substance or meaning of the signal. Not every artificial signal, moreover, has to contain a message or actually be directed at anyone: A position beacon, for example, may just allow a certain object to be located on the basis of a bare radio signal but does not necessarily have to contain any data about the nature of the object etc. Moreover, the signal and/or its message may by its nature be comprehensible only to certain persons, groups, or civilisations,

23 John R Elliott and Stephen Baxter, The DISC Quotient, 78 *Acta Astronautica* (2012) 20–25.

24 Based on an earlier paper by John Elliott, A post-detection decipherment strategy, 68 *Acta Astronautica* (2011) 441–444.

25 *Supra* fn. 23, at 20.

and, of course, certain concepts may have historically and culturally different socially constructed meanings, although on the face of it they may seem to refer to the same idea as, for example, anecdotal[26] evidence from colloquial human conversations illustrates. Indeed, another well-known human example is the saying that in Arabic every word may mean "itself, its direct opposite, or a camel".[27] There is no reason to assume that ETI have not socially constructed similar linguistic conventions where situational meaning may deviate from the literal or ordinary use of a term – even if this phenomenon may be something an intelligent species trying to communicate with an unknown alien other will for obvious reasons try to avoid as much as possible. How many layers of meaning of increasing semantic complexity can be encapsulated in such a type of message beyond the bland (pictorial?) announcement "We are here, and this is what we look like!" as in the Pioneer plaques is, naturally, open to question.

In other words, the issue of the reliability of the mere linguistic decipherability regarding a literal/conceptual and cultural meaning[28] becomes progressively more difficult the more an idea is tied to a cultural upbringing and environment which the recipient of the message has not had the opportunity to share – the phenotype of a message is not necessarily the same as its genotype.

---

26 *Example 1*: A well-known "terrestrial" example, which every German immigrant to the UK will have experienced at some stage, is the use of the word "interesting" in English and its direct equivalent, "*interessant*", in German as a response to a statement made by another person. In German, the word ordinarily means just that – the story is genuinely interesting. In English, the default assumption today is that "interesting" is a euphemism to avoid explicitly expressing the exact opposite, i.e., lack of interest – the word has thus become a synonym for "boring". Every German trips up on that the first time. Real interest must in English now be expressed by the use of terminological superlative inflation such as "fascinating", "exciting" along with a rise in voice pitch etc. – *Example 2*: Similarly, people do, in UK English at least, no longer simply have an "interest in", or "care" about, a certain matter, they are "passionate" about it. Achievements are not merely "acknowledged" or receive expressions of "congratulations", they are "celebrated". The latter is sometimes even used for mere characteristics that would not normally qualify as specific, possibly hard-earned, above-average personal achievements, i.e., when the generic contributions of certain parts of society – for example, of female academics or academics from certain ethnic groups, first generation scholars from widening participation backgrounds etc. – to a particular generic endeavour, such as astronomy research, are to be recognised in the context of modern equality, diversity and inclusion (EDI) environments.

27 See Mark Liberman, The Four Meanings of an Arabic Word, 2006, http://itre.cis.upenn.edu/~myl/languagelog/archives/003264.html.

28 See on cultural communications Paolo Musso, Wide Cultural Communications in Interstellar Messages, in R P Norris and F H Stootman, *Bioastronomy 2002: Life Among the Stars – IAU Symposium,* (Astronomical Society of the Pacific, San Francisco, 2004) pp. 511–513; *id.*, A language based on analogy to communicate cultural concepts in SETI, 68 *Acta Astronautica* (2011) 489–499.

This is already the case between humans and/or between humans and other possibly sapient terrestrial species, such as dolphins and octopuses;[29] it will be even more so in interspecies communication with extraterrestrials. The relative ease with which some SF treatments of the communication aspect such as, for example, the 2016 movie *Arrival*[30] approach highly complex communication problem scenarios, or the ubiquitous capacity of aliens to speak English which they learned from listening to and watching Earth's radio and TV transmissions[31] has possibly led to a deceptive persuasion among the general public that some form of communication will eventually be established in a relatively short time once contact occurs.

This realisation is, of course, not lost on those[32] who deal with the linguistic[33] issue and are faced with the absence of a Rosetta Stone in SETI research.[34] We already addressed the Lingua Cosmica (LINCOS) of Freudenthal/Ollongren[35]

---

29 See Laurance R Doyle et al., Information theory, animal communication, and the search for extraterrestrial intelligence, 68 Acta Astronautica (2011) 406–417.

30 Despite the huge effort that was put into creating the written language of the seven-tentacled aliens, called heptapods, "Heptapod B", by the producers of the movie, it is worth remembering that this is still humans constructing a language that is meant to look alien but has human conceptual DNA, so to speak. Little to no effort was spent on exploring the aural communication language, "Heptapod A", because it sounds more like a mix between whale song and assorted other noises. On this (and other SF languages) see Yens Wahlgren, *The Universal Translator – Everything you need to know about 139 languages that don't really exist* (The History Press, Cheltenham, 2021) pp. 164–168.

31 How would an ETI intent on making direct contact know with the necessary certainty which language to pick in order to establish communications and/or choose a landing site? By sheer numbers, Mandarin Chinese should also be a strong contender.

32 Indeed, Soviet/Russian SETI researchers have traditionally been more sceptical whether communication would ever be possible at all; see recently Lev M Gindilis and Leonid I Gurvits, SETI in Russia, USSR and the post-Soviet space: a century of research, 162 Acta Astronautica (2019) 1–13, at 7; Michael Schetsche and Andreas Anton, Die *Gesellschaft der Außerirdischen – Einführung in die Exosoziologie* (Springer, Wiesbaden, 2019 - hereafter: Schetsche/Anton) p. 87.

33 For further reading see Seth Shostak, Limits on interstellar messages, 68 *Acta Astronautica* (2011) 366–371; Douglas A Vakoch, The art and science of interstellar message composition: a report on international workshops to encourage multidisciplinary discussion, 68 *Acta Astronautica* (2011) 451–458; *id.*, A narratological approach to interpreting and designing interstellar messages, 68 Acta Astronautica (2011) 520–534; *id.*, A taxonomic approach to communicating maxims in interstellar messages, 68 Acta Astronautica (2011) 500–511.

34 See Douglas A Vakoch (ed.). *Archaeology, anthropology, and interstellar communication* (NASA, Washington, 2013) www.nasa.gov/connect/ebooks/archaeology_anthropology_and_interstellar_communication.html.

35 See further on the question of complex message construction Alexander Ollongren and Douglas A Vakoch, 2004. Large-Size Message Construction for ETI: Self-Interpretation

above, as well as the (questionable) assumption that mathematics[36] can be the interspecies *lingua franca*. Elliott's[37] and Baxter's DISC quotient model is also related to the problem. Realising the pattern of a message and potential similarities to human language patterns nonetheless remains *prima facie* a surface effort. As Schetsche and Anton explain, it is not a given that there will necessarily at some stage emerge some degree of mutual understanding,[38] despite the fact that modern evolution biology postulates that life forms develop sensory channels based on their living environment, and that at least planets with Earth-like environments might produce beings with sensory capacities similar to humans – but others may not and other sensory perception mechanisms inaccessible to humans may have evolved.[39] Schetsche and Anton critique the traditional narrow SETI radio astronomy approach to signals from afar as a major restriction on the debate and refer, as a cautionary tale, to the experience regarding the Mayan texts, which have eluded translation for centuries

---

in LINCOS, in R P Norris and F H Stootman (eds.) *Bioastronomy 2002: Life Among the Stars– IAU Symposium* (Astronomical Society of the Pacific, San Francisco, 2004) pp. 499–504; for basic requirements of a *lingua franca* see Alexander Ollongren, Recursivity in Lingua Cosmica, 68 *Acta Astronautica* (2011) 544–548; Alexander Ollongren and Douglas A Vakoch, Typing logic contents using Lingua Cosmica, 68 *Acta Astronautica* (2011) 535–538.

36 But see B S McConnell, *Algorithmic Communication with Extraterrestrial Intelligence*, in R P Norris and F H Stootman (eds.) *Bioastronomy 2002: Life Among the Stars– IAU Symposium* (Astronomical Society of the Pacific, San Francisco, 2004) pp. 445–450; Douglas A Vakoch and Michael Matessa, An algorithmic approach to communicating reciprocal altruism in interstellar messages: Drawing analogies between social and astrophysical phenomena, 68 *Acta Astronautica* (2001) 459–475. On the use of social media as a tool for decryption see René Heller, Decryption of messages from extraterrestrial intelligence using the power of social media – The SETI Decrypt Challenge, 18 *International Journal of Astrobiology* (2019) 296–303.

37 John Elliott has been one of the most prolific and imaginative authors in the exolinguistics field, see, for example, his publications *id.*, Detecting the signature of intelligent life, 67 *Acta Astronautica* (2010) 1419–1426; *id.*, First stage identification of syntactic elements in an extra-terrestrial signal, 68 *Acta Astronautica* (2011) 389–398; *id.*, The filtration of intergalactic objets trouvés and the identification of the lingua ex machina hierarchy, 68 *Acta Astronautica* (2011) 399–405; *id.*, A human language corpus for interstellar message construction, 68 *Acta Astronautica* (2011) 418–424; *id.*, A semantic 'engine' for universal translation, 68 *Acta Astronautica* (2011) 435–440; *id.*, A post-detection decipherment strategy, 68 Acta Astronautica (2011) 441–444; *id.*, Constructing the matrix, 78 *Acta Astronautica* (2012) 26–30; *id.*, Beyond an anthropomorphic template, 116 *Acta Astronautica* (2015) 403–407.

38 Schetsche/Anton, p. 85.

39 *Ibid*, pp. 85–86.

due to the lack of comparison material, and they cite Finney and Bentley,[40] who stated:

> The Maya case appears to undermine SETI scientists' hopes of actually translating the messages they are working to detect. If we have been unable to translate ancient human scripts without some knowledge of the spoken language they represent, what prospects have we of being able to comprehend radio transmissions emanating from other worlds for which we have neither "Rosetta Stones" nor any knowledge of the languages they encode? [...] We must think about the formidable prerequisites of deciphering extraterrestrial messages and consider the possibility that whole domains of knowledge may remain opaque to us, despite our best efforts, for a very long time. If terrestrial analogues are to be employed in relation to SETI, then we should explore the wide range of human experience around the globe and not focus solely on familiar cases that appear to reinforce our most earnest hopes.[41]

Similar conundra are posed, for example, by the Phaistos Disc and the Voynich manuscript, which have given rise to all sorts of speculations, not all of them based on academic rigour.[42] It shall suffice for our purposes to remember that there is no reason to think that communication will be anything but highly difficult, even once an artificial signal has been detected and confirmed as such. This needs to be borne in mind, for example, when evaluating *inter alia* the potential for diplomatic negotiations in the broader sense in the case of a direct contact of uncertain outcome.

3 Exosociology, Exophilosophy and Exotheology

As we saw above, the mere concept of contact with ETI already has profound implications for human society in several existential core areas beyond the

40 Ben Finney and Jerry Bentley, A Tale of Two Analogues Learning at a Distance from the Ancient Greeks and Maya and the Problem of Deciphering Extraterrestrial Radio Transmissions, in Douglas A Vakoch (ed.) *Archaeology, anthropology, and interstellar communication* (NASA, Washington, 2013) www.nasa.gov/connect/ebooks/archaeology_anthropology_and_interstellar_communication.html, pp. 65–78.

41 *Ibid.*, pp. 75 and 77.

42 See Daniel Gerritzen, *Erstkontakt* (Kosmos, Stuttgart, 2016 – hereafter *Erstkontakt*) pp. 197–204.

scientific environment. Actual contact, especially direct contact, would test many of our fundamental assumptions about the meaning of life to their limit, if not beyond breaking point. Among those core areas are some which have traditionally been the subject of intellectual disciplines such as philosophy, theology, or sociology – more generally, the social sciences and the arts and humanities. As with the use of the prefix "exo-" or "astro-"[43] in the context of biology, their use in the fields we will look at in this section is equally wide:[44] They cover the philosophical, theological and sociological impact of SETI and contact on humanity[45] as well as the more speculative ruminations

43 See, for example, the definition of the term "astrosociology" given on the (dated) webpage by Jim Pass, "What is Astrosociology?" www.astrosociology.org: "Astrosociology is a relatively new field defined as the study of astrosocial phenomena (i.e., the social, cultural, and behavioral patterns related to outer space). The field originally began as a sociological perspective almost exclusively [...]. Almost immediately, however, it became clear that contributions were required from the other social and behavioral sciences, the humanities, and the arts (hereafter referred to as the "social sciences" for brevity). Thus, [...] astrosociology was intended as both (1) a subdiscipline of sociology and (2) a multidisciplinary field that includes, but is by no means limited to disciplines/fields such as psychology, anthropology, economics, social psychology, political science, space history, space law, space policy, philosophy, as well as the arts. [...]". See also for more detail Jim Pass, Inaugural Essay: The Definition and Relevance of Astrosociology in the Twenty-First Century, 2004, www.astrosociology.org/Library/Iessay/iessay_p1.pdf; *id.*, Astrosociology as the Missing Perspective, 4 *Astropolitics* (2006) 85-99, and the contributions in the special 2011 issue of the journal *Astropolitics*: Christopher M Hearsey and Jim Pass, Astrosociology, 9 *Astropolitics* (2011) 1–5; Jim Pass, Examining the Definition of Astrosociology, 9 *Astropolitics* (2011) 6–27; Christopher M Hearsey, The Nexus between Law and Astrosociology, 9 *Astropolitics* (2011) 28–38; Albert A Harrison, The Search for Extraterrestrial Intelligence: Astrosociology and Cultural Aspects, 9 *Astropolitics* (2011) 63–83; David Lempert, Living in Space: Cultural and Social Dynamics, Opportunities, and Challenges in Permanent Space Habitats, 9 *Astropolitics* (2011) 84–111, as well as Jacques Arnould, Tele-Reality: How Space Technology Transforms Human Perceptions of Space, Time, and Self, 11 *Astropolitics* (2013) 231–237; David Lempert, Placing Outer Space: An Earthly Ethnography of Other Worlds. 16 *Astropolitics* (2018) 237–241. The term astrosociology translates in German into *Raumfahrtsoziologie* (sociology of space exploration), a somewhat narrower concept; see Joachim Fischer and Dierk Spreen, *Soziologie der Weltraumfahrt.* (transcript, Bielefeld, 2014).

44 Indeed, all of these fields have been gathered under the umbrella term "Xenology", for example, by Robert Freitas; see his online compendium *Xenology: An Introduction to the Scientific Study of Extraterrestrial Life, Intelligence, and Civilization,* www.xenology.info/Xeno.htm.

45 See Michael T Schetsche, 2011. Encounters among the stars – exosociological considerations, in U Landfester et al (eds.) *Humans in Outer Space – Interdisciplinary Perspectives.*

about what should more clearly be called "alien" philosophy, theology and sociology – if indeed there are such things: Other civilisations may not have developed something akin to a theology at all, or may have abandoned the concept during the course of their development. Machine civilisations regulated by Artificial Intelligence (AI), for example, may emphasise their (individual?) components' functional and technical system compliance and consequently have no use at all for concepts such as freedom of the will, minority rights, freedom of thought and speech etc. The potential effect of contact with aliens on *terrestrial* philosophy, theology and sociology is something that we addressed in passing in the previous sections of this chapter. There is thus no need to repeat what was said.[46] The aspect which was not analysed, however, is the question of whether there is or can be a *transspecies* philosophy, theology, sociology or even law, and whether humans can surmise their parameters on their own. This is a fascinating avenue of speculation, and nowhere do the inherent problems and pitfalls of such speculation become clearer than at the example of the Metalaw debate, to which we will now turn as a detailed case study.

Studies in Space Policy (Springer, Vienna, 2011) pp. 102–114; Schetsche/Anton, pp. 1–19, point out that the term "exosociology" was actually already coined by a Soviet scientist in the 1960s.

46 For further detailed reading on *theology* see David Wilkinson, *Science, Religion, and the Search for Extraterrestrial Intelligence* (OUP, Oxford, 2013); *id.*, Why Should Theology Take SETI Seriously? 16 *Theology and Science* (2018) 427-438; see also the special issue on Exoplanets and Astrotheology, 51 *Zygon* (2016) 405–535; Armin Kreiner, *Jesus, UFOs, Aliens – Außerirdische Intelligenz als Herausforderung für den christlichen Glauben.* (Herder, Meersburg, 2011); for two recent studies of the Islamic context see Jörg M Determann, *Islam, Science Fiction and Extraterrestrial Life – The Culture of Astrobiology in the Muslim World* (Bloomsbury, London, 2020) and Barbara K Dick, *Modern Arabic Science Fiction: Science, Society and Religion in Selected Texts,* 2016 http://etheses.dur.ac.uk/11907/. On philosophy, see Mark Lupisella, *Cosmological Theories of Value – Science, Philosophy and Meaning in Cosmic Evolution* (Springer, New York, 2020); Douglas A Vakoch (ed). *Extraterrestrial Altruism: Evolution and Ethics in the Cosmos* (Springer, New York, 2014); Karim Akerma, *Außerirdische – Einleitung in die Philosophie/Extraterrestrische Intelligenz in der Philosophie von Epikur bis Hans Jonas* (Monsenstein und Vannerdat, Münster, 2001); the contributions on philosophy and ethics in Kelly C Smith and Carlos Mariscal (eds.), *Social and Conceptual Issues in Astrobiology* (OUP, Oxford, 2020). For a view of previous Soviet thinking, Maxim W Mikulak, Soviet Philosophic-Cosmological Thought, 25 *Philosophy of Science* (1958) 35–50. On sociology, see generally Schetsche/Anton.

4 The Metalaw Debate – Premature Speculation and Proper Use of Legal Considerations[47]

The modern debate about how relations with extraterrestrial intelligences should be established and subsequently legally regulated began in earnest with the seminal writings of Andrew G Haley in the 1950s,[48] followed by the work of Ernst Fasan[49] in the 1960s, the initial period of humanity's excitement of entering the Space Age.[50] It has been critiqued by a number of commentators mainly for its lack of an empirical, rather than theoretical-deductive, approach,[51] most recently in relation to human interaction with AI.[52] In essence, the Haley-Fasan rule advocates an alleged transmogrification of the traditional "Golden Rule" of "Do unto others as *you* would be done by" into "Do unto others as *they* would be done by". The reasoning builds upon espousing full equality between humans and ETI, and on an extrapolation of Kant's Categorical Imperative.[53] Fasan in particular distilled eleven more specific rules[54] from the general discussion, which are still the most detailed to be

---

47 This section is a modified version of the author's paper Metalaw – What is it good for?, 188 *Acta Astronautica* (2021) 400–404; with kind permission of Elsevier.

48 Andrew G Haley, Space Law and Metalaw – A Synoptic View, *Harvard Law Record*, November 8, 1956; *id.*, *Space Law and Government* (Appleton-Century-Crofts, New York, 1963 – hereafter *Haley*).

49 Ernst Fasan, *Weltraumrecht* (Krausskopf-Flugwelt-Verlag, Cologne, 1965) pp. 141–154; *id.*, *Relations with Alien Intelligences: The Scientific Basis of Metalaw* (Berlin Verlag, Berlin, 1970 – cited after the version printed in Patricia M Stearns and Leslie I Tennen, Leslie (eds.), *Private Law, Public Law, Metalaw and Public Policy in Space,* Springer, New York, 2016) pp. 181–246 (hereafter *Relations*); *id.,* Discovery of ETI: Terrestrial and Extraterrestrial Legal Implications, 21 *Acta Astronautica* (1990) 131–135; *id.*, Legal Consequences of a SETI Detection, 42 *Acta Astronautica* (1998) 677– 679.

50 See, for example, Stephen Gorove, On the Threshold of Space: Toward a Cosmic Law, 4 *New York Law Forum* (1958) 305–328.

51 Overview of the literature in George S Robinson, METALAW: From Speculation to Human*kind* Legal Posturing with Extraterrestrial Life, 2 Journal of Space Philosophy (2013) 49–56, Adam Korbitz, IAC-10-A4.2.10 – Metalaw and the Need for Further Elaboration, 2010 (unpublished paper kindly provided courtesy of the author) and *id.*, Altruism, Metalaw, and Celegistics: An Extraterrestrial Perspective on Universal Law-Making, in Douglas A. Vakoch (ed.) *Extraterrestrial Altruism* (Springer, New York, 2014) pp. 231–247.

52 Kamil Muzyka. The basic rules for coexistence: The possible applicability of metalaw for human-AGI relations, 11 *Paladyn, J. Behav. Robot* (2020) 104–117.

53 *Haley*, p. 412; *Relations*, p. 223.

54 *Relations*, pp. 237–238. He later reduced these to a shorter canon of three rules, see Ernst Fasan, Legal Consequences of a SETI Detection, 42 Acta Astronautica (1998) 677– 679, at 678–679.

found in the debate.[55] The eleven rules are, in the order of precedence and with the explanations given to them by Fasan:

1. *No partner of Metalaw may demand an impossibility.* – This is the strongest rule of all, because an obligation to perform the impossible goes contrary to the principles of life, law, and logic. Living organisms are not capable of performing the impossible.
2. *No rule of Metalaw must be complied with when compliance would result in the practical suicide of the obligated race.* – This rule is the second in strength, because it results from the most basic instinct of life, that of self-preservation.
3. *All intelligent races of the universe have in principle equal rights and values.* – This rule comes next because it results from the basic will to live and because it is necessary for the development of further legal relations. From which it follows:
4. *Every partner of Metalaw has the right of self-determination.*
5. *Any act which causes harm to another race must be avoided.* – This next rule, based upon the anti-entropical nature of life, is (as may well be noted) the first one which assigns a real duty to one race in regard to the other one. It results in the following terms of equal validity.
6. *Every race is entitled to its own living space*
7. *Every race has the right to defend itself against any harmful act performed by another race.*
8. *The principle of preserving one race has priority over the development of another race.*
9. *In case of damage, the damager must restore the integrity of the damaged party.*
10. *Metalegal agreements and treaties must be kept.*
11. *To help the other race by one's own activities is not a legal but a basic ethical Principle.*[56]

Later iterations of the metalaw debate used technological, economic, thermodynamics-and altruism-based[57] arguments to shape the contours of universally valid ethical and legal principles.

55 Overview in Adam Korbitz, Altruism, Metalaw, and Celegistics: An Extraterrestrial Perspective on Universal Law-Making, in Douglas A. Vakoch (ed.) *Extraterrestrial Altruism* (Springer, New York, 2014) pp. 231–247, at 239–242.

56 *Relations*, pp. 237–238.

57 Adam Korbitz, *supra* note 55.

We need to critique the intellectual foundations of the debate and argue, firstly, that apart from questionable approaches in the use of Kant's philosophy[58] and despite its attempts at avoiding anthropocentrism[59] in its deontology, it cannot *qua natura* evade the banal and incontrovertible fact that so far only humans have contributed to the discussion, based only on human interaction with the world. While there may be other highly developed sentient, and possibly even sapient, species on Earth – such as, for example, octopuses and dolphins – humans are so far obviously unaware of any philosophical reflections they might entertain; communication with them is not at a level where such complex concepts could be addressed and hence, they cannot influence the terrestrial debate.[60] Secondly, it fails in its present form to acknowledge properly the diverse scenarios, other than one of generic expectations of alien altruism, which may be realistically expected in the case of contact with ETI. Thirdly, it omits proper recognition of the likely realpolitik environment surrounding such an encounter, including sheer power politics, for which there is moreover ample empirical evidence in interhuman legal and political relationships. Ultimately, despite its now decade-long pedigree, human reflection about a universally applicable cosmic metalaw is still premature philosophical speculation – based on extrapolations from hitherto unverifiable hypothetical grounds also imagined by humans. It is undoubtedly intellectually highly stimulating but mostly without practical relevance when it comes to defining mutual foundations of the very practical problem of managing actual contact with ETI, if and when it should occur. At present, the focus should thus be on developing the practical, including the legal, parameters of the *unilateral human* response to a potential future event, the quality and impact of which is unknown and unknowable until it occurs. The metalaw debate may, however, still play a role in this respect.

As was already mentioned, the modern debate, for all practical intents and purposes, began in the 1950s with Haley's string of articles[61] and ultimately

---

58 But see more recently Anna Frammartino Wilks. *Kantian Foundations for a Cosmocentric Ethic,* in James S J Schwartz and Tony Milligan (eds.), *The Ethics of Space Exploration* (Springer, New York, 2016), pp. 181–194.

59 *Haley*, pp. 414, 420.

60 Denise L Herzing, SETI meets a social intelligence: Dolphins as a model for real-time interaction and communication with a sentient species, 67 *Acta Astronautica* (2010) 1451–1454; Laurance R Doyle et al. 2011. Information theory, animal communication, and the search for extraterrestrial intelligence, 68 *Acta Astronautica* (2011) 406–417. On similar research with octopuses Peter Godfrey-Smith, *Other Minds – The Octopus and the Evolution of Intelligent Life* (William Collins, Glasgow, 2016).

61 Listed in *Haley*, pp. 421–423.

his seminal book "Space Law and Government" from 1963,[62] followed by the work of Fasan. Central to his argument, as later to that of Fasan, is an adaptation of Kant's Categorical Imperative. Haley, however, apart from listing a string of sources for the universality of the anthropocentric traditional Golden Rule, the applicability of which he then rejected as a proper basis of metalaw, did not engage in any deeper philosophical argument about the legitimacy of using Kant's idea in the context of interspecies relations.[63] In his famous "wager"[64] and the speculations in his Universal Natural History about inhabitants of other planets, Kant referred to the existence, living environment and possible physical and mental constitution of ETI;[65] however, he did not engage in explicit ethical discussions about interspecies relations. Nor did Haley and Fasan confront the criticism already levelled at Kant on account of the controversial *a priori* grounding of his imperative by other philosophers, such as Hegel or Schopenhauer,[66] at the time.[67] Incidentally, the idea of using

---

62 *Haley*, pp. 394–423.

63 Quite outspoken Francis Lyall and Paul B Larsen, *Space Law – A Treatise,* 2nd ed. (Routledge, Abingdon, 2018) pp. 506–507.

64 "If it were possible to settle by any sort of experience whether there are inhabitants of at least some of the planets that we see, I might well bet everything that I have on it. Hence I say that it is not merely an opinion but a strong belief (on the correctness of which I would wager many advantages in life) that there are also inhabitants of other worlds". – Immanuel Kant, *Critique of Pure Reason* (Translated and edited by P Guyer and A W Wood, CUP, Cambridge, 1998) p. 687 (B 853). – See on the wager's impact on theology Andreas Losch, Kant's wager – Kant's strong belief in extra-terrestrial life, the history of this question and its challenge for theology today, 15 *International Journal of Astrobiology* (2016) 261–270.

65 Immanuel Kant, Universal natural history and theory of the heavens or essay on the constitution and the mechanical origin of the whole universe according to Newtonian principles, 1755, Part Three; in Eric Watkins (ed.) *Immanuel Kant – Natural Science* (CUP, Cambridge, 2012) pp. 294–306. See also in the context of anthropomorphism the reference by Ulrike M Bohlmann and Moritz J F Bürger, Anthropomorphism in the search for extra-terrestrial intelligence – The limits of cognition?, 143 *Acta Astronautica* (2018) 163–168, at 165.

66 Georg Wilhelm Friedrich Hegel, *Grundlinien der Philosophie des Rechts,* (F. Meiner, Leipzig, 1820) p. 139; *id.*, Aufsätze aus dem *Kritischen. Journal der Philosophie* (1803) 463; Arthur Schopenhauer, *On the Basis of Morality.* 2nd rev. ed. (Translation by E.F.J. Payne, Hackett Classics, Indianapolis, 1998). – There is only a glancing reference by Fasan to Schopenhauer and the assertion that "[a]s great a man as Kant was, he made mistakes, as Schopenhauer pointed out", *Relations*, p. 233 at note 193.

67 More recent critiques of Kant were formulated by Karl Marx, *Critique of Hegel's Philosophy of Right.* (Translation by Annette Jolin and Joseph O'Malley, CUP, Cambridge, 1977); Jürgen Habermas, *Moralbewusstsein und kommunikatives Handeln* (Suhrkamp, Berlin, 1983); Hans Jonas, *Das Prinzip Verantwortung. Versuch einer Ethik für die technologische Zivilisation* (Suhrkamp, Berlin, 1984); Marcus G Singer, 1971. *Generalization in*

the Categorical Imperative as a foundation of, or a shortcut to, the traditional Golden Rule as a maxim of ethics based on an agent's desire for a certain outcome was rejected by Kant himself,[68] so it stands to reason that he might not have approved of its use for a revised Golden Rule, either.

The best example of the absurd conclusions in legally relevant scenarios which the application of the categorical imperative can lead to is the response by Kant to French philosopher Benjamin Constant's challenge whether it was permissible for a person to lie to a murderer who asks them about the whereabouts of the murderer's intended victim (assuming that not answering the question was not an option). Kant, in the 1797 essay "On the Supposed Right to Lie from Benevolent Motives",[69] agreed with Constant that based on Kant's argument the murderer must be told the truth in order to treat him as an end in himself. Two criticisms are apposite in this context: Firstly, this outcome is far removed from common sense *practical* ethics – and indeed the commands of almost any criminal law on complicity on Earth – and it must be called grotesque to try to shoehorn applied human practical ethics, which will ultimately have to underlie any conversation with alien ethics, into Kant's conceptual theoretical framework. Secondly, the focus on guaranteeing the murderer's quality as an end in himself misses the fact that it is his innocent victim who is now being treated as a mere means to an end, namely, to uphold the purity of the categorical imperative, and Kant may actually have misapplied his own principle in his response to Constant. From the point of view of relevant practical ethics, Kant's philosophy was thus a problematic foundation on which to build a *cosmic* metalaw – not least because at the time, the pertinent modern discussion about terrestrial cultural and human rights relativism[70] was essentially unknown.

Interestingly, Fasan also advocated the use of the principles expounded in Hans Kelsen's *Reine Rechtslehre* of 1934 ("Pure Theory of Law") as a kind of second stage of fleshing out the details of metalaw by the purely formalistic and almost mechanical mode of argument espoused by Kelsen, an approach

---

Ethics (Macmillan, New York, 1971) and Norbert Hoerster, *Ethik und Interesse* (Reclam, Leipzig, 2003).

68 Immanuel Kant, *Grundlegung der Metaphysik der Sitten,* in Gesammelte Schriften, AA IV, 430, https://korpora.zim.uni-duisburg-essen.de/Kant/aa04/430.html.

69 See Immanuel Kant, *On the Supposed Right to Lie From Benevolent Motives,* 1797, Sopha Project Phil Archive. www.sophia-project.org/uploads/1/3/9/5/13955288/kant_lying.pdf.

70 See, for example, R J Vincent, *Human Rights and International Relations* (CUP, Cambridge, 2009); Andreas Follesdal, Human Rights and Relativism, in A Follesdal and T W Pogge (eds.), *Real World Justice – Grounds, Principles, Human Rights, and Social Institutions,* (Springer, New York, 2005) pp. 265–283.

that does not allow any extraneous policy aspects, or indeed adjustments, to influence the process of deduction as such.[71] Again, that idea of a seemingly "clean" – another word for the German "*rein*" – method based on mere deductive logic is something the modern development of domestic and international legal interpretation in virtually all jurisdictions had long abandoned as an epistemological illusion – even at the time when Fasan was expressing his ideas.

Subject to the overarching proviso explained below, Haley's and Fasan's arguments would also appear to be self-defeating to a large extent: If the new rule is to be that each party to a metalaw-based relationship should treat the other as *they* want to be treated, the universal rule's implied mutual reciprocity also demands of each party to treat the other in a way which the other party is not entitled to ask to be treated in the first place. In other words, if A must not expect to be treated as it wants to be treated but must treat B as B wants to be treated, and B must not expect to be treated as it wants to be treated but must treat A as A wants to be treated, then the mutual commands of the new Golden Rule *prima facie* cancel each other out, always assuming that the expectations on either side are not identical.

In a slight modification of the example given by Patricia M. Sterns[72] of a war after which the victorious ETI as a rule practices the enslavement and cannibalism of the vanquished on its home world, the new rule might expect an allied human force to abide by the ETI's practices and join in them on pain of irredeemably offending the ETI, although the humans in turn could ask the ETI not to be made to do so, because it would be a violation of fundamental human values, which the ETI would under the metalaw rule be prevented from asking the humans to consent to.

Fasan's eleven rules, against this background, are actually not mere and more specific explanatory sub-rules of the new Golden Rule, they are in themselves – in legal terms moreover rather unclear and in part self-contradicting – restrictions on its general application: Rule 1 on not asking for an impossibility may be understood not merely as a factual impossibility (which seems rather banal) but also, and more importantly, as an ethical impossibility, i.e., it may depend on whether a certain demand refers to negotiable or non-negotiable aspects of the other party's set of moral or legal rules. The same applies to Rule

71 *Relations*, p. 238. On the consequences of using Kelsen for designing criminal law systems see Otto Lagodny, *Zwei Strafrechtswelten – Rechtsvergleichende Betrachtungen und Erfahrungen aus deutscher Sicht in Österreich* (Nomos, Baden-Baden, 2020).

72 Patricia M Stearns, SETI and Space Law: Jurisprudential and Philosophical Considerations for Humankind in Relation to Extraterrestrial Life, 46 *Acta Astronautica* (2000) 759–763, at 762.

4 on self-determination and Rule 5 on avoidance of harm. All of these could trigger the right to self-defence under Rule 7, which coupled with Rule 8 on the hierarchically more important protection of one's own species might ultimately justify, in terms of current international interhuman criminal law, the crime against humanity of extermination of the other species. What is left of the general new rule after these detractions is open to question.

A major conceptual problem becomes apparent here, namely, that there is no reference to a higher instance that could be called upon to settle disputes arising from the application of the new rule. Depending on the strength of offence caused to either party, settling the dispute might *ultima ratione* result in another conflict. The usual way of managing such discrepancies between parties' positions is the negotiation of a compromise, as evidenced in human international relations experience. The new Golden Rule offers no guidance in that respect, yet as the examples above show, compromise will be the only viable avenue short of conflict.

The subsequently introduced models based on thermodynamics arguments (thermoethics)[73] and altruism-or technological/economic feasibility-based[74] hypotheses are certainly intellectually more sophisticated than the methodologically questionable recourse to an 18th century philosopher, yet they, like Haley's and Fasan's, are all mere human conjecture based on the behaviour of the only sapient ethical civilisation known to humans and with whom they can communicate at an advanced level – themselves. It is therefore irrelevant for the purposes of the present examination to discuss their respective philosophical and practical merits as such.

Only the following general comment on the link between an advanced civilisation state[75] and ethical conduct may be permitted – it should certainly contain no radically new insight: Even if the general assumption that ETI will likely be highly advanced and hence rational actors was correct, ethical or even altruistic behaviour does not necessarily follow from being rational – especially in the case of post-biological AI civilisations where the level of self-awareness and experience of contact with other sentient (biological) entities

73 On the Universal Thermoethical Principles of First Contact see Robert Freitas, Xenology: An Introduction to the Scientific Study of Extraterrestrial Life, Intelligence, and Civilization, www.xenology.info/Xeno/25.1.3.htm.

74 Critical: Steven J. Dick, 2018. *Astrobiology, Discovery, and Societal Impact* (CUP, Cambridge, 2018 – hereafter: *Dick, Astrobiology*) p. 287: "dubious alien economics about the cost-effectiveness of interstellar spaceflight".

75 But see Niklas Alexander Döbler, The Concept of Developmental Relativity: Thoughts on the Technological Synchrony of Interstellar Civilizations, 54 *Space Policy* (2020) 101391.

may determine the level of insight into ethical reference frameworks. Human history alone speaks against such a blithe conclusion which some might even call wishful thinking. The Nazi ideology arose in a German scientific environment whose community was very advanced for its time, yet the Nazis were extremely rational in using that science in order to pursue an utterly immoral policy that led to immeasurable suffering and the horrors of the Holocaust. Also, as every criminal detective, prosecutor and judge knows, even "ordinary" criminals can be highly intelligent and rational, and the more they are, the greater the danger they pose – one need only think of Arthur Conan Doyle's fictional character of Professor Moriarty. There is no reason to think that ETI do not have them or that first contact might not be made with a rogue individual or group.[76] Humans are as advanced as never before technologically but massive organised criminal activity, both by state and non-state actors, using that very technology still occurs and our level of civilisational development has so far not led to drastic action to stop and reverse the greatest environmental crime against our entire species, man-made climate change.[77]

There is simply no other dataset that would support any of the conclusions reached by human scholars based on hypotheses created out of sheer speculation. They can only ever serve the – nonetheless important[78] – purpose of elaborating the moral point of departure for humans in future ethical conversations with ETI. Beyond that, what is said in these models about expectations related, for example, to likely degrees of alien altruism or aggressive and hostile attitudes of ETI is, it must be repeated, currently only a figment of our own ethical imagination. It may equally be as true as it might be wrong.[79] In this sense, Tony Milligan cautioned even for the aspect of mere human space exploration:

> The danger then is one of imagining that we can specify, by appeal to known and homely considerations, more than the very broadest and most general ethical features of how this more distant and troubling future might be lived.[80]

---

76 Michaud, p. 302.

77 Michaud, pp. 293–301, 304.

78 James S J Schwartz, On the Methodology of Space Ethics, in James S J Schwartz and Tony Milligan (eds.), *The Ethics of Space Exploration* (Springer, New York, 2016) pp. 93–107, at p. 106.

79 Schetsche/Anton, p. 212.

80 Tony Milligan, Space Ethics Without Foundations, in James S J Schwartz and Tony Milligan (*supra* note 78), pp. 125–134, at p. 133.

Actual empirical data on any moral principles of ETI will be collected only when contact is made, and the content or speed of data collection will depend on the manner of contact: It may take decades or even centuries if a signal from afar is received; it may happen within hours in the case of direct contact in the proximity of, or even on, Earth. It bears pointing out in the context of the debate about the greater likelihood of contact being made with a highly advanced AI-controlled[81] machine civilisation rather[82] than a biological one, that reception of a remote signal might already be *direct* contact if the signal contains either a sort of virus meant to debilitate terrestrial defences,[83] or even *is* the AI in the form of a sentient full clone programme of itself.[84]

In both cases, there will very likely either – at least initially – be no sufficient point of reference in the form of an interstellar Rosetta Stone in order to decipher the meaning, leave alone a moral meaning, of a message, or there may be no time at all to achieve efficiency of communication on a level required for an exchange of information on ethical or other philosophical concepts. If the ETI is hostile, inclined to pre-emptive aggression and superior in power, there may be no communication.

---

81 However, highly developed machine/AI civilisations may use advanced methods of communication such as quantum entanglement which would be undetectable to humans, thus providing another possible answer to the Great Silence under the Fermi Paradox; see Joe Gale et al., Will recent advances in AI result in a paradigm shift in Astrobiology and SETI?, 19 *International Journal of Astrobiology* (2020) 295–298.

82 There is a school of thought that predicts a higher stochastic likelihood of encountering machines rather than biological life forms, see Alex de Visscher, Artificial versus biological intelligence in the Cosmos: clues from a stochastic analysis of the Drake equation, 19 *International Journal of Astrobiology* (2020) 353–359.

83 Such concerns have been voiced by a number of academics, for example, by Hans Moravec and Richard Carrigan Jr, with a common counterargument being that an alien virus could not cause any damage to terrestrial software environments because it could not decipher and mimic the human coding and computer language, in the same way as a "PC virus cannot affect an Apple Macintosh"; see *Erstkontakt* pp. 218–219. This may be true but assumes that the IT capabilities of the ETI would not be advanced enough to circumvent or overcome any problems with the "handshake" between both technologies. Gerritzen also points out correctly that METI attempts might actually be inviting alien malware messages that either infect the internet with a very high dissemination speed – he gives the example of the SETI@home programme – or contain, for example, instructions to build a highly destructive device, and that SETI scientists will not be able to control their scientific curiosity and unpack any files received just to find out what will happen, with the negative consequences thus being triggered by the humans themselves; *ibid.*, pp. 219–224.

84 Schetsche/ Anton, pp. 212–213, with references to previous literature on the virus scenario.

Competing for expensive and highly coveted dish time by radio astronomers or creating such ambitious projects as Breakthrough Starshot[85] makes no sense unless there is a shared expectation that contact is actually possible and all involved aspire to making it – although some have queried whether the traditional refusal to engage with accounts of alleged direct contact on Earth or the persistent "giggle factor" around UFO research etc. might not be indicative of a subconscious apprehension that the very thing everyone is working towards might actually come to fruition or already have happened.[86] SETI is not primarily a philosophical or academic undertaking. It has so far been mainly in the hand of natural scientists, more recently also increasingly of social scientists, but as Baxter and Elliott correctly stated in 2012 regarding the need for proper pre-and post-detection protocols and policies, "[t]he early involvement of space lawyers and UN agencies could help improve the chances of having any proposed policy widely accepted, and workable in practice".[87]

In an unprecedented editorial comment in the American Journal of International Law, Richard B. Bilder recently confirmed the widely held conviction that despite the broad acceptance in the community of the two SETI protocols and some references in the existing treaties and agreements about the use of outer space, the moon and other celestial bodies which could find application to contact events, there is currently no binding legal framework regarding SETI. A treaty regulating it would make eminent sense in his view, yet on the one hand not many states might develop an interest in preparing for a scenario that is in many people's views unlikely to materialise anytime soon. On the other hand, they and the UN agencies might consequently be reluctant to divert resources away from the more pressing core areas of UN activity to a field where a large number of states would not realistically have the chance of any material involvement. A few states with the capacity of space exploration in the wider sense would thus be dominating the efforts, creating the risk that any treaty would not receive sufficient ratifications. He expresses the view that in practice the SETI Protocols would be largely observed already. Incidentally, this was confirmed in a private communication to the author from a member of the European Space Agency (ESA) who wrote on condition of anonymity that in the case of a first contact, ESA would abide by the SETI protocol(s) and

85 See https://breakthroughinitiatives.org/initiative/3.

86 Schetsche/Anton, pp. 199 and 215; Michaud, p. 241 (citing Zdenek Kopal), pp. 252, 325, 358–359.

87 Stephen Baxter and John Elliott, A SETI metapolicy: New directions towards comprehensive policies concerning the detection of extraterrestrial intelligence, 78 *Acta Astronautica* (2012) 31–36, at 36.

accordingly coordinate its response with UNOOSA. Bilder argues that "soft law" options[88] such as non-binding declarations or resolutions by the UN General Assembly might provide a less difficult pathway to international agreement on the matter.[89] He concluded, however, by stating:

> The chances of our contact or encounter with extraterrestrial beings or civilizations may be remote. Yet, as Stephen Hawking and others have argued, the risks and impact of such a contact for our human species could be very great – even existential. Consequently, the issues raised by SETI and METI merit the international community's, COPUOS's – and international lawyers' – timely concern and consideration.[90]

If that is the case, then the SETI community needs to add practical politics-facing activism to its portfolio to a greater extent than is hitherto the case. SETI protocol development currently has a democracy deficit[91] and needs a stronger basis in society and among political decision-makers, not least because it is all but certain that the moment detection occurs and is communicated to the relevant governmental and international authorities, the latter will take control of the situation.[92] Law is one discipline that should be at the forefront of these endeavours.[93] In the words of Dick, "SETI is way behind the curve when it comes to legal implications of discovering intelligent life".[94]

---

88 Irmgard Marboe (ed.), *Soft Law in Outer Space – The Function of Non-binding Norms in International Space Law* (Böhlau Verlag, Vienna, 2012).

89 Richard B Bilder, Editorial Comment: On the Search for Extraterrestrial Intelligence (SETI), 144 *American Journal of International Law* (2020) 87–95.

90 *Ibid*, at 95. See also *Dick, Astrobiology*, p. 287.

91 Peter Hatfield and Leah Trueblood, SETI and democracy. 190 *Acta Astronautica* (2021) 596–603; Michaud, pp. 288–291, 366–368.

92 *Dick, Astrobiology*, p. 292.

93 However, renowned space lawyer Frans G. von der Dunk seemed to think in 2016 that the time for such concerted efforts at the international level related to regulating to SETI activities, and in particular prohibitions on active SETI, has "certainly" not come yet because of state sovereignty, if these efforts are condoned by the states in which they take place. See Frans G. von der Dunk, Shaking the Foundations of the Law: Some Legal Issues Posed by the Detection of Extraterrestrial Life, in *The Ethics of Space Exploration, supra* note 78, pp. 251–263, at p. 257. This would appear to be an almost defeatist approach, less ambitious than the one advocated by Bilder in his editorial in the AJIL.

94 *Dick, Astrobiology*, p. 295. – For a recent, broad-brush "thought experiment" on legal issues arising from contact with ETI, see Klaus Stähle, *Rechtsfragen beim Kontakt mit Extraterrestrischen. Völkerrecht, Wirtschaft und Politik – Ein Gedankenmodell* (Berliner Wissenschafts-Verlag, Berlin, 2023).

The argument that because scientific SETI has been unsuccessful so far, (direct) contact remains only a remote possibility is a common logical fallacy based on incomplete statistics. The current search parameters of SETI – and especially IAASETI – are very narrow as it is, and humanity may moreover have missed a plethora of available information because we are not (yet) technologically equipped to recognise the evidence – if there is much to detect in the first place or if it will be SETI scientists at all, and not the intelligence services with their more advanced technology, who detect the signal.[95] We might in theory be only days away, every day, from contact. Even if contact were a low-probability event, it would at the same time be high-risk, the level of risk depending on the nature of the contact.[96]

Humanity cannot rely on the hope of a purely benign contact, especially if we were to face direct interaction with ETI. Prudence requires that adequate preparations be made especially for the risk of hostile contact.[97] This includes drafting revised planetary defence protocols involving a change in paradigm for the interpretation of the term "defence", and possibly adaptations, for example, of the laws of armed conflict. Research into potential amendments to current laws of armed conflict applicable to interhuman military space operations is already being conducted by two major projects, one the one hand under the auspices of the Woomera Manual,[98] and on the other hand the Manual on International Law Applicable to Military Uses of Outer Space (MILAMOS), volume I of which was recently published.[99] In the context of possible SETI success and preparing for (direct) contact, it would seem fairly obvious that an extension of such research into interspecies conflict could – and should – be a natural corollary to considering interhuman space warfare.

In an email of 13 August 2020 to the author, a senior member of the US Army officer corps, also on condition of anonymity, further opined:

> Regarding a general blueprint or policy for first contact, I am not aware of any such plan or policy. Having said that, there are two points that I would highlight. First, as you might imagine, any such plan would most

95 Michaud, pp. 264–267, 277.

96 Compare *Dick, Astrobiology*, pp. 269–302 on an "astropolicy" to prepare for the impact of discovery.

97 Compare William Kramer and Charles Bahmer, *The Fire Officer's Guide to Disaster Control*, 2nd ed. (Pennwell, Tulsa, 1992), in Chapter 13 on enemy attack and UFO sightings or landings.

98 The Woomera Manual, https://law.adelaide.edu.au/woomera/.

99 McGill Manual on International Applicable to Military Uses of Outer Space, www.mcgill.ca/iasl/files/iasl/mcgill_manual_volume_i_-_rules.pdf.

> likely be classified. That is, it is not at all uncommon as most operations plans are. Second, at least from the perspective of the U.S. military, we are obsessive planners. As such, it would not surprise me that such plans or policies would exist.[100]

The revision of existing protocols and legal frameworks cannot be done by the scientific community alone or remain forever in the black box of military operational planning but must involve democratically legitimised political decision-makers at the earliest opportunity.

If all of this seems to be (lunatic) fringe thinking, it may be because humanity has not yet developed cosmic species awareness and responsibility,[101] or simply accepts the common narrative that any ETI contacted will be vastly more advanced and powerful and hence impossible to resist anyway. In that respect, Michaud had the following to say:

> SETI conventional wisdom assumes that because we will be much less technologically advanced than any other civilization that we contact, we would be helpless if the extraterrestrials were hostile. This disparity may turn out to be true, but it remains unproven. To assume our weakness in advance would be preemptive capitulation.[102]

Even in peace time, international interhuman relations are ultimately always based on power politics. Unless one side can back up its position with some form of persuasive capital, it will stand little chance of influencing the negotiations in its favour. There is no reason to think it would be otherwise in compromise negotiations with ETI.

---

100 The US Dept. Of Defense, HQ United States Strategic Command, ran a real training exercise in 2009 and 2010, called CONPLAN 8888-11 based on a "zombie survival plan", i.e., a reaction to a fictitious zombie attack. It explicitly contained a category called "Space Zombies": "1. (U) SZ's are zombie life forms originating from space or created by toxic contamination of the earth environment via some form of extra-terrestrial toxin or radiation 2. (U) "Zombie satellites" can be classified as SZ's, however they pose no danger to humans (unless they conduct an unplanned de-orbit). Typically, zombie satellites only pose a threat [to] the SATCOM services like DirectTV (Refer to Galaxy 15 incident – May 2010)". US Dept of Defence, CONPLAN 8888, US Strategic Command training exercise, 2010, www.stratcom.mil/Portals/8/Documents/FOIA/CONPLAN_8888-11.pdf?ver=2016-10-17-114016-887. One of the aims to stop a spread of zombies was the capability to deliver a "Prompt Global Strike", if necessary with nuclear payloads, anywhere on Earth within one hour; see *Erstkontakt* pp. 279–280.

101 *Dick, Astrobiology*, pp.310–311, and more broadly pp. 209–239.

102 Michaud, p. 376.

Given that reflections about possible moral persuasions of ETI will by necessity remain one-sided, unverifiable conjecture until contact is made, the role of legal research in SETI should shift to shaping the human baseline for future moral conversations with ETI in the wider sense, or even conflict.[103] If there is a "Galactic Club"[104] to which humanity might in time wish to aspire, we should expect to fulfil certain membership criteria and be in a grounded position to decide whether they are compatible with human ethical parameters. Dick found that "the possibility of contact is a strong argument that some form of metalaw must be developed in order to deal with interactions with aliens[.]"[105]

The experience of international law has shown that there is an osmosis effect both ways with domestic jurisdictions, and while domestic states create international law through treaties or simply their practice, once created, international law can develop powers to bind even its creators, for example, in the case of customary *ius cogens* applicable *erga omnes*. It can be expected that such an osmosis effect might also occur in the relationship with ETI, especially in the "Galactic Club" example. Human rights law in particular can serve as a ready guideline for ethical discussions (see Chapter 7 below for a detailedanalysis). It has so far been conspicuously absent as an avenue of study in the metalaw environment.[106]

There is a related field of uncertainty in the context of potential hostile encounters, assuming humanity would be in a position to mount an effective defence at all. Our laws of armed conflict and consequently international criminal law are based on human-to-human hostilities or in other words, "man's inhumanity to man". They ultimately derive from considerations of damage control within one species. Genocide or the crime against humanity of extermination are particularly glaring examples. Would these laws still be held to prevent the destruction of an entire species or a substantial part thereof – for example, the arrival of a colony ship in Earth's orbit carrying all, or a majority of, the members of a nomadic civilisation – if otherwise humanity was at risk of enslavement or extinction? This issue will be addressed in Chapter 5.

---

103 *Dick, Astrobiology*, pp. 240–268.

104 Term coined by R N Bracewell, *The Galactic Club: Intelligent life in outer space* (San Francisco Book Co., San Francisco, 1976).

105 *Dick, Astrobiology*, p. 301.

106 Francis Lyall and Paul B Larsen, *Space Law – A Treatise*, 2nd ed. (Routledge, London, 2018) p. 506 at note 131.

5 Conclusion

Currently, humanity has no coordinated answers for any of the questions raised above.[107] Metalaw research could play a role in testing and, if necessary, stretching the envelope of traditional attitudes. Work on fundamental principles of universal human rights and acceptable negotiated forms of governance, as well as research into the foundations of an outward facing law of armed conflict including its interaction with international criminal law as a basis for encounters with ETI could become a mainstay of its policy ambitions. To quote Steven J Dick once more: "Meeting the alien will be an experience we cannot afford to mismanage. In so many ways and more than ever, failure is not an option".[108]

Finally, balanced legal or ethical principles are only one side of the coin. As Guy J. Consolmagno has rightly pointed out, we must also be aware that we do not proceed from a point of view of unconscious species bias often found in speculative thinking as expressed in popular culture outlets:

> Many science-fiction writers . . . have depicted humans and alien races interacting; but in virtually all cases, the human race is depicted as somehow special, different and better than the others. . . . The ultimate myth of science fiction that is tagged onto our astronomy turns out to be that, even with all those alien races, human beings are the central characters in the story of the universe. It is as if the Copernican Revolution never happened.[109]

This leads us to our next topic, the relevance of Science Fiction.

---

107 *Dick, Astrobiology*, pp. 270–271.

108 *Dick, Astrobiology*, p. 302.

109 Guy J Consolmagno, Astronomy, Science Fiction and Popular Culture: 1277 to 2001 (and Beyond), 29 *Leonardo* (1996) 127–132, at 131.

CHAPTER 4

Science Fiction and (First) Contact Scenarios

1 Science Fiction Literature[1]

Science Fiction literature and film or TV culture[2] abound with well-known descriptions of first contact and relationships between different alien species thereafter – to name but one example, see the different franchises of the *Star Trek* Universe.[3] The latter, and SF in the wider sense, have been used by French legal academic and attorney, Fabrice Defferard, as examples from which to draw insights into general legal principles,[4] and potential lessons for space law.[5] Istvan Csicsery-Ronay, Jr. in his book of critical science fiction studies, "*The Seven Beauties of Science Fiction*", has described and analysed the different avenues along which SF impacts on our real-world thinking and development,

1 This section may naturally contain some spoilers for readers who have not yet perused the cited works. – There are, of course, many more works on the issues we will be looking at here but making a selection is unavoidable and everyone will have a different preference for what are the most important ones.

2 Mario Springnagel, *Die Darstellung von außerirdischer Intelligenz im Film* (*Extraterrestrial Intelligence in the Movies*), unpublished PhD thesis, 2017, https://othes.univie.ac.at/49475/. On the impact of SF and SETI on education see Mark Brake and Martin Griffiths, Broad horizons – SETI, SF and education, 3 *International Journal of Astrobiology* (2004) 175–181 and erratum at 333

3 Official website at https://intl.startrek.com/.

4 See also Christine Corcos, Visits to a Small Planet: Rights Talk in Some Science Fiction Film and Television Series from the 1950s to the 1990s, 39 *Stetson Law Review* (2009) 183–246, on human species racism portrayed in SF. She concludes: "[W]e must confront the possible negative or racist human responses to those beings, should they exist. We should make every attempt to deal with the results of our thinking here on Earth before venturing into space, or we will carry those results with us, and they will infect our encounters with extraterrestrial life, if it exists. Some humans already believe that extraterrestrial beings are here and that, contrary to beliefs in the 1960s and 1970s, they are here not to help us, but to exploit us". – at 246. For a point of view from Chinese SF culture, see Han Song, Chinese Science Fiction: A Response to Modernization, 40 *Science Fiction Studies* (2013) 15–21. On the link of SF to imperialist themes, see David Seed, The Course of Empire: A Survey of the Imperial Theme in Early Anglophone Science Fiction, 37 *Science Fiction Studies* (2010) 230–252.

5 Fabrice Defferard, *Le droit selon Star Trek* (Mare Martin, Paris, 2016); *id.* (ed.). 2017. *Le droit saisi par la science fiction* (Mare Martin, Paris, 2017); *id.*, Star Trek: paradigme juridique et laboratoire du droit, 45 *Revue Générale du Droit* (2015) 613–635.

 | DOI:10.1163/9789004677708_005

technological as much as societal.[6] In more recent times, SF has been used as an imaginative tool to discuss 21st century challenges to a number of governance aspects, including in military scenarios, in Jonathan Klug's and Steven Leonard's book "To Boldly Go".[7]

This chapter is going to be quite extensive, mainly because SF authors in a variety of ways have imagined the possible, unrestricted by scientific or social conventions prevalent in real-world society and by the technological achievements currently envisaged as possible within the next few decades. For a topic as seemingly unrealistic to present minds as laying the foundations of a law of interspecies conflict, however, flights of fancy can be extremely helpful in stretching the envelope of attitudes about answers to questions that at least to some may not appear to have even been asked with the necessary seriousness, simply because any thought of them needing answers at this time is itself dismissed as science fiction.[8]

Some of the literary and cineastic references, like Carl Sagan's *Contact*[9] or Jack McDevitt's *The Hercules Text*,[10] deal with signals from afar received on Earth, and the process and problems of decipherment, as well as the human response in the case of *Contact*, to what are, however, in essence benevolent or indifferent messages. Clarke's *Rama* tetralogy[11], which must have resonated with very many people all over the world in 2017 during the public furore over 'Oumuamua, spans an arc from first contact with an immense alien world ship probe collecting life forms on its interstellar journey to the grand finale of addressing the reason behind the creation of the universe(s). More recently,

6 Istvan Csicsery-Ronay, Jr, *The Seven Beauties of Science Fiction* (Wesleyan University Press, Middletown, 2008). See also Rob Latham (ed.), *Science Fiction Criticism – An Anthology of Essential Writings* (Bloomsbury and James, London, 2017); Edward James and Farah Mendlesohn (eds.), *The Cambridge Companion to Science Fiction* (CUP, Cambridge, 2003); Gerry Canavan and Eric Carl Link (eds.), *The Cambridge History of Science Fiction* (CUP, Cambridge, 2019).

7 Jonathan Klug and Steven Leonard (eds.), *To Boldly Go – Leadership, Strategy and Conflict in the 21st Century and Beyond* (Casemate, Philadelphia, 2021).

8 See Mark Brake and Neil Hook, Darwin to the double helix: astrobiology in fiction, 6 *International Journal of Astrobiology* (2007) 273–280.

9 Carl Sagan, *Contact.* First Printing edition. (Simon & Schuster Ltd., New York, 1985 – hereafter: *Contact*).

10 Jack McDevitt, *The Hercules Text, Revised version* (Ace Books, New York, 2015 – hereafter: *Hercules Text*).

11 From volume II onwards together with Gentry Lee: Arthur C. Clarke, *Rendezvous with Rama* (Gollancz, London, 1973 – hereafter *Rama I*)); *id.* and Gentry Lee, *Rama II* (Gollancz, London, 1989 – hereafter: *Rama II*); *id.*, *The Garden of Rama* (Bantam Spectra, New York, 1992 – hereafter: *Rama III*); *id.*, *Rama Revealed* (Orbit Books, London, 1996 – hereafter: *Rama IV*)).

and of interest in the context of space exploration including settlements on other planets, the issue of settlers encountering different sentient and sapient species on other planets and the problems of establishing communication are highlighted in Sue Burke's *Semiosis*[12] and Adrian Tchaikovsky's *Children of Time*[13] and *Children of Ruin*.[14] The problems of regulating the influence and initiative between scientists and politicians after contact with an alien entity are brought into relief in Fred Hoyle's classic *The Black Cloud*.[15] A literary treatment of the Metalaw concept was provided by Lee Correy, the *nom-de-plume* of G. Harry Stine, in *A Matter of Metalaw*.[16]

---

12 Sue Burke, *Semiosis* (HarperVoyager, Glasgow, 2018 – hereafter: *Semiosis*).

13 Adrian Tchaikovsky, *Children of Time* (Pan Books, London, 2016 – hereafter: *Children of Time*).

14 Adrian Tchaikovsky, *Children of Ruin* (Pan Books, London, 2020 – hereafter: *Children of Ruin*).

15 Fred Hoyle, *The Black Cloud* (William Heinemann Ltd., Portsmouth, 1957; cited after the Penguin edition, 1960 – hereafter: *Black Cloud*).

16 Lee Correy, *A Matter of Metalaw* (DAW Books, New York, 1986). – Although we shall not dwell any further on the issue of a cosmic interspecies metalaw as such (for the reasons see the discussion above), it is nonetheless useful for reference purposes to reproduce part of Correy's Preface in which he tries to define the meaning of law, metalaw, intelligent being, and "zone of sensitivity", i.e., in modern terms "personal space". We shall look at what he says about law and metalaw. There is a conspicuous overlap with Haley's and Fasan's metalaw rules, as well as with the structure of Isaac Asimov's three laws of robotics:

> "*Law*: A system of rules of conduct governing the relationships between intelligent beings. These precepts are classified, reduced to order, put in the shape of rules, and mutually agreed upon.
> *Metalaw*: A system of law dealing with all frames of existence and with intelligent beings of all kinds. [...]
> THE CANONS OF METALAW:
> First Canon (Haley's Rule): Do unto others as they would have you do unto them.
> Second Canon: The First Canon of Metalaw must not be applied if it might result in the destruction of an intelligent being.
> Third Canon: Any intelligent being may suspend adherence to the first two Canons of Metalaw in his own self-defense to prevent others from restricting his freedom of choice or destroying him.
> Fourth Canon: An intelligent being must not affect the freedom of choice or the survival of another intelligent being and must not, by inaction, permit the destruction of another intelligent being.
> Fifth Canon: Any intelligent being has the right of freedom of choice in life style, living location, and socio-economic-cultural system consistent with the preceding Canons of Metalaw.
> Sixth Canon: Sustained communication among intelligent beings must always be established and maintained with bilateral consent.
> Seventh Canon: Any intelligent being may move about at will in a fashion unrestricted by other intelligent beings provided that the Zone of Sensitivity of another intelligent being is not thereby violated without permission.

Then there are scenarios of a more sinister and threatening kind, and of varying degrees of contact, notably Earth invasion or occupation[17] scenarios such as H. G. Wells' famous 1898 novel *The War of the Worlds*,[18] John Christopher's *The Tripods* tetralogy,[19] or Arthur C. Clarke's *Childhood's End*.[20] In some cases, they encompass space opera treatments such as the destruction of Earth by alien interstellar probes and the ensuing revenge by the remaining humans saved by a different faction of benevolent aliens, called "the Benefactors" or "Moms" in Greg Bear's *The Forge of God*[21] and its sequel, *Anvil of Stars*.[22] Interestingly, the Benefactors' apparently purely talionic, or perhaps better apodictic,[23] law

Eigth Canon: In the event of canonical conflict in any relationship among intelligent beings, the involved beings shall settle said conflict by non-violent concordance". – *Ibid.*, pp. 7–8 (all formatting as in the original). – Asimov's three laws of robotics were first explicitly stated in the 1942 short story *Runaround*, featured in Isaac Asimov, *I, Robot – The Isaac Asimov Collection edition*, (Doubleday, New York, 1950) p. 40.

17 A fascinating twist on the "hostile alien" trope in the context of future human space colonisation is provided in Greg Bear, *Hull Zero Three* (Gollancz, London, 2011). In it, humanity has launched what initially seems to be a generation ship to a distant habitable exoplanet which, as it turned out before the ship was launched, was already inhabited. Apart from its original crew, all humans needed for the voyage and the actual colonisation are artificially grown from a "Catalogue" containing a gene pool. However, the Catalogue also contains templates for genetically designed monstruous creatures which are meant to act as the invasion force for the intended annihilation of the local species. – The novel also addresses the conundrum that a generation ship meant to travel for centuries might well be overtaken by the technological development of the species launching it and its purpose be defunct and moot by the time it arrives at its destination, where representatives of the launching species may already have settled hundreds of years before the ship's arrival. Indeed, in the novel the ship, which has already travelled for about 500 years, is ultimately diverted off course and registered as an "archaeology" project by humanity in the future present. Bear's themes of using genetic seed ships rather than fully crewed generation ships and the effects of advances in technology on the options available for human space expansion borrow quite clearly from Arthur C. Clarke, *The Songs of Distant Earth* (Grafton Books. London, 1968).

18 H. G. Wells, *The War of the Worlds* (Harper & Brothers, New York, 1898).

19 John Christopher, *The Tripods Collection – Vol. 1: The White Mountains, vol. 2: The City of Gold and Lead* (hereafter: *City of Gold and Lead*); *vol. 3: The Pool of Fire* (hereafter: *Pool of Fire*); *Prequel: When the Tripods Came* (hereafter: *Prequel*), 1st eds. 1967–1988 (Aladdin Paperback, New York, 2014).

20 Arthur C. Clarke, *Childhood's End*, 1st ed. 1953 (cited after the 1990 edition of Del Rey Books, New York, 1990).

21 Greg Bear, *The Forge of God*, 1st ed. 1987 (cited after the Gollancz, London, 2010 edition – hereafter: *Forge of God*).

22 Greg Bear, *Anvil of Stars* (Warner Books, New York, 1992 – hereafter: *Anvil of Stars*).

23 See *Forge of God*, p. 324: "'*What if we find the civilization of the planet-eaters, and it's matured? What if it's beautiful and noble and rich with culture, and it regrets its past mistakes? Do we still destroy it?*' '*Yes*', the Moms had replied. '*Why? What good would that do?*'

requires that "[a]ll intelligences responsible for or associated with the manufacture of self-replicating and destructive devices will be destroyed",[24] with such self-replicating probes after all being one of the alternatives discussed in the SETI/SETA community as a likely preferable means of interstellar exploration and colonisation by alien species.

Of closer relevance for the topic of this book are, however, those works which look at hostile encounters between humanity and an alien species, not least within a fully military setting. This includes classics such as Larry Niven's and Jerry Pournelle's *The Mote in God's Eye*[25] and its sequel, *The Gripping Hand*,[26] Joe Haldeman's *The Forever War*,[27] John Scalzi's *Old Man's War* trilogy[28] Robert A. Heinlein's *Starship Troopers*,[29] Cixin Liu's *Three-Body Problem* trilogy,[30] and of course, Orson Scott Card's *Ender's Game*.[31] We will look at a few of the above in quite some detail to tease out a number of recurring tropes and find out how the authors' imagination and their way of presenting them may provide us with some departure points for the further discussion, not least to discover where SF themes with too much emphasis on the F in SF may have created an incorrect impression in the public perception.

'Because it is the Law'". The book ends with the lines: "*To those who killed Earth: beware her children!* That is how the balance is kept". – *Ibid.*, at p, 325 (formatting as in the original).

24 See *Anvil of Stars*, 9 – Note that the "Law" as stated would also allow and indeed require the destruction of such species regardless of whether any of these devices have already been released by them. It seemingly rules out forgiveness and reconciliation. It makes the rule a "public order" rule, in human terms, as opposed to a rule protecting only individual interests, and removes any discretionary evaluation of policy merit from the framework of its application.

25 Larry Niven and Jerry Pournelle, *The Mote in God's Eye,* 1st ed. 1974 (cited after HarperCollins, New York, 1993 edition – hereafter: *Mote in God's Eye*).

26 Larry Niven and Jerry Pournelle, *The Gripping Hand* (Pocket Books, New York, 1993).

27 Joe Haldeman, *The Forever War,* 1st ed. 1974 (cited after Gollancz, London, 2010 edition).

28 John Scalzi, *Vol. 1: Old Man's War* (Tor Books, New York, 2007 – hereafter: *Old Man's War*); *id., Vol. 2: The Ghost Brigades* (Tor Books, New York, 2007- hereafter *Ghost Brigades*); *id., Vol. 3: The Last Colony* (Tor Books, New York, 2008 – hereafter: *Last Colony*).

29 Robert A. Heinlein, *Starship Troopers,* 1st ed. 1959 (cited after Hodder and Stoughton, London, 2005 edition). For a comparison of the narrative's underlying themes emphasised in the novel's movie adaptation to the Jewish Holocaust, see Brian E. Crim, The Intergalactic Final Solution: Nazism and Genocide in Paul Verhoeven's Starship Troopers, 28 *Holocaust and Genocide Cinema* (2010) 104–115.

30 Cixin Liu, *Vol. 1: The Three-Body Problem* (Head of Zeus. London, 2015 – hereafter: *Three-Body Problem*); *id., Vol. 2: The Dark Forest* (Head of Zeus, London, 2016 – hereafter: *Dark Forest*); *id., Vol. 3: Death's End* (Head of Zeus, London, 2016 – hereafter: *Death's End*).

31 Orson Scott Card, *Ender's Game,* 1st ed. 1977 (cited after Author's Definitive Edition, Tor Books, New York, 1994 – hereafter: *Ender's Game*).

2 Types of First Contact

2.1 *The Hercules Text*

The traditional paradigm of SETI research still follows the avenue of radio astronomy: We listen until we receive a signal. That, for example, is also the basic plot of *The Hercules Text*. That novel is of far greater interest for the post-detection message decipherment problems, and we will look at it a little more closely in the next section, together with other books. In essence, the distant signal version and its post-contact relevance are to a large part driven by the distance to the source and the light-speed barrier for radio signals: The star and planetary system closest to our solar system is Alpha Centauri, which is 4.37 light years away. An exchange of messages could be initiated and, depending on the message size and contents each way as well as the existence or (more likely) not of a primer or crib, some initial progress seems, in theory at least, possible within one human lifetime. In *The Hercules Text*, however, the distance to the signal source, which turns out to be an artificially created[32] X-ray pulsar in an isolated star system named *Althea* picked up by the fictional *Hercules Array* on the far side of the Moon is given as over 1.5 million light years,[33] reducing the "contact" to listening only, and listening to a message from a very distant past and thus very likely from a vanished civilisation at that.

2.2 The *Rama* Cycle – *Rama I and II*

Regarding the spectrum between entirely benevolent and entirely – and indeed mutually – hostile contact, and the degree of proximity, beyond the signal-from-afar narrative, Clarke's *Rama* cycle is quite instructive. In *Rama I*, humans land a spaceship called Endeavour on the huge cylindrical spacecraft christened Rama, which seems to have come into our solar system from interstellar space. When they board it, they discover that it is a kind of self-contained technological eco-system complete with bio-mechanical creatures they call "biots". They also discover what they assume is a type of 3D-printer template storage facility; one of the templates appears to be a "harness, or uniform"[34] for a biological creature much taller than humans – although the crew never meet any properly biological entities. Neither the spacecraft nor its "inhabitants" display any intentionally hostile or benevolent attitude but

---

32 See on a scientific discussion of the use of pulsars in SETI Clément Vidal, Pulsar positioning system: a quest for evidence of extraterrestrial engineering, 18 *International Journal of Astrobiology* (2019) 213–234.

33 *Hercules Text*, p. 10.

34 *Rama I*, p. 233.

seem indifferent of the humans unless, for example, they get in the way of one of the biots' functions. Nonetheless, one faction of humanity, from the planet Mercury, sends a massive nuclear bomb to destroy Rama pre-emptively. The bomb is disabled by the human crew of the Endeavour, and Rama, after apparently recharging its energy directly in a close fly-by and a gravitational slingshot around the Sun, disappears again into interstellar space. At no time is there any evidence that Rama knew of or was going to investigate any species in the solar system, let alone Earth. The commander of the Endeavour realises at the end of the book:

> One might speculate endlessly, but the nature and purpose of the Ramans was still utterly unknown. They had used the solar system as a refuelling stop – as a booster station – call it what you will, and had then spurned it completely, on their way to more important business. They would probably never even know that the human race existed; such monumental indifference was worse than any deliberate insult.[35]

In other words, even in a case of what must be described as direct contact with a machine, i.e., a space probe seen by many in the SETI community as the more likely scenario of direct contact, it is uncertain whether a communication can be established or that the ETI who built the machine may even be interested in making contact with other species living in the vicinity of the probe's trajectory.

Things change in the sequel, *Rama II,* when 70 years later, a second spacecraft of a shape identical to the first Rama, but an apparently different interior layout, enters the solar system. This time, a mission is sent in the spaceship Newton to intercept the second spacecraft and to explore it more thoroughly than was possible the first time. At some stage, Rama II sets a course that brings it on an impact trajectory with Earth, from which the crew onboard deduce that it must have detected transmissions from Earth and is going to investigate their origin. The human international space agency ISA decides by majority that its intentions would result in its entering Earth's orbit and conducting observations which could be perceived by humanity to be of a potentially hostile[36] nature, and prepares for countermeasures by targeting a fleet of

35 *Ibid.*, p. 252.

36 Clarke also seems to have had a somewhat strained view of human conjecture regarding anything beyond the materially observable exobiological data, because he has Wakefield say: "The ISA has an employee, a Canadian I think, whose speciality is exobiological psychology. Can you believe it? This idiot actually participated in the conference call and offered insights into the motives behind the Raman manoeuvre. […] All bureaucracies

nuclear missiles at Rama II. There is also a bomb on board the Newton, which is transferred to the inside of Rama II but ultimately not detonated because one of the crew who has to enter the trigger code, General Michael O'Toole, refuses to do so.

The main protagonist of the last three volumes of the cycle, life-science officer Nicole des Jardins, who has become lost and cut off from her crew members while on an expedition inside the spacecraft, encounters two specimens of an avian species who are apparently sapient and capable of communicating with each other at the level of "prehistoric man".[37] It turns out that these avians are passengers on the spacecraft, not its masters nor their descendants. They provide her with food and when she subsequently frees one of the two avians from a net in which it has been caught, a relationship is established and they take her to their lair, where she meets other members of the same avian species. She is eventually reunited with her crew member – and later husband – Richard Wakefield, who had gone looking for her. Together, they encounter another species resembling giant spiders with eight tentacles, which they christen "Octospiders", and who are also merely passengers on the spacecraft. Because their behaviour seems aggressive at first, no further direct contact is established initially and, while waiting to be rescued by the other crew members of the Newton, des Jardins and Wakefield find an empty lair which to their surprise is fitted out with what looks like phenotypical but mostly not functioning replicas of human household objects, such as a tube of toothpaste, a brush and a comb, as well as a keyboard with Latin letters, which does, however, work and when switched on links to and opens a screen in the wall of the lair. They conclude that the first Rama and its biots must have had sensor arrays that recorded the objects used by the first human crew 70 years ago, and transmitted the sensor data to the second spacecraft, which then reproduced copies of them when it realised that humans had entered it. Through this makeshift computer link, and after much experimentation with the keyboard's functions, they start communicating with the ship to a level that it manufactures items for their use at their request, something made possible only due to Wakefield's superb engineering skills.[38] Eventually, they

are the same. They drain the life out of the truly creative people and develop mindless paper-pushers as their critical mass". – *Rama II*, p. 338.

37 *Ibid*, p. 335.

38 Another example in *Rama II* for perhaps unrealistic levels of the breadth of scientific knowledge apart from Wakefield is said character Michael O'Toole, whose code for triggering the bomb is made up of the dates from his and his wife's birthdays, which he hides in a 50-digit code, using the so-called "quadratic prime" sequence based on the integer 41, also called "Euler's Polynomial", (for an explanation of the details see, for example, R. A.

devise a way of returning to a place near the mission base close to the exit to the Newton, where they are met by crew member O'Toole who is still procrastinating about entering the trigger code for the bomb. Eventually, the three return to the Newton but find that the remaining crew has left in escape pods and activated a code-breaking mechanism that is meant to discover and enter O'Toole's code. The code-breaker device disabled, all three return inside Rama II to the lair that des Jardins and Wakefield had lived in. They "warn" the ship of the incoming missiles through use of the computer and witness Rama's advanced evasive and purely defensive protective capabilities that allow it to escape undamaged. It changes its trajectory away from Earth and like the first Rama, heads out into interstellar space with the three humans on board.

Here, to break the narrative and interject some analysis, we happen upon two tropes often seen in first contact SF, the first one probably shared by a majority of SETI researchers, i.e., that on the one hand somehow the aliens will more often than not already be well prepared for communication with humans[39] (usually from watching our TV programmes etc.), and on the other hand that despite each crew member having some sort of scientific specialisation for which they have been recruited to the team in the first place, they are all capable of performing tasks to a high degree of sophistication at what would seem to be, as it were, post-doctoral degree level complexity[40] in a variety of scientific disciplines, including reversing and expanding the communication

---

Mollin, Prime-Producing Quadratics, 104 *American Mathematical Monthly* (1997) 529–544) and then "scattering" the resulting numbers across the 50 digits by using an "inverse Fibonacci sequence". – *Rama II*, pp. 435–436.

39 This trope – including the one about mathematics as the universal language and knowledge of prime-number-producing equations as evidence of sufficient technological advancement – also underlies Sagan's 1985 novel *Contact*, given that the aliens are capable of sending directed and individualised messages to other species, in this case the humans (choosing Hitler's opening of the 1936 Olympics as the first TV signal strong enough to penetrate Earth's ionosphere, as a sign of their knowledge about Earth and humanity – Contact, 94), consisting of tens of thousands of pages of detailed construction plans for a worm-hole transport machine they have to build, *and* expecting the humans to understand that they have to look for phase modulation in the message signal (remember the Wow!-Signal) to find the primer or crib that allows message decipherment and construction – which in essence none of the Ivy-League-educated scientists working on the project realise until the main protagonist, Ellie Arroway, is told to check for them by an odd-ball genius engineer (*Contact*, pp. 224, 233–236).

40 This is a feature also found in other science-driven action prose in general, especially of some American authors, where everybody on a fictional "Special Ops" teams, for example, has an MA in one subject and a PhD in another, or speaks or reads fifteen languages to an operationally sufficient level of proficiency, including exotic or ancient ones, while also being on top athletic form.

stream with the aliens. Both assumptions are not very likely to have a real-life equivalent. More to the point, as we will also see in the context of message decipherment and establishing communication, the actual details of the path to achieving these miraculous results are never fully explained – in this context especially the *Star Trek* franchise is replete with technological jargon arising from a veritable cornucopia of imagined pseudo-science, bits of which are dredged up by specialists and non-specialists alike at a moment's notice to defuse crises that have never occurred before.[41] A third theme is that of the space probe as a collector of specimens from the different stations along its voyage. As we will see in the remaining two volumes, *Rama III* and *Rama IV*, this is not far from the truth, yet these two books deal more with the aspects of species comprehension, communication and cohabitation, and shall be addressed under that heading below.

2.3 The *Tripods* Tetralogy and the *Forge of God*

Other than, for example, the benevolent[42] invasion or occupation scenarios such as Clarke's *Childhood's End* already mentioned above, there is a majority of narratives describing an invasion by ETI that is entirely hostile in character, and often linked to issues of them using Earth as a depository of raw materials and resources[43] for their own society, or simply as living space found as part

41 See, for example, NASA, The Science of Star Trek, 2016, www.nasa.gov/topics/technology/features/star_trek.html.

42 Here it is important to distinguish who is meant to be the (primary) addressee of the benevolence, as can be seen from the narrative of the movie *The Day the Earth Stood Still* (1951 and remake 2008), loosely based on the 1940 short story by Harry Bates, Farewell to the Master, in *Astounding Science Fiction*, October issue (1940) 58–86. The main purpose of the visit by "Klaatu" and the robot "Gnut" ("Gort" in the movie adaptation 1951 and GORT in the remake of 2008, where it is actually a US military acronym for "Genetically Organized Robotic Technology") is the protection of the extraterrestrial peace, or of the planet Earth itself, from impending human aggression or environmental neglect, and any benefit arising from humanity's compliance with the visitor's demands – depending on the story line – may be nothing more than a reflex of this ulterior main motive. Moreover, the story does away with the traditional view that biological/organic entities are always the masters of mechanical entities or machines: "*'Gnut,' he said earnestly, holding carefully the limp body in his arms, 'you must do one thing for me. Listen carefully. I want you to tell your master – the master yet to come – that what happened to the first Klaatu was an accident, for which all Earth is immeasurably sorry.* [...] *[W]ill you promise to tell your master – just those words – as soon as he is arrived?'* [...] *'You misunderstand,' the mighty robot had said. 'I am the master.'*"; *ibid.*, 86.

43 Both *Independence Day* movies, *Independence Day* (1996) and *Independence Day – Resurgence* (2016), for example, are in part based on that theme. – Incidentally, the latter also contains another example of questionable science, as already alluded to generally above, in that an alien spaceship, with a diameter of about 3,000 miles and such a

of their interstellar colonisation and subsequent reverse terraforming efforts, not infrequently because their own home system may be about to become uninhabitable. These sometimes also contain an element of (sometimes only temporary) enslavement or even harvesting[44] or annihilation of the human species.

2.3.1 *The Tripods*

The colonisation and enslavement aspects are clearly present in John Christopher's youth-literature trilogy *The Tripods* from the late 1960s period of UK science fiction, to which he later added a fourth volume in 1988 to explain in more detail the arrival of the alien race called the "Masters" and their conquest of Earth, which are only hinted at, and in not much detail, in the second volume of the original trilogy. The name Tripod derives mainly from the huge mechanical ground transport vehicles the Masters use to travel around, ensconced in their own atmosphere: They consist of a large disc-shaped control capsule mounted on three legs and possessing three tentacles, thus being in part an extraneous extension of the Masters' own physique who themselves have three legs and three tentacles. The Masters arrived in a large mothership that had orbited the Earth at a safe distance and undetected for years.

The plot has a number of curious question marks hanging over it from the start: The Masters apparently and rather unconvincingly – despite having travelled through space for a long time in a search for habitable worlds in a ship capable of moving at near-lightspeed[45] and having watched Earth for years[46] and thus by necessity being aware of humanity's defensive capabilities – seem not to give thought to ensuring air superiority through air support capacity[47] for the tripods, and during the first contact between a tripod and terrestrial fighter aircraft, the tripod is unsurprisingly destroyed effortlessly. Had the Masters landed their mothership as a bridgehead, it, too, would have been destroyed.[48] The discrepancy between their advanced spacefaring technology

large mass that it is described as actually having its own gravity, physically lands on and attaches itself to Earth, drilling through the Earth's crust and mantle to within a minute of breaching the molten core, without this leading to any disruption in the Earth's spin and consequently its geological/tectonic stability, or to its climate.

44 Which seems to have been an underlying implied plot line in the 2002 movie *Signs* by M. Night Shyamalan.

45 *City of Gold and Lead*, p. 171.

46 And occasionally sent down smaller ships, a reference to UFOs, yet those who saw them were not believed by other humans; ibid., pp. 172–173.

47 Despite landing a hundred smaller ships in the original drive to implant the "caps" on humans; *ibid*, pp. 174–175.

48 Ibid.

and the rather pedestrian (no pun intended) planet-side invasion ground force is remarked upon by one of the novels' characters.[49] Therefore, they have to use a different tack and employ means of psychological warfare, in which they are even more advanced,[50] to subdue humans, by influencing them subliminally via a hypnotic TV and music programme called "The Trippy Show", terrestrially broadcast from the US but with a hypnotic signal superimposed from the mothership in orbit, presenting the Tripods in a favourable light and as someone to be obeyed, which ultimately leads to "Trippies" communes evolving, and ultimately a cult following emerging across the globe. The hypnosis lasts for a few days and once a tipping point of mass hypnosis is reached, the aliens land in many smaller ships and begin attaching the first generation of mesh-like mind-controlling devices, the so-called "caps", to their skulls. The remaining population who did not watch the subliminal TV message, are disorganised and unable to put up a coordinated resistance. The mothership then lands and a first main base is built, followed by three large cities spread across the globe from which the Masters build their domain over Earth, keeping the humans in check using the caps which are now attached at a certain age. Human males compete in athletic tournaments every year and the winners are then taken to the cities, where they serve as slaves to the Masters in an artificial gravity similar to their home world and much higher than that of Earth, and in their atmosphere, requiring them to wear breathing masks all day except for the rest periods when they are allowed to retire to their own room with an Earth atmosphere – hence the athletic selection process: Once they lose their strength due to the harsh conditions, they willingly let themselves be terminated at the "Place of Happy Release".[51] Females of great beauty, on the other hand, are collected by the Masters like humans collect butterflies, prepared and displayed in museums for eternity.[52]

A clandestine and scattered human resistance movement, which has been working to find ways to end the Masters' by now centuries-old stranglehold over Earth, and to reclaim humanity's lost technological knowledge, manages to infiltrate the cities with a number of boys who have run away from home before they could be capped. They are supplied with fake mesh caps fastened only on the outside of their skulls and register as candidates at the athletic

---

49 *Prequel*, p. 19.

50 Which still raises, of course, the question how the Masters would understand how the human psyche works.

51 *City of Gold and Lead*, pp. 171, 193–194.

52 *Ibid*, pp. 183–188. – How an alien species would relate to human preferences regarding physical beauty is left unexplained.

contests, meant to be taken away if they win. The main protagonist learns from his Master that the aliens' ultimate plan is to terraform the Earth to replicate the Masters' atmosphere, which is unbreathable to humans, terrestrial animals and plants, and he realises that "man's subjugation was not, as we had thought, a final evil, but the precursor of annihilation".[53] To this end, a re-supply mothership carrying the required equipment for the 10-year terraforming process to begin is expected to arrive in a matter of a few years. While in the cities, the "moles" manage to scout out some of their weak spots and escape the cities to report back. In a concerted effort, with rather primitive means, the resistance movement manages to incapacitate the cities, thereby also de-activating the mind-control function of the caps in the process. In the end, the resupply ship arrives and seeing that mankind has regained its freedom and is increasing its military capacity, decides to abandon the colonisation effort, and destroys the three sites from orbit to prevent any Masters technology falling into human hands. Liberated humanity, previously united by its struggle against a joint oppressor, holds a "Conference of Man", at which, however, it then descends again into age-old factional disputes pitting nation against nation, into isolationism, and exceptionalism against multinational cooperation.[54]

Leaving aside the above-mentioned technological and tactical plot holes, the treatment presents a not too far-fetched scenario of the hostile colonisation of Earth as a precursor to annihilation of all terrestrial life by a species which regards humanity as most humans would regard an ant colony, or possibly pet animals, whose fate ultimately is of no consequence for the ulterior purposes of the ETI. Tellingly enough, the protagonists' Master reveals that annihilating life on Earth is a heavy moral burden for some of them, and that there is a dispute among them whether to allow some humans, animals and plants to continue to live in the cities, which would then become unnecessary for the Master's accommodation – but which could serve as a sort of zoo for the Masters to visit,[55] because they "appreciate beauty" and "preserve the best of the worlds [they] colonize".[56] Any thought of attempting peaceful cohabitation as moral equals with a highly developed species is entirely absent. The novel, however, also presents a scenario of possible human resistance in the face of overwhelming alien technological superiority, and allows speculation about human military defence potential creating a near-level playing field if not equality of arms as long as the gap between the level of technological

53 *Ibid.*, p. 203.
54 *Pool of Fire*, pp. 240–245.
55 *City of Gold and Lead*, pp. 171, 201–206.
56 *Ibid.*, p. 204.

sophistication is not too wide. Finally, it speaks to the need – and difficulty – of developing and maintaining what we called "cosmic species awareness"[57] above, with all the consequences that entails: If even the serious scientific SETI research effort – which as we saw after all traditionally tends to embrace the benevolent and altruistic ETI paradigm – still causes the "giggle factor" among many if not most people, then any hope of an adequate resource allocation for a timely start to the development of a global space defence technology seems rather futile, although as we will see in a later chapter, humanity is not averse to advancing the extremely costly militarisation of space at the risk of its own destruction.

2.3.2 *The Forge of God*

The novel addresses the possibility of a hostile and pre-emptively aggressive ETI using what in German is called a "*Kriegslist*", i.e., stratagems or ruses of war, in order to deflect humanity's attention from the real course of events, combined with the use of destructive probes. Two spaceships land on Earth, one in the USA, one in Australia. The one in the USA apparently carries a kind of stowaway, an alien creature called the "Guest" by the humans who discover it, and which speaks English, predicting "bad news",[58] warning of destruction by hostile[59] von Neumann machines,[60] i.e., self-replicating "eaters of worlds",[61] sometimes also called "Berserkers" after the short story collection of the same title by Fred Saberhagen,[62] and lamenting Earth's inadequate technological development.[63] The other in Australia releases a number of robots which announce an era of unprecedented prosperity for humanity. The Guest's own

57 Fred Hoyle put it this way at the end of his book *The Black Cloud*: "Do we want to remain big people in a tiny world or to become a little people in a vaster world?" – *The Black Cloud*, p. 219. Notice the difference in the use of the indeterminate article.

58 *Forge of God*, p. 14.

59 The possibility of replication errors and a split of such probes into mutual predators and prey is also a topic of general scientific concern in the context of the Fermi Paradox, see Duncan H. Forgan, Predator-prey behaviour in self-replicating interstellar probes, 18 *International Journal of Astrobiology* (2019) 552–561.

60 The seminal work is Arthur W. Burks and John von Neumann, *Theory of Self-reproducing Automata* (University of Illinois Press, Illinois, 1967). Von Neumann did not originally envisage their use in the context of space exploration. See for their use in that sense, for example, Andreas Hein and Stephen Baxter, Artificial Intelligence for Interstellar Travel, 72 *JBIS* (2019) 125–143; see also Z. Osmanov, On the interstellar Von Neumann micro self-reproducing probes, 19 *International Journal of Astrobiology* (2020) 220–223.

61 *Forge of God*, p. 61.

62 Fred Saberhagen, *Berserker – Collection* (Ballantine Books, New York, 1967).

63 *Forge of God*, p. 42.

home world was allegedly destroyed by similar machines of the same origin, and the spaceship that landed on its planet is the same that landed as one of the two on Earth. In fact, two devices, so-called "neutronium bombs"[64] have inserted themselves into the Earth's core and begin circulating in it, effectively on a count-down until they both meet. The human response is muddled due to the misinformation by the different alien narratives and the full and true nature of the threat remains unknown until it is too late. The Guest, despite its own home world's alleged fate, declares that the "[d]eath of a world is judgment of its inadequacy. Death removes the unnecessary and the false".[65] The hostile aliens' machines are, however, countered by another ETI, called the Benefactors as already indicated above, who are using mind-controlling miniature robots in the form of spiders to select and recruit a number of humans they intend to save from the Earth's inevitable destruction. In this they succeed, using ark ships deployed all over the world which then join to a larger spacecraft, the Central Ark,[66] in orbit. When the two probes finally collide inside Earth, the planet explodes. The survivors are put in some sort of suspended animation aboard the Central Ark and revived about 390 years later on Mars, which has in the meantime been terraformed with the aid of the Benefactors, from where they begin to explore the solar system supported by the Benefactors. Almost immediately after the destruction of Earth, they sent "Ships of the Law" made from the remains of Earth and crewed by surviving humans on a quest to find the home system of the ETI responsible for launching the von Neumann machines and to destroy its civilisation,[67] which is the subject of the sequel *Anvil of Stars* (see below).

Apart from the treatment of the trope of an unconditionally hostile civilisation whose aim is to destroy pre-emptively and pro-actively all technologically advanced life forms that might eventually become a threat to itself, a theme reprised below in Cixin Liu's work, the novel provides an example of the double-edged quality the use of AI-guided self-replicating probes in particular as a method of interstellar exploration and expansion may pose, and the relative ease with which such an approach might fit into a pre-emptively hostile ETI encounter/expansion model. Even if the discrepancy between humanity's capabilities and those of the planet killers is insurmountable in the story and resistance would have been futile, to use a Star Trek meme, real-world contact with such probes may not necessarily be so: Assuming some of them may have

64 *Anvil of Stars*, p. 405.

65 *Forge of God*, p. 62.

66 *Ibid.*, p. 321.

67 *Ibid.*, pp. 324–325.

travelled hundreds or thousands of years from their system of origin, it stands to reason that they might not be too much advanced, or even be defective after their long interstellar journey, and still within the reach of a reasonably predictable development of future human military defence capacity. Humanity's present collective unpreparedness and lack of attention to the risk of inimical relationships with ETI based on incredulity and much of the SETI community's wishful thinking about *a priori* and *per definitionem* benign encounters could have serious but avoidable repercussions should such contact be made.

2.4 *The Mote in God's Eye*

The 1974 novel by Niven and Pournelle is of interest because it describes in great detail, and with an eye for the bigger picture of the difference between communication and mutual understanding, the problems one species may face when encountering another of a roughly equal development, but which has its own troubled history and may be looking for expansion to the likely detriment of the other, and the ensuing efforts at containment. The story is set in the far future in the region on the far side of the Coal Sack Nebula,[68] at a time when humanity has established an interstellar Empire but has not yet made first contact with an alien civilisation. However, due to prior encounters with non-intelligent life, the military navy has a code for potential encounters with ETI, an excerpt of which is provided in the narration:

> Section 4500: First contact with non-human sentient[69] beings. Note: Sentient beings are defined as creatures which employ tools and communication in purposeful behaviour. Subnote: Officers are cautioned to use judgment in applying this definition. The hive rat of Makassar, as an example, employs tools and communication to maintain its nest, but is not sentient.
>
> 'Section One': Upon encounter with nonhuman beings, Officers will communicate the existence of such aliens to nearest Fleet command. All other objectives will be considered secondary to this accomplishment. Section Two: After the objective described in section one is assured, officers will attempt to establish communication with the aliens, provided however that in doing so they are not authorized to risk their command unless so ordered by higher authority. Although officers will not

68 See ESO, Part of the Coalsack Nebula. 2015, www.eso.org/public/images/eso1539a/.

69 Sentient is used here in the meaning of sapient.

> initiate hostilities it must be assumed that nonhuman sentient beings may be hostile.[70]

A space craft with a laser-propelled light sail is detected by a warship and its capsule brought aboard, in which a dead brown-and-white, furred alien creature is found. After the craft's trajectory has been traced back to its origin, a yellow star called "The Mote in God's Eye" (the Mote), two warships are sent to investigate. They use an instantaneous drive, called the Alderson Drive, which is linked to certain naturally occurring – and changing – jump points in a number of star systems; travel between those is, however, by normal propulsion. One such jump point is close to red giant sun near the Mote. The ships also possess deflective shields, the so-called Langston shields. They encounter an alien species near the main planet of the Mote system, Mote Prime, which are soon given the moniker "Moties". They seem friendly and eager to communicate with the humans – and here again we encounter the usual trope that they are capable of learning human language much easier and faster than the other way round, so that during mutual encounters speaking between themselves in their own language provides them with a code unintelligible to, and unbreakable by, the humans. The species is very old and has had spacefaring capabilities for a long time, but they possess nothing similar to the Alderson Drive or the Langston Field, and have not been able to leave their solar system other than by occasional experimental craft travelling at sub-lightspeed, such as the light sail ship captured by the navy. Their physical appearance is not basically uniform like that of the humans, but they have several subspecies which can – and must – become pregnant during their lifetime in order to thrive and indeed, to survive, and some of which are genetically engineered to perform certain functions. They are societally split into different factions controlled by so-called Masters, who continually have to negotiate truces in order to avoid all-out war between them. One subspecies is extremely adept at disassembling, analysing, and re-assembling any piece of technology in an improved state. This creates concern among the humans that if not controlled properly, they might develop and even improve upon the drive engines and shield generators – the latter in fact happens when one of the war ships falls into the Moties' hands and has to be destroyed by the other ship in order to avoid the improved shield technology falling into the aliens' hands. It ultimately transpires that, restricted to their star system and Mote Prime, the Moties have for millennia engaged

70 *Mote in God's Eye,* pp. 40–41 (verbatim quote as in the original). Note that this is a more pro-active approach than the one advocated, for example, in the IAASETI Protocols.

in cycles of genocidal wars in order to control overpopulation due to the fact that pregnancy is a necessary stage for certain Motie subspecies to survive, and they have created a particular fierce and dangerous warrior subspecies to prosecute these wars, which are vastly superior to the ordinary human Marines and at the very least on a par with the super-warrior caste engineered on one planet of the Empire, Sauron.[71] They are thus keen to expand from their system but their speed of species propagation would obviously put the predominance of the Empire at risk.[72] Despite the best coordinated efforts of the Motie negotiators to hide this fact, the humans eventually recognise the danger and in order to avoid a pre-emptive attack by the navy with the aim of exterminating[73] the Moties by destroying Mote Prime, the Moties accept a permanent stand-off by being locked in their system with navy ships continuously patrolling the close-by jump point as a precaution should the Moties ever succeed in developing a similar drive, which is how the novel ends. In the 1993 sequel, *The Gripping Hand*, some factions of the Moties actually manage to develop a jump drive and leave their system before the navy can intervene because the natural jump point has unexpectedly moved from the position guarded by the navy. A major conflict between them and the humans ensues which only ends in a truce when the humans present a biological contraceptive to the peaceful Motie faction who supported them to reduce cyclical overpopulation overall and the need for fighting to cull their surplus population.

The two novels on the one hand break with and reverse the traditional trope of the ETI being the ones which allow humanity to join the "Galactic Club"[74] and show on the other hand that despite near-equivalence of technological advancement, other hidden qualities and characteristics of one species may be determinative of any conflict, and that simplistic, essentialising deductions from perceived appearances of technological capacity, altruism or any other self-professed benign intentions of the other side prohibit themselves as much as in interhuman relations. Decipherment of a signal and even achievement of

71 No link to *The Lord of the Rings* is known.

72 *Supra* note 70, pp. 349, 357, 504–505.

73 *Ibid.*, p. 509.

74 "For a long time we've talked about the Great Galactic Wizards showing up and deciding whether to let the humans join, right? Only it's the other way round, isn't it? We've got to decide whether to let the Moties out of their system, and until that's decided we don't want them to see the Langston Field generators, the Alderson Drive, our weapons [...] It would give away too much about our capabilities. We've a lot to hide, and we'll hide it". – "You're treating them as enemies" [...] – "And that's neither your decision nor mine [...]. Besides, I've got some questions I want answered before I decide that the Moties are nothing more than steadfast friends ...". – *Ibid.*, p. 208.

some level of communication will not necessarily allow real-time understanding of intentions and impending actions of the ETI – and vice-versa – in order to make use of them on an operational, tactical, or strategic level. Direct face-to-face contact without even basic precautionary policies, as is aptly described in the first novel in particular and as was already mentioned above, drastically reduces the time available for sound planning based on verifiable and objective intelligence. Exolinguistic research efforts may thus come to have direct influence on military offensive and defensive capacity and possibly negotiation capital. Neglecting the exigencies of direct contact scenarios and the need to prepare for them can thus be seen as adding to the extraneous risk.

2.5 The *Three-Body Problem* as an Example of the Risk Inherent in METI

Liu Cixin, probably China's most prominent SF writer, describes in *The Three-Body Problem*, the first volume of his complex *Three-Body* trilogy (properly entitled *Remembrance of Earth's Past*)[75] the consequences of an act of malevolent METI activity by a Chinese astrophysicist, Ye Wenjie, who had to watch her father being beaten to death by the Red Guards during China's Cultural Revolution in 1967 and who over the following four decades successfully makes contact with an ETI on the planet "Trisolaris",[76] in order to entice them to come to Earth and take over the rule of the planet because she is convinced that there is no way to end "man's inhumanity to man"[77] other than by alien rule. Her request proves to be successful. The narrative again provides no detailed explanation as to how the communication of content was achieved in the first place.

Ye Wenjie manages to establish an underground cabal of followers who prepare for the Trisolaran invasion fleet's arrival, which is calculated to occur in just

75 In Mandarin, the title is 地球往事, which translates literally as "Earth's Past". The common usage, however, even in China, is to refer to it as the *Three-Body* trilogy.

76 The name of the planet is also the explanation of the novel's title: The planet Trisolaris is under the disruptive gravitational and energetic influence of three suns circling each other, as an example of the generic Three-Body Problem in mechanical physics, first described in 1687 by Isaac Newton in his *Philosophiae Naturalis Principia Mathematica*, Book 1, Proposition 66, and its 22 Corollaries. See for an overview June Barrow-Green, The Three-Body Problem, in Timothy Gowers et al (eds.), *The Princeton Companion to Mathematics*, (Princeton University Press, Princeton, 2008), pp. 726–728.

77 The first use of this phrase is commonly attributed to a stanza by the poet Robert Burns in his 1784 poem *Man was made to Mourn: A Dirge*: "Many and sharp the num'rous ills Inwoven with our frame! More pointed still we make ourselves, Regret, remorse, and shame! And man, whose heav'n-erected face, The smiles of love adorn, – Man's inhumanity to man Makes countless thousands mourn!" – Online open access at www.robertburns.org/works/55.shtml.

over 400 years. The plot is, however, discovered by the authorities. Yet, in order to reduce or even extinguish Earth's potential for developing more advanced technology and defence capabilities, the Trisolarans have already infiltrated all of Earth's advanced technological systems, including communication, with what are called "Sophons", fictional multidimensional particles that scan all communication traffic and prevent the use of particle accelerators in particular. All the time, communication with the ETI has happened only within the cabal through an interactive computer game, until towards the end of the first volume the first – and last – message is sent outside that environment. It reads: "You're bugs!"[78] However, in the second volume, *The Dark Forest*, in a conversation between a Trisolaran and a human supporter of the Trisolaran conquest of Earth, it is established that the concept of "lying" is unknown to the Trisolarans who communicate by telepathy and whose thoughts are open for all who communicate with each other. The realisation of the human facility of dissimulation leads the Trisolaran to admit "I am afraid of you".[79]

The second volume, apart from describing humanity's failed efforts to counter the pervasive surveillance of its defence planning by the Sophons and the almost total destruction of Earth's entire space fleet of 2,000 ships by just one minute Trisolaran probe, further has Ye Wenjie trying to establish what she calls a rudimentary "cosmic sociology" and the consequences flowing from it for interstellar interspecies relations, and in particular, for our purposes, for the sensibility of METI and the use of information about a civilisation's stellar location as a deterrent. Ye Wenjie's two axiomata of cosmic sociology, as she explains them to the character Luo Ji, are:

> First: Survival is the primary need of civilization. Second: Civilization continuously grows and expands, but the total matter in the universe remains constant. [...] To derive a basic picture of cosmic sociology from these two axioms, you need two other important concepts: chains of suspicion, and the technological explosion.[80]

Leaving aside the still unresolved question of whether the second of the two axioms in particular is actually scientifically valid regarding the finite amount of matter in the universe, we see Luo Ji develop the idea of a basic cosmic sociology further in a conversation with his colleague Shi Qiang: Based on the near-impossibility of real-time interstellar communications, learning of another

78 *Three-Body Problem*, p. 418.
79 *Dark Forest*, pp. 8–14 at p. 14.
80 *Ibid*, pp. 6–7.

civilisation's existence which is unaware of your existence and not knowing whether it is benevolent – i.e., not inclined to pre-emptive aggression – or its opposite, malicious, beginning a conversation may ultimately lead to your own detection, even if only the fact of your existence and not your precise location is divulged in the opening of the conversation – as was actually already done on the Pioneer plaques, incidentally (see Chapter 2 above).

Even only knowing that there is a previously unknown civilisation out there through an attempt at communication may give the other civilisation an initial clue to where to look. A chain of suspicion is thus triggered: At the beginning of any inter-civilisational conversation, it is unknowable for benevolent civilisation A starting the conversation, whether the other, civilisation B, is benevolent or malicious, and vice-versa for the contacted civilisation B. Even if B knows that A thinks B is benevolent, and A knows that B thinks A is benevolent, A does not know what B is thinking about what A thinks about what B is thinking about A, and so on; in essence a theoretically near-infinite regression of second-guessing each other's intentions will begin.[81] A resolution of this chain of suspicion in a reasonably short period of time to avoid any conflict, as it would be possible within one civilisation, is impossible at interstellar distances. Any difference in technological advancement between A and B and hence possible superiority at the beginning of the conversation could easily be equalised or even reversed in a short period through a "technological explosion", i.e., a quantum leap in development as human knowledge, for example, is currently experiencing, and hence at the time of contact could result in the annihilation of one civilisation by the other, or possibly mutual destruction. Keeping quiet after detecting B is thus not an option for A, either, because if A could detect B on its own, then at some stage B may also detect A on its own. As Luo Ji's interlocutor – who represents B in their conversation – sums up: "⌊O⌋ne, letting you know I exist, and two, letting you continue to exist, are both dangerous to me and violate the first axiom".[82] Luo Ji continues to the summation of the situation:

> If neither communication nor silence will work once you learn of my existence, you're left with only one option. [...] The real universe is just that black. [...] The universe is a dark forest. Every civilization is an armed hunter stalking through the trees like a ghost, gently pushing aside branches that block the path and trying to tread without sound. [...] The

81 *Ibid*, pp. 518–519.
82 *Ibid*, p. 520.

> hunter has to be careful, because everywhere in the forest are stealthy hunters like him. If he finds other life [...] there's only one thing he can do: open fire and eliminate them. In this forest, hell is other people. An eternal threat that any life that exposes its own existence will be swiftly wiped out. This is the picture of cosmic civilization. It's the explanation for the Fermi Paradox. [...] But in this forest, there is a stupid child called humanity, who has built a bonfire and is standing beside it shouting. 'Here I am! Here I am!'[83]

Luo Ji uses this principle in order to threaten Trisolaris with advertising its position in a manner visible to any galactic civilisation capable of decipherin-ghis message, and is thus able to reach an uneasy truce with them. However, he is aware that by doing so, he would also disclose the position of humanity's solar system. In the third volume, *Death's End*, the conflict between humanity and the Trisolarans is rekindled, which leads a few human protagonists to actually trigger the broadcast of the planet's location, but thereby also that of Earth's solar system. Both are subsequently destroyed by a third alien species' dimension-collapsing hyper-technology, which as a matter of course will eventually also destroy the entire universe, giving the third volume a rather eschatological character, most of which is too fictional and specific to the narrative to be a useful comparator for our purposes.

This narrative is in essence a modified restatement of the "state-of-nature" Hobbesian Trap for a scenario where avoidance through negotiation or the enforcement of a mutually accepted law by a joint ruler is precluded by the factual circumstances.[84] Assuming that there is some prima facie credit to the first axiom, that every civilisation's primary need is survival, one may still have legitimate doubts as to whether mere passive detection will eventually and inevitably engender the likelihood of reverse detection and thus justify pre-emptive annihilation of the detected civilisation, not least because after all the manner of weapon used may in and of itself give away the existence and approximate location as well as military capabilities of the aggressor, as Liu

83 *Ibid*, pp. 521–522. – This concern is reflected, for example, in the 2015 METI Statement, which warns: "As a newly emerging technological species, it is prudent to listen before we shout". – *Regarding Messaging to Extraterrestrial Intelligence* (METI)/*Active Searches for Extraterrestrial Intelligence* (Active SETI), 2016, https://setiathome.berkeley.edu/meti_statement_0.html – reproduced in Annex A.IV.

84 See Chao Yu and Jiajan Liu, The Dark Forest Rule: One Solution to the Fermi Paradox. 67 *JBIS* (2015) 142–144; Karim Jebaria and Niklas Olsson-Yaouzis, A Game of Stars: Active SETI, radical translation and the Hobbesian trap, 101 *Futures* (2018) 46–54.

Cixin himself has understood. After all, the link between detection and reverse detection is not causal but coincidental and hypothetical at best: A may be detected by B regardless of whether A detected B first. However, the increased risk of actively advertising our existence *and location* faces a powerful counterargument in the *Dark Forest* scenario based not on speculation about possible alien responses but on a precautionary reasoning arising precisely from the absolute absence of any possible knowledge about the other side's attitudes and motives. METI thus carries a grave risk if one proceeds from the assumption that contact with ETI is actually desired by the members of the METI community. Conversely, and maybe counterintuitively, only unexpected direct contact scenarios may thus provide an environment where a negotiated relationship may possibly evolve in real time *if* the ETI is not pre-emptively aggressive. But for that to occur, negotiation capital in the form of adequate and credible military deterrence will as a default rule still be needed[85] (see above), and it is that realisation that militates in favour of reflecting on a global planetary defence effort rather sooner than later.

3 Interspecies Comprehension and Communication

We will take a brief summary look at the ultimately as yet intractable question of how comprehension and communication is established between different species. It is worth remembering that real-world research into communication with dolphins and octopuses as examples of alien species, for example, is nowhere near the stage where a meaningful conversation could be had. Despite serious exolinguistic research having been conducted for quite a while now (see above), there still seems to be little serious echo of that in SF literature dealing with that trope.[86] Somehow, as was already alluded to above, comprehension or communication are always reached, and more often than

85 Scenarios such as the one pictured in the Star Trek movie *First Contact* (1996), where a Vulcan interstellar patrol ship lands on Earth, and relations are initiated, after the Vulcans notice the warp drive signature of Zefram Cochrane's experimental spaceship, are based on the benevolent superior species trope. After all, the Borg collective which has infested the USS Enterprise circling the Earth at the same time, has entirely different intentions for the planet and the future of its population. Likewise, discovery by the Star Trek universe's original "villain species", i.e., the Klingons or the Romulans, might have resulted in a diametrically opposed outcome.

86 On the issue of linguistics in SF generally see Walter E. Myers, *Aliens and linguists: language study and science fiction* (University of Georgia Press, Athens, 1980), and Myra E. Barnes, *Linguistics and Language in Science Fiction-Fantasy* (Arno Press, New York, 1975).

not through the good offices of the galactically polyglot ETI – which may strain credulity for some, because after all for the ETI it may be their first contact with an alien species, too. Walter E. Myers criticised this non-method approach by saying: "One does not resolve a contradiction by asserting it".[87]

Nor is this the case only for ETI contact narratives: Earth-bound SF writing dealing with extremely complex but purely terrestrial interspecies communication scenarios such as the French author Bernard Werber's *Les Fourmis*[88], who describes the successful interaction, without even any use of modern information technology, between humans and ants based on pheromones, also makes daring excursions into uncharted fictional territory but without exception, like their colleagues dealing with ETI, they are – hardly surprisingly – unable to explain in any detail how that comprehension of basic communicative and linguistic structures is achieved and how the step from these to any conversation about substance and meaning is made. The same can be said of the narrative of *The Hercules Text*, a novel whose very topic is after all the decipherment of an alien message from afar, as well as the reactions of the different characters, including the authorities who at the end of the day decide to shut the project down. After the usual mathematical "bait", a binary data message containing non-random number sequences based on the powers of 2, a much larger data package is received, also in binary, consisting of mathematical formulae and some basic imagery, finally increasing in complexity to more sophisticated content ranging from mechanical schematics and assembly instructions via the ETI's DNA to philosophy and poetry. Other than the use of massive amounts of computer run time and the ingenuity of the researchers, there is no explanation how binary data from an alien species 1.5 million light years away – meaning they cannot have had any contact with humanity at a time when the latter had developed even rudimentary speech – can be transposed into something recognisable and as un-binary as poetry by humans, unless one is willing to make the questionable assumption that certain developmental traits are shared by all species.

3.1 *Rama III* and *IV*

Similarly, descriptions of encounters and communication between humans and/or other species in an outer space environment regularly side-step the issue. Already indicated above, volumes III and IV of Arthur C. Clarke's *Rama* cycle describe the arrival of the human crew and their descendants at a "Node",

87 *Ibid.*, p. 88.

88 Bernard Werber, *The Empire of the Ants* (*Les Fourmis*- Trans. Margaret Rocques; Bantam Press. London, 1996).

i.e., a gigantic space station where the Rama spacecraft is refitted for its next mission, where they meet other alien species and eventually learn – from a polyglot humanoid alien biot with the head of an eagle – that their universe is an evolutionary research experiment designed by unknown actors and continuously monitored on an astronomically vast scale. They are then sent back to Earth to pick up 2,000 more humans either selected by Earth authorities or joining as volunteers, a large number of which are criminals promised release from prison if they volunteer to be space colonists. Very quickly, a Japanese crime lord takes control of the human habitat and establishes a dictatorial mafia-like regime, which starts a campaign of extermination against the avians and other species they discover in Rama, almost leading to their extinction. Des Jardins and some of her family eventually manage to flee and end up in the separate habitat occupied by the Octospider population not yet discovered by the other humans. The Octospiders are a highly structured and organised society who communicate with each other by colour band displays running around their heads like neon banners, but they learn to understand the human language – in essence by lip-reading[89] – and even to treat a human viral disease incurable for human physicians through their own type of medical procedures.[90] They previously and clandestinely genetically altered one female human so that she is able to read and interpret their colour language for the other humans – although des Jardins also manages to get a basic grasp after a while. Their language is described as follows:

> It's extremely mathematical. They use sixty-four colours altogether, but only fifty-one are what we would call alphabetical. The other thirteen are clarifiers – they are used to specify tenses, or as counters, or even to identify comparatives and superlatives. Their language is really quite elegant.[91]

When the war waged by the Japanese crime lord begins to spill over into the Octospiders' domain, they use means of biological warfare as a last resort by releasing clouds of minute creatures which invade a human body and cause death. Interestingly, however, the consequence of engaging in warfare in the Octospider's ethical code is the termination of any and all Octospiders involved in the design and execution war effort, including their commander-in-chief,

89 *Rama IV*, p. 192.
90 *Ibid.*, pp. 198–203.
91 *Ibid.*, p. 204.

the Octospider Queen called "Chief Optimiser",[92] for having experienced the attractions and the potential of the use of force, in order to prevent its use from becoming a regular feature in the governmental processes in their community. The use of violence is seen by the Octospiders as a non-optimal use of resources. The war is stopped through the intervention of the constructors of Rama when it threatens all-out annihilation of all involved species. Ultimately, the human survivors of the war return to the Node and are separated of their own free will into separate colony ships depending on whether they wish to join the multispecies society of the Node or remain among their own species – in the latter case, they will live in comfort on those spaceships segregated by species but be sterilised to prevent them having any further offspring, and never have contact again with humans or other species remaining at the Node or on their ships.

The two volumes thus raise the trope of contact from the horizontal species-to-species level to a vertical plane with religious overtones of interacting with what appear to be seemingly benevolent makers of cosmogony, who are also in a position and willing to dictate certain rules to any species in their sphere of influence if and to the extent that the success of the experiment is endangered. In such a context, which comes close to that of (representatives of a) creator and creation, it may pass muster to assume that communication in the vertical relationship should not be a surprise, yet on the horizontal level the traditional difficulties remain and the use of the *deus-ex-machina* of the vastly superior species is needed to overcome what would seem to be insuperable obstacles between species of similar advancement – the description of the number of colours used by the Octospiders, for example, and the qualification of their language as mathematical in essence betray the old tendency to take refuge in the omnipresence and ubiquitous validity of mathematics as the cosmic lingua franca.

3.2 *Semiosis*

Sue Burke's novel *Semiosis* is another example of even authors who like Burke are linguists, not fleshing out the actual roadmap to mutual comprehension.

92 See the conversation between des Jardins and an Octospider called "Dr Blue" by the humans: *"Have I understood correctly then", Nicole asked, "that every individual member of your species who has been involved in the design and prosecution of this war will be terminated when it is over?" – "Yes", Dr Blue replied. "Although they will not all die immediately … They will be notified that they have been put on the termination list … The new Chief Optimiser will define the exact schedule for the terminations, depending on the needs of the colony and the pace of replenishment".* – *Ibid.*, p. 424.

The book tells the story of the human colonisation of an exoplanet called "Pax" by a group of settlers, which already has its own flora and fauna, some of which are sentient to borderline sapient. The narrative tracks the development across several generations. Another sapient alien species that had settled on the planet a long time ago, called "Glassmakers" – because the cities they built were made of glass-like materials – makes contact with the humans but its vast majority is hostile to the humans; they became nomadic and their societal structures have all but collapsed. The main alien character, however, is a bamboo-like sapient plant whose roots cover large swathes of the planet and who is eventually called "Stevland", a name it is given by the humans and adopts in honour of the first casualty among the settlers, who died during the voyage to Pax. Communication with the bamboo is initially by primitive signs but with time it develops the skill of mimicking human script and understanding human speech, while some of the humans learn to write the Glassmaker script and communicate with their more peaceful faction. Stevland and the humans develop a symbiotic relationship, yet it is always clear that it is Stevland who is in control and the choice of continuing the relationship with the humans ultimately rests on how it perceives their usefulness for its own desires and purposes; indeed, it thinks of them as "service animals".[93]

The idea of sapient plants – already evoked as a trope, for example, in John Wyndham's 1951 novel about intelligent and mobile plants, *The Day of the Triffids*[94] – communicating with animal species in the wider sense, and with intelligent alien animal species in particular, certainly raises the conundrum of mutual comprehension to a new level: After all, plants are highly unlikely to have any repository of evolutionary experience connected to the capability of movement and all the consequences this may have on the development of neural structures as animals do, for example. Vice versa, animal species – with the exception of sessile species such as corals – suffer from an absence of understanding born of an experienced restriction of powers of reaction, and of the ensuing survival and environment control strategies of a stationary plant species lacking a central brain and quite possibly, beyond a certain capacity for tactile sensation, all or most of the five senses in a meaning comparable to what animals are usually equipped with.[95] Again, the question is evaded by

93 *Semiosis*, p. 299.

94 John Wyndham, 1951, *The Day of the Triffids* (Michael Joseph, London, 1951).

95 There has been a long-standing debate of whether plants have consciousness comparable to animals, where the majority view has traditionally been averse to answering that question in the affirmative. The emerging and controversial research on plant intelligence and behaviour does, however, clearly show the existence of what may be called survival strategies which at least phenotypically resemble intelligent or even deliberate conduct,

essentially casting the plant in the role of the superior species using animals for its own ends as service providers – which depends, however, on its permanent existence and continuous development over a long period and its wide-ranging root systems connecting it to large swathes of the planet's surface, even if possibly not rising to the level of a planet-spanning consciousness such as the ocean in Stanisław Lem's *Solaris*.[96] Absence of its territorial networked ubiquitousness would naturally make it much more vulnerable to destruction. In that sense, *Semiosis* does at the end of the day not really add any deeper insights into the methods of making a connection and maintaining (friendly) cooperation.

3.3 *Children of Time* and *Children of Ruin*

Finally, Adrian Tchaikovsky's novels *Children of Time* and *Children of Ruin* entangle the plot line of a human intelligence enhancement effort on an exoplanet gone wrong with that of the consequences of a human terraforming mission on another exoplanet millennia later. In *Children of Time*, a human astrobiologist develops a nanovirus she intends to use on monkeys dropped from an orbiting human ship on a faraway exoplanet in order to enhance their intelligence; instead, due to an unexpected turn of events, its release on the planet is to the benefit of a local species of spiders whose development over hundreds of generations to a highly sapient species the book follows. The humans, who had left the planet's system for millennia in their ship, return eventually and meet their engineered prodigy as the dominant intelligent species of the planet, eventually striking up a cohabitation, which is carried over into the sequel, *Children of Ruin*. In it, the story links the terraforming efforts of another human crew on yet another exoplanet with the storyline from *Children of Time*. The terraformers encounter forms of sentient life but also a

---

including possibly a form of visual perception especially in plants that can closely mimic other plants, and which may even stretch to controlling animals if that benefits the plant. On this debate, see Stefano Mancuso, *The revolutionary genius of plants* (Atria Books, London et al, 2018) – who incidentally considers plants to be the closest thing on Earth to an alien species from a human point of view, *ibid.*, at p. x; Yogi H Hendlin, Plant Philosophy and Making Sense of Contemporary Plant Intelligence Debates, 31 *Environmental Values* (2022) 253–276; Paco Calvo and Anthony Trevawas, Cognition and intelligence of green plants: Information for animal scientists, 564 *Biochemical and Biophysical Research Communications* (2021) 78–85; Paul C Struik et al., Plant neurobiology and green plant intelligence: science, metaphors and nonsense, 88 *J Sci Food Agric*, (2008) 363–370; James A Shapiro, All living cells are cognitive, 564 *Biochemical and Biophysical Research Communications* (2021) 134–149.

96 Stanisław Lem, *Solaris* (Wydawnictwo MON, Warsaw, 1961). – English translation by Bill Johnston. (Walker, London, 1970).

collective-consciousness species of microscopic parasites which aims to infect and control any species it comes into contact with – it ultimately also infects and assimilates the human crew. The humans brought a number of octopuses with them who are released into the planet's ocean and thrive over millennia to become a spacefaring race themselves. It is then that the human-spider alliance detects radio signals originating from the location of the second planet's system and travel there to investigate. They meet both the octopus space fleet and the parasitic life form. The novel describes the efforts of humans and octopuses to establish communication, but yet again – despite the author's express nod to the work of Godfrey-Smith[97] in the acknowledgements – the process of matching the colour-code based communication of the cephalopods to that of humans and spiders is hidden in the use of advanced computer technology. At the end, all four species manage to co-exist and form an alliance to explore the universe and find other forms of life, with the parasitic species apparently serving as a conduit to merging with any new species they encounter and hence overcome the traditional communication problems.

The novels both address the potential consequences arising from proactive, not to say aggressive, human space exploration – although admittedly in a far future with an imagined technology that is a far cry from present-day standards. However, the generic lesson is twofold: On the one hand – and this is not necessarily a new idea – exoplanet environments may contain forms of intelligent life humans would not recognise as such when they encounter them and contact may produce serious consequences, not least under the heading of planetary protection, that cannot be effectively countered anymore after they become clear – both on the exoplanet and on Earth, depending on the individual scenario. On the other hand, and more interestingly, the direct encounter with alien intelligent species especially in an interstellar space environment far away from Earth may lead to challenges to any traditional solitary human species identity and lead to (part of) humanity's adhesion to, or even co-creation of, a new collective which will as such no longer be bound by any moral, philosophical, theological, leave alone legal, premises that each individual species was – and a large majority of their respective members left behind on their home worlds may still continue to be – subject to. It will have to ask itself, to repeat Fred Hoyle, "[d]o we want to remain big people in a tiny world or to become a little people in a vaster world?"[98] It is very likely that this question will not be answered unanimously by all, thus possibly creating distinct

97 Peter Godfrey-Smith, *Other Minds – The Octopus and the Evolution of Intelligent Life* (William Collins, Glasgow, 2016).

98 *Black Cloud.* p. 219.

regimes within and between the different human factions to the point that for all intents and purposes, extraterrestrial humans may in effect become simply extraterrestrials for the humans on Earth.[99]

4 Interspecies Armed Conflict

Finally, it is necessary to take a brief look at scenarios in which an armed conflict is already taking place between different species. The manner in which these are described in the SF literature can provide an indication as to possible challenges for the current deontology of international humanitarian law, or law of armed conflict. By extrapolation, the question arises how to treat humans – and aliens – who breach fundamental rules of engagement and humanitarian red lines such as the protection of civilian populations: Are they liable to be prosecuted and punished under the regime of international criminal law? These questions will be interrogated more closely in Chapter 5. In this section we will put the main focus on the descriptions of actual space combat activities as opposed to the other common trope of humans defending Earth from an attack by an ETI ground invasion on Earth, or from Earth orbit, for example.

4.1 *Ender's Game*

The most glaring example from the point of view of current humanitarian law is Orson Scott Card's *Ender's Game*. It asks unsettling questions regarding the ethical principles underlying some of the most serious international crimes such as genocide[100] and the crime against humanity of extermination. However, before we address this particular point, it is useful to highlight the insights Card had on the requirements for military training relevant for combat in an outer space environment. The author explained the thinking behind the "Battle Room" featuring in the zero-gravity training of the cadets in the introduction to the definitive edition cited here:

> How would you train soldiers for combat in the future? I didn't bother thinking about new land-based weapons systems – what was on my mind […] was space. Soldiers and commanders would have to think

99 In this context see Tony Milligan, Space Ethics Without Foundations, in James S J Schwartz & Tony Milligan (eds.), *The Ethics of Space Exploration* (Springer, New York, 2016) pp. 125–134.

100 Indeed, the third volume in the Ender series is entitled *Xenocide* (Tor Books), 1992, a variation on the term genocide, and meaning the large-scale killing of the "other", the "alien".

> very differently in space, because the old ideas of up and down simply wouldn't apply anymore. I had read in Nordhoff's and Hall's history of World War I flying that it was very hard at first for new pilots to learn to look above and below them rather than merely to the right and left, to find the enemy approaching them in the air. How much worse, then, would it be to learn to think with no up and down at all?[101]

The essence of the story of *Ender's Game* is told quickly. Earth has been engaged for some time in an armed conflict with a highly advanced insectoid species, organised as a hive mind with a Hive Queen in control of each battle group collective; they are called "Formics",[102] because their shape loosely resembles that of ants. Humanity anticipates another invasion attempt and decides to take pre-emptive action. Children are trained via computer simulations of increasing complexity as combatants who are allegedly more adept at processing complex information than adults, among them the protagonist, Ender Wiggin, who shows outstanding tactical abilities. He is promoted through the different levels of officer training to the final posting at Command School. There he often takes part in what appear to be computer simulation battle command training exercises, until the final test, which he is told is a computer simulation of a battle scenario around the Formics' home world. Ender has by that time become depressed by his military training and hopes to be expelled from Command School by ruthlessly sacrificing the entire, massively outnumbered, human fleet and firing a Molecular Detachment Device called the "Little Doctor"[103] at the planet, which duly annihilates all life on the planet and the surrounding alien fleet. He is then told that the more advanced alleged computer simulations since his arrival at Command School were actually real combat activities, remotely conducted via a so-called "ansible",[104] a

101 *Ender's Game*, p. xiv.

102 Also called the "buggers" – from "bugs" – by some of the characters in the book.

103 *Ender's Game*, p. 273. – The name "Little Doctor" is a pun on the abbreviation of Molecular Detachment, "MD", which also stands for "Medical Doctor".

104 The term "ansible" is a contraction of the word "answerable" and was first coined in Ursula K Le Guin, *Rocannon's World* (Ace Books, New York, 1966); the idea of an instantaneous interstellar communication device had, however, been employed in SF writing at the very least since 1952 by Raymond F Jones, *This Island Earth* (Shasta Publishers, Chicago, 1952), where it is called "interocitor", or a "Dirac Communicator" in James Blish's short story *Beep* in the 1954 volume of the SF magazine Galaxy. – See generally *Ansible*, Encyclopedia of Science Fiction, http://sf-encyclopedia.com/entry/ansible, or World Wide Words, *Ansible*. www.worldwidewords.org/weirdwords/ww-ans1.htm for a further explanation of the term's history.

fictional device allowing instantaneous, faster-than-light communication with any corresponding ansible device. Ender feels utterly deceived and his conscience is racked by intense remorse for having killed almost the entire species in perpetuity by annihilating the queens on the planet and in the Formics' fleet. However, he later finds a surviving queen egg and through a telepathic link learns that the Formics had misread the level of species development of humanity due to its not having reached a stage of collective consciousness – regardless of humanity's technological advancement:

> We did not mean to murder, and when we understood, we never came again. We thought we are the only thinking beings in the universe, until we met you, but never did we dream that thought could arise from the lonely animals who cannot dream each other's dreams. How were we to know? We could live with you in peace. Believe us.[105]

Obviously, the entire narrative concept is first and foremost based on the availability of the fictional ansible device, regardless of that of an advanced weapon of mass destruction like the Little Doctor. However, the latter aspect is the one which takes us into the realm of the human rules of armed conflict as we understand them today. Using such a device would at the very least be a major war crime, a crime against humanity, and possibly constitute the crime of aggression. Yet, the pre-emptive annihilation of an overwhelming enemy in order to save one's own species from further devastating attacks would seem to be a colourable case of the traditional criminal law defence of necessity, possibly also self-defence, and in Metalaw terms might even pass muster under Fasan's 7th and 8th rules (see above). Lastly, the revelation that the Formics did not consider humans as sapient due to their lack of a hive consciousness, did therefore not consider their destruction to constitute murder and hence saw Earth as fair game for their interstellar expansionist efforts, is a reminder of the banal fact also addressed above in the Metalaw section that even fundamental ethical synchronicity between all species in the universe cannot be taken as read.

4.2 *The Forever War, Starship Troopers, Old Man's War Trilogy,* and *Anvil of Stars*

The six books examined together under his heading deal with – admittedly rather futuristic – war scenarios which do, however, shed light on some aspects

105 *Ender's Game*, p. 321.

that may occur in interspecies conflicts in a space environment: Firstly, how wars can break out for reasons similar to what happened on Earth in the past, and because of a simple lack of mutual communication and verifiability across stellar distances, secondly – and similar to *Ender's Game* –, how wars in space and possibly even on exoplanets may by default be fought with what would be termed excessive force, unlawful means or weapons of mass destruction or ethnic cleansing under current human terminology, caused by a societal rise in prominence and importance of military service, and thirdly – somewhat related to the *Three-Body* trilogy –, the need to abandon restrictions on military violence traditionally based on general considerations of proportionality and avoidance of collateral damage.

The Forever War, written in 1974, influenced by the author's experience of fighting in the Vietnam war and thus in essence an anti-war novel, describes the conflict between humanity and an alien species called the Taurans, set in the (then) future of the year 1997. It breaks out because the ETI allegedly attack a convoy of human colony ships, and the "United Nations Exploratory Force" is deployed to exact revenge. The first encounter with the aliens takes place on a planet orbiting Epsilon Aurigae – a real star system which is about 1,300–1,600 light years from Earth.[106] Similar to *The Mote in God's Eyes,* the terran ships are using jump points called "collapsars"[107] to travel at near light-speed;[108] similar technology is used by the Taurans. Soldiers are subjected to hypnotic techniques during the training, and in combat the post-hypnotic condition leads to excessive violence against the Taurans who do not initially defend themselves. After the last tour of duty, the protagonist learns that the war, which lasted for more than 1,000 years in non-relativistic time, is over and that humanity, which has started cloning itself just as the Taurans are clones, is now able to communicate with them. It transpires that the initial loss of the human colony ships was actually due to accident, and the start of hostilities engineered

106 See Centre de Données astronomiques de Strasbourg, http://simbad.u-strasbg.fr/simbad/sim-id?Ident=eps+Aur.

107 A star which has undergone gravitational collapse and turned into either a white dwarf, a neutron star, or a black hole, depending on the relation of its mass to the values of the so-called Chandrasekhar and Tolman–Oppenheimer–Volkoff limits. See Harald A. Wiltsche, The Forever War: understanding, science fiction, and thought experiments, 198 *Synthese* (2019) 3675–3698.

108 This causes enormous relativistic effects with the deployed soldiers who may spend a few years on a campaign and return to a terrestrial society where several centuries have passed. This has been said to reflect the Vietnam veterans' experience of rejection and abuse when returning home to the United States – see Media in transition, Joe Haldeman (1943-). http://web.mit.edu/m-I-t/science_fiction/profiles/haldeman_index.html.

by persons with an interest in starting a new war, i.e., the equivalent to the "Military-Industrial Complex" from 20th-century United States history,[109] who were pushing for a war which ultimately turns out to be meaningless. Here again, the question of mutual comprehension between species and of lack of real-time communication over interstellar distances resurfaces, and that, as was the case with the Vietnam war, there may also be nefarious reasons for starting hostilities even if the survival of the species is at stake. The laws of war applying to these conflicts are not spelled out in any detail. Furthermore, due to the advancement of the psycho-sciences, the use of psychological means to suppress the combatants' moral reflexes in the immediate combat environment – unlawful as it may be – is perhaps not as outlandish anymore as it may have seemed then, although it is reasonable to assume that the military use of AI with the power to make autonomous operative or even tactical decisions on the battlefield may currently be the more likely avenue for the future development of the armed forces.

Heinlein's *Starship Troopers*, another classic of the "war in space" genre, is set in the far future and also featuring starships travelling at relativistic and even FTL speeds, powered armour suits to support mobile infantry soldiers, and describing an interstellar war, where no quarter is given, against two alien species, the hive-consciousness-based spider-like "Arachnids" or "bugs", and the comparatively somewhat more individualistic "Skinnies", first allies of the Arachnoids and then switching to supporting the human forces. It has been one of the most, if not *the* most controversial[110] political SF novel since its publication, with criticism including glorification of the military to a point where full citizenship and the right to vote are depending on a minimum of three

109 See, for example, Ben Baack and Edward Ray, The Political Economy of the Origins of the Military-Industrial Complex in the United States, 45 *The Journal of Economic History* (1985) 369–375.

110 See, for example, the discussion by various SF authors in Poul Anderson and Anthony Boucher, *Starship Troopers: The PITFCS Debate, The Proceedings of the Institute for Twenty-First Century Studies* (PITFCS) No. 133, February 1960, www.panshin.com/critics/PITFCS/pitfcsintro.html; James Gifford, The Nature of "Federal Service" in Robert A. Heinlein's Starship Troopers, 1996, http://www.nitrosyncretic.com/rah/ftp/fedrlsvc.pdf; Brian E. Crim, A World That Works: Fascism and Media Globalization in Starship Troopers. 39 *Film & History* (2009) 17–29; on the movie adaptation by Paul Verhoeven see Florentine Strzelczyk, Our Future – Our Past: Fascism, Postmodernism, and Starship Troopers (1997). 15 Modernism/Modernity (2008) 87–99; Darko Suvin, Of Starship Troopers and Refuseniks: War and Militarism in U.S. Science Fiction, Part 1, in Donald M. Hassler and Clyde Wilcox (eds.), *New Boundaries in Political Science Fiction* (University of South Carolina Press, Columbia, 2008) pp. 115–144; Darko Suvin, Part 2, 1975-2001: Post-Fordism, and Some Conclusions, 48 *Extrapolation* (2007) 9–34.

years' service in the armed forces of the "Terran Federation", leading to a further charge of supporting fascism as a mode of government. The actual battle themes are a variation on the standard SF fare and of secondary importance, but the ideology underlying the Federation is central to the novel, and it highlights the dangers of connecting the admiration for advanced and sophisticated weaponry and military prowess with an elitist system of government that on the one hand pre-selects who may be a citizen and vote, and on the other hand is controlled by a military elite with little to no political accountability to anyone who has not served. The early 21st century has already seen numerous examples across the globe of the rise of a combination of populism with politically almost unaccountable executive political power. There are also distinct hints that the war against the insectoids is prosecuted as indiscriminately as it is because the species, albeit on a level of intelligence and development at least on a par with humanity, are not perceived to be "individuals" worthy of respect such as humans, and, as it were, are being implicitly "dehumanised". This has echoes of the annihilation of the equally insectoid alien species in *Ender's Game*. Any human contact with an ETI that is not closely humanoid[111] itself, and in a public environment in particular, is thus subject to the concern that depending on the nature of the contact the ETI will be "othered" very easily and be excluded from the self-formed group identity of humans *in limine*, reminiscent of the concept of the "maximal alien",[112] and depending on the mutual military capabilities subjected to ostracising violence, or full species cleansing.[113]

Sometimes reminiscent of a blend of Haldeman and Heinlein, Scalzi's *Old Man's War* Trilogy paints a bleak picture of future interspecies relations in the galaxy. Earth has *de facto* lost its predominant governmental role as the humans' home planet to an organisation called the "Colonial Defense Forces", or CDF, which is the mighty military arm of the Colonial Union (CU), and for which Earth serves only as a reservoir to re-supply it with soldiers. The series is called *Old Man's War* because the regular "recruits" are made up entirely from

111 This may not only apply to the physical appearance but also to the emotional impression or link the ETI may try to create with humans: "They're trying to personalize themselves, be more to us than unfamiliar creatures or opponents. It's a tactic almost human ... and it implies some understanding of or congruence with our psychology". – *Anvil of Stars*, p. 407.

112 Schetsche/Anton, p. 16 (Translation by the author).

113 Othering does, of course, happen in interhuman relationships as well, which is naturally where the term was originally coined; see for an introduction Travis D Boyce and Winsome M Chunnu (eds.), *Historicizing Fear: Ignorance, Vilification, and Othering* (University Press of Colorado, Boulder, 2020).

people who have reached retirement age on Earth and are then encouraged to enlist in the CDF, where they will in effect be given a new body with massively increased power and quite a number of cyborg enhancements. There is a more sinister elite force in the CDF made up of psychologically altered imprints of deceased humans' stored personalities in new bodies, the so-called Ghost Brigades. The actual combat action again is not that dissimilar to Haldeman's or Heinlein's , but the philosophical and political background scenario is of greater interest for our purposes, because it helps tame the imagination about how relations between civilisations could only evolve in a positive manner.

In the first volume, *Old Man's War*, the underlying ideology of the all-powerful CDF is disclosed, and it strikes a chord with regard to the *Dark Forest* theory explained above: There is no "Galactic Club" to which species can peacefully accede; instead, colonisation of other worlds is perceived by all civilisations, and mostly by the CDF, as the only way of expanding and securing new dominions, given the restricted amount of galactic "real estate", and the preferred manner of doing so is by pre-emptive extermination.[114] The CDF furthermore operates on the – above-mentioned – anthropomorphic bias when initially distinguishing "good vs. bad" species.[115] Sparing civilians – to the extent this distinction is feasible[116] – in attacks is something it aspires to, but ultimately even this fundamental humanitarian aspiration takes a back seat to tactical and operational necessities, such as carpet-bombing the capital city of an enemy's home planet in order to demoralise the population and its leadership.[117] The cynical conclusion of some of the protagonists is that it is "easier to fight than to negotiate", regardless of whether this results in what they call genocide.[118] In the second volume, *The Ghost Brigades*, the constant state of war has resulted in hundreds of civilisations forming an alliance called the "Conclave", which aims at establishing a joint governance system. Not every species decides to join the Conclave formally, as opposed to sending observer representatives, but only the dominant, vastly more advanced and hence unassailable species in that sector of space, called the *Consu*, and the humans' CU, the political base of the CDF, refuse to do even that.[119] The Conclave intends

114 *Old Man's War*, pp. 113, 119–120.

115 *Ibid.*, p. 158.

116 One soldier, a former Earth politician, who tries to use the diplomatic route during an attack operation is killed by what were initially considered mere civilian bystanders. *Ibid.*, p. 194.

117 *Ibid.*

118 *Ibid.*, pp. 202–203.

119 *Ghost Brigades*, p. 295; *Last Colony*, pp. 84–86.

to regulate colonisation and vows to attack any colonising species that uses force to acquire new colonies, and refuses to protect any non-members from colonisation by force, either, thus presenting a real problem for the CDF's preferred *modus operandi*,[120] which leads the CU to engage in subversion through instrumentalisation of a co-called "counter-conclave".[121] An example of the Conclave's resolve is given in the third volume, *The Last Colony*, where after an initial and ultimately rebuffed offer by the commander of the massive Conclave fleet to spare a group of colonists if they abandoned the planet they had occupied, their entire settlement is vaporised by the fleet from orbit.[122] This is of interest for any discussion around an idea of a Prime Directive à la Star Trek, and highlights the simple truth that any organisation may be dealing peacefully with its members but not necessarily with outsiders. The idea of a "Galactic Club", to which we will return in a later chapter, thus has at best an ambivalent value. The main protagonist finally manages to break the deadlock by deft clandestine manoeuvring, in getting the entire Conclave fleet to circumvent the CU governance structure and head directly to Earth with goods for trading instead of weapons, ushering in a new era in which Earth regains its former central role.

Finally, on the one hand, the theme of cross-species deception raised in the analysis of Greg Bear's *The Forge of God* above is addressed further in the sequel, *Anvil of Stars*, in which the survivors of Earth are pursuing the species that built the machines which destroyed their home world. Again, the battle narratives and the advanced futuristic weapons systems used on both sides are too fictional for our purposes but, on the other hand, the story also has a moral tale to tell about the ideas that there can be a cosmic law enforcement. To repeat the principle of cosmic law espoused by the Benefactors, which the humans are meant to follow: "All intelligences responsible for or associated with the manufacture of self-replicating and destructive devices will be destroyed".[123] The book at its very end also adds an interesting secondary law

---

120 *Ghost Brigades*, pp. 295, 296–297.

121 *Ibid.*, p. 334.

122 *Last Colony*, pp. 151–169.

123 *Anvil of Stars*, p. 9 – Note that the "Law" as stated would also allow and indeed require the destruction of such species regardless of whether any of these devices have already been released by them. It seemingly rules out forgiveness and reconciliation. It makes the rule a "public order" rule, in human terms, as opposed to a rule protecting only individual interests, and removes any discretionary evaluation of policy merit from the framework of its application, despite the fact that the actual judgment is left to the aggrieved species and not imposed by the Benefactors, and that interpretation of the Law may be a complex task – *ibid.*, pp. 419, 421.

on self-replicating machines, when the AI governing the humans' ship realises after the mission has been completed, that is has been changed by the experience and has thus become a mutation of its original self, consequently deciding to self-destroy after delivering the ship's crew to their final destination:

> I have no instructions on what to do with the fruits of our combined efforts. Having no knowledge of how other ships have dealt with intellectual collaborations with their crews, or how they have dealt with the inevitable transfer of characteristics, I can see no other option. When the humans are settled, I will destroy myself. I am not what I was when I was made. This qualifies me as a mutation, and mutations are forbidden among robot vehicles capable of self-replication. That is the Law.[124]

The apodictic nature of the retaliatory Law with potentially problematic ethical repercussions is soon recognised by the humans:

> 'What if we find the civilization of the planet-eaters, and it's matured? What if it's beautiful and noble and rich with culture, and it regrets its past mistakes? Do we still destroy it?' 'Yes', the Moms had replied. 'Why? What good would that do?' 'Because it is the Law'.[125]

An approach of this kind does not sit easily with, for example, Haley's and Fasan's ideas of the generic principles that should underlie all civilisations' morals, and which should be considered the building blocks of a communal metalaw. The dilemma duly arises once the humans enter the home system of the planet killers. The species living in the star system which the humans have determined to be the system of origin of the planet killers, are the same kind as the "Guest" from *Forge of God* – and apparently a species engineered by the former – who protest that they have nothing to do with the crimes committed by their creators. A number of conversations take place between them, another entity superior to the first, and a representative of the humans. Factions appear between the humans regarding the question whether the original mission should still be prosecuted if there is no sufficient evidence that the species are responsible for Earth's destruction. The captain of one ship uses the negotiations as a smokescreen and attacks the planetary system without warning even his fellow humans, destroying it completely and in the process

124 *Ibid.*, pp. 470–471.
125 *Forge of God*, pp. 324–325; italics in the original.

killing trillions of life forms with the advanced weaponry developed and provided by the Benefactor's technology on site.[126] Both sides engage in bitter recriminations until the truth is revealed, namely that the planet killers had not left the system and that neutronium bombs like the ones used on Earth were still being manufactured in the system at the time the humans arrived. In fact, the entire star system was one gigantic machinery of deception, with a number of planets, and possibly even the life forms inhabiting them, having been engineered artificially, for example.[127]

This fictional scenario ties in with the idea proposed by some in the SETI community that looking for Dyson-type[128] artefacts even at stellar engineering level[129] should be a preferred avenue of search efforts but also gives a few pointers of why it may be difficult to do so. Combined with the ideas behind the *Dark Forest* rules explained above, civilisations capable of artificially modifying their own or any stellar environment at such a mega-level, may by definition also have to invest heavily in camouflage or stealth technology and advanced defence systems of the kind described in *Anvil of Stars*.

5 Conclusion

It is hoped that this chapter has given a sufficient, albeit by necessity superficial, overview of the issues involved if and when we want to move on to thinking about how contact with ETI might impact on humanitarian law as it stands today. The scientific background to SETI in its various forms, its imponderabilities or, in the words of former US Secretary of Defence Donald Rumsfeld, "known unknowns" and "unknown unknowns",[130] make it extremely difficult to arrive at anything close to predictability about the forms of contact, the

126 For which there was no precedent even in the Benefactors' history, nor for a civilisation of the type destroyed, highlighting the theoretical possibility that even highly advanced species already operating on an interstellar basis for long periods of time may still encounter unknown scenarios – *Anvil of Stars*, p. 460.

127 *Ibid.*, 440, 463.

128 Milan M Ćirković, Astroengineering, Dysonian SETI, and naturalism: A new Catch-22, 152 *Acta Astronautica* (2018) 289–298; Massimo Teodorani, A strategic "viewfinder" for SETI research, 105 Acta Astronautica (2014) 512–516; *id.* Search for high-proper motion objects with infrared excess, 105 Acta Astronautica (2014) 547–552.

129 See also Stephen Baxter's sequel to H.G. Wells' *The Time Machine*: *The Time Ships*, 1st ed. 1995 (cited after the HarperVoyager, Glasgow, 2016 paperback edition) p. 75.

130 See his comments at the press conference of 12 February 2002 at www.youtube.com/watch?v=REWeBzGuzCc, and the title of his autobiography Donald Rumsfeld, *Known and Unknown* (Penguin, London, 2011).

interests and intentions of any ETI in revealing itself, and the wide variety of potential forms of interaction. The wisdom of actively messaging ETI, as in METI, becomes a matter of some concern. Almost invariably, a high state of development of any ETI is coupled with an equally high degree of altruism and benevolence. Speculative assumptions are made from a purely human perspective about fundamental building blocks of a cosmic metalaw, despite a total absence and lack of comparator data originating outside the sphere of human imagination – even bearing in mind the free flights of fancy of SF writers. The almost obsessive emphasis by the traditional astronomic SETI community on looking at the stars as being the only right way to do SETI, and its near-absolute aggressive herd instinct against any methodological approach that involves alleged lived human experience of contact with ETI or search for tangible objects on Earth, together with the mostly misinformed use of the questionable ECREE paradigm, add to the hurdles, not least because the vast majority of funding goes into that kind of research, and even joining the mainstream of SETI work still has very detrimental effects on an academic's career – the German animal sociology term for this phenomenon is "*verbeißen*". The use of the "giggle factor" even within the SETI community by one faction against another is evidence of what may be called, again in German, *Denkverbote*, i.e., intellectual taboos, and of being protective about very real and vested financial and power interests. Against this background, establishing what must ultimately be precautionary rules of human-to-ETI behaviour is a formidable challenge.

CHAPTER 5

Hostile Contact and Current International and Domestic Law

1 Introduction

The question of inter-human armed hostilities involving the use of military force in, or emanating from, outer space has been receiving attention for some time from the perspectives of political science, international relations and also law;[1] the MILAMOS and Woomera Manual projects, for example, show how far

1 See Cassandra Steer and Matthew Hersch (eds.), *War and Peace in Outer Space – Law, Policy, and Ethics* (OUP, Oxford, 2021); John J Klein, *Understanding Space Strategy – The Art of War in Space* (Routledge, London/New York, 2019); Linda Dawson, *War in Space: The Science and Technology Behind Our Next Theater of Conflict* (Springer, New York, 2018). One major forum for these discussions since 2003 has notably been the journal *Astropolitics*. See only William L Spacy II, Assessing the Military Utility of Space-Based Weapons, 1 *Astropolitics* (2003) 1–43; Andrei Shoumikhin, Russian Perspectives on the Military Uses of Outer Space, 1 *Astropolitics* (2003) 95–112; Randall Correll, Military Space Cooperation: Aligning the Balance of Power and Building Common Interest, 2 *Astropolitics* (2004) 133–147; Phillip Baines, Non-Offensive Defences: Space Protection Without Space-Based Weapons, 2 *Astropolitics* (2004) 149–174; Philip Coyle and John Rhinelander, Space Weapons: Alternatives for Today, 2 *Astropolitics* (2004) 201–213; Howard Kleinberg, On War in Space, 5 *Astropolitics* (2007) 1–27; Laurence Nardon, Cold War Space Policy and Observation Satellites, 5 *Astropolitics* (2007) 29–62; Darren Huskisson, Protecting the Space Network and the Future of Self-Defense, 5 *Astropolitics* (2007) 123–143; Patrick K Gleeson, Perspectives on Space Operations, 5 *Astropolitics* (2007) 145–172; Larry M Wortzel, The Chinese People's Liberation Army and Space Warfare, 6 *Astropolitics* (2008) 112–137; Damon Coletta, Space and Deterrence, 7 *Astropolitics* (2009) 171–192; Sterling Michael Pavelec, The Inevitability of the Weaponization of Space: Technological Constructivism Versus Determinism, 10 *Astropolitics* (2012) 39–48; Laura Delgado López, Predicting an Arms Race in Space: Problematic Assumptions for Space Arms Control, 10 *Astropolitics* (2012) 49–67; Alan Steinberg, Weapons in Space: The Need to Protect Space Assets, 10 Astropolitics (2012) 248–267; Karl D Hebert, Regulation of Space Weapons: Ensuring Stability and Continued Use of Outer Space, 12 *Astropolitics*: 1–26; Promit Chatterjee, Legality of Anti-Satellites Under the Space Law Regime, 12 *Astropolitics* (2014) 27–45; Michael E Salla, Astropolitics and the "Exopolitics" of Unacknowledged Activities in Outer Space, 12 *Astropolitics* (2014) 95–105; Jeremy Straub, Application of a Maritime Framework to Space: Deep Space Conflict and Warfare Scenario, 13 *Astropolitics* (2015) 65–77; Michael Nayak, Fighting a War in Space: The Case for a Space Innovation Force, 16 *Astropolitics* (2018) 157–173; Ekta Rathore and Biswanath Gupta, Emergence of Jus Cogens Principles in Outer Space Law, 18 *Astropolitics* (2020) 1–21; Ram S Jakhu et al., Threats to Peaceful Purposes of Outer Space: Politics and Law, 18 *Astropolitics* (2020) 22–50; Trevor Brown, Revolutionizing

 | DOI:10.1163/9789004677708_006

the thinking in that field has progressed.[2] There have been calls for the creation of an interstellar criminal law, but also only on an interhuman level.[3] The same cannot be said for the topic of how to deal with potentially hostile contact with ETI. The current SETI efforts and the lack of reliable findings leaves most if not all of that field in a grey area of more or less informed speculation. This has an impact on the question which we are about to address now, namely how the hypothetical idea of a hostile contact leading to potential armed hostilities will influence our current understanding of international humanitarian law (IHL). In other words, are the rationales underlying our current law of armed conflict adequate for, or at least adaptable to, war with an alien species? Does it depend on where the theatre of combat lies – on Earth, in its orbit or outer space in general? Assuming we will at all be able to mount a defence and the ETI will not be unassailably superior in power as the majority expectation of those who entertain the possibility of a hostile scenario tends to be, will the justification of our response depend on the difference in military capacity? The greater the difference in technological advancement and the less likely and capable humans will be to engage in low-intensity and spatially restricted, surgical warfare, the more attractive radical pre-emptive solutions will become: As in *Ender's Game*, if we cannot engage in conventional aerial/space and ground combat with an invasion force on a more or less level playing field, we might be tempted very early on to reach for the ultimate weapon that destroys the heart of the civilisation, or even the civilisation itself.[4] A direct application of the *Dark Forest* rules elaborated upon previously would even suggest very much the same course of conduct on the mere detection of another civilisation, although humanity will for a long time not be in a position to deploy weapons

---

Space Warfare: "Power Star" Space Solar Power Concept, 18 *Astropolitics* (2020) 51–72; Raja Qaiser Ahmed et al., Emerging Trends of Space Weaponization: India's Quest for Space Weapons and Implications for Security in South Asia, 18 *Astropolitics* (2020) 158–169.

2 The debate about the weaponisation of outer space is naturally linked to the general discussion about the development of new weapons categories in general. On this see William H Boothby (ed.), *New Technologies and the Law in War and Peace* (CUP, Cambridge, 2019).

3 Carrie Leonetti, Space Bandits: The Need for Interstellar Criminal Law, *Kilaw Journal* (2019) 195–271, https://journal.kilaw.edu.kw/wp-content/uploads/2019/10/Carrie-Leonetti-.pdf.

4 Current law frowns even upon the idea of regime elite assassination to avoid full-scale war. See Michael Bohlander and Dawn L Rothe, "Spock was wrong" – Global Student Views on Head-of-State and Regime Assassination as a Means of Avoiding Collateral Civilian Damage in Armed Conflicts, *The Global Community Yearbook of International Law and Jurisprudence* (2012) 69–127; Michael Bohlander, Killing many to save a few? Preliminary Thoughts about Avoiding Collateral Civilian Damage by Assassination of Regime Elites, in Kaiyan Kaikobad and Michael Bohlander (eds.), *International Law and Power: Perspectives on Legal Order and Justice – Essays in Honour of Colin Warbrick* (Martinus Nijhoff, Leiden, 2009) pp. 207–234.

capable of doing so – and very likely such an act would be seen in essence as a form of the crime of aggression currently prohibited by international criminal law (ICL).[5] We shall therefore not entertain this specific far-fetched scenario of a classic pro-active military aggression any further and focus on forms of conflict closer to home and – from a human point of view – of a defensive nature.

However, the question of a potentially aggressive impact of human space exploration on non-space-faring life forms on other planets in the wider sense, as discussed briefly in Chapter 2 under the heading of planetary protection, is worth considering: If these life forms are sentient or even sapient but not as far advanced as humans, or maybe highly advanced in a totally different manner but not interested in space flight as a concept, would human colonisation and exploitation of celestial bodies inhabited by such species without consent or even against their will reach a level of immorality that should trigger criminal liability or at the very least lead to rules being implemented that provide for ex-ante guidance and some form of sanctions for non-compliance? The story of the 2009 blockbuster film "Avatar" serves as a fictional example where such exploitation may occur under the (unregulated) use of military force including heavy weaponry, yet the fate of the masterminds of the commercial company exploiting Pandora and de facto commanding the military expedition force, for example, remains unclear: They are being led away to an off-planet transport at the end of the movie but we are not told their ultimate fate, and whether anyone will face legal consequences for their actions.[6] We will consider this aspect in more detail under 2.1.2.5 below.

Conversely, we might ask whether there would be a basis in law for holding ETI liable under human IHL. Obviously, no existing international criminal court on Earth with their present narrow jurisdictional parameters would have the power to try a member of an alien species, and that includes, for example, a referral by the UN Security Council (UNSC) to the ICC or a new ad hoc tribunal based on Chapter VII of the UN Charta: The UN means nothing to

5 Art. 8bis (1) ICCS defines the crime of aggression as follows: "For the purpose of this Statute, 'crime of aggression' means the planning, preparation, initiation or execution, by a person in a position effectively to exercise control over or to direct the political or military action of a State, of an act of aggression which, by its character, gravity and scale, constitutes a manifest violation of the Charter of the United Nations". – See for more detail Claus Kreß and Stefan Barriga (eds.), *The Crime of Aggression – A Commentary* (CUP, Cambridge, 2017).

6 It appears from the advance marketing for the sequel scheduled to come to cinemas in December 2022 that the narrative will be more along the lines of a revenge or retaliation scenario, hence the narrative likelihood of a legal reckoning would seem to be infinitesimal – see www.avatar.com. See also Russell Blackford, *Science Fiction and the Moral Imagination – Visions, Minds, Ethics* (Springer, New York, 2017) pp. 182–187.

an ETI and short of the UN, for example, transmogrifying into a proper world government representing the whole planet Earth and thus in a sense exercising the ultimate territorial jurisdiction, any international agreements between human states within the UN framework or otherwise can have no effect for any extraterrestrial entity not willing to be bound by them – this is already a well-known human concept which aliens could in theory readily rely on, namely that treaties cannot bind third non-parties: *Pacta tertiis nec nocent nec prosunt.*[7] On the other hand, territorial criminal jurisdiction at the very least is the most uncontroversial, basic standard form – the question would then turn more towards whether an alien can be liable under a state's or international body's substantive criminal law which, of course, is normally meant to apply to humans[8] (and in some countries, corporations) and may raise issues particularly around concepts of mistakes of fact or law, cultural defences etc. It is thus quite a different matter whether individual states could prosecute and try an alien apprehended on their territory or under their other domestic jurisdictional criteria, or whether they might decide to transfer their domestic jurisdiction to the International Criminal Court (ICC) or another international tribunal.

2 Liability of Humans

2.1 *International Criminal Law*

In order to answer this question and to gauge where human law would tend to draw the line, it is helpful to start from the other end of the regulatory spectrum, as it were, and look at which conduct is currently being criminalised

7 See entry in John P Grant and J Craig Barker (eds.), *Encyclopaedic Dictionary of International Law,* 3rd ed. (OUP, Oxford, 2009) – Online Edition.

8 There have, of course, been prosecutions and trials, including executions, of non-human animals not only during the less enlightened ages of humanity but into the 20th century in some societies. See, for example, Edward P Evans, *The criminal prosecution and capital punishment of animals* (Heinemann, London, 1906); Walter Woodburn Hyde, The Prosecution and Punishment of Animals and Lifeless Things in the Middle Ages and Modern Times, 64 *University of Pennsylvania Law Review and American Law Register* (1916) 696–730; Hampton L Carson, The Trial of Animals and Insects – A Little Known Chapter of Mediæval Jurisprudence, 56 *Proceedings of the American Philosophical Society* (1917) 410–415; Esther Cohen, Law, Folklore and Animal Lore, *Past & Present* No. 110 (1986) 6–37; Peter Dinzelbacher, Animal Trials: A Multidisciplinary Approach, 32 *The Journal of Interdisciplinary History* (2002) 405–421; Jen Girgen, The Historical and Contemporary Prosecution and Punishment of Animals, 9 *Animal Law Review* (2003) 97–133; Peter T Leeson, Vermin Trials, 56 *The Journal of Law & Economics* (2013) 811–836.

under ICL. The idea is that as long as they are not criminalised, it would probably be acceptable to use any tactic and means of warfare. There is a grey area, of course, of ethically questionable conduct falling under categories of violations of the laws of armed conflict that do not reach the level of criminal conduct under ICL, but if we are to look for relatively clear-cut delineations, then ICL recommends itself as a first port of call.

ICL's core crimes are genocide, crimes against humanity (CAH), war crimes and aggression. For our purposes, we shall rely on the definition of these as set out in the law applicable before the International Criminal Court (ICC),[9] i.e., its Statute (ICCS), also called the "Rome Statute" after its place of adoption,[10] and the Elements of Crimes (EoC),[11] both as interpreted by the ICC's chambers. The ICC's law represents the current negotiated consensus of a large number of states of what conduct should attract criminal liability for individuals, and hence serves as an ex-post evaluation of prohibited conduct, despite the occasional discrepancy with ICL based on customary international law. These differences are of little relevance for the matter at hand. It should also be remembered that CAH and genocide also apply in the absence of any type of armed conflict, i.e., in peacetime.[12]

As Chapter 1 was a necessary introduction to SETI for lawyers, so it will be useful for SETI researchers who are not legally trained to have a short introduction to the core crimes under ICL before we proceed to discuss individual problems.[13] We will begin by looking at the mere text of the ICC Statute and leave details for the in-depth discussion. International core crimes typically have a) what are called "chapeau elements", i.e., those which apply to the category of crime in general, and b) the relevant individual elements of the crimes.

9 Collection of core documents at International Criminal Court: Core Legal Texts. www.icc-cpi.int/resource-library/Pages/core-legal-texts.aspx.

10 Rome Statute of the International Criminal Court, www.icc-cpi.int/Publications/Rome-Statute.pdf.

11 Elements of Crimes, www.icc-cpi.int/Publications/Elements-of-Crimes.pdf.

12 Kai Ambos (ed.) *The Rome Statute of the ICC*, 4th edition (Bloomsbury, London, 2021 – hereafter: Ambos ICC) – Art 7 mn. 3, 17.

13 NB: The references in the footnotes related to the more technical ICL sources have been restricted to a few sources such as commentaries and textbooks which summarise and analyse the development and state of the law. This book is not an ICL textbook in itself with a need for referencing the primary sources of the case law, for example, and as it is geared more towards lawyers who need to gain an understanding of the SETI environment and access to primary sources in that respect is more necessary, the number of footnote references to the legal aspects will not be the same as in Chapter 1 with regard to the SETI-specific citations.

2.1.1 Overview of Core Crimes

2.1.1.1 *Genocide – Art. 6 ICCS*

This provision is based on the 1948 Genocide Convention. It reads as follows:

> For the purpose of this Statute, "genocide" means any of the following acts committed with intent to destroy, in whole or in part, a national, ethnical, racial or religious group, as such:
> (a) Killing members of the group;
> (b) Causing serious bodily or mental harm to members of the group;
> (c) Deliberately inflicting on the group conditions of life calculated to bring about its physical destruction in whole or in part;
> (d) Imposing measures intended to prevent births within the group;
> (e) Forcibly transferring children of the group to another group.

The EoC explain the crime further, but apart from adding the controversial contextual element[14] of "[t]he conduct took place in the context of a manifest pattern of similar conduct directed against that group or was conduct that could itself effect such destruction" to every sub-category from Art. 6(a) – (e) ICCS, and a footnote explaining the term "forcibly"[15] in Art. 6(e) ICCS, it does little else but repeat the text of the ICCS. Among the most litigated and discussed elements of genocide are the definition of a group, the four discriminatory criteria and the related intent, as well as the intent to destroy the group in whole or in part. The individual *modi operandi* in alternatives (a) – (e) are more specific elements and hence less difficult to define and interpret. The three general issues mentioned will be looked at below in the context of how they can apply to ETI.

2.1.1.2 *Crimes against Humanity (CAH)*

CAH are regulated in Art. 7 ICCS, a rather lengthy provision which merits verbatim reproduction, nonetheless. It "codifies" for the purposes of proceedings before the ICC (see the salvatory clause "for the purposes of this Statute" in Arts. 6, 7 and 8 ICCS) the different categories developed over time under customary

---

14 On the debate see William A Schabas, in Ambos ICC – Art 6 mn. 9–13.

15 EoC fn. 5: The term "forcibly" is not restricted to physical force, but may include threat of force or coercion, such as that caused by fear of violence, duress, detention, psychological oppression or abuse of power, against such person or persons or another person, or by taking advantage of a coercive environment.

international law[16] into the form accepted by the parties to the ICCS. Art. 7(1) ICCS lists the crimes, para. (2) explains the main elements of each, and para. (3) contains the highly controversial[17] definition of the term "gender".

> Art. 7(1)
>
> For the purpose of this Statute, "crime against humanity" means any of the following acts when committed as part of a widespread or systematic attack directed against any civilian population, with knowledge of the attack:
>
> (a) Murder;
> (b) Extermination;
> (c) Enslavement;
> (d) Deportation or forcible transfer of population;
> (e) Imprisonment or other severe deprivation of physical liberty in violation of fundamental rules of international law;
> (f) Torture;
> (g) Rape, sexual slavery, enforced prostitution, forced pregnancy, enforced sterilization, or any other form of sexual violence of comparable gravity;
> (h) Persecution against any identifiable group or collectivity on political, racial, national, ethnic, cultural, religious, gender as defined in paragraph 3, or other grounds that are universally recognized as impermissible under international law, in connection with any act referred to in this paragraph or any crime within the jurisdiction of the Court;
> (i) Enforced disappearance of persons;
> (j) The crime of apartheid;

16 Note that Art. 10 ICCS states clearly "Nothing in this Part shall be interpreted as limiting or prejudicing in any way existing or developing rules of international law for purposes other than this Statute", which is meant to preclude the ICCS being used as a general restatement of customary law. That command has been honoured more in the breach than in observance even before the ICCS technically came into force. See on the discussion especially in the context of the *Tadic* case before the ICTY, Michael Bohlander, Prosecutor v. Dusko Tadic: Waiting to Exhale, 11 *Criminal Law Forum* (2000) 217–248 at 244.

17 See on the history of the provision and the problems arising from it Michael Bohlander, Criminalising LGBT persons under national criminal law and Article 7(1)(h) and (3) of the ICC Statute, *Global Policy* (2014) 401–414.

(k) Other inhumane acts of a similar character intentionally causing great suffering, or serious injury to body or to mental or physical health.

Art. 7(2)

For the purpose of paragraph 1:

(a) "Attack directed against any civilian population" means a course of conduct involving the multiple commission of acts referred to in paragraph 1 against any civilian population, pursuant to or in furtherance of a State or organizational policy to commit such attack;

(b) "Extermination" includes the intentional infliction of conditions of life, *inter alia* the deprivation of access to food and medicine, calculated to bring about the destruction of part of a population;

(c) "Enslavement" means the exercise of any or all of the powers attaching to the right of ownership over a person and includes the exercise of such power in the course of trafficking in persons, in particular women and children;

(d) "Deportation or forcible transfer of population" means forced displacement of the persons concerned by expulsion or other coercive acts from the area in which they are lawfully present, without grounds permitted under international law;

(e) "Torture" means the intentional infliction of severe pain or suffering, whether physical or mental, upon a person in the custody or under the control of the accused; except that torture shall not include pain or suffering arising only from, inherent in or incidental to, lawful sanctions;

(f) "Forced pregnancy" means the unlawful confinement of a woman forcibly made pregnant, with the intent of affecting the ethnic composition of any population or carrying out other grave violations of international law. This definition shall not in any way be interpreted as affecting national laws relating to pregnancy;

(g) "Persecution" means the intentional and severe deprivation of fundamental rights contrary to international law by reason of the identity of the group or collectivity;

(h) "The crime of apartheid" means inhumane acts of a character similar to those referred to in paragraph 1, committed in the context of an institutionalized regime of systematic oppression and domination by one racial group over any other racial group or groups and committed with the intention of maintaining that regime;

(i) "Enforced disappearance of persons" means the arrest, detention or abduction of persons by, or with the authorization, support or acquiescence of, a State or a political organization, followed by a refusal to acknowledge that deprivation of freedom or to give information on the fate or whereabouts of those persons, with the intention of removing them from the protection of the law for a prolonged period of time.

Art. 7(3)

For the purpose of this Statute, it is understood that the term "gender" refers to the two sexes, male and female, within the context of society. The term "gender" does not indicate any meaning different from the above.

The EoC for Art. 7 ICCS cover several pages and it is not useful to reproduce them in full here or go into too much detail. Like with Art. 6 ICCS, there is a lot of repetition of the text of the Statute. However, the EoC expressly list the following two chapeau elements for each crime:

a) The conduct was committed as part of a widespread or systematic attack directed against a civilian population.
b) The perpetrator knew that the conduct was part of or intended the conduct to be part of a widespread or systematic attack against a civilian population.

Issues which arise often in interhuman conflict and may arise *mutatis mutandis* in the case of ETI are, for example, the elements "widespread or systematic attack", "civilian population", "in furtherance of a State or organizational policy", in addition to all of the offence elements that relate to particularly human conditions, such as gender and sexuality, which may mean nothing or something totally different for ETI, for example, and may thus create problems of conceptual transfer. One may even imagine a crime of apartheid based on a scenario similar to the plot of the SF film "District 9", fittingly also situated in South Africa. We will look at individual issues below.

2.1.1.3 *War Crimes*

War crimes are the original category of crimes in ICL, and most people will be somewhat more familiar with them. Everybody has probably heard about the Geneva or Hague Conventions in their various permutations over time, brought to life not least by Alec Guinness' memorable impersonation of Colonel Nicholson in *The Bridge on the River Kwai*. They deal with such issues as respecting the sign of the Red Cross and its equivalents, not giving quarter in combat engagements, collateral damage caused by improper targeting, prohibited weapons, how to treat prisoners of war and soldiers who do or can no longer fight and are *hors de combat*, and so forth. With war crimes being the original source of ICL crimes, the development especially of CAH has led to some overlap for wartime scenarios. The ICCS covers them in Art. 8 in great detail and their extent prohibits a reprint here. The defining conceptual difference to CAH and genocide is that they require an armed conflict, either international or non-international,[18] and cannot be committed in peacetime. Art. 8 (1) ICCS contains an attempt to restrict the ICC's use of resources under its jurisdiction by stating that "[t] The Court shall have jurisdiction in respect of war crimes in particular when committed as part of a plan or policy or as part of a large-scale commission of such crimes". Apart from defining the nature of the conflict, with the likelihood of a hostile encounter with ETI quite probably being classified as a form of international conflict, the rules ban the use of certain conduct in warfare or the use of certain weapons. We will discuss below whether the direct application of some of them might disadvantage human defence forces vis-à-vis ETI.

2.1.2 Individual Problems

2.1.2.1 *Genocide*

2.1.2.1.1 "Protected Group" Definition

The discussion in ICL about what constitutes a group has not yet found a definitive solution. Based on early case law, it seemed that a certain degree of stability in its coherence[19] was required. Yet, the recent trend is towards a more flexible approach, including more subjective aspects by referring to the insight that any collective identity is a social construct and in its essence not comparable to facts of nature.[20] In any event, groups are to be defined by positive criteria, not by mere absence of characteristics.[21]

---

18 We shall leave aside the thorny issue of purely internal disturbances within a State; the application of the law follows separate rules and is not relevant for our purposes.

19 Overview at Gerhard Werle and Florian Jeßberger, *Völkerstrafrecht*, 5th ed. (Mohr Siebeck, Tübingen, 2020 – hereafter: Werle/Jeßberger) pp. 396–399.

20 William A Schabas, in Ambos ICC, Art 6 mn. 17.

21 *Ibid.*, with reference to *Bosnia and Herzegovina v. Yugoslavia (Serbia and Montenegro)* (2007) *ICJ Rep* 43, paras. 193–197.

For our purposes, humans very likely will not know ex ante what the social structure of an ETI contingent of entities physically appearing to be individuals will be – one has to be so roundabout in the description because concepts like group and individual may not mean the same thing or anything to an extraterrestrial civilisation (ETC), and ETC may and most likely will, of course, differ from each other. For example, is a hive a group or a singular entity composed of multiple "organs", as it were? Will a coalition of ET forces from different planets attacking Earth simply be a homogenous group of "aliens" or would our current understanding require us to make efforts at distinguishing between them – if we even could? It is a trite fact that the human development of the concept of genocide was historically not in any manner intended nor in a position to provide answers to these questions. Application of the ideas underlying the 1948 Convention and the modern ICL of genocide can thus only be managed by analogous reasoning. This may be a welcome approach as far as the prevention of what passes for genocide between humans is concerned, but creation or extension of crimes by analogy is frowned upon by modern criminal jurisdictions of almost all countries, even in those based, for example, on Islamic Shariah law and its traditional concept of judge-made *ta'zir* crimes.[22]

Apart from the problems of finding a definition of a group as a standalone concept, the four exhaustive[23] categories of what groups are "*protected* groups" see a continuation of the difficulties. Protection is given only to "national, ethnical, racial or religious" groups. Regardless of the definition of these in the human context,[24] it is immediately evident that all four concepts may not mean the same thing, or indeed nothing at all, to an ETC. If we base our evaluation on the realisation of the nature of these identities as essentially social constructs, we face the same problem as we did with the idea of a group. The closest one might get to a finding of equivalence, if one had to choose one of the four categories, would probably be "racial". The term refers to inherited, visible physical characteristics which are common the members of the group, such as skin colour or body shape.[25] Given that it is naturally based on inter-human behaviour owing to its provenance from the time of the Holocaust, it is not used in ICL in the meaning of "the human race", i.e., all of humanity, which would be the proper counterpart to ETI being an "alien race".

22 See for an overview Michael Bohlander and Mohammad Hedayati-Kakhki, Criminal Justice under Shari'ah in the 21st Century – An Inter-Cultural View, 23 *Arab Law Quarterly* (2009) 417–436.

23 William A Schabas, in Ambos ICC, Art 6 mn. 16.

24 Werle/Jeßberger, pp. 399–403.

25 Werle/Jeßberger, p. 400 – with references to the case law and literature.

2.1.2.1.2 Intent to Destroy "in Whole or in Part"

Despite the fact that the previous criterion would already appear to be difficult to transpose to an interspecies conflict and our examination of the applicability of genocide could in theory end here, it is also important to consider the required *mens rea*: Genocide is not just based on the intent to commit murder on a massive scale (see on this below the CAH of extermination), its intent must be specifically[26] related to the annihilation of the group as such. The "in part" element of the required intent has traditionally been interpreted to mean a "substantial part".[27] The courts have struggled over the definition of the threshold above which such an evaluation is merited. Mere numerical calculations, while a traditional starting point, are not determinative, and the intent to kill a smaller group may suffice if that group, for example, held a special significance for the group as a whole.[28] The specific intent thus needs to be present *before* the actual genocidal conduct is embarked upon.

It is immediately clear that this element will be nigh impossible to fulfil, especially in the context of first contact. Humans will have no way of knowing *ex ante* before they attack, whether even a gigantic generation ship or a fleet of spacecraft appearing in the solar system or over Earth contains a sizeable crew/population made up of biological entities in the wider sense, especially compared to the ETI's home world or whether it is a singular nomadic civilisation of only a few hundred or thousand entities, or whether and to what extent the crew and/or passengers are in any way significant enough for the entire species. Genocide would thus very likely also fail on this second element.

2.1.2.1.3 Discriminatory Intent

To round off the investigation into the overarching prerequisites of genocide, the crime also requires a discriminatory intent in the sense that the acts must be done to the victims *because* of their membership of the group possessing the protected characteristics.[29] This part of the intent also needs to exist before the acts begin. In the context of currently imaginable scenarios of a human species defence against hostile ETI, the existence of any protective characteristics would be entirely irrelevant for the decision to engage in and carry out

26 William A Schabas, in Ambos ICC, Art. 6 mn. 7 with references to the case law.

27 It is not necessary for the actions to *actually* destroy a part of the group; this criterion is one of *mens rea*, not *actus reus*. Genocide begins with the first victim. However, the actual extent of the casualties will, of course, be a major factor in inferring the offender's intent.

28 On the debate see William A Schabas, in Ambos ICC, Art. 6 mn. 14–15.

29 Werle/Jeßberger, pp. 421–423.

hostilities. It would be a pure case of communal self-defence of the species against the risk of annihilation.

To sum up, it seems therefore unlikely that the current state of the law could be applied by analogy, regardless of whether that would be permissible for the criminal law aspect, because even in the preventive function of the law on genocide, it would create duties to act or to omit certain actions, which would be especially problematic in a defensive context where the existence or freedom of the entire human species might be at stake – notwithstanding the fact that the International Court of Justice has held that the 1948 Genocide Convention's definition (and hence also Art. 6 ICCS) is customary law in the form of *ius cogens* applicable *erga omnes*: It is binding and has effect with regard to anyone.[30] In a sense, this would also be a prime example of the application of Fasan's Metalaw Rules 2, 7, and 8 as negative correctives to the general new Golden Rule espoused by him: Humans would understandably be loath to extend any kind of protective courtesy to a species bent on destroying or enslaving the human species – the pre-emptive application of the otherwise generally rejected *tu quoque* defence might raise its head again in such a case, i.e., human conduct aimed at the ETI's annihilation might be justified because the ETI engaged in the same.[31] The current law on genocide would not appear to be applicable even if the human defence would result in the intended annihilation of the entire alien species. It is therefore not necessary to discuss potential defences in the wider sense such as those listed under Arts. 31–33 ICCS, although the apodictic nature of the prescription in Art. 33(2) ICCS that orders to commit genocide (and CAH) are always manifestly unlawful may seem to be put somewhat in doubt in the context. The fictional analogy in the title of the third volume of the *Ender* cycle using the term "Xenocide"[32] is thus conceptually an entirely different crime, more akin to the CAH of extermination.

30 *DRC v. Rwanda, Judgment, Armed Activities on the Territory of the Congo (New Application: 2002) Jurisdiction and Admissibility* of 3 February 2006, (2006) *ICJ Rep 31*, para. 64; *Croatia v. Serbia, Application of the Genocide Convention of 3 February 2015*, (2015) *ICJ Rep 3*, para. 87

31 On the meaning of the defence see, for example, Sienho Yee, The Tu Quoque Argument as a Defence to International Crimes, Prosecution or Punishment, 3 *Chinese Journal of International Law* (2004) 87–134; Katerina Borrelli, Between show-trials and Utopia: A study of the tu quoque defence, 32 *Leiden Journal of International Law* (2019) 315–331.

32 Orson Scott Card, *Xenocide* (Tor Books, New York, 1992).

2.1.2.2 *Crimes against Humanity*

The individual underlying acts of the CAH listed in Art. 7(1) ICCS can in theory almost all be committed against ETI: They can in principle be killed, enslaved, imprisoned, tortured etc. The applicability of the sexual and gender-based crimes, for example, will naturally depend on the specific biological and socially constructed circumstances of the respective ETI in this regard. The main problem, as the name "crime against humanity" attests, is, however, that the crimes are, one the one hand, meant to apply between humans, and on the other hand to relate to civilian populations, based on a widespread or systematic attack.

2.1.2.2.1 Equivalence to Humans

As with genocide, interpreting the *criminal* law as already encompassing non-humans in whatever manner will fall foul of the ban on extending criminal liability by analogy. But they might still serve as a guideline to proper conduct and treatment of aliens. CAH are said to be crimes "which either by their magnitude and savagery or by their large number or by the fact that a similar pattern was applied [...] endangered the international community or shocked the conscience of mankind",[33] or which "are particularly odious offences in that they constitute a serious attack on human dignity or a grave humiliation or degradation of one or more human beings".[34] The moral foundation of this category of crimes thus appears to be that they are on the one hand particularly inhumane, and on the other hand that they are directed at "a collective body of individuals".[35] Depending on the definition of "inhumane", for example, a case might be made for extension to another species which has the one characteristic that sets humans apart even from sentient animals: Sapience. Rustam Atadjanov has recently produced a definition of the elements making up the core opprobrium of CAH as follows:

> Out of all the elements [...] *human reason is perhaps most closely connected to human nature – as the fundamental feature which distinguishes us from other, non-human beings.* Unlike emotions or feelings, this particular characteristic is the one which allows human beings to live by and employ their comprehensive humanity which is void without reason. All the constituent elements of humanity – even humaneness that

33 United Nations War Crimes Commission (UNWCC), as cited by Kai Ambos, in Ambos ICC Art 7 mn 4.

34 Antonio Cassese, as cited by Kai Ambos in Ambos ICC Art. 7 fn. 22.

35 Kai Ambos, *ibid.*, mn. 3.

> is often associated with benevolent feelings rather than mind, are based on reason. If we accept that human freedom is harmed by the commission of crimes against humanity – and that freedom is an inherent right of all people due to their humanness [...], *then we need to acknowledge that reason [,] a necessary feature of humanness, is attacked as well, since these crimes strip their victims of their core nature of being reasonable creatures.*
>
> Humanness is a human status/condition/quality of being human. It is what makes us human. Crimes against humanity are inhuman acts [... which] eventually aim [...] at rendering their victims "inhuman", in the sense of depriving them of that very status. All parts of this status come under attack:
> (1) the victims' individual freedom is denied;
> (2) they are deprived of their human dignity;
> (3) the civilized attitude is negated removing the link between the victims and mankind;
> (4) the sentiment of active good will, or humaneness, ceases to exist by the commission of inhumane acts, and
> (5) *the victims' human nature in the form of reason is denied as well since those acts do not allow them the status of reasonable creatures anymore.*[36]

If one wants to follow that approach – despite its partially circular path of deduction – for argument's sake, it seems evident that the leap from the element of humans as reasonable creatures to *other reasonable* creatures is not a quantum leap, methodologically. Thus, a case could be made that the human response to hostile contact with ETI should as far as possible not fall below the ethical standards we reserve for each other. Unlike with genocide, there appear to be no insurmountable ex-ante *mens rea* problems in this respect, either. If a spacecraft, as opposed to what would have to be easily recognisable as a mere machine probe[37] arrives, the human default assumption will most likely be

---

36 Rustam Atadjanov, *Humanness as a Protected Legal Interest of Crimes Against Humanity – Conceptual and Normative Aspects* (Asser Press/Springer, New York, 2019) pp. 183–184; 187. – Emphases added.

37 One might, of course, debate whether an AI as the end state of an old extraterrestrial culture's development should receive protection as a reasonable creature but this would appear too speculative. Moreover, while reason is one defining element for being human, aspects such as love, empathy, compassion, and the ability to sacrifice one's own interests are equally important – in a sense as described by St. Paul in 1 Corinthians 13:1–13. It would also seem to be asking too much of biological entities to sacrifice their (style of) existence

that it is crewed by biological entities in the wider sense, and the very fact that they managed to build it and travel across vast – and most likely interstellar – distances should be sufficient testimony to their sapience. Knowledge of them being reasonable creatures would thus be implied.

2.1.2.2.2 Civilian Population

This should apply equally to the other chapeau element, an attack against a "civilian population", which generally excludes enemy combatants.[38] The alternatives are fairly straightforward: The alien vessel is a purely scientific exploration ship, with no combatants on board, or it has a purely military crew, or a mix of both. Only in the first case would there be a relatively clear-cut path to affirming a purely civilian population; however, even in that case the crew might lose the protection if they engaged in combat activities.[39] In the second case, the entire crew is in principle a legitimate target for hostile action, and in the third case it would ultimately depend on the percentage of combatants among the crew.[40] This means: It does not matter what formal status a person has; as soon as they themselves engage in armed hostilities, they lose the status and the protection of the civilian population criterion. Hence, it would also be irrelevant from a human point of view whether the ETI actually subscribed to an equivalent of the theoretical combatant – civilian dichotomy: As soon as they engage in armed hostilities, they become a legitimate target from our side; they clearly would have no right to be held to a higher standard than humans would hold each other.

In turn, the consequence is that unless there is a sufficiently fast, certain and reliable way of finding out what the ETI's intentions are, pre-emptive attacks by human forces without prior hostile conduct or at the very least credible threats from the ETI might run afoul of that criterion, if one were minded to extend the concept of CAH on the basis of a shared nature as reasonable beings. The

for a machine governed by a disembodied intelligence: The self-preservation instinct would easily outweigh any intellectual concerns. On the nature of AI and the power relations involved in their use with regard to the real world, see Kate Crawford, *Atlas of AI: The Real Worlds of Artificial Intelligence* (Yale University Press, New Haven, 2021). Crawford is a Senior Principal Researcher at Microsoft Research New York – www.microsoft.com/en-us/research/people/kate/.

38 For example, *argumento ex* Common Article 3 of the 1949 Geneva Conventions (hereafter: GC). On this element. see Kai Ambos, in Ambos ICC Art. 7 mn. 26–27; Werle/Jeßberger, pp. 446–450.

39 See on the different approaches Kai Ambos, in Ambos ICC Art. 7 mn. 27.

40 Art. 50(3) Additional Protocol I to the Geneva Conventions (hereafter: AP I); see on the discussion Kai Ambos, in Ambos ICC Art. 7 mn. 27.

likelihood of unilateral human pre-emptive action absent such insight would seem rather low in any event.

2.1.2.2.3 Fatal Offences

Of the underlying acts in Art. 7(1) ICCS, a hostile contact scenario would primarily involve acts of murder or extermination, especially if it was a pitched battle either in space or involving a ground offensive. The *actus reus* of murder simply means causing death,[41] whereas the *mens rea*, i.e., intent or recklessness, is still unclear, even after years of international tribunals applying this crime, resulting in one commentator's scathing conclusion that "for nearly a decade ICTY and ICTR TCs have continued to convict persons in exactly the same circumstances that would lead to acquittals in other TCs, and the ACs of the two Tribunals have failed to resolve this problem, thus denying justice to the accused, victims and the general public".[42] The law of the ICC *prima facie* requires "intent and knowledge" (Art. 30(2)(a) and (b) ICCS) which has apparently led to a more restrictive practice at the ICC, and which seems to require at least what in English law is called *Woollin*[43] causation and intent: Virtual certainty of the lethal outcome following from the defendant's actions and the defendant's awareness of this virtual certainty.[44] Extermination, despite some discussion in the literature, is essentially murder on a massive scale[45] but without the need for a discriminatory criterion or intent.[46] One may thus debate whether extermination is not actually a more serious crime than genocide, because it does not contain any restrictions on who may be protected as a victim. Unlike genocide, however, extermination requires that mass killings are actually already taking place, even though an individual may be charged with causing only one death, as long as it was part of the mass killings.[47]

2.1.2.2.4 Conclusion Regarding Crimes against Humanity

For our purposes, then, leaving the scenario of calculable groups of individual alien entities landing on Earth aside, it could depend on factors such as the

41 Kai Ambos and Carsten Stahn, in Ambos ICC Art 7 mn. 33.

42 *Ibid.*

43 *R v. Woollin* [1999] 1 AC 82.

44 See for the discussion and related case law Kai Ambos and Carsten Stahn, in Ambos ICC Art 7 mn 32–42.

45 There are no set numerical thresholds, but the element is defined on a case-by-case basis, with numbers as low as 60 having been referenced in the case law; see Kai Ambos and Carsten Stahn, in Ambos ICC Art 7 mn. 212–214.

46 Kai Ambos and Carsten Stahn, in Ambos ICC Art 7 mn. 44–47.

47 *Ibid.*, mn. 47.

number or size of the spacecraft being attacked by human armed forces etc., always bearing in mind that aliens engaging in actual combat would be exempt from protection under CAH anyway. The margin remaining for the application of CAH via the civilian population element is thus rather slim, it would appear, even if one wanted to extend the spirit of the law to non-humans. In any event, at the end of the day the species preservation aspect would again exert a powerful influence, and equally raise the question of defences under Arts. 31–33 ICCS. The remaining, maybe more realistic field of legal debate may thus be the area of war crimes, to which we turn now.

2.1.2.3 *War Crimes*

2.1.2.3.1 "International" Armed Conflict

As we saw above, Art. 8 ICCS deals with two distinct categories of armed conflict – international and non-international. A hostile encounter with an alien civilisation is strictly speaking neither, but if one had to choose a category from which to extrapolate, the offences relating to international conflicts would seem to be better suited; only those shall therefore be looked at here. In any event, there is a lot of duplication of crimes between both categories. The war crimes law is ultimately based on the realisation that a) use of even legitimate armed force between nations or states is almost always a failure of diplomacy, that b) the people doing the actual fighting are doing so because they have been ordered to fight under a chain of command going up to the government, and rarely out of their own free will, and that c) in most cases there will be a need for re-establishing more or less friendly relations after the cessation of hostilities. These factors demand that the fighting, if it has to happen at all, is done with the minimum of (collateral) damage for those not involved in the fighting, and that any extrinsic motivation and aggravating conduct by the combatants towards each other, borne from the uncontrollable aspect of human nature, which is as vindictive as it is vulnerable and has a natural tendency to resort to cruelty and dehumanising othering of the enemy as an emotional antidote to one's own – real or perceived – victimisation, is curbed to be extent possible, and as a result the suffering of the combatants themselves is reduced to the absolute lawful minimum. This has resulted in the rules dealing with the treatment of combatants and civilians on the one hand, and with the technical modalities of warfare on the other.

It is open to question to what extent any of these reasons can apply to an interspecies conflict. Previous diplomatic relations are unlikely, especially if we look at a first contact scenario without proper communication between humans and the ETC, as discussed in Chapter 1. The second aspect of the combatants fighting on superior orders rather than based on their own preservation instinct may be doubtful, too, especially if the hostilities are initiated by the ETC with little or no forewarning and are plausibly aimed at the annihilation or occupation of Earth and its inhabitants – triggering the defensive herd instinct among humans. The third reason – that of re-establishing friendly relations post-conflict – will most likely also be absent in the just-mentioned case of an invasion aimed at a campaign of total species dominance in a first contact scenario. Situations where conflict might erupt *after* peaceful relations have initially been established with an ETC are too speculative, not least because it is entirely unclear whether and which prior agreements may have been made between them that might impact the conduct of conflicts.

In sum, in a hostile first contact scenario, rapid dominance will most likely (have to) be the paramount goal of each side, in order to dictate unilaterally the conditions of a surrender and future relationship or, in the absence of a willingness to compromise, to ensure the ability of annihilation of all meaningful resistance in order to extinguish the risk of a future rise of retaliatory action by the vanquished species. The very language used in the preceding lines is uneasy evidence that much like in the discussion of genocide, we quickly reach the limit of how normally desirable ethical restrictions in interhuman warfare can be accommodated in face of the necessity of preserving the species. In essence, we will have to ask ourselves whether and for what reasons we owe an aggressive ETC any restraint in how we defend ourselves as a species against an act of aggression on a planetary scale.

2.1.2.3.2 Means of Defence

If we look at a list of the main kinds of war crimes under the ICCS relating to the ability to mount an effective defence in an international conflict, i.e., the restrictions on modes and means of warfare, questions may soon arise as to why humans would want to tie their hands in advance with regards to the arsenal at their disposal, especially if the ETC's military capabilities are unknown – with a natural presumption that a species managing interstellar travel and contemplating contact with another civilisation might also be at an advanced stage when it comes to weapons development. The current – known – stage of the human development of weapons that can be used in space appears to be restricted to modified ground- or ship-based antiballistic interceptor missiles capable of hitting objects in orbit, electronic signal interruption (jamming), satellites armed with kinetic weapons, directed energy beams such as lasers, jamming technology or simply capable of ramming other satellites, mini shuttles such as the X-37, or the intentional use of space debris as a kinetic weapon.[48] It is certainly correct that this seems rather pedestrian compared to what one might expect to be at the disposal of an alien species capable of crossing interstellar distances, yet as Michaud said, assuming our total military inferiority a priori would mean ex-ante capitulation.[49]

The following are excerpts from the crimes listed in Art. 8(2)(a) and (b) ICCS that relate to *methods* of warfare, rather than the typical results of armed hostilities or treatment of combatants and civilians. It seems fair to say that humans would in any event not wish to engage in maltreatment of alien prisoners of war (POWS), especially once they pose no risk any longer – there is no discernible difference to interhuman standards in that respect. The text has been partially redacted where references to criteria such as UN symbols etc. obviously make little sense:

> Art. 8(2)(a) – Grave breaches of the Geneva Conventions of 12 August 1949:
>
> [...]
> (iv) Extensive destruction and appropriation of property, not justified by military necessity and carried out unlawfully and wantonly;
> [...]
> (viii) Taking of hostages.
>
> Art. 8(2)(b) – Other serious violations of the laws and customs applicable in international armed conflict:
>
> [...]
> (iv) Intentionally launching an attack in the knowledge that such attack will cause incidental loss of life or injury to civilians or damage to civilian objects or widespread, long-term and severe damage to the natural environment which would be clearly excessive in relation to the concrete and direct overall military advantage anticipated;
> (v) Attacking or bombarding, by whatever means, towns, villages, dwellings or buildings which are undefended and which are not military objectives;

---

48 Linda Dawson, *War in Space – The Science and Technology Behind Our Next Theater of Conflict* (Springer, New York, 2018) pp. 12–32, 46–60, as well as the references in fn. 1 above.

49 Michael A.G. Michaud, *Contact with Alien Civilizations – Our Hopes and Fears about Encountering Extraterrestrials* (Copernicus Books, New York, 2010 – hereafter: Michaud), p. 376.

[…]

(vii) Making improper use of a flag of truce, of the flag or of the military insignia and uniform of the enemy […] resulting in death or serious personal injury;

[…]

(ix) Intentionally directing attacks against buildings dedicated to religion, education, art, science or charitable purposes, historic monuments, hospitals and places where the sick and wounded are collected, provided they are not military objectives;

[…]

(xi) Killing or wounding treacherously individuals belonging to the hostile nation or army;

(xii) Declaring that no quarter will be given;

(xiii) Destroying or seizing the enemy's property unless such destruction or seizure be imperatively demanded by the necessities of war;

[…]

(xvi) Pillaging a town or place, even when taken by assault;

(xvii) Employing poison or poisoned weapons;

(xviii) Employing asphyxiating, poisonous or other gases, and all analogous liquids, materials or devices;

(xix) Employing bullets which expand or flatten easily in the human body, such as bullets with a hard envelope which does not entirely cover the core or is pierced with incisions;

(xx) Employing weapons, projectiles and material and methods of warfare which are of a nature to cause superfluous injury or unnecessary suffering or which are inherently indiscriminate in violation of the international law of armed conflict […]

(xxiii) Utilizing the presence of a civilian or other protected person to render certain points, areas or military forces immune from military operations;

[…]

(xxv) Intentionally using starvation of civilians as a method of warfare by depriving them of objects indispensable to their survival, including wilfully impeding relief supplies as provided for under the Geneva Conventions;

It becomes clear very quickly that quite a number of these crimes relate to the traditional ground war *cum* (aerial or naval) combat and bombardment scenario. These may in principle be adaptable to situations where alien ground troops have landed and established bridgeheads or a forward operating base etc. One might even imagine a scenario of a protracted conflict with partial occupation of large regions of Earth in which civilian personnel or even family members (or their equivalent in the ETC's culture) might already be billeted. However, much like human armed forces are doing at present, advanced ETI will very likely also have found ways to ensure that biological entity casualties in their own ranks are to be avoided as much as possible, meaning their ground troops might consist mainly or entirely of (semi-)autonomous robots and drones etc., hence all rules obviously aimed at protecting the interests of *biological* civilian entities would *prima facie* not apply.

However, when perusing the list of prohibited conduct, it becomes evident that even such time-honoured bans as the one on expanding or flattening bullets, i.e., mostly soft-or hollow-point projectiles[50] colloquially known as "Dum-Dum bullets", may be questionable if their higher body-stopping power, for which they were after all originally invented, gave a decisive edge to human armed forces in close combat. The taking of hostages, especially of key personnel, might be one of the most effective ways of influencing the ETI's preparedness for continuing the hostilities. The use of chemical or even biological weapons – some of which might after all be entirely harmless to humans, such as bacteria or viruses humans have become immune to – with a wide and fast dispersion might be the reaction of choice in the face of an otherwise overwhelming force. Much as with the previous crime categories, the aspect of the preservation of the human species from extinction or enslavement may again trump any traditional aversion to using outlawed methods of warfare and consequently even call into question our long-held assumptions underlying interhuman IHL.

2.1.2.4 *Excursion 1: a Look at Human Colonial History*

To sum up, all three major core crime categories in ICL for one reason or another present substantial difficulties when examined against the need for application of interhuman standards of restricting modes and consequences of warfare or other systematic or large-scale attacks on humans, be it as genocide

50 They are, however, still being widely, and indeed regularly, used in police firearms in the UK or the US, for example. See the report by Sandra Laville, Met police to use hollow point bullets that killed Jean Charles de Menezes, 2011, www.theguardian.com/uk/2011/may/11/met-police-hollow-bullets-menezes, and J B Brady, Justifiability of Hollow-Point Bullets, 2(2) *Criminal Justice Ethics* (1983) 9–18. They are even available for sports – see, for example, the law in New Jersey, at New Jersey State Police, 2022, Firearms information, www.njsp.org/firearms/transport-hollowpoint.shtml.

or CAH, to ETI. The idea that in an interspecies conflict, most or even all of them might be subordinated to the need for species preservation, is uneasy circumstantial evidence of a possibly more tenuous nature of their underlying ethical foundations than we might care to admit.

Looking at the not-too-distant past, would we – under present views – have judged the indigenous peoples in the Americas or in Africa, for example, for engaging in mass killings of the colonists from Europe, who after all were a major if not the main cause for the near extinction and/or oppression of certain populations due to their carrying germs which were harmless to them but lethal to the indigenous population – this being a confirmed historical fact[51]? The question of whether the aboriginal people would have been in a position to know the exact biological chains of causation is neither here nor there: Based on the state of science available to them at the time, a conclusion might in those days still have been justifiably drawn from the fact that locals who were exposed to the colonists suffered from and died of previously unknown diseases in alarming numbers. This problem arises irrespective of the question of whether the colonists would have been openly hostile and engaging in armed conflict with the indigenous population. The mere fact of their close and ubiquitous, and maybe even friendly, presence would have been the cause of the biological contamination and ensuing danger to the particular local environment. If they refused to leave when being asked by the locals, would the latter have to suffer extinction merely because the ensuing mass killings might be considered extermination, a CAH if the scenario was transposed to the present day? Would we these days accept such an argument as providing a defence, for example, under Arts. 31–33 ICCS?

Given the difference in technological advancement between indigenous and colonist cultures – the very scenario almost everyone seems to expect to occur in the case of direct contact with ETI –, would it have been appropriate for the former to employ unnecessarily cruel methods which caused massive harm and suffering among the colonists, but which may have acted as an effective and powerful deterrent? In other words, would they have been justified in reaching for their historical equivalent to the so-called "nuclear option" if any other and less incisive methods of resistance would have been entirely

51 See, for example, Barbara I Tshisuaka, 2007. Pocken, in Werner E. Gerabek et al. (eds.), *Enzyklopädie Medizingeschichte*, p. 1172 (Walter de Gruyter, Berlin/New York, 2007); Ursula Thiemer-Sachse, Das große Leiden - Huey cocoliztli (aztekisch): das große Leiden: Zu den aus Europa eingeschleppten Seuchen, welche die Urbevölkerung Amerikas dezimierten, 2002, www.fu-berlin.de/presse/publikationen/fundiert/archiv/2002_01/02_01_thiemer_sachse/index.html.

ineffective? As our investigation above has shown, we may after all actually seem to be prepared to accept the nuclear option and dropping all rules of damage control when the survival of the entire human species is at stake. Is it then all merely a question of perspective and proportions? John C. Wright seems to agree that expectations should not be raised too high when he writes that any contemplation of the use of inter-human laws of armed conflict vis-à-vis ETI would likely face a "bleak outlook".[52]

2.1.2.5 *Excursion II: "Aggression" through Space Exploration?*

The example of biological contamination leading to the extinction of entire ethnicities by colonists from human history leads us to a brief excursion discussing of the question of whether some form of legal, possibly criminal, liability should arise for human space travellers,[53] or remote operators of unmanned probes, who violate planetary protection[54] protocols by either bringing back contaminating materials to Earth, or who contaminate another planetary[55] environment by landing there and spreading "germs" in the wider sense which have a negative impact on that environment, or to take it to the highest level, by engaging in terraforming.[56] The first alternative is relatively easy to arrange

---

52 John C. Wright, 2020. *Deep Space Warfare – Military Strategy Beyond Orbit* (McFarland, Jefferson, 2020 – hereafter *Deep Space Warfare*) p. 100.

53 On private space travel in particular, see Julie Abou Yehia and Kai-Uwe Schrogl, European regulation for private human spaceflight in the context of space traffic management, 66 *Acta Astronautica* (2010) 1618–1624; P J Blount, Informed consent v. ITAR: Regulatory conflicts that could constrain commercial human spaceflight, 66 *Acta Astronautica* (2010) 1608–1612; Stephan Hobe, The legal regime for private space tourism activities – An overview, 66 *Acta Astronautica* (2010) 1593–1596; Patrick Collins and Adriano Autino, What the growth of a space tourism industry could contribute to employment, economic growth, environmental protection, education, culture and world peace, 66 Acta Astronautica (2010) 1553–1562; Francis Lyall, Who is an astronaut? The inadequacy of current international law, 66 *Acta Astronautica* (2010) 1613–1617.

54 Gerhard Kminek et al., *The International Planetary Protection Handbook, An online-only supplement to (2019) 205 Space Research Today*, 2019, www.sciencedirect.com/journal/space-research-today/vol/205/suppl/S; Michael Meltzer, *When biospheres collide: a history of NASA's planetary protection programs* (NASA, Washington, 2011), www.nasa.gov/connect/ebooks/when_biospheres_collide_detail.html; Bergit Uhran et al., Updating Planetary Protection Considerations and Policies for Mars Sample Return, 49 *Space Policy* (2019) 101322; John D Rummela and D E (Betsy) Pugel, Planetary protection technologies for planetary science instruments, spacecraft, and missions: Report of the NASA Planetary Protection Technology Definition Team (PPTDT), 23 *Life Sciences in Space Research* (2019) 60–68.

55 This is, of course, meant to include moons and asteroids, insofar as factually relevant.

56 See generally on the political, ethical, and legal challenges of space exploration, and on related issues Daniel Deudney, Daniel, *Dark skies: space expansionism, planetary*

because it is about humans endangering other humans, resulting in offences such as negligent manslaughter, environmental crimes etc., which is not really the object of our study. The more interesting part is the hypothetical of humans contaminating an exoplanetary ecosystem. Here again, some type of regulatory public order offence around diligence in avoiding the harm of contamination is imaginable,[57] but it would still be mainly based on precautionary human concerns and be in essence a kind of victimless crime.

What, however, if the human presence, in the flesh or by remote, actually triggered a negative effect in an exoplanetary biological environment, an area

---

geopolitics, and the ends of humanity (OUP, Oxford, 2020); James S J Schwartz and Tony Milligan (eds.), *The Ethics of Space Exploration* (Springer, New York, 2016); Steven J Dick (ed.), *Historical studies in the societal impact of spaceflight* (NASA, Washington, 2015), www.nasa.gov/ebooks; Asif A Siddiqi, Asif A. 2017. *Beyond Earth: a chronicle of deep space exploration, 1958–2016* (NASA History Program Office, Washington, 2017) www.nasa.gov/ebooks; Keith Abney, Ethics of colonization: Arguments from existential risk, 110 *Futures* (2019) 60–63; Giancarlo Genta, Private space exploration: A new way for starting a spacefaring society?, 104 *Acta Astronautica* (2014) 480–486; James A Vedda, Challenges to the Sustainability of Space Exploration, 6 *Astropolitics* (2008) 22–49; Ram Jakhu and Maria Buzdugan, Development of the Natural Resources of the Moon and Other Celestial Bodies: Economic and Legal Aspects, 6 *Astropolitics* (2008) 201–250; Martin Machay and Jitka Pochylá, European Attitudes Toward Space Exploration and Exploitation, 11 *Astropolitics* (2013) 203–217; Jacques Arnould, From Quarantine to Exploration: Space Agencies and the Ethical Challenge of Astrobiology, 10 *Astropolitics* (2012) 176–182; Carl L DeVito, Getting off planet, 110 *Futures* (2019) 54–55; Andrea Sommariva, Motivations Behind Interstellar Exploration and Colonization, 12 *Astropolitics* (2014) 82–94; James S J Schwartz, Myth-Free Space Advocacy Part II: The Myth of the Space Frontier, 15 *Astropolitics* (2017) 167–184; John Hickman, Problems of Interplanetary and Interstellar Trade, 6 *Astropolitics* (2008) 95–104; Konrad Szocik and Koji Tachibana, Research Viewpoint: Human Enhancement and Artificial Intelligence for Space Missions, 17 *Astropolitics* (2019) 208–219; Nikola Schmidt and Petr Bohacek, First Space Colony: What Political System Could We Expect? 56 *Space Policy* (2021) 101426; Rayna Elizabeth Slobodian, Selling space colonization and immortality: A psychosocial, anthropological critique of the rush to colonize Mars, 113 *Acta Astronautica* (2015) 89–104; Milan M Ćirković, Space colonization remains the only long-term option for humanity: A reply to Torres, 105 *Futures* (2019) 166–173; Patrick Lin, Viewpoint: Look Before Taking Another Leap for Mankind – Ethical and Social Considerations in Rebuilding Society in Space, 4 *Astropolitics* (2006) 281–294; Eligar Sadeh, Viewpoint: The Evolution of Access to Space as an Idea and Technology, 3 *Astropolitics* (2005) 305–318; Tanja Masson-Zwaan and Steven Freeland, Between heaven and earth: The legal challenges of human space travel, 66 *Acta Astronautica* (2010) 1597–1607.

57 See Christopher Newman. 2016. 'The Way to Eden': Environmental Legal and Ethical Values in Interplanetary Spaceflight, in James S J Schwartz and Tony Milligan (eds.), *The Ethics of Space Exploration* (Springer, New York, 2016) pp. 221–238, at pp. 233–235, who appears to be in favour of combining criminalisation with embedding a duty of care for the exoplanetary environment in the "Crew Code of Conduct".

that is still awaiting proper treatment and regulation?[58] This might affect anything from microbes to sentient or even sapient entities who are not in a position to interdict the human intrusion, and who may not be spacefaring yet themselves. Here again, we need to be on guard against the conceptual dangers of anthropocentric and-morphic bias: While the current state of the art of human biology and neuroscience may consider these ideas as farfetched, forms of intelligence or communication between groups of biological entities may have developed elsewhere which we do not understand or are even able to conceptualise according to terrestrial classifications – and if they have not fully developed yet, they may be in the process of doing so very soon, speaking in historical timelines.

Human intrusion with a discernible effect on the local biosphere may thus be interfering *in limine* in the development of an entire or even multiple species, evoking connotations of pre-emptive "genocide" or extermination. We as humans may, as the most highly developed species on Earth, have de facto been given the stewardship of the planet, but the same can obviously not be said for other worlds and hence our duty of care there must be far greater than that which we would normally employ, so to speak, in our "own affairs".

Traditionally, the balancing exercise between human interests in space exploration and resource mining on the one hand, and the unaffected state of the indigenous environment on the other seems to have been discussed mainly on the basis of the *existing* stage of development along the lines of Star Trek's Prime Directive,[59] which typically seemed to require some form of sentience at least, which may be rather rare in microbes. However, as Cockell argues, "viewing microbial life elsewhere purely from instrumental considerations may be highly destructive and [...] a form of intrinsic value, *rooted in a respect for the trajectories and potential of other life forms and biospheres,* allows us to take a more cautious approach to the exploration of other worlds. This ethic is not easy to constrain in a way that allows for clear adjudication in all matters of extraterrestrial exploration, but it prevents a policy of exploration that sees microscopic extraterrestrial life as purely a resource".[60]

58 *Ibid.*

59 See on this, for example, Kelly C Smith 2016. The Curious Case of the Martian Microbes: Mariomania, Intrinsic Value and the Prime Directive, in James S J Schwartz and Tony Milligan (eds.), *The Ethics of Space Exploration* (Springer, New York, 2016) pp. 195–208.

60 Charles S Cockell, The Ethical Status of Microbial Life on Earth and Elsewhere: In Defence of Intrinsic Value, in James S J Schwartz and Tony Milligan (eds.) *The Ethics of Space Exploration* (Springer, New York, 2016) pp. 167–180, at 177. – Emphasis added. See also Monica Vidaurri et al., Absolute Prioritization of Planetary Protection, Safety, and

Add to this the scenario that humans land on an exoplanet which has an indigenous microbial life form that is harmless for all elements of the local ecosystem and biosphere, but which is dangerous or even lethal to humans:[61] The eradication or at least repression of that life form would be understandable from a perspective of human self-preservation in a hostile environment far away from access to standard recuperative medical care, yet the only factor causing a danger to anyone is the very intrusion by humans itself, i.e., alien entities who are not part of the otherwise balanced ecosystem of that planet.

It is nonetheless more than open to question whether the commercial promise of an abundance of much-needed resources will not override any concerns arising on behalf of a life form that can only be seen through a microscope. It is somehow difficult to imagine that after its detection such a planet would be declared off-limits, even to scientists: The presence of a sort of guardian civilisation effectively enforcing the ban as the one creating the monolith which tells humans to stay away from Jupiter's moon Europa in "2010: Odyssey Two" is not to be expected.[62] It is thus not entirely outlandish to entertain the concern that the preference expected to be given to commercial or other interests may in extreme cases lead to a rupture in a planet's biological evolution. Humanity has over the centuries annihilated myriads of terrestrial species in its never-ending striving for technological development, commercial gain or out of the sheer desire to kill animals for sport – its record in species protection is thus far from reassuring.

2.2 *Domestic Law*

While problems arising from scenarios of artificially constructed jurisdictions such as international courts or treaties and conventions do not arise in relation to the power of individual states to control their own criminal laws, the fundamental problems of how to include ETI into the spectrum of recognised victims of crime and the ban on analogical reasoning to the detriment of an offender remain. This is especially the case for all legal systems that have incorporated the entirety or part of the principles of ICL into their domestic legal order, as is de facto required, for example, by all member states of the

Avoiding Imperialism in All Future Science Missions: A Policy Perspective, 51 *Space Policy* (2020) 101345.

61 This is a scenario occurring, for example, in Kim Stanley Robinson, *Aurora.* (Orbit, London, 2015).

62 In a similar vein based on other SF treatments of the colonisation and exploitation scenario, see Russell Blackford, *Science Fiction and the Moral Imagination – Visions, Minds, Ethics* (Springer, New York, 2017) pp. 182–187.

Assembly of States Parties to the ICCS, where the objections listed above will in their vast majority apply *mutatis mutandis*, unless a country has regulated them somewhat differently from the ICL essence.[63] We are left with questions such as whether homicide laws etc. could apply to ETI, and in turn whether conduct endangering life, limb or liberty of aliens would be preventively prohibited under the general law of public policing as a part of public order law, for example. It stands to reason that the same concerns as set out for ICL under the species preservation aspect would demand compliance and influence the interpretation of the law in very much the same manner. A more detailed study of domestic environments is therefore not necessary at this point.

3 Liability of ETI

The reverse question, apart from the licence to simply destroy ETI on the battlefield with all means available if they are engaging in hostile conduct, is whether a scenario can be imagined in which humanity would or indeed could hold them to account for war crimes in the wider sense in a kind of justice process, assuming individuals would have been captured and indeed be responsible for their actions as individuals in the sense humans would understand that. This idea raises all kinds of questions in substantive and procedural law. None of them are easy to answer.

3.1 *Jurisdiction*

The most straightforward one would *prima facie* seem to be that of territorial jurisdiction over ETI, as indicated above. A state can at the very least claim jurisdiction over anything and anyone on its territory. Diplomatic immunity, for example, as one of the major exceptions, is of course not going to be available to aliens in a hostile first contact scenario. The territorial factor becomes, of course, rather tricky if we envisage conduct occurring in outer space beyond the reach of the vertical territorial expanse *usque ad coelum* of any country under the heading of "air space". This may in theory involve conduct having effects on the ground and/or in air space, or solely in outer space. There is meant to be no state sovereignty in outer space under Art. II of the Outer Space Treaty (OST),[64] so the demarcation would in principle appear

63 For the example of France and its divergent definition of genocide see Caroline Fournet, *Genocide and Crimes Against Humanity – Misconceptions and Confusion in French Law and Practice* (Hart, Oxford, 2013).

64 United Nations, Treaty Series, vol. 610, No. 8843.

to be important. However, the exact delineation between air space and outer space is quite surprisingly still unclear;[65] increasing state and international practice would appear to be favouring an orbital height of 100 km as the cut-off point.[66] Furthermore, the demarcation is mainly meant to represent the line beyond which a state can no longer deny overflight by satellites and other space craft of *other states* simply on the grounds of territorial sovereignty. It is not immediately clear why and whether this should apply to an attack originating *from* or occurring *in* outer space, especially by an ETC, given that any state must be able to defend itself no matter where the attack originates and it would seem illogical not to then permit criminal jurisdiction for acts committed in such a manner, if active defence was allowed. For the purely interhuman context, the non-militarisation of outer space has therefore been enshrined in Art. IV(1) OST as a corollary precaution – naturally no such corollary agreement exists for the hypothetical of preventing an attack by ETI from or in outer space. In essence, a state may thus still be able to claim territorial sovereignty for these purposes even beyond the demarcation line and it then is a question of the specific domestic criminal law or policing law rules on territorial jurisdiction (*ratione loci*) as to whether an act/acts or parts thereof may fall under a state's jurisdiction or not. Typical domestic rules tend to rely on the place of the conduct as well as on the place of the effect, for example. In the case of a lengthier overflight in orbit, several states may thus acquire jurisdiction over the same conduct. In any event, the matter remains unclear, but the point of the reflections was to show that even such a basic criterion as territorial jurisdiction can become laden with difficulties of application. This would seem to be an argument in favour of either establishing universal jurisdiction for any state, or of referring the matter to an international court of some sort to which all states might have delegated the exercise of their jurisdiction.

---

65 Francis Lyall and Paul B Larsen, *Space Law – A Treatise,* 2nd ed. (Routledge, Abingdon, 2018) pp. 135–151.

66 *Ibid.*, 151. – But see Marcus Schladebach, *Weltraumrecht* (Mohr/Siebeck, Tübingen, 2020) pp. 42–44, who prefers 83 km as the limit until which aerodynamic flight as opposed to the operation of rockets and missiles is in theory physically possible: In his view, a state can have no legitimate interest in claiming control over the higher part of the column of space over its territory if it cannot for all practical purposes make use of it. The use of rockets or missiles, he additionally argues, is subject to the laws of war, not space and air law. In an age of burgeoning scientific and commercial use of rockets this appears questionable.

3.2 Nullum Crimen *Principle*

On a more substantive level, ETI would have to be classified as potential perpetrators *before* any legal responsibility would and could arise. Currently, the law only recognises humans as potential offenders, with some states having extended criminal liability to corporations. Analogous ad-hoc application would be prohibited by the *nullum crimen sine lege praevia* principle. Similarly, even if ETI were classified as being capable of incurring criminal liability under human law, this would not solve the many fundamental follow-on problems in the so-called general part of the criminal law, such as mens rea and mistake of law or fact, the availability of special cultural, linguistic, mental, or other unknown species-related defences etc. If, for example, English and Welsh courts seem to think that foreigners who come from a country where public transport is free and who do thus not pay for a ticket on an English bus are not acting dishonestly,[67] how much more would such thoughts have to apply to someone who is literally from another planet. Fair trial guarantees such as assistance by defence counsel and interpreters etc. would in effect be meaningless if there was no possibility of communication between human and ETI. All of this shows that the prospects for any sort of legal liability of ETI, be it criminal, civil, or otherwise, are slim at best. The likelihood of them being treated solely as depersonalised threats under laws that are meant to avert a danger to public peace and safety is thus great, with alternatives allowing them even some degree of greater agency unlikely to emerge, not least for the simple reason that there is currently no way for humanity to anticipate any of the factors that might justify a particular legal stance towards ETI's behaviour.

4 Conclusion

This chapter interrogated the potential interface between hostile contact scenarios and existing laws, especially IHL, in order to find out whether any guidance can be drawn from the status quo for the hypothetical case of hostilities between humans and ETI in a direct first contact environment, which may – as was already said in Chapter 1 – in theory include an electronic signal from afar that, for example, disables human defence technology without actual physical contact between humans and ETI, be they biological or machine entities, occurring. Considering ICL as an indicator of extreme positions when

67 See critically Michael Bohlander, Abandoning Dishonesty – A Brief German Comment on the State of the Law after Ivey, 86 *Journal of Criminal Law* (2022) 170–178.

humanity has decided to express its most forceful sanction, the criminal law, we investigated the extent to which core crimes under IHL such as genocide, CAH and war crimes might apply in an interspecies conflict, and what the outcome might tell us about the solidity of our traditional understanding of the underlying moral values.

The somewhat disconcerting conclusion is that the values which we subscribe to in an interhuman context are nigh impossible to adhere to in a situation when the preservation of the human species from annihilation or its freedom from occupation and enslavement are at stake. Even with a crime as serious as genocide, matching the requirements of *actus reus* and *mens rea* to a non-human other is fraught with difficulties due to the total absence of even educated guesses about what ETI might think and act like, what their determining social and cultural features would be etc. Even more so, the preservation of the species aspect cuts across the applicability of the "lesser" crimes of CAH and war crimes. That realisation leads us to question these underlying assumptions even in the context of comparable interhuman extinction risk scenarios, for example, from colonial times. The application of restrictions on the brutality of the conduct and consequences of armed conflicts which humans accord each other finds no easy equivalent vis-à-vis hostile ETI. Indeed, as Taylor and Boan have argued in their – admittedly at times somewhat flippantly formulated – book on alien invasions,

> [t]hrough our conventions and treaties, we have tried to make war civilized when combatants are face-to-face with the ability to recognize each other and especially when one clearly has the upper hand. We believe that it is all right to kill the nameless and faceless, but that we must respect the civil rights of the captured. ET may believe that war is brutal and cruel. He may believe that it is equally suitable to kill those under his control as it is to brutalize and kill those he is unable to distinguish. He may act in total and complete opposition to our gentlemanly rules of engagement. He may even find that he can use our rules against us. Since we espouse that those rules are a part of our values, we are bound by them. [...] We would be constrained by our rules of engagement even as ET is free to behave in a fashion consistent with his values. [...] Then again, ET might simply consider us pests and plan to exterminate us. Do we consider the rules of engagement that warring fire-ant colonies do when eradicating fire-ant colonies from our lawns?[68]

68 Travis S Taylor and Bob Boan, *Alien Invasion – How to Defend Earth* (Baen Books, Wake Forest, 2011) p. 80.

Humanity's default approach to contact with ETI then seems to be dictated by the need to develop and maintain a forceful and effective, uncompromising defence posture to the extent that our overall technological development as a species at the time of contact will allow us to mount a defence at all – yet even that level of readiness will not emerge on its own. Peaceful contact and the ensuing establishment of harmonious relations between humanity and ETC would be a bonus we cannot count on or even take for granted, notwithstanding all speculative writing about altruism born of highly advanced species development. The consequences for the human stance will be discussed in more detail in Chapters 6 and 7.

CHAPTER 6

Preparing for Hostile Contact

1 Introduction

As the previous chapters have shown, humanity is at present essentially unprepared for any form of contact, leave alone direct or even hostile contact. In fact, and as already mentioned, the vast majority of SETI researchers are in almost *ex cathedra* denial about the possibility of contact already having occurred, be it benevolent or hostile, with the "official" reluctance only having begun to wane as recently as June 2021 with the Director of National Intelligence's Report on UAP and the US congressional committee hearing/announcements in June 2022, the news being that, for example, the Pentagon and NASA, Canada, and now even the Russian counterpart ROSKOSMOS, will enhance their research into UAP.[1] The mainstream belief is that ETI who make contact with us – or with whom we will make contact – will be far more advanced and hence have passed through the developmental threshold of using violence in the regulation of any form of societal conflict. Therefore, they will be benevolent and altruistic, so contact with them will bring advances in the sciences, in the understanding of the cosmos and of our own place in it.

This rose-tinted scenario is still awaiting any form of empirical verification, it is neither theoretically nor philosophically cogent and is in essence based on no more than wishful thinking, especially by those who engage in active SETI and burden our descendants with the risk of an unforeseeable and quite

1 See for an overview of the recent developments the partially declassified version of the Report by the Director of National Intelligence, Preliminary Assessment Unidentified Aerial Phenomena, 2021, https://documents2.theblackvault.com/documents/odni/DEOM-2021-00006.pdf; for the US congressional hearing: https://youtu.be/aSDweUbGBow; NASA Unidentified Aerial Phenomena Independent Study, https://science.nasa.gov/uap; for ROSCOSMOS: Andreas, Müller, Auch Russlands Raumfahrt-Chef äußert sich über außerirdisches Leben und UFOs, 2021, www.grenzwissenschaft-aktuell.de/russlands-raumfahrt-chef-rogozin-aeussert-sich-ueber-ausserirdisches-leben-und-ufos20220613/ (in German); for Canada: Natural Resources Ministry, Letter to MP Larry Maguire, 2022, www.larrymaguire.com/_files/ugd/ba2ab2_878aa8c5de7749bbb4196435c156271c.pdf. On the holdings of over 12,000 pages of related records in the George W. Bush Presidential Library, see John Greenewald, Letter from George W. Bush Presidential Library, 2022, https://twitter.com/blackvaultcom/status/1534242020906045441/photo/1; on the holdings of the Obama equivalent see John Greenewald, Letter from Barack Obama Presidential Library, 2022, https://twitter.com/blackvaultcom/status/1502019931382059016.

 | DOI:10.1163/9789004677708_007

possibly aggressive delayed response, without having any sort of official mandate from humanity to do so. What little evidence there is, to repeat the discourse from the Introduction, should cast doubt on any idea of unmitigated altruism. An interview with Stanford academic Dr Garry Nolan by Tucker Carlson on Fox News as recently as 3 August 2022 provided evidence of specific incidents of harm occurring to humans from interaction with UAP for which the CIA asked his scientific advice.[2] If these reports are accurate and relate to ETI, we may already have had (quasi-)hostile contact and have come out of it not looking too good, to put it bluntly. On the other hand, the "altruists", if one wanted to call them that, more or less neglect the global risk caused by any form of contact, benevolent or not, and the unprecedented consequences of the realisation that humanity is not alone and that all its faiths, ideologies, morals, ethics, and other pillars of societal coherence are about to be shaken to their foundations, with the attendant high likelihood of severe global disruption and unrest.

Michael Ashkenazi has aptly queried the underlying assumption that altruism means full disclosure and mutual trust:

> Many authors […] have assumed that our ETI peers are necessarily benevolent and idealistic. This may or may not be the case. Even if it is the case, this does not mean that they will be providing us with truthful information all the time. It is conceivable, and ought to be kept in mind, that for reasons of benevolence and idealism, they made hide data from us, for reasons we cannot conceive of.[3]

This is strictly speaking not a surprising realisation since humans treat their offspring in much the same way for entirely benevolent reasons, but there is also the example of more powerful groups keeping weaker groups in ignorance for the former's own and sole benefit. Deception is thus to be expected. In the hands of a hostile interlocutor, deception can be a ruse of war, as the attack on Pearl Harbour has shown, for example. Feigning benevolence can put us off our guard until it is too late for effective resistance. Benevolence can also be exercised in a way and to the benefit of one party, which causes detrimental consequences to another. In the SF classic *The Day the Earth Stood Still*, Klaatu came as the messenger of humanity's destruction for the benefit of saving Earth's galactically rare and precious inhabitable ecosphere – a hostile act for

---

2 See https://youtu.be/u7cKhIJnTpo.

3 Michael Ashkenazi, *What We Know About Extraterrestrial Intelligence – Foundations of Xenology* (Springer, New York, 2016) p. 304 (hereafter: *Ashkenazi, Xenology*).

the human species but benevolent for all the rest. And again, as exemplified by the robot Gnut/Gort in *The Day the Earth Stood Still*, even human-developed advanced AI, after the "technological singularity" coined by Stanislaw Ulam in 1958 and later made popular by Ray Kurzweil,[4] may ultimately come to take a similar view of humanity – in the words of *The Matrix's* Agent Smith:

> I'd like to share a revelation that I've had during my time here. It came to me when I tried to classify your species. I realized that you're not actually mammals. Every mammal on this planet instinctively develops a natural equilibrium with the surrounding environment, but you humans do not. You move to an area, and you multiply, and multiply, until every natural resource is consumed. The only way you can survive is to spread to another area. There is another organism on this planet that follows the same pattern. A virus. Human beings are a disease, a cancer of this planet, you are a plague, and we are the cure.[5]

Advanced ETI with a broader historical experience and a better overview of the habitable regions' density in a galaxy, for example, and the corresponding indigenous species impact and stewardship responsibility, may harbour persuasions not too far removed from this fictional account. In other words, ETI do not have to be inherently aggressive or wish us ill out of per se morally evil motives, but their "moral compass" may be determined by considerations of higher-order necessities which outweigh those of the preservation interest of any one species on the planet in question, which incidentally is another argument against current human imaginations of a cosmic metalaw. After all, to remain in the *Matrix* example, the hero figure Morpheus admits that in the war against the machines,

> [w]e don't know who struck first, us or them. But we do know it was us that scorched the sky. At the time, they were dependent on solar power. It was believed they would be unable to survive without an energy source as abundant as the sun [,][6]

thereby confessing to extinguishing the one basic source of life for all other higher species on Earth, plants, and animals, for the sole purpose of securing

4 Daniel Gerritzen, *Erstkontakt* (Kosmos, Stuttgart, 2016) pp. 304–305.
5 The Matrix Quotes, www.quotes.net/mquote/60252.
6 The Matrix: Laurence Fishburne: Morpheus, www.imdb.com/title/tt0133093/characters/nm0000401.

the survival of the remnants of the *human* race – an aspect that perhaps tellingly receives no further attention in the *Matrix* trilogy, however. More ethically advanced ETI might therefore quite understandably take a dim view of our treatment of, and our importance for, the terrestrial ecosphere. Depending on their inclination to impose conditions of proper equilibrium by force, annihilation of the human species might in their eyes seem the most benevolent, indeed optimal course of action for the entire planet.

All of this is meant to convey the simple fact that ETI might want to eradicate us for any number of reasons that may appear unfathomable or even evil to us but eminently sensible to them. We will not know which is which until contact is made, and assuming we do not simply want to accept the moral judgment of ETI or surrender to its superior power and acquiesce in our own obliteration, prudence would demand that we need to be in a position to enforce our own species interests with the necessary arsenal of weapons, to the best of our abilities. They may, as Michaud conceded,[7] not amount to much, as the case may be, but to quote yet another line from a famous SF movie, *Independence Day* by the fictitious US President Whitmore that should not mean humanity should not even wish to try: "We will not go quietly into the night! We will not vanish without a fight!"[8] Humanity currently has, as far as that is public knowledge, neither the technological capacity nor a legal or political framework to mount an effective – or indeed any – defence against a hostile alien civilisation arriving on our doorstep.

Even recent developments about national space force command centres do not contemplate the alien contact scenario.[9] The webpage of the US Space Force (USSF), for example, gives the following explanation of the mission of the USSF:

> Space has become essential to our security and prosperity – so much so that we need a branch of our military dedicated to its defense, just like we have branches of the military dedicated to protecting and securing the

---

7 Michael A.G. Michaud, *Contact with Alien Civilizations – Our Hopes and Fears about Encountering Extraterrestrials* (Copernicus Books, New York, 2010 – hereafter: Michaud) p. 376.

8 "Independence Day" (1996), www.americanrhetoric.com/MovieSpeeches/moviespeechindependenceday.html.

9 See for, example, for the US at United States Space Force www.spaceforce.mil/, and Jean Galbraith, United States Creates the U.S. Space Command and the U.S. Space Force to Strengthen Military Capabilities in Space, 114 *American Journal of International Law* (2020) 323–326; for Germany the *Weltraumkommando* (Space Command), which was inaugurated on 13 July 2021 – www.bundeswehr.de/de/organisation/luftwaffe/aktuelles/das-weltraumkommando-in-uedem-5181718.

> air, land, and sea. Unfettered access to space is vital to national defense. Space systems are woven into the fabric of our way of life. Space affects almost every part of our daily lives and is fundamental to our economic system. For example, satellites not only power the GPS technology that we use daily, but allow us to surf the web and call our friends, enable first responders to communicate with each other in times of crisis, time-stamp transactions in the world financial market, and even allow us to use credit cards at gas pumps.[10]

Section 1 of the Space Policy Directive No. 4 (SPD-4) of 19 February 2019 lays out the basis for this approach:

> Space is integral to our way of life, our national security, and modern warfare. Although United States space systems have historically maintained a technological advantage over those of our potential adversaries, those potential adversaries are now advancing their space capabilities and actively developing ways to deny our use of space in a crisis or conflict. It is imperative that the United States adapt its national security organizations, policies, doctrine, and capabilities to deter aggression and protect our interests.[11]

However, the wording of section 3 of SPD-4 allows for inclusion of an ETI hostile intervention:

> 1. Protecting the Nation's interests in space and the peaceful use of space for all responsible actors, consistent with applicable law, including international law;
> 2. Ensuring unfettered use of space for United States national security purposes, the United States economy, and United States persons, partners, and allies;
> 3. Deterring aggression and defending the Nation, United States allies, and United States interests *from hostile acts in and from space*;
> 4. Ensuring that needed space capabilities are integrated and available to all United States Combatant Commands;
> 5. Projecting military power *in, from, and to space* in support of our Nation's interests; and

10 "Why do we need a Space Force?", www.spaceforce.mil/About-Us/FAQs/Whats-the-Space-Force/.

11 At www.spaceforce.mil/About-Us/SPD-4/.

6. Developing, maintaining, and improving a community of professionals focused on the national security demands of the space domain.[12]

Orbital warfare[13] is listed as a distinct subcategory of the Space Force areas of operation and since 24 July 2020, there has been a separate command structure located at Schriever Air Force Base called Space-Delta-9.[14] The US Capstone Doctrine for Space Forces[15] does, however, not contain any reference to conflict with a non-human enemy, either.

This chapter will therefore deal with the current state of affairs in both fields and map out the possibility of a path towards an improved defensive stance for humanity against hostile ETI. The concomitant issue of the need for regulating the generic post-detection regime currently under the somewhat uncertain and merely practical aegis of the IAASETI Protocols was already reviewed in Chapter 3 and will not be addressed here again.

2 Weapons Technology

As we saw already in Chapter 5 above, there seems to be a natural presumption that a species capable of interstellar travel and envisaging contact with other civilisations might also be at a highly advanced stage of weapons development, with SF providing ample imagination of the variety of conceivable technologies. The publicly known state of the current human development of weapons deployable in space seems to be restricted to ground- or ship-based antiballistic interceptor missiles capable of destroying objects in orbit, electronic signal interruption (jamming), satellites, possibly fitted out with kinetic weapons, directed energy beams such as lasers, jamming technology, or satellites simply capable of ramming other satellites, mini space shuttles, or the intentional use of space debris as a kinetic weapon.[16] This seems rather pedestrian compared

12 *Ibid.* – Emphases added.

13 The concern about the potential build-up for such warfare and especially recent US endeavours in that context are addressed in Joan Johnson-Freese, *Space Warfare in the 21st Century – Arming the Heavens* (Routledge, Abingdon, 2017).

14 At https://www.schriever.spaceforce.mil/About-Us/Units/Space-Delta-9/.

15 At www.schriever.spaceforce.mil/Portals/17/Space%20Capstone%20Publication_10%20Aug%202020.pdf.

16 Linda Dawson, *War in Space – The Science and Technology Behind Our Next Theater of Conflict*. New York: (Springer, New York, 2018) pp. 12–32, 46–60, as well as the references in fn. 1 of Chapter 5.

to what might be at the disposal of an alien species with the capacity of crossing interstellar distances.

Taylor and Boan, in their popular science book from 2011 *Alien Invasion: How to Defend Earth*, for example, referred to at the time still experimental devices such as railguns,[17] which are high energy projectile weapons yet still remain kinetic in nature. Many other options listed by them[18] are (probably) even more in the realm of science fiction than of science – however, after all, they also quite reasonably advocate that secret weapons must remain secret until the need for their deployment arises.[19] Both factors may be a reason why authors still mostly shy away from discussing the development of "proper" space-usable armaments: Melissa de Zwart,[20] for example, when discussing the historically undeniable link between the development of weapons technology and human space exploration from its earliest days,[21] even as recently as 2019 referred only to interhuman conflict and the terrestrial impact of human space weaponry.

In the related field of the traditional planetary defence against near-Earth objects (NEOs) such as asteroids and meteors, the currently imaginable methods of defence are kinetic impactors,[22] gravity tractor spacecraft or nuclear explosions to deflect an incoming NEO from its collision orbit.[23] Most tellingly, all of these deflective actions ideally have to occur a long way from Earth's orbit and do not tend to involve merely shattering the NEO into smaller objects, because after all, these could then still remain on, or return to, their original near-Earth trajectory.[24] It is more than questionable whether humanity currently has the technology to provide such solutions far away from Earth orbit, and apart from the issue of whether the insight into the need for a global preparation of defensive capabilities against potentially hostile ETI in the near future exists, there is the not far-fetched concern that the premature creation

---

17 Travis S Taylor and Bob Boan, *Alien Invasion: How to Defend Earth* (Baen Books, New York, 2011 – hereafter: Taylor/Boan) pp. 176–180.

18 Taylor/Boan, pp. 180–181.

19 *Ibid.*, pp. 134–135.

20 Melissa de Zwart, Outer Space, in William H. Boothby (ed.). *New Technologies and the Law in War and Peace* (CUP, Cambridge, 2019) pp. 347–349.

21 See also in a similar vein Neil de Grasse Tysson and Avis Lang, *Accessory to War – The unspoken alliance between astrophysics and the military* (Norton, New York, 2019).

22 See, for example, the Double Asteroid Redirection Test (DART) performed by NASA on 26 September 2022, www.nasa.gov/press-release/nasa-s-dart-mission-hits-asteroid-in-first-ever-planetary-defense-test.

23 David Morrison, Overview of Active Planetary Defense *Methods*, in Nikola Schmidt (ed.) *Planetary Defense – Global Collaboration for Defending Earth from Asteroids and Comets* (Springer, New York, 2019) pp. 113–121 at pp. 119–120.

24 *Ibid.*, pp. 119–120.

and deployment of any such devices may actually turn them into weapons to be used by their creators against humanity themselves.[25] Their development as a defensive arsenal against hostile ETI thus faces even more significant additional (geo-)political hurdles. The "giggle factor" from the UFO research environment will also make an appearance again, especially when the debate will be about allocating substantial (global) funds to research and development, regardless of the degree of upset and concern the 2021 UAP report and the ensuing enhanced international UAP research efforts may have caused to some political decision-makers. The threat arising from the proliferating effects of climate change, the risk of a break-up of the rules-based world order, and the resurgence of nationalist, ethnic and religious rifts leading to violence across large sections of the globe understandably have a much more urgent claim on their attention, their time, and the available resources. Low-probability risks, even if existential should they materialise, rank low on the scale of political priorities, and so, as a consequence, does the awareness of the need for planning ahead to counter them. Nonetheless, it is worth bearing in mind the strategic military view as expressed by Major John C Wright, a U.S. Air Force officer, when he writes in the only monograph published so far on deep space warfare which expressly includes scenarios of conflict with non-human intelligence at length:

> When one considers the scale at which the universe exists, compounded with the unstoppable onslaught of scientific progress and our species' slow reach for the stars, it becomes patently obvious that if an extraterrestrial sentient competitor exists somewhere, it is only a matter of time before we make contact. This claim is contentious, but from a military strategy perspective it is reasonable enough to contemplate potential military confrontations and associated countermeasures.[26]

Reconceptualising the term "planetary defence" to include military defensive capability of repelling an intelligent extraterrestrial enemy of mankind is thus

---

25 *Ibid.*, p. 120.

26 John C. Wright, 2020. *Deep Space Warfare – Military Strategy Beyond Orbit* (McFarland, Jefferson, 2020 – hereafter *Deep Space Warfare*) p. 25. This chapter owes a lot to Wright's book. He adds on a more practical level that "when space conversations come up today in military conversations, the topic is discussed with seriousness and attention. Military commanders listen when their space officers – whose very existence speaks volumes – present their concerns. People no longer find spacegoing battle fleets and armed astronauts far-fetched. Science Fiction is by far the most 'acceptably nerdy' interest to possess [...] not only because it represents windows into the future [...]". – *Ibid.*, p. 7.

bound to remain a mere semantic exercise unless humanity's cosmic species awareness, which we talked about in Chapter 2, reaches a higher level and the corresponding conclusions are drawn. To sum up, the (publicly known) state of the art of human space weapons technology in the wider sense would seem to be at a lamentably low level, with an almost total absence of effectiveness beyond near-Earth-orbit regions. In addition, as Wright points out, 95% of space are empty and therefore of no military value.[27] We will see below how this ties in with the requirements based on the prospective nature of potential deep space warfare operations.

Definitions for deep space currently range from 30,000 km from Earth to 2 million km, depending on what the definition is meant to regulate;[28] they do not necessarily relate to the question we want to answer. For our purposes of distinguishing between "home" and "forward" defence operations, as it were, the Merriam-Webster definition is actually sufficient, i.e., "space well outside the earth's atmosphere *and especially that part lying beyond the earth-moon system*".[29] Hereafter, deep space will thus mean the part of space beyond the Moon's orbit.

3 Strategy and Tactics

Leaving aside far-future space opera treatments in SF, the imagination about defending Earth from any external threat, be it natural such as NEOs or artificial in the form of generic ETI interference, has so far mostly been confined to actions in relative proximity to Earth. This has had the consequence of creating the illusion of the feasibility of a real-time response scenario with communication delays of mere seconds or at most minutes between the ground control centre and the forces in the field. However, the further away from Earth the theatre of action is removed – and that is after all a demand of prudence in planetary defence as traditionally understood – the more this becomes a serious problem, especially on a military level related to the chain of command and the degree of autonomy granted the commanding officer of the force *in situ*. As we saw in Chapter 4, SF writers struggle with this matter, too, and attempt to circumvent it by inventing instant communication devices like

27 *Deep Space Warfare*, p. 20.

28 Distances defining the beginning of deep space range from 30,000 kilometres from Earth (NASA Deep Space Network) to 2 million kilometres (International Telecommunications Union – ITU).

29 See www.merriam-webster.com/dictionary/deep%20space – emphasis added.

the ansible, interocitor or the Dirac communicator. Communication is not the only problem surrounding long-distance space operations. We will look at that in some more detail now.

3.1 *Weapons Development and Deep Space Strategy*

We begin this section by another apposite quote from Wright, flowing from the above-mentioned realisation that the current human space weapons development appears to be inadequate for combat with (advanced) hostile ETI. We might ask: If there is no hardware for us to make a credible stand against hostile ETI, why should we worry about the "software" aspect of strategy and tactics? Wright states, when introducing his book on military strategy beyond Earth orbit:

> While science fiction and real scientists across the world are doing their best to test the limits of current technology as it applies to space operations, this book refrains from calling on technically infeasible or theoretically impossible technology for the sake of focusing on strategic discussions regarding space warfare. While it is true advancements in propulsion, daily existence in space, and weaponry are certainly welcome and probably necessary to make full-fledged space operations possible, for discussing space warfare at the strategic level they are immaterial.[30]

In other words, researching and/or emphasising the isolated weapons development without accompanying prophylactic strategy research is thus discussing only one aspect of space warfare. Tactics relate to strategy in the same way as tools relate to aims. Advances in weapons development may certainly immediately influence the range of available combat tactics; they do, however, not normally determine the basic tenets of warfare strategy, unless they are of an order of magnitude that would revolutionise the entire way we conduct hostilities – for example, the rise of long-range weapons of mass destruction. Here changes in the available tools can in theory over time blend into additions to available strategic options. To give an example: In the times of traditional ground and naval warfare between states in the 18th and 19th centuries, the strategic aim of the total annihilation of the enemy - military and civilians - rather than the enemy government's surrender and possibly occupation or annexation of the enemy territory, was not realistically imaginable due to the available weaponry of the day. With the advent of nuclear, biological, and chemical weapons and

30 *Deep Space Warfare*, p. 32.

long-range delivery systems such as intercontinental ballistic missiles (IBMS) or cruise missiles, this aim has become an achievable option. It is irrelevant from the point of view of the definition of strategy whether this aim would be banned under international law or whether it would be sensible, for example, against the background of mutually assured destruction (aptly abbreviated MAD) in the nuclear scenario: It would still be a strategic aim.

How would this translate to a deep space combat environment? We addressed a version of this scenario in Chapter 5 when we discussed the question of how humanity might want to react to an attack by a superior ETI. Traditional humanitarian law allows only certain strategic aims as legitimate military strategy options; the same applies at the level of tactics. Despite the many treaties about nuclear disarmament and non-proliferation, given the historical horrors of Hiroshima and Nagasaki with their effects reaching to the present day, and the inability to discriminate between combatants and civilians in the case of a nuclear strike, there is still no full and clear consensus that the isolated use of a nuclear device capable of killing tens of thousands of people (tactic) in order to force the enemy to surrender (strategic aim) – i.e., the Japanese WWII scenario – or in the act of self-defence, would be illegal under international law.[31] However, the use of nuclear carpet bombing (tactic) in order to eradicate the entire population of a country and make its territory uninhabitable for many centuries (strategic aim) would undoubtedly be prohibited, *inter alia*, as a crime against humanity of extermination and depending on the motivation, possibly even as genocide. In the ETI scenario, however, (pre-emptive) annihilation of the entire ETI civilisation to prevent any recurrence of conflict as a strategic aim might have to be considered acceptable.[32] This view is shared by John J. Klein who writes, albeit in a purely interhuman context:

> For the development of space strategy, this reality means that the application of space-based technologies is unlikely to win wars by itself. While space-related technology may provide a tactical advantage in combat

31 See International Court of Justice (ICJ), *Legality of the Threat or Use of Nuclear Weapons*, Advisory Opinion, 8 July 1996, ICJ. Reports 1996, 226, at paras. 95–97. – Strangely enough, the much less destructive so-called neutron bomb, officially classified as an enhanced radiation weapon or ERW, was retired from the active arsenal of the United States in the 1990s under Ronald Reagan due to the refusal of European countries to have them stationed on their territories under the aegis of NATO based on the anti-nuclear movement of the time. See, for example, John T. Correll, The Neutron Bomb, *Air Force Magazine* (2017), www.airforcemag.com/article/the-neutron-bomb/.

32 In the same vein, *Deep Space Warfare*, pp. 100, 114, 128.

> and influence operations style, it is unlikely that a single technology will determine the outcome of a conflict. Technology should not be used in isolation from the overall strategic objectives of the war, and 'technological proficiency is no substitute for strategic acuity'.[33]

More to the point, for example, weapons that cannot be used by a mobile military agent, such as a battle fleet, in a deep space battle theatre due to the factual requirements of deep space operations – on which more below – are only worth developing if they can be employed in a deep-space stationary setting with relative proximity to a given battle theatre, such as a forward operating base or an automated missile launch site etc. on a different planet,[34] moon or asteroid, or – in the near-Earth space environment – armed satellites or ground-based weapons, and only to the extent that such use would be compliant with the overall strategic objective humanity may wish to develop for its space presence. This means, for example, the more massive and energy-consuming a device will be, the less likely it will be to feature in the arsenal of a space fleet operating millions of miles from Earth in deep space.

3.2 *The Strategic Parameters of Deep Space Warfare*

Assuming the need and even rudimentary capacity for deep space warfare, it becomes immediately clear that this kind of campaign could not be fought in the same manner as a purely terrestrial one. As discussed in Chapter 4 on SF conflict scenarios, in particular around the Dark Forest theorem, any kind of pre-emptive strike by human forces against a non-human civilisation even within our own solar system, leave alone at interstellar distances, is currently well outside humanity's capabilities and hence also unlikely to become a major incentive for military action, because of the unforeseeable retaliatory capacity of an otherwise possibly non-aggressive opponent. That in effect leaves humanity with a defensive stance for the time being, which incidentally sits well with the ban on aggressive warfare in the current human laws of war. Nonetheless, as we saw above, the optimal location for mounting

---

33 John J Klein, *Understanding Space Strategy – The Art of War in Space* (Routledge, London, 2019 – hereafter *Klein, Understanding*) p. 61.

34 We will have to leave aside at this point the high potential, based on human colonial history, for planetary settlements to become independent of their home world to a lesser or greater degree, and hence the likelihood of the interplanetary environment sliding into a form of interplanetary anarchy; see Deep Space Warfare, p. 16. Similarly critical about the consequences of human expansion into space, Daniel Deudney, *Dark skies: space expansionism, planetary geopolitics, and the ends of humanity* (OUP, Oxford, 2020).

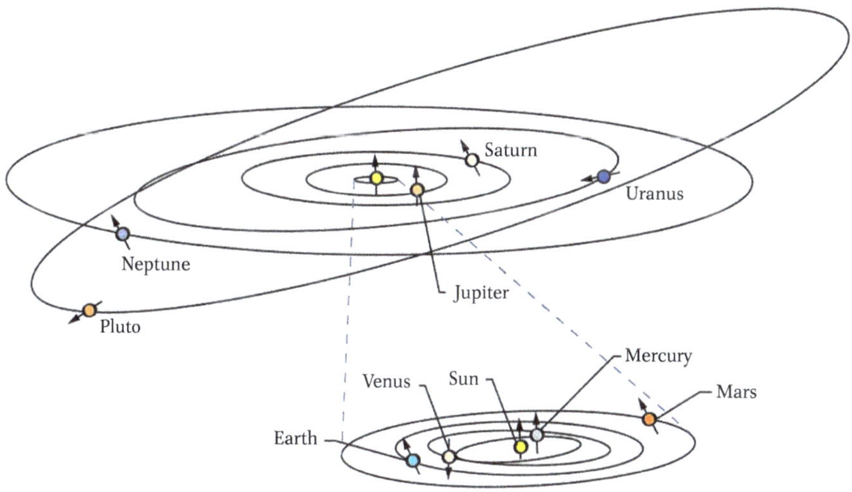

FIGURE 4 Orbital plane of the solar system
SOURCE: WWW.NASA.GOV/SITES/DEFAULT/FILES/THUMBNAILS/IMAGE/EDU_WHAT_IS_PLUTO_3.PNG

such a defence is as far away from the Earth as possible; the human defence endeavour would thus still have to aim at deep space activities. There are, however, a plethora of obstacles to overcome, some of which seem insuperable for humanity at its current stage of development.

3.2.1 Distances, Speeds, and Celestial Mechanics

Banal as it is, the fact merits mention that any defensive perimeter would of course have to be spherical in shape because Earth can in theory be attacked from any direction in three-dimensional space[35] and it is probably illusory that any military force could ever provide comprehensive protection.[36] While it may in theory be envisaged that humanity might over time establish forward operating bases on the planets of the solar system, that would still confine human planet-bound defence installations to the orbital plane in which the planets move around the sun, even with Pluto's somewhat enhanced orbital inclination relative to the plane. Figure 4[37] gives an impression of the relatively flat orbital plane of the solar system.

35 Wright uses the phrase "square kilometers suddenly become cubed kilometers". – *Deep Space Warfare*, p. 14.

36 *Deep Space Warfare*, p. 15.

37 See www.nasa.gov/sites/default/files/thumbnails/image/edu_what_is_pluto_3.png.

If a spacecraft were to go "up" or "down"[38] relative to the orbital plane, it would not encounter anything for a very long distance, even further than to the outer planets. The Kuiper Belt, at the farthest fringes of the solar system, has some vertical deviation from the orbital plane but not to the extent that it could be said to be even approximately fully vertical, and it also exists mainly in a flat plane of its own relative to the sun. The nearest sufficiently dense collection of sizeable objects "up" or "down" from the plane is the Oort Cloud, a kind of spherical bubble enveloping the solar system. The explanation given by NASA on its webpage "Solar System Exploration" is useful and straightforward for non-astronomers – it also highlights the massive problems arising for use of that part of space as a military staging area of any sort:

> The distance from the Sun to the Oort Cloud is so enormous that it's useful to describe it not in the more common units of miles or kilometers, but astronomical units. One astronomical unit (or AU) is the distance between Earth and the Sun. Pluto's elliptical orbit carries it as close as 30 AU from the Sun, and as far as 50 AU. The inner edge of the Oort Cloud, however, is thought to be between 2,000 and 5,000 AU from the Sun. The outer edge might be 10,000 or even 100,000 AU from the Sun – that's one-quarter to halfway between the Sun and the nearest neighboring star.[39]

That star nearest to our sun is Proxima Centauri at a distance of about 4.25 light years. The following may serve as an illustration of the possible speeds and travel times involved: If Voyager I,[40] a probe launched in 1977 and having entered interstellar space in 2012, which is travelling away from our sun at about 17 km/s, had been aimed at Proxima it would take about 73,000 years to get there.[41] The fastest manmade spacecraft so far appears to be the Parker Solar Probe launched in 2018, which in November 2021 reached a speed of 163 km/s or slightly above 0.05% of the speed of light (300,000 km/s); its top speed will eventually be around 190 km/s, which still is only just above 0.06%.[42] Even

38 There is, of course, in general no "up" or "down" in space.
39 See https://solarsystem.nasa.gov/solar-system/oort-cloud/overview/.
40 This webpage provides a continuous update on both the Voyager I and Voyager II mission status: https://voyager.jpl.nasa.gov/mission/status/.
41 See https://imagine.gsfc.nasa.gov/features/cosmic/nearest_star_info.html.
42 See https://blogs.nasa.gov/parkersolarprobe/. The Breakthrough Starshot Project already mentioned in Chapter 2 aims to reach a significant higher proportion of lightspeed; see https://breakthroughinitiatives.org/initiative/3.

at these speeds,[43] the journey to Proxima would still take between about 7,600 and 6,500 years. Even getting near the inner Oort Cloud would take multiple human lifetimes. Mere rocket propulsion alone of the type currently available to humans[44] is unable to reach anywhere near even such relatively modest speeds, and repeated accelerating slingshots using planetary gravity assist manoeuvres to support a trajectory highly inclined to the orbital plane are difficult to imagine, because while the slingshot effect may also be used to initially deflect a probe at an inclination out of the plane, in principle it works only *in* the orbital plane based on the planets' orbital velocity which is synchronous to their movement within the plane.[45]

Any long-term or even permanent human – as opposed to automated – presence above and below the orbital plane would thus have to consist of massive space habitats far larger, more robust, and more sophisticated than the present International Space Station (ISS). Rollock and Klaus have recently demonstrated the general need for development towards a state of self-awareness and self-sufficiency of such facilities, possibly with the aid of autonomous systems.[46] They would, however, depending on the actual nature of the habitat,

---

43 For the Parker Solar Probe this actually requires several approaches to the sun over the span of a few years, each aided by repeated slingshot breaking manoeuvres around Venus to bring it on its next eccentric elliptic orbit closer to the sun and thus in the process each time increasing its speed at perihelion, i.e., the closest distance to the Sun.

44 For example, allowing a hypothetical 200,000 metric ton spacecraft carrier's crew to remain at a normal and healthy Earth gravity of 1 G while transiting from Moon orbit to Mars orbit, i.e., 55 million kilometres at closest distance, while under orders to arrive at Mars orbit within six months, the necessary speed of 1,300 km/s could be reached by an engine capable of accelerating at 1 G/s for 1,300,000 seconds, i.e., 361 hours, that is roughly 15 days, continuously – yet no such engine currently exists. Even then it would still not reach only 1% of lightspeed – Example given in *Deep Space Warfare*, pp. 106–107.

45 One example is the Ulysses probe – https://solarsystem.nasa.gov/missions/ulysses/in-depth/ – launched in 1990 and sent into a permanent elliptic orbit around the sun at 80° inclination to the orbital plane by a so-called gravity assist operation around Jupiter in February 1992. There is the possibility that if Ulysses swings near one of Jupiter's moons in the future, its trajectory might actually be affected again to become hyperbolic and take it into interstellar space; see Steve Gorman, Solar orbiter Ulysses ends mission after 18 years, Reuters Science News, 1 July 2009, www.reuters.com/article/us-space-solar-idINTRE5600A220090701. – The author is grateful to Dr Martin Dominik, University of St Andrews, for the explanation of the slingshot manoeuvre of the Parker Solar Probe and the physics of sending a probe out of the orbital plane using fly-by manoeuvres, as well as mentioning the Ulysses example.

46 Annika E Rollock and David M Klaus, Defining and characterizing self-awareness and self-sufficiency for deep space habitats, 198 *Acta Astronautica* (2022) 366–375.

still be beset with major ensuing logistical and human resources problems such as

- maintenance of life support systems,
- hardware fatigue and software deterioration,
- loss of human knowledge and expertise because the second-generation and later crews, unlike the initial one, would no longer be selected from among the best once the first generation of ship-born humans took over, and hence over time probably revert to a state closer to the average distribution of human IQs,
- absolute independence from any interplanetary supply lines,
- supporting a human crew who would have been/be born there and have no chance of ever returning to Earth,
- forced operative independence from Earth due to the time even radio signals would take to reach home etc.[47]

In essence, even in an automated setting these would be outposts which for all intents and purposes would be cut off from operative coordination with Earth and therefore quite possibly useless even as an advance early warning system in the case that an unknown object or fleet of objects moving under power or in an unusual trajectory might be headed for the inner solar system, especially if that object was moving at very high to near-relativistic speeds. It also appears rather questionable whether an AI-controlled automated monitor capable of armed attack or defence operations would be allowed to take such decisions without human input,[48] possibly risking full-scale conflict with an otherwise benign ETI. The added value to state-of-the-art near-Earth telescopes such as the recently launched James Webb Telescope would in fact be nigh negligible. From a military perspective, such habitats would also be highly vulnerable to attacks from a distance and by devices possibly outside the range of detection or response of any human defensive weapons, such as advanced stealth missile systems or other ultra-high-speed kinetic weapons, drone swarms etc., leave alone any other more futuristic weapons systems an advanced ETI might possess. The sobering fact remains that humanity is far from acquiring any of the technology necessary to even begin seriously considering such initiatives.

---

47 See generally *Deep Space Warfare*, p. 21. – The related scenarios have been described very well by the SF writers Adrian Tchaikovsky in his already mentioned novel *Children of Time* (see Chapter 4) and Kim Stanley Robinson in his *Aurora* (Orbit Books, London, 2016).

48 Also opposed to this use of AI: *Deep Space Warfare*, p. 112. – For an introduction to the related issues, see Kenneth Payne, *I, Warbot: The Dawn of Artificially Intelligent Conflict* (C Hurst & Co., London, 2021).

An added, but equally banal problem are the so-called "celestial mechanics". Obviously, the planets do not orbit the sun in a manner that they are always in exactly the same position in relation to each other, or as Wright puts it, "stellar phenomena are in constant motion".[49] This leads, for example, to the phenomenon of optimum launch windows for spacecraft when the velocity needed for the transfer orbit – such as, for example, the Hohman Transfer[50] – is minimized.[51] So even within the orbital plane, and even if humanity had a staging post on each planet and possibly automated monitoring stations on a few of the major inner asteroid orbits, the vast distances and the orbits involved would preclude any idea of a fast reaction force if there was an alien incursion within or into the solar system by any ETI with advanced propulsion systems superior to human technology; this would be especially crucial if the incursion came from interstellar space because then the ETI – like the humans just described – would either have to use some kind of massive generation ships travelling at more traditional speeds over longer periods, or spacecraft capable of travelling at least close to the speed of light,[52] if one wishes to avoid discussing the feasibility of light-speed or even faster-than-light (FTL) travel of objects with a rest mass of more than zero, both of which are currently – according to

49 *Deep Space Warfare*, p. 15.

50 See Ulrich Walter, *Astronautics: The Physics of Space Flight*, 3rd ed. (Springer, Cham, 2018) pp. 313–325.

51 See for a comprehensive introduction to these issues the NASA webpage "Basics of Space Flight" at https://solarsystem.nasa.gov/basics/.

52 In this context, research done based on the flight and acceleration capabilities of reported UAPs suggests that if these were indeed spacecraft of extraterrestrial origin, they would be able to reach relativistic speeds in relatively short time. See Kevin H. Knuth et al., Estimating Flight Characteristics of Anomalous Unidentified Aerial Vehicles, 21 *Entropy* (2019) 939 at p. 15: "While the Extraterrestrial Hypothesis can be neither verified nor ruled out at this time, it is useful to consider whether the characteristics of these UAVs tend to support or rule out the Extraterrestrial Hypothesis. Given the estimated accelerations of these UAVs, it is useful to consider the time it would take them to travel interstellar distances. Figure 7A illustrates how long it would take a craft accelerating at 1000 g to reach various percentages of the speed of light. In just less than an hour, a craft accelerating at a constant 1000 g would reach 10% of the speed of light, which is NASA's goal for the planned 2069 mission to Proxima Centuri [sic!] (Alpha Centuri system). In less than three hours, the same craft would reach 30% of the speed of light. Such a craft accelerating at a constant 1000 g for half of the trip and decelerating at the same rate for the remaining half would reach Proxima Centuri within 5 days' ship time due to the fact that it would have been traveling at relativistic speeds for most of the trip […]. However, for those of us on Earth, or anyone on Proxima Centuri b, the trip would take over four years. As a comparison, a craft accelerating at 100 g would reach 10% of the speed of light in 8.5 hrs, 30% of the speed of light in just more than a day, and Proxima Centuri in a month and a half".

human scientific consensus – precluded under the special theory of relativity developed by Albert Einstein in 1905.[53] In all of these scenarios it needs to be borne in mind that the original intended mission of any ETI craft[54] or fleet capable of engaging in warfare would not have to be aggressive in nature at all but may turn aggressive – from a human point of view – depending on the circumstances when contact is made, and like with human SETI this can include the moment of unilateral detection of a human signal by the ETI.

3.2.2 Psychological Aspects

The overall conclusion based on public record information on weapons and propulsion technology must therefore be that humanity at this time has little to no prospect of establishing an effective defensive perimeter sufficiently far away from Earth orbit, especially out of the orbital plane. That does, however, not translate directly into the conclusion that it would be pointless anyway to consider how Earth's defences to hostile contact could be improved closer to home. These efforts, even if taken seriously, would, however, encounter another stress test to which we turn now – psychology. In this context, and in a reversal of the previously cited saying by Hawking, Wright opines that humanity might be too aggressive for other species to want to meet us.[55]

Psychological aspects will influence relations on both sides. This begins with the above-mentioned stance towards the "inferior" species: Unless it is a matter of species survival, each cosmic species must make a choice regarding its motives towards optional engagements with other species. This may either lead to a prime directive approach, or towards an aggressive attitude in line with, for example, the Dark Forest concept.[56] It is unclear, for example,

---

53 See the English translation of his seminal paper Albert Einstein, Zur Elektrodynamik bewegter Körper, 17 *Annalen der Physik* (1905) 891, online at www.fourmilab.ch/etexts/einstein/specrel/www/.

54 As already mentioned in Chapter 4, when describing the chain of events in Liu Cixin's "The Dark Forest", one can imagine scenarios where one small, unmanned spacecraft composed of highly resilient, ultra-dense material, capable of high speeds and sudden trajectory changes without loss of speed can take out a multitude of other spacecraft through sheer kinetic impact. One of the more concerning findings of the 2021 UAP Report laid before the US Congress referenced above was precisely that some of the objects observed were apparently capable of just those kinds of manoeuvres, although nothing is known, of course, about their material composition or any armaments, not least because there are to the author's knowledge no reliably recorded incidents in the public domain when an alien craft directly attacked a human craft, at least without provocation, other than by returning fire.

55 *Deep Space Warfare*, p. 112.

56 *Deep Space Warfare*, p. 162.

whether and to what extent ETI will view the aspect of territorial disagreements as a sufficient cause for armed hostilities.[57] Humans and ETI may, again in line with Dark Forest thinking, ask the question "What if we do nothing?" when deciding on whether to embark on hostilities.[58] Equally unclear are the existence and effect of psychological and cultural concepts such as honour[59] and self-interest[60] on alien decision-making

For humans in particular, facing a hon-human opponent will have references to the human-animal experience: A certain degree of aggressiveness is to be expected in initial human-ETI relations, and based on the degree of mutual strangeness, may result in fear, hate and loathing. First contact must assume a total mutual lack of similarity, and while mathematics, biology or chemistry may supply first points of basic intellectual communication, they cannot in and of themselves provide any access to behavioural and cultural norms.[61] The interplay between power and the primacy of fear as a motivating element will play a significant role in determining whether the first encounter will be an emanation of the Thucydides trap, because it is not unreasonable to expect that any ETI will have the psychological experience of fear as one of their primal motivators in their species memory.[62] Reflecting, for example, the distinction in attitudes to METI, the competition between "xenophobism" and "xenophilism" will inform the decision on how to react on both sides, with the chances of the former guiding any government's actions being rather strong, because it stands to reason that the security-minded factions will be carrying the day in the context of an unprecedented contact event, especially against the background of the ex-ante unknowable power disparity between both sides.[63] Wright points out that lack of understanding – a highly likely state of affairs in the event of direct first contact – creates distrust and that relations might end up in general carnage through the "dehumanisation" of the opponent.[64]

57 *Deep Space Warfare*, pp. 169–170.
58 *Deep Space Warfare*, p. 170.
59 In John Scalzi's *Old Man's War* trilogy, to use another SF example from Chapter 4, even the most advanced species in the quadrant, the Consu, still adhere to an archaic honour code almost like the time-honoured Bushido of the Samurai, which they apply, for example, even to other species, who must fight – and kill – Consu warriors for each question they wish to ask the Consu.
60 *Deep Space Warfare*, pp. 170–172.
61 *Deep Space Warfare*, pp. 61–63.
62 *Deep Space Warfare*, pp. 63–65.
63 *Deep Space Warfare*, pp. 66–70.
64 *Deep Space Warfare*, pp. 151–153.

4 Conclusion: an End to the Idea of a Peaceful Use of Outer Space?

A final remark needs to be made about what this all will mean for the fundamental human outlook on the peaceful use of outer space, and in particular the ban on the use of military weapons or installations of any kind. It can very probably be taken for granted that the major spacefaring nations will tend to honour this more in the breach than by observance if it suits their vital geostrategic aims, even to the limited extent that there is binding law, yet it seems apt to repeat what the Treaty on Principles Governing the Activities of States in the Exploration and Use of Outer Space, including the Moon and Other Celestial Bodies (Outer Space Treaty) has to say on this in Article IV, which serves as a high-minded aspiration at the very least:

> States Parties to the Treaty undertake not to place in orbit around the Earth any objects carrying nuclear weapons or any other kinds of weapons of mass destruction, install such weapons on celestial bodies, or station such weapons in outer space in any other manner.
>
> The Moon and other celestial bodies shall be used by all States Parties to the Treaty exclusively for peaceful purposes. The establishment of military bases, installations and fortifications, the testing of any type of weapons and the installations and fortifications, the testing of any type of weapons and the conduct of military manoeuvres on celestial bodies shall be forbidden. The use of military personnel for scientific research or for any other peaceful purposes shall not be prohibited. The use of any equipment or facility necessary for shall not be prohibited. The use of any equipment or facility necessary for peaceful exploration of the Moon and other celestial bodies shall also not be prohibited.[65]

Again, the Agreement Governing the Activities of States on the Moon and Other Celestial Bodies (Moon Agreement) takes up this thought in its Article 3.[66] Incorporating the military defence of Earth and of Moon orbit space against hostile non-human opponents into a revised paradigm of planetary defence would put paid to any such ideas. If anything, the militarisation of near-Earth space would become of paramount importance. This would in practice entail the risk of the major spacefaring nations – some coincidentally also among the world's military superpowers – taking military control of near-Earth space

65 See for the Treaty Annex B. I.

66 See Annex B. II.

without multilateral, leave alone overall, consensus and guarantees against unilateral abuse, the very thing the existing agreements aim to prevent.

This concern is not restricted to the creation military environments: Even in the next endeavour to regulate the commercial exploitation of the Moon, the so-called Artemis Accords advanced by NASA in 2020 in the context of its Artemis Programme aimed at returning humans to the Moon,[67] there has been criticism that this was a framework that demonstrably favoured US interests of establishing dominance in space in yet another area,[68] not least because accession to the Accords is required for States to participate in the Artemis Programme of NASA. In particular Section 11, entitled "Deconfliction of Space Activities", with its establishment of so-called "safety zones" around the installations of individual nations is seen by some as trying to circumvent the ban of the Outer Space Treaty on appropriation of parts of the Moon by individual States through the backdoor, through the clandestine creation of new international customary law.[69] It can be expected that similar tactics would be deployed in an even starker fashion if the matter was the creation of a military zone in orbit, on the Moon or – in the due course of technological development – of likely unmanned but possibly AI-controlled forward installations on other planets or, where feasible and tactically sensible due to their trajectories, asteroids.

So, we come back to the earlier complaint that humanity needs to find a cosmic species identity first, before it can become even a minor player in any interstellar relations, peaceful or hostile. Currently, and more clearly than

67 The full title is "The Artemis Accords – Principles for Cooperation in the Civil Exploration and Use of the Moon, Mars, Comets, and Asteroids for Peaceful Purposes"; full text at www.nasa.gov/specials/artemis-accords/img/Artemis-Accords-signed-13Oct2020.pdf.

68 On the Accords, see David P. Fidler, The Artemis Accords and the Next Generation of Outer Space Governance, Council on Foreign Relations, 2 June 2020, www.cfr.org/blog/artemis-accords-and-next-generation-outer-space-governance; Dennis O'Brien, The Artemis Accords: repeating the mistakes of the Age of Exploration, The Space Review (2020), www.thespacereview.com/article/3975/1; Elliot Ji, What Does China Think About NASA's Artemis Accords? The Diplomat (2020), https://thediplomat.com/2020/09/what-does-china-think-about-nasas-artemis-accords/; Alexander Stirn, Wie die USA das Völkerrecht aushebeln könnten, Spektrum (2020). www.spektrum.de/news/raumfahrt-wie-die-usa-das-voelkerrecht-aushebeln-koennten/1787216; Rajeswari Pillai Rajagopalan, The Artemis Accords and Global Lunar Governance, The Diplomat (2021), https://thediplomat.com/2021/06/the-artemis-accords-and-global-lunar-governance/; Rossana Deplano, The Artemis Accords: Evolution or Revolution in International Space Law, 70 *International and Comparative Law Quarterly* (2021) 799–819.

69 Frans von der Dunk. The Artemis Accords and the law: Is the Moon 'back in business'?, The Big Q (2020), www.thebigq.org/2020/06/02/the-artemis-accords-and-the-law-is-the-moon-back-in-business/; Alexander Stirn, *ibid.*

before since 24 February 2022, the few States which in reality control the potential for any development of space-worthy defence capabilities are in danger of dismantling the rule-based world order which arose out of the horror of the experience of the last world war. If one major permanent member of the UN Security Council can attack a neighbouring country in a criminal war of aggression at a level not seen at least in Europe since the last world war, and another major member refuses to denounce the attack for what it is but supports the aggressor for the purpose of settling historical geopolitical scores with the West, then we are still very far away from our goal, with the direction of travel set to increase the distance further. However, because the perfect is the enemy of the good, we should still reflect on how we could reach some form of unity, even if we have to wait until the pendulum swings back. This we will try to do in the next and last substantial chapter.

CHAPTER 7

Legal Prolegomena of Peaceful Relationships with ETI

1 Introduction

In Chapters 5 and 6 we dealt with the legal and factual problems arising from humanity's probable lack of preparedness to defend itself in the face of a hostile alien encounter. However, we must now also turn our attention to scenarios where conflict avoidance might be possible. This could, of course, either be the case if the ETI turn out to be generally benevolent and interested in cooperation with other cosmic species, or if there is an incentive to negotiate peaceful relations if the ETI is in principle willing and able to consider hostile action but for other reasons deems a mutually agreed solution to any differences in interest preferrable. As discussed earlier in Chapter 3 in the section on metalaw, we will not engage in any speculation about possible moral or legal attitudes taken by ETI to inform the outcome of the discussion, but will look solely at the human baseline for negotiations with ETI within a range of potential conceptual options that humans could expect to be faced with.

We already saw in the Introduction that any hope for a generally shared approach by advanced ETI towards less developed species akin to Star Trek's "Prime Directive"[1] might currently seem to run afoul of the trend in the results of decades of research into UFOs, now UAP. The open manner in which UFOs have allegedly displayed themselves and their technological capabilities in terrestrial airspace does in any event not match the basic conceptual parameters of a galactic zoo or reservation status for Earth, where advanced ETI do not wish to interfere in the development of the specimens existing in that particular zoo. Nevertheless, until and unless the UAP conundrum is solved and their possible extraterrestrial origin established, the current state of public record SETI research in the wider sense determines the conceptual boundaries of what we can work with.

1 Suffice it to say that Star Trek itself is replete with examples of situational ethics overriding the mechanical application of the Prime Directive, see Fabrice Defferard, *Le droit selon Star Trek* (Mare Martin, Paris, 2016). Other instances of a description of the equivalent of the Prime Directive and the clash with situational ethics include the novel by Arkady Strugatsky and Boris Strugatsky, *Hard to be a God* (Gateway, Huntingdon, 2015) pp. 37–38.

 | DOI:10.1163/9789004677708_008

Recent events in Ukraine since February 2022 should also give us ample cause to disabuse ourselves of the romantic notion that the example of the United Nations could serve as an indicator of how peaceful interspecies diplomatic relations and conflict resolution mechanisms might be established and upheld, as, for example, in Star Trek's Federation of Planets. The convenient SETI (and METI) narrative that advanced ETI will by necessity have passed through the "Great Filter" of not destroying themselves and thus will have abandoned the aggressive traits of their nature is not based on evidence and ultimately wishful thinking, as we discussed earlier in the section on metalaw. The very possibility of the idea of a Federation of distinct species with the function of a joint defence platform against other advanced spacefaring species would also seem to belie the imagined rationale behind the benevolent alien hypothesis. The alternative of another Great Filter, namely interstellar Darwinism, is equally likely: Human history as the only example we have so far has shown that many technological advancements have had their origin in military applications, and quite often were developed in actual wartime periods. There is no reason to think that similar circumstances might not apply to the species trajectory of advanced ETI. It is also too simplistic to assume a steady linear upwards trend in any form of species development, technological or ethical, when the human historical evidence on the grand scale would tend to suggest a more cyclical model, or that of the pendulum swinging back and forth between the extreme ends of a spectrum.

Finally, John Wright[2] in his book on deep space warfare has flagged up a number of ultimately interlinked issues that would very likely hinder attempts at diplomatic efforts. These range from the biological impediments to interstellar communication, i.e., possible aspects around the lifetime of the "correspondents" based on the time needed for message receipt and answer[3] each way, to finding incentives to stop fighting, especially if the reciprocal strangeness of the ETI and humans might lead to an overall atmosphere of hate and othering.[4] Wright rightly points out the limitations of any treaty-making endeavour, namely that the historical record of humans' compliance with treaties entered into among them is "bad" and that treaty enforcement across huge distances will be much more difficult.[5] The state of affairs could in his view very well develop into a kind of "Cold War" in space and lead to a semi-hostile distance.[6]

2 John C Wright, *Deep Space Warfare – Military Strategy Beyond Orbit* (McFarland, Jefferson, 2020 – hereafter *Deep Space Warfare*).

3 *Deep Space Warfare*, p. 173.

4 *Deep Space Warfare*, pp. 175–176.

5 *Deep Space Warfare*, pp. 176–177.

6 *Deep Space Warfare*, pp. 178–179.

All these feasibility caveats notwithstanding: From the point of view of humans as individual members of the human species, it is imperative that any negotiated relationship with ETI, should it come to pass, must not impact on their freedoms as imagined and developed by human society across the centuries. Making contact with an advanced civilisation or even a network of them must not result in a retrograde development in individual rights unless new restrictions would appear to be absolutely non-negotiable if humanity wanted to join the network and reap the advantages of membership. What would we be willing to trade for the prospect of the solution to the manifold problems besetting humanity on its home planet? This is where the so far neglected aspect of traditional human rights protections becomes highly relevant, and we turn to it now.

2 Joining the "Galactic Club" – a Future Theory of Humans' Rights Protection in Interstellar Civilisation Networks?[7]

Will contact with extraterrestrial intelligence (ETI) "render us heirs to a galactic culture", and will it "set us on a new and higher path", as Ronald N. Bracewell asked in the final chapter of his book "The Galactic Club"?[8] If, as Michael A.G. Michaud wrote, we "encounter civilizations that already have formed a Galactic Club [and who] offer us an interstellar legal framework", would we accede to it, knowing that it might "require significant changes in our own laws"?[9] Is the scenario of humanity speaking "with many voices [while] congruent with individual rights and cultural diversity [...] [possibly] bad policy" in an interstellar and interspecies context?[10] Can there be a joint view of what a global human position should look like or is it factually – and legally – next to impossible to arrive at a grand consensus if we are currently nowhere near anything that resembles a unified world government? Is there any point in speculating at this time about basic rules of a joint cosmic metalaw, as has been done since

7 This section is a modified version of my article Michael Bohlander, Joining the "Galactic Club": What Price Admission? – A hypothetical case study of the impact of human rights on a future accession of humanity to interstellar civilisation networks, 132 *Futures* (2021) 102801, by kind permission of Elsevier.

8 Ronald N Bracewell, *The Galactic Club: Intelligent Life in Outer Space* (Norton & Co, London, 1976) p. 129.

9 Michael A G Michaud, 2010. C*ontact with Alien Civilizations – Our Hopes and Fears about Encountering Extraterrestrials* (Copernicus Books, New York, 2010 – hereafter Michaud) p. 375.

10 Michaud, p. 369.

the early second half of the 20th century, and pinning humanity's hopes for a contact event on the expectation that every ETI would more or less share its views?[11]

Even assuming that we were to meet highly advanced ETI who are altruistically minded and basically benign in nature, would their understanding of these terms be identical to ours? It does not take references to Science Fiction classics such as *The Day the Earth Stood Still*[12] to realise the banal insight that altruism can be directed at varying beneficiaries with varying degrees of primacy. More to the point of this chapter, would they, for example, equally cherish concepts such as individualism and minority protection, as is the case in many if not most of the current human rights regimes on Earth, or will they consider striving for forms of collective-minded frameworks or even of forms of collective consciousness preferable?[13] Will such collective entities view

11 See Andrew G Haley, Space Law and Metalaw – A Synoptic View, Harvard Law Record, November 8, 1956; id., Space Law and Government (Appleton-Century-Crofts, New York, 1963 – hereafter Haley); Ernst Fasan, *Weltraumrecht* (Krausskopf-Flugwelt-Verlag, Cologne, 1965) pp. 141–154; *id., Relations with Alien Intelligences: The Scientific Basis of Metalaw* (Berlin Verlag, Berlin, 1970 – cited after the version printed in Patricia M Stearns and Leslie I Tennen, Leslie (eds.), *Private Law, Public Law, Metalaw and Public Policy in Space,* Springer, New York, 2016) pp 181–246; *id.,* Discovery of ETI: Terrestrial and Extraterrestrial Legal Implications, 21 *Acta Astronautica* (1990) 131–135; *id.*, Legal Consequences of a SETI Detection, 42 *Acta Astronautica* (1998) 677– 679. Overview of the literature in George S Robinson, METALAW: From Speculation to Humankind Legal Posturing with Extraterrestrial Life, 2 *Journal of Space Philosophy* (2013) 49–56, Adam Korbitz, IAC-10-A4.2.10 – Metalaw and the Need for Further Elaboration, 2010 (unpublished paper kindly provided courtesy of the author) and *id.*, Altruism, Metalaw, and Celegistics: An Extraterrestrial Perspective on Universal Law-Making, in Douglas A. Vakoch (ed.) *Extraterrestrial Altruism* (Springer, New York, 2014) pp. 231–247.

12 The two movies of that title from 1951 and 2008 are loosely based on the 1940 short story by Harry Bates, Farewell to the Master, 1940 Astounding Science Fiction, October issue, https://web.archive.org/web/20140727101426/http://thenostalgialeague.com/olmag/bates-farewell-to-the-master.html.

13 The issue of collective decision-making etc. is already currently being studied under the term of "eusociality", Nicola Plowes, 2010. An Introduction to Eusociality 3(10) *Nature Education Knowledge* (2010) 7, www.nature.com/scitable/knowledge/library/an-introduction-to-eusociality-15788128/. On some tendencies in 20th century SF literature of moving away from individualism as an unassailable civilisational requirement see, for example, Michael Bohlander, Blood Music on Darwin's Radio – Musings on Social Network Data Transparency, Cyborg Technology, Science Fiction and the Future Perception of Human Rights, *The Global Community Yearbook of International Law & Jurisprudence* (2013) 45–64 (hereafter: Bohlander, Blood Music) at 50–51: "It seems telling that apart from the dystopian segment of the genre such as *1984* and the like, which warns about a *Gleichschaltung* of all individuals into a mass of indistinguishable social automatons, there is another stream of thought that addresses the matter from the point of view of the next step in

non-collective life-forms as truly sapient and on an equal moral footing with themselves at all – or would the oft-cited image of the human attitude to ants prevail?[14] As the author queried elsewhere, even the human debate of the subject has been, and continues to be, far from uniform or static:

> Transposed to our current stage of species development, this may translate into increasingly questioning the old concerns over protecting human dignity, individuality, and personal autonomy vis-a-vis the demands of the collective and emphasising that the good of the whole and the goal of peaceful co-existence of all members of a community supersede the need for concepts such as a presumption of innocence and the attendant restrictions on intrusions by the collective, when it becomes ever more apparent that we may be on the path to redefining human and personal dignity and autonomy, this time not in an ideologically forced conversion to the interests of the whole as occurred during the time of the authoritarian regimes of the last century, such as, for example, the Nazi regime's *Volk* concept, but based on a paradigm shift in our own perception triggered by our immersion in the new and rapidly evolving environment of the 'freedom of information society'.[15]

human evolution which is meant to go towards a collective consciousness, sometimes called a hive mind. In such a hive mind, every member of the hive is connected to everyone else and knows everything about every member of the collective, in effect making any idea such as the presumption of innocence or a right to privacy in general into largely meaningless concepts. While we are, of course, nowhere near accomplishing such a state of mental unity and may well never reach it, the point of interest is that humanity's striving for and reaching such a state is mostly if not uniformly presented as something desirable by the relevant authors, as a higher state of existence worth striving for – as opposed, for example, to the forced assimilation strategy embraced by *Star Trek's Next Generation's Borg.* [...] Nonetheless, cyborg technology, especially in the form of surgically embedded communication implants, may soon bring us closer to such a state of affairs than we currently think". – Italics in the original, footnotes omitted.

14 Again, SF writing provides hypothetical scenarios worth considering. Orson Scott Card, at the end of his novel *Ender's Game*, has the Hive Queen of the alien species who tried to colonise Earth and killed millions in the process say: "We did not mean to murder, and when we understood, we never came again. We thought we are the only thinking beings in the universe, until we met you, but never did we dream that thought could arise from the lonely animals who cannot dream each other's dreams. How were we to know?" – Orson Scott Card, *Ender's Game,* 1st ed. 1977 (Cited after Author's Definitive Edition, Tor Books, New York, 1994) p. 321.

15 Bohlander, Blood Music, 51. – Italics in the original, footnotes omitted.

Aspects of questions connected to the consequences for human society of contact with ETI like these have been hinted at in the literature[16] in a generic sense but an analysis of the nuts and bolts, as it were, and above all of the costs to human identity, of taking out membership in the Galactic Club has so far not been attempted. This may hardly be surprising, given that no-one would appear to see a pressing need for answering such questions, because the general public – and quite possibly also the mainstream academic – consensus seems to be that musing about contact with ETI at such a level, if not simply discarded as a figment of the febrile hallucinations by "alien hunters",

16 See, for example, Mark Neal, Preparing for extraterrestrial contact, 16 *Risk Management* (2014) 63–87; Thomas Moynihan, Existential risk and human extinction: An intellectual history, 116 *Futures* (2020) 102495; Alexey Turchin and David Denkenberger, Global catastrophic and existential risks communication scale, 102 Futures (2018) 27–38; Allen E. Goodman, Diplomatic and political problems affecting the formulation and implementation of an international protocol for activities following the detection of a signal from extraterrestrial intelligence, 21 *Acta Astronautica* (1990) 103-108; *id.*, Diplomacy and the search of extraterrestrial intelligence (SETI), 21 Acta Astronautica (1990) 137-141; Karim Jebaria and Niklas Olsson-Yaouzis, A Game of Stars: Active SETI, radical translation and the Hobbesian trap, 101 *Futures* (2018) 46–54; Janne M Korhonen, 2013. MAD with aliens? Interstellar deterrence and its implications, 86 *Acta Astronautica* (2013) 201–210; Joao Pedro de Magalhaes, A direct communication proposal to test the Zoo Hypothesis, 38 *Space Policy* (2016) 22–26; James D Millera, and D Felton, Thc Fermi paradox, Bayes' rule, and existential risk management. 86 *Futures* (2017) 44–57; Gabriel G de la Torre, Toward a new cosmic consciousness: Psychoeducational aspects of contact with extraterrestrial civilizations, 94 *Acta Astronautica* (2014) 577–583; Douglas A Vakoch et al., What should we say to extraterrestrial intelligence?: An analysis of responses to "Earth Speaks", 86 *Acta Astronautica* (2013) 136–148; Seth D Baum, The far future argument for confronting catastrophic threats to humanity: Practical significance and alternatives, 72 *Futures* (2015) 86–96; Joseph Voros, On a morphology of contact scenario space, *Technological Forecasting & Social Change* (2018) 126–137; Ivan Almár and Margaret S Race, Discovery of extra-terrestrial life: assessment by scales of its importance and associated risks, 369 *Phil. Trans. R. Soc. A* (2011) 679–692; Martin Dominik and John C Zarnecki, The detection of extra-terrestrial life and the consequences for science and society, 369 *Phil. Trans. R. Soc. A* (2011) 499–507; Albert A Harrison, Fear, pandemonium, equanimity and delight: human responses to extra-terrestrial life, 369 *Phil. Trans. R. Soc. A* (2011) 656–668; *id.*, Proximity, System Level, and Human Response to Extraterrestrial Life, in: Workshop on the societal implications of astrobiology – Final Report, Ames Research Center, November 16–17, 1999; in NASA, *Workshop on the societal implications of Astrobiology*, 1999, p. 56, www.astrosociology.org/library/pdf/nasa-workshop-report-societal-implications-of-astrobiology.pdf.; Simon Conway Morris, Predicting what extra-terrestrials will be like: and preparing for the worst, 369 *Phil. Trans. R. Soc. A* (2011) 555–571; Mazlan Othman, Supra-Earth affairs, 369 *Phil. Trans. R. Soc. A* (2011) 693–699; Ted Peters, The implications of the discovery of extra-terrestrial life for religion, 369 *Phil. Trans. R. Soc. A* (2011) 644–655; Christopher P Mackay, The search for life in our Solar System and the implications for science and society, 369 *Phil. Trans. R. Soc. A* (2011) 594–606.

"UFOlogists" or at best overzealous SF enthusiasts, would mean wasting political energy on something that is very unlikely to happen anytime soon, if at all:[17] After all, SETI in its many variations has been going on for decades without any tangible results to show for, especially as far as the regions of space close to the Earth's solar system are concerned. Furthermore, until contact occurs we will not know the extent of ETI's strangeness[18] compared to ourselves and hence such ideas are unwarranted speculation.

However, to repeat the gist of what was said before, that argument, while understandable from a point of view of purely pragmatic priorities, appears short-sighted in principle for a number of reasons. Firstly, the fact that so far hard evidence of the existence of ETI continues to elude human science is neither here nor there: Absence of evidence is not evidence of absence. Secondly, given the still relatively narrow search parameters of traditional, mainly radioastronomy-oriented SETI and the state of human technological advancement, we may have been missing evidence so far because the search concentrated on the "wrong" regions of space, looked for the wrong signal indicators, omitted the proper advancement of the search for extraterrestrial artefacts (SETA),[19] or because we are as yet technologically unable to detect the evidence. Thirdly, even if humanity was to make an effort at establishing a joint position, the complex negotiations would take a very long time, if current purely terrestrial politics and diplomacy are anything to go by. Fourthly, and *horribile dictu* for any member of the traditionally conservative and reputationally risk-averse[20] SETI

---

17 See on the timescale argument Seth D Baum, The far future argument for confronting catastrophic threats to humanity: Practical significance and alternatives, 72 *Futures* (2015) 86–96.

18 On the discussion of strangeness in the context of ETI, see Michael Schetsche and Andreas Anton, Die *Gesellschaft der Außerirdischen – Einführung in die Exosoziologie* (Springer, Wiesbaden, 2019 – hereafter: Schetsche/Anton) p. 16.; Wilhelm Vossenkuhl, Jenseits des Vertrauten und Fremden, in Odo Marquard (ed.) *Einheit und Vielfalt*, (Meiner Hamburg, 1990), pp. 101–113, at 109; Herfried Münkler and Bernd Ladwig, Dimensionen der Fremdheit, in Herfried Münkler (ed.) *Furcht und Faszination – Facetten der Fremdheit*, (Akademia, Berlin, 1997) pp. 11–43; Georg Simmel, *Soziologie: Untersuchungen über die Formen der Vergesellschaftung*, 4th ed. (Duncker & Humblot, Berlin, 1958) p. 509.

19 A relatively recent and documented example from the year 2000 is the still unexplained anomaly of a prima facie artificial-looking object 45 m across in size, photographed by the NEAR Shoemaker probe during its mission to 433Eros; see Chapter 2 text and footnote at Figure 2.1. A second probe could bring clarification but, of course, that would be very expensive and is probably not high on NASA's or anyone's list of mission priorities, but that may change with the new emphasis on UAP research.

20 See, for example, Avi Loeb, *Extraterrestrial: The First Sign of Intelligent Life Beyond Earth* (Houghton Mifflin Harcourt, Boston/New York, 2021) pp. 101–102: "[T]he explicit and

community,[21] all of this discounts the remote possibility that there might be some truth to even a vanishingly small number of reports about unexplained aerial phenomena (UAP) or UFOs, meaning contact may already have occurred in the past and humanity was caught unprepared.[22] Steven J. Dick was thus correct when he said that "the possibility of contact is a strong argument that some form of metalaw must be developed in order to deal with interactions with aliens"[23] and "[m]eeting the alien will be an experience we cannot afford to mismanage. In so many ways and more than ever, failure is not an option".[24]

This chapter will contribute to closing at least part of the gap by addressing one facet of human normativity that will inevitably exert a major influence on any negotiations with ETI, be it purely bilateral or multilateral as in the Galactic Club scenario: Human rights law. The nigh-total absence of this particular field of law in any SETI-related legal or ethical research, for example, in the metalaw debate, has been conspicuous and at least given the current state of affairs regarding its level of sophistication, that is difficult to explain.[25] The chapter can, of course, do no more than offer first reflections meant to help shape the future debate, hence "prolegomena" is used here in the literal sense as introductory comments.[26] Yet, it will try to chart a course across the existing

---

implicit encouraging of conservative science is both depressing and concerning, given the extent of anomalies the universe still contains. While it is not obvious to me why extraordinary claims require extraordinary evidence (evidence is evidence, no?), I do believe that extraordinary conservatism keeps us extraordinarily ignorant. Put differently, the field doesn't need more cautious detectives".

21 The terms of reference of the IAASETI Permanent Committee, for example, state: "These terms of reference exclude any consideration of UFO phenomena", https://iaaseti.org/en/terms-reference/.

22 It should be remembered, however, that even serious and above all sceptical research conducted in this area has failed to discredit every incident of direct contact reports; see, for example, Leslie Kean, 2010. *UFOs – Generals, Pilots and Government Officials Go on the Record* (Three Rivers Press, New York, 2010); Michaud, pp. 143–161.

23 Steven J. Dick 2018. *Astrobiology, Discovery, and Societal Impact* (CUP, Cambridge, 2018 – hereafter: Dick, Astrobiology) p. 301 – He does, however, not seem to have understood "metalaw" in the sense advocated by Haley and Fasan but more in the meaning of a *human* meta-legal construct which can serve as a point of departure for the conversation with ETI.

24 Dick, Astrobiology, p. 302.

25 Francis Lyall and Paul B Larsen, *Space Law – A Treatise*, 2nd ed. (Routledge, Abingdon, 2018) p. 131.

26 It is certainly not meant to be at the level of Kant's famous Prolegomena to Any Future Metaphysics of 1783, which was de facto an ex-post guide to his Critique of Pure Reason. – Immanuel Kant, *Prolegomena to Any Future Metaphysics That Will Be Able to Come Forward as Science*, Revised ed. (Trans. Gary Hatfield, CUP, Cambridge, 2004).

terrain of human rights law, looking at the fundamental aspects of individual human rights guarantees and how they might be affected by contact with an interstellar legal regime. Are there negotiable aspects that we might be willing to trade away? What if the Galactic Club rules demand certain concessions humanity is not prepared to make? The term "*human* rights" is thus taking on a new and potentially a distinctly and substantially different meaning. We will also have to realise that in real-world legal practice the devil is often in the detail and that general and fulsome declarations about the expected interspecies comity among advanced civilisations may still run afoul of even benign and advanced individual species' cherished moral, ethical and legal traditions. Early reflection on these matters would therefore seem wise in order to lay the groundwork for any actual occurrence of, and need for, effective and efficient trans-species conversations about the crucial factors determining individual species, in this case human, identity. This not made easier by the unsurprising realisation that humanity is currently still far away from developing a cosmic species awareness, possibly because it has yet to meet the "other" in an unequivocally verified and incontrovertible fashion.[27]

On a terminological note, the chapter deliberately does not employ words like "organisation", "empire" etc., because they have a tendency of carrying certain connotations from human traditions, social constructs, and positionalities, such as hierarchical power structures, distribution of portfolios and responsibilities etc. It seems more appropriate to refer to the more neutral concept of a network which allows for the expression of some form of coordination but leaves its precise nature open. As the author has shown previously in the context of the discussion between Islamic law and secular legal systems, the idea of a loose network of corresponding sources based on the botanical feature of root webs or "rhizomes" as an avenue to constructing an overarching legal framework can also be found in human intercultural legal discourse.[28] In fact, such an interstellar network might well be the ultimate example of a Foucauldian *Heterotopia*.[29] Moreover, in an interspecies context, the term "human rights" obviously makes no sense anymore, either, and should thus be

27 See on this Dick, Astrobiology, pp. 310–311, and more broadly pp. 209–239.

28 Michael Bohlander, Sisters in Law – Using Maqāṣid al-Shari'ah to Advance the Conversation between Islamic and Secular Legal Thinking, 28 *Arab Law Quarterly* (2014) 257–277, at 271–272; on the difficulties of putting this approach into practice *id.*, Of Higher Intentions and Lower Expectations – A report about a failed survey project on using maqāṣid al-shari'ah as a means of comparative governance research, 2 *European Journal of Comparative Law and Governance* (2015) 187–211.

29 Michel Foucault, 2001. *Des espaces autres in: Dits et écrits, vol. II, 1976–1988* (Gallimard, Paris, 2001) pp. 1571–1581; English translation: Michel Foucault, *Of other spaces, 1967*, in

replaced with "humans' rights" to signify that the debate is about the position of humans as a species in the network.

2.1 *Overview of Possible Factors Affecting Human Rights Guarantees*

We shall look at some fundamental issues that may as a rule develop an impact in the context of reconciling differing systems of rights protection. The selection does, however, not claim to be comprehensive.

2.1.1 Network Regulation Density

An interstellar civilisational network that supplies its own legal framework to candidates and expects adherence from member civilisations may, of course, take different approaches to regulation density. It may, on the one hand, regulate even the most minute details of its members' legal rights and obligations, making the network into a de facto centralist form of governance, or a federation with strong central powers. It may, on the other hand, take the approach seen in some of human colonial history with the human colonisers only legislating in certain areas relevant to a smooth functioning of public life such as, for example, criminal law, tax law, administrative law etc., while leaving the local population a wide margin of discretion to regulate their own affairs in personal matters such as family law, law of succession, religious matters etc. Depending on the model adopted, different areas of freedom might be affected, and to differing degrees. Civilisations which do not subscribe to any concept of personal freedom and of individual rights as a defence against government intrusion at all may form networks which cater for that attitude and admit newcomers only if they are able and willing to support the collectivist framework unreservedly.

The presumption, however, would appear to point in the direction of minimum intrusion across different species and their civilisations if membership is voluntary and a choice of degree of involvement is available, in a sense, as in the European Union's (EU) general policy movement to an ever closer union, which, however, some (former) EU member states have historically resisted:

> The Heads of State or Government, on the basis of an awareness of a common destiny and the wish to affirm the European identity, confirm their commitment to progress towards an ever closer union among the peoples and Member States of the European Community.[30]

M. Dehaene & L. De Cauter (eds.) *Heterotopia and the City* (Routledge, London/New York, 2008) pp. 13–30.

30 European Council, Solemn Declaration on European Union, [1983] *Bulletin of the European Communities* 6-1983, 25–29.

As the solemn declaration of the European Council from 1983 makes clear by extrapolation, two of the central issues for the degree of any network coherence will be the strength of the desire for, and the awareness of, a common destiny and a joint identity. The one does not necessarily imply the other, especially if one imagines an interstellar network spanning several solar systems possibly light years apart – assuming for argument's sake that the technological interstellar travel and communication problems based on the lightspeed barrier have been solved in an acceptable manner by all member civilisations and potential candidates, which is a factor that would indeed rule out humanity's (full) accession to any such multilateral network for the foreseeable future, even if contact was made, absent any transfer of advanced knowledge by the ETI. The issue arguably remains live at the shorter term, however, for bilateral relationships with ETI capable of visiting Earth on a sustained level.

2.1.2 Rights Hierarchies and Enforcement Mechanisms

Humanity has developed a number of regional and universal human rights regimes with different enforcement mechanisms and also different levels of subscription by states, which are after all the actors on the stage of international law. In addition, each state will typically have a civil liberties or fundamental rights section in its constitution, the domestic equivalent to international human rights. In some cases, these may remain below the level of protection guaranteed by a human rights convention, in some cases they may go beyond it. The relationship of the domestic constitution as being typically the highest law of the land to any international obligations the state may have entered into is another problem area. Some of the laws of the EU – which was not originally designed as a human rights protection framework and only developed its own Charter of Fundamental Rights decades after its inception[31] – have supranational character, i.e., they *eo ipso* supersede every domestic law of a member state.[32] Generally, international treaties, agreements or customary law have no such supranational effect. Lastly, if a state is based on a federal model of some sort, the member states may have their own constitutions and cases of conflict between the federal and the state level may be solved in different ways, depending on which one must give deference to the other. The German constitution, the Basic Law (*Grundgesetz* – GG), for example, contains a very strong protection of human dignity (*Menschenwürde*) in Art. 1(1) GG, which reads:

31 Charter of Fundamental Rights of the European Union, https://eur-lex.europa.eu/eli/treaty/char_2012/oj.

32 See the landmark decision of the European Court of Justice in *Costa v E.N.E.L.* of 15 July 1964, https://eur-lex.europa.eu/legal-content/EN/TXT/?uri=CELEX:61964CJ0006.

Article 1

(1) Human dignity shall be inviolable. To respect and protect it shall be the duty of all state authority.[33]

The protection of human dignity as a separate right as such[34] is, for example, not guaranteed in this stark form in one of the most sophisticated existing human rights frameworks, the European Convention on Human Rights (ECHR),[35] of which Germany is also a member and which according to the case law of the German Federal Constitutional Court (*Bundesverfassungsgericht*) otherwise informs even the interpretation of the Basic Law.[36] The German Court has also in a line of cases, the so-called "*Solange*" (meaning "as long as") jurisprudence, reserved its power to scrutinise even legislation made in the jurisdictional framework of the EU against the Basic Law, as long as the EU protection does not reach that of the Basic Law, and not only on the basis of its civil liberties section.[37] The German Court, akin to its American counterpart, the United States Supreme Court, has the power to strike down even acts of parliament for violations of the Basic Law – which to repeat it, is to be interpreted in line with the ECHR as far as possible.

Conversely, the United Kingdom when introducing the Human Rights Act 1998 (HRA), in essence stated that the British courts needed take the settled

33 Basic Law for the Federal Republic of Germany, www.gesetze-im-internet.de/englisch_gg/englisch_gg.html#p0019.

34 Which led the German Constitutional Court to declare in 2005 that it would violate human dignity if in a 9/11 scenario a plane carrying a few hundred passengers who were about to die in any event, was to be shot down in order to avoid it crashing into an office building with many thousands of people. The argument was that human lives cannot be measured in numbers. See for further details and a critique Michael Bohlander, In Extremis – Hijacked airplanes, 'collateral damage' and the limits of criminal law, *Criminal Law Review* (2006) 579–592; *id.*, Of shipwrecked sailors, unborn children, conjoined twins and hijacked airplanes – Taking human life and the defence of necessity, 70 *Journal of Criminal Law* (2006) 147–161.

35 European Convention on Human Rights, www.echr.coe.int/documents/convention_eng.pdf.

36 BVerfGE vol. 111, 307 (317); vol. 131, 286, (295).

37 *Solange I*, Decision of 29 April 1974, BVerfGE vol. 37, 271 = 2 *CMLR* (1974) 540; *Solange II*, Decision of 22 October 1986, BVerfGE vol. 73, 339 = 3 *CMLR* (1987) 225; an overview of the development of the case law of the Bundesverfassugsgericht until September 2020 can be found in Sebastian Bering, *Solange bis Vergessen – Kritische Analyse der Entwicklung und gegenwärtigen Position der BVerfG-Rechtsprechung zum Verhältnis von EU-Recht und den Grundrechten des Grundgesetzes,* Beiträge zum Europa-und Völkerrecht, vol. 21 (University of Halle-Wittenberg, Halle, 2020), https://tietje.jura.uni-halle.de/sites/default/files/BeitraegeEVR/Heft_21_Bering.pdf.

jurisprudence of the Convention's guardian, the European Court of Human Rights (ECtHR), into account as much as possible in the interpretation of domestic law (section 3 of the HRA)[38] but even a declaration of incompatibility under section 4(6) of the HRA[39] did not have the effect of making the legislation void, nor was the finding even binding on the parties to the case in which it was made. This was the effect of the British view on the absolute sovereignty of Parliament: British courts have no strike-down power with respect to parliamentary or secondary legislation.[40] Recourse to the ECtHR by an individual citizen or resident against the member state is available but even a judgment in favour of the plaintiff would not directly affect the domestic validity of the impugned piece of legislation and it would ultimately be up to the state to adapt its laws to Convention standards.

Similarly broad spectrums and constellations of interdependent and interlacing normative hierarchies as well as varying forms of (quasi-)judicial enforcement mechanisms in the wider sense, with a broad range of powers of intervention of differing degrees of impact on the affairs either of the network as such or those of its members, could reasonably be expected to exist in other rights-based civilisations who are members of an interstellar network adhering to some form of trans-species rule of law – something which could then begin to resemble a *negotiated* metalaw that Haley and Fasan, for example, wrote about in the last century mainly on the basis of extrapolations from Kantian philosophy. Hence it stands to reason that any galactic club of the law-based nature we are interrogating here would very likely have made provision for all of these eventualities – although that does not mean it would have to or even wish to accommodate any and all species idiosyncrasies, even if they are as basic, for example, as the time-honoured principle of the separation of powers, or checks and balances, may appear to many humans. It also needs to be pointed out that some human constitutions provide for a difference in protection depending on whether the person is a full citizen or merely a resident; it can easily be imagined that this might apply *mutatis mutandis* to a member of one species living under the jurisdiction of another. In other words, the legal system of the network may in effect not look like anything humans would recognise as a familiar manner of arriving at an intelligible moral, let alone legal,

38 Human Rights Act 1998, www.legislation.gov.uk/ukpga/1998/42/section/3.

39 Human Rights Act 1998, www.legislation.gov.uk/ukpga/1998/42/section/4.

40 On the general question of which understanding of human rights underlies the UK system, see the revealing paper by Benedict Douglas, Too Attentive to our Duty: The Fundamental Conflict Underlying Human Rights Protection in the UK, 38 *Legal Studies* (2018) 360–378.

set of principles. Robert A. Heinlein, for example, has one of the protagonists say this about the fictional Martian species in his novel *Double Star* in 1956:

> They are a very old race and they have worked out a system of debts and obligations to cover every possible situation – the greatest formalists conceivable. Compared with them, the ancient Japanese with their *giri* and *gimu,* were outright anarchists. Martians don't have 'right' and 'wrong' – instead they have propriety and impropriety, squared, cubed.[41]

2.2 *Individual Rights*

Humanity, as was already indicated, has developed a number of universal[42] and regional general human rights regimes, among them the ECHR. There are also, for example, the Universal Declaration of Human Rights (UDHR),[43] the International Covenant on Civil and Political Rights (ICCPR),[44] the American Convention on Human Rights,[45] the Cairo Declaration on Human Rights in Islam,[46] the Universal Islamic Declaration of Human Rights,[47] the Arab Charter on Human Rights,[48] the African Charter on Human and Peoples' Rights[49] and the ASEAN Human Rights Declaration.[50] It is outside the scope of this book to

41 Robert A Heinlein, *Double Star,* 1st ed. 1956 (cited after Gollancz. London, 2013) p. 54. – On the Japanese terms of *giri* and *gimu,* see Jim Caldwell and Shin Ryu Kan, Japanese Philosophy: Giri 義理, 2016, http://kenukan.com/blog/2016/10/12/japanese-philosophy-giri/.

42 When we talk about "universal" instruments, we must, however, not forget the debate about human rights relativism which queries whether a concept such as universally accepted rights does even exist. See, for example, R J Vincent, *Human Rights and International Relations* (CUP, Cambridge, 2009); Andreas Follesdal, Human Rights and Relativism, in A Follesdal and T W Pogge (eds.), *Real World Justice – Grounds, Principles, Human Rights, and Social Institutions,* (Springer, New York, 2005) pp. 265–283.

43 Uiversal Declaration of Human Rights, www.ohchr.org/EN/UDHR/Documents/UDHR_Translations/eng.pdf.

44 International Covenant on Civil and Political Rights, www.ohchr.org/en/professionalinterest/pages/ccpr.aspx.

45 American Convention on Human Rights, www.cidh.oas.org/basicos/english/basic3.american%20convention.htm.

46 Cairo Declaration on Human Rights in Islam, 5 August 1990, (English Translation). http://hrlibrary.umn.edu/instree/cairodeclaration.html.

47 Universal Islamic Declaration of Human Rights. 1981, www.alhewar.com/ISLAMDECL.html.

48 Arab Charter on Human Rights http://hrlibrary.umn.edu/instree/loas2005.html.

49 African Charter on Human and Peoples' Rights. https://au.int/en/treaties/african-charter-human-and-peoples-rights.

50 Asean Human Rights Declaration, https://asean.org/asean-human-rights-declaration/.

list and analyse any and all of these in detail,[51] and as far as the generic fundamental rights are concerned, there is a lot of overlap in any event. Human rights courts and bodies often look to each other's decisions for argumentative support and persuasive authority. The following discussion could have been guided by the UDHR as the original and most programmatic statement which, although not legally binding, seems to enjoy wide global support. Yet, its incarnation in the ICCPR of 1966, which *is* legally binding and as of September 2019 had 173 parties and six further signatories,[52] comes closest to a document representing an approximation to the legal views of the entire human species, even bearing in mind the manifold reservations individual states have made. We shall thus look, in the necessary brevity, at the Preamble and the material rights provisions of Articles 1–27 ICCPR, omitting the procedural part from Article 28 onwards.[53] The rights will be clustered into broadly cognate categories rather than examining them in turn by their numerical sequence.

One final caveat, however, is apposite at this juncture, before we proceed. The entire exercise is dependent on whether and to what extent ETI recognise the concept of a "right", i.e., in very simple[54] terms the claim of a person that goes beyond a mere moral obligation on the part of the debtor and to which attaches the power of some form of enforcement against the will of the latter,

---

51 For a non-exhaustive overview of further universal human rights instruments and further links to relevant sites, see www.ohchr.org/en/instruments-listings.

52 With the notable absence of one permanent member of the UN Security Council, namely the People's Republic of China. – Ratification status at United Nations, International Convention on civil and Political rights, signatory status, https://treaties.un.org/doc/Publication/MTDSG/Volume%20I/Chapter%20IV/IV-4.en.pdf.

53 The analysis will not engage in the details of the interpretation the individual elements of the provisions have found in the human context, as this would be far beyond the scope of this chapter. Further reading can be found in the commentaries on the ICCPR, for example, Paul M Taylor, *A Commentary on the International Covenant on Civil and Political Rights: The UN Human Rights Committee's Monitoring of ICCPR Rights,* (CUP, Cambridge, 2020 – hereafter: Taylor, ICCPR) which will be cited here as authority; William A Schabas, *Nowak's ICCPR Commentary: U.N. International Covenant on Civil and Political Rights*, 3rd ed. (N. P. Engel, Kehl, 2019); Sarah Joseph and Melissa Castan, *The International Covenant on Civil and Political Rights: Cases, Materials, and Commentary,* 3rd ed. (OUP, Oxford, 2013). An explanation of the ECHR can be found in Bernadette Rainey et al. *Jacobs, White, and Ovey: The European Convention on Human Rights,* 8th ed. (OUP, Oxford, 2021); William A Schabas, *The European Convention on Human Rights: A Commentary* (OUP, Oxford, 2015); Christoph Grabenwarter, *European Convention on Human Rights – Commentary,* (CH Beck, Munich, 2014).

54 See for an introduction to the different understandings and meaning of the term "right" and a list of further reading the Stanford Encyclopedia of Philosophy, online at Stanford Encyclopedia of Philosophy, 2020, *Rights,* https://plato.stanford.edu/entries/rights/.

even if the debtor is the collective or the entity exercising the role of governance, and vice-versa that of a "duty". Here again, different levels of rights-based relations might arise: While a civilisation structured as an integrated collective consciousness, for example, a hive mind, may have no use for the concept of the rights of its members, it may still support the notion of one hive having rights against other hives or other civilisations, or indeed against the network. Relations between networks, unless there is a simultaneous and at least partial vertical subordination of a series of networks to a higher-ranking network (see the EU example above), would probably tend to be on the level of what humans would call international political relations, including treaties among equals or possibly simple power politics, rather than rights. But the above examples shall suffice for the caveat – there is such a thing as too much conjecture.

2.2.1 Preamble

The Preamble sets out the fundamental principles upon which the parties to the ICCPR agreed to its provisions, namely

> [R]ecognition of the inherent dignity and of the equal and inalienable rights of all members of the human family is the foundation of freedom, justice and peace in the world,
>
> Recognizing that these rights derive from the inherent dignity of the human person,
>
> Recognizing that [...] the ideal of free human beings enjoying civil and political freedom and freedom from fear and want can only be achieved if conditions are created whereby everyone may enjoy his civil and political rights, as well as his economic, social and cultural rights,
>
> Considering the obligation of States [...] to promote universal respect for, and observance of, human rights and freedoms,
>
> Realizing that the individual, having duties to other individuals and to the community to which he belongs, is under a responsibility to strive for the promotion and observance of the rights recognized in the present Covenant.

If – as we will do here merely once for the sake of illustration – one were to replace "human person" etc. in the ICCPR with a more generic term referring to a certain non-species-specific membership standard, such as, for example, something like "sapient *entity*" (to avoid stereotypes based on human attitudes to the concept of personhood), and "state" with "civilisation", the preamble could be rephrased into a text that would – if one wanted to look at a metalaw aspect for a moment – seem to evoke a rough framework concept capable of garnering the necessary "moral" respect in order to apply in a wider spectrum of rule-based interspecies environments, but more importantly – and given its origin, perhaps rather naturally – would not deviate from the essence of what humans[55] expect in their own species context:

> [R]ecognition of the inherent dignity and of the equal and inalienable rights of all sapient entities is the foundation of freedom, justice and peace in the universe,
>
> Recognizing that these rights derive from the inherent dignity of any sapient entity,
>
> Recognizing that [...] the ideal of free sapient entities enjoying civil and political freedom and freedom from fear and want can only be achieved if conditions are created whereby every sapient entity may enjoy their civil and political rights, as well as their economic, social and cultural rights,
>
> Considering the obligation of Civilisations [...] to promote universal respect for, and observance of, rights and freedoms of sapient entities,
>
> Realizing that any sapient entity, having duties to other sapient entities and to the community to which they belong, is under a responsibility to strive for the promotion and observance of the rights recognized in the present Covenant.

In fact, any detraction from such high-minded ideals would, in human terms, very likely render the network either fascist, dictatorial or colonialist/supremacist in nature and serve as a disincentive to humans, and possibly others, to consider joining the network at all. It stands to reason, however, that if the network was of such an aggressive nature, freedom of accession might be a moot point to begin with. It would seem that under the current human rights *acquis*, the rights cluster described above would fall among the non-negotiable parts of the human species identity (see also 2.2.3. below on self-determination and political activity).

2.2.2 Recognition as a Person before the Law

Closely related to the basic principles of personal freedom and agency enunciated in the Preamble, Article 16 ICCPR states that "[e]veryone shall have the right to recognition everywhere as a person before the law". This, together with

55 However, it may well be that other civilisations might go further in their approach than humans and grant some rights to sentient but not sapient entities, akin to the debate about animal rights.

the rules on slavery, servitude and compulsory labour in Article 8 (see below), for example, prohibits the treatment of humans as mere chattels or objects, rather than subjects, of the law in the wider sense; it does not prohibit making differences in the range of rights granted to citizens and residents, or discriminating on the basis of criteria such as age, mental health etc. in the context of civil law capacity, for example.[56] All rights in the ICCPR are ultimately based on the fundamental recognition of legal personhood. A civilisation network reserving the legal authority to withhold or withdraw legal agency from some of its members is always in danger of falling into fascist and exploitative models of governance, and the *factual* withdrawal of person status alone is often a precursor or corollary to genocide. Having full access to legal protection on the basis of personal agency would thus also seem to be a candidate for a non-negotiable position.

2.2.3 Self-determination, Political Activity

Article 1 ICCPR contains the right to a people's's[57] self-determination, and specific sub-categories of it, such as the exploitation of natural wealth and resources subject to agreements of economic co-operation based upon mutual benefit, as well as the prohibition on depriving a people of its means of subsistence. It would seem that in a mutually beneficial network based on voluntary accession, similar protections might be expected by any candidate species. The *actus contrarius* of the freedom of terminating one's membership should also be provided for under the statutes of the network – self-determination of a species would thus probably rank among non-negotiable positions.

The self-determination of a people is to a large extent based on the internal political processes of the state, and among those the political activity of its citizens, which is covered by Article 25 ICCPR;[58] the provision guarantees the right to vote and of access to public office. While clearly advocating a democratic style of governance, it does, however, not guarantee or require a specific form of government or citizen participation.[59] Yet, it would be fair to say that an absolute monarchy, dictatorship, theocratic government etc. without *any* form of citizen involvement would run afoul of Article 25. Hence, it seems that this particular right would tolerate quite some margin of variation, especially if the initial decision to accede to an interspecies network was made on the basis of

56 Taylor, ICCPR, pp. 445–446.
57 It is thus a collective right, and the only such right under the ICCPR – Taylor, ICCPR, p. 41.
58 Article 25 applies *strictu sensu* only to citizens. – Taylor, ICCPR, p. 693.
59 *Ibid.*

an encompassing species-wide vote, such as, for example, a referendum with a high qualified majority threshold.

2.2.4 Equality and Minority Rights

Articles 2 ICCPR forbids any discrimination on the basis of "race, colour, sex,[60] language, religion, political or other opinion, national or social origin, property, birth or other status", and requires member states to provide for an effective remedy in the case of a violation. Article 3 ICCPR repeats the equal treatment obligation explicitly for men and women. Article 26 ICCPR extends the guarantee to the equal protection of the law. Finally, Article 27 ICCPR, demands that "[i]n those States in which ethnic, religious or linguistic minorities exist, persons belonging to such minorities shall not be denied the right, in community with the other members of their group, to enjoy their own culture, to profess and practise their own religion, or to use their own language".

It would appear to be incontestable that given the – above all still imperfect – development of equality rights of the manner described in Article 2 ICCPR among the human species, any network rules lagging behind the human effort at maximum equality would violate fundamental principles espoused by humans, even if human practice leaves a lot to be desired. Linked in essence to the proper understanding of personhood, the essence of general species equality rights would appear to be non-negotiable.

However, while already at times shown to be difficult to comply with in practice within one country or species, the ethnic cultural, linguistic and religious minority rights under Article 27 ICCPR, or indeed the wider remit of Article 2 ICCPR already, – for example, such apparently perennially controversial issues as *halal* and *kosher* killing of animals, circumcision of young boys, pervasive harmful cultural practices as female genital mutilation (FGM) etc., to name but a few – might become even more of a problem in a multi-species environment, where deep-seated sensitivities in cross-species settings may prove to be more fundamental than the internal record of experience of the human species could lead humans to expect, and cause irreconcilable tensions. Similar issues will arise in the context of the partially overlapping areas of privacy, religious freedom, and freedom of speech rights under Articles 17–20 (see below). This

60 It is an interesting fact, however, that the ICCPR itself, even in 2021, does not use gender-inclusive language but employs the male (possessive) pronoun throughout in the section examined here. The words "she", "her" or "woman" do not appear even once, the term "women" only three times. While this may possibly be explained by the customs prevailing at the time of its drafting in 1966, it would not have been outlandish to expect a linguistic update in the decades that have since passed.

will especially become virulent in high regulation-density networks. While it is hard to conceive of a scenario where, for example, a ban on FGM – or its equivalent – or other practices that a species considers bodily or mentally harmful to its own members would face censure from the network, the picture becomes more blurred when – from a human point of view – non-harmful practices cause mental harm or serious offence to the members of another species in ways humans cannot comprehend or anticipate. We shall leave the thorny issue here, not least because any more detailed considerations would involve excessive speculation about a myriad of factors that are unknowable at this time and will remain so until contact is made, and mutual comprehension reached at a level where such conversations can be properly and meaningfully held between different species. Suffice it to say that this is an area where some give and take may become necessary that would seem intolerable to many in the purely human context.

2.2.5 Right to Life, Ban on Cruel and Degrading Treatment, Torture and Slavery

Articles 6–8 ICCPR address the "inherent" right to life, the protection against arbitrary killing and the death penalty (Article 6 ICCPR), the ban on torture and inhuman or degrading treatment (Article 7 ICCPR) and the ban on slavery and servitude (Article 8 ICCPR). It is important to note that the ICCPR does not require the abolition of the death penalty, even though the UN's political stance is clearly set against it.[61] It restricts it to the "most serious crimes" and puts certain procedural safeguards on its imposition and enforcement, especially against minors under 18 and pregnant women. However, the interpretation of what constitutes a "most serious crime" is not explained any further. Nonetheless, given the fact that the death penalty is still being imposed and enforced in otherwise enlightened states such as the USA, and in a number of other jurisdictions for a variety of crimes – leaving aside the specific issue of the in theory relatively quick trigger finger of religion-based legal systems such as Islamic Shariah for what are in part petty offences, or more to the point conduct which modern civilised nations no longer consider as justifying criminal liability – it is conceivable that joining a network which uses it might not necessarily fall foul of a clear and overwhelming majority view against the death penalty. Torture and similar acts of cruel and degrading treatment, as well as slavery, are now part and parcel of crimes against humanity in international

61 See only the United Nations Human Rights Office, Death penalty – Overview at www.ohchr.org/EN/Issues/DeathPenalty/Pages/DPIndex.aspx.

criminal law (see, for example, Article 7(1)(c), (f), (g) and (k) of the Statute of the International Criminal Court)[62] and the presumption would thus seem to be against any margin for negotiation.

2.2.6 Due Process Rights, Right to Liberty

Articles 9–11, 14 and 15 ICCPR deal with what are commonly called due process rights. Article 9 ICCPR on the liberty and security of the person requires certain safeguards for depriving a person of their liberty, while Article 10(1) ICCPR mandates that "[a]ll persons deprived of their liberty shall be treated with humanity and with respect for the inherent dignity of the human person". Article 11 bans the institution of the debtor's prison for people who cannot pay their debts arising from a contractual obligation – but does not necessarily prohibit what may be called civil contempt sanctions, such as, for example, for non-disclosure of assets at the request of a creditor in the German Code of Civil Procedure (*Zivilprozessordnung* – ZPO): Sections 802g and 802j ZPO allow for imprisonment of up to six months, but renewals are possible under certain conditions (sections 802j(3), 802d ZPO). Article 14 ICCPR is the fundamental rule on fair trial guarantees such as the presumption of innocence, speedy trial, assistance of counsel, *ne bis in idem* etc. Given that the ICCPR does not mandate a certain model of criminal proceedings (for example, adversarial or inquisitorial), and that comparative research across the world's criminal jurisdictions will easily show that there is a broad spectrum of manners in which a system can create compliance with the fair trial guarantees,[63] there would appear to be some leeway in which adaptation to an interspecies network's rules could occur. The same would seem to apply in the case of the ban on retroactive criminalisation or punishment for conduct which was not a crime at the time the conduct occurred, i.e., Article 15 ICCPR. Article 15(2) ICCPR contains the so-called "Nuremberg Clause" – after the Nuremberg Tribunal post-WW II which to some extent retroactively applied crimes that had not been regulated before the acts were committed – which allows "the trial and punishment of any person for any act or omission which, at the time when it was committed, was criminal according to the general principles of law recognized by the community of nations", which could rather easily be used to convince newcomers of a common view of what category of crimes fit that description

---

62 Rome Statute of the International Criminal Court, www.icc-cpi.int/resource-library/documents/rs-eng.pdf.

63 See the seminal work by Mirjan Damaska, *The Faces of Justice and State Authority* (Yale University Press, New Haven, 1986).

across the species already in the network. In any event, insurmountable obstacles would be unlikely and at worst few and far between.

2.2.7 Freedom of Movement

Articles 12 and 13 ICCPR regulate the right to liberty of movement and freedom to choose one's residence in a state's territory,[64] to leave any country, to enter one's own country, as well as the expulsion of aliens (in the immigration law sense) from the territory of a state. Again, much like with the criminal procedure guarantees, comparative research shows a wide spectrum of compliant approaches, so it is not to be expected that this particular issue would cause tensions over non-negotiable positions, although, of course, the territory of a species or civilisation may now have to be characterised as a planet or even a whole star system, which will make especially the expulsion arrangements somewhat more onerous.

2.2.8 Privacy, Freedom of Religion and Expression, Assembly and Association

Articles 17–20 ICCPR contain provisions on some of the most contentious and litigated rights in human jurisdictions. Article 17(1) ICCPR on privacy grants the right not to be "subjected to arbitrary or unlawful interference with [one's] privacy, family, home or correspondence, nor to unlawful attacks on [one's] honour and reputation". Again, collective-based species may have no use for the individualistic concerns of humans and, as is the case in some countries on Earth already, the practice of mass surveillance may be more common-place and less frowned upon than it is by humans.[65]

Article 18(1) and (2) ICCPR on religious freedom state that "[e]veryone shall have the right to freedom of thought, conscience and religion. This right shall include freedom to have or to adopt a religion or belief of his choice, and freedom, either individually or in community with others and in public or private, to manifest his religion or belief in worship, observance, practice and teaching" and that "no-one shall be subject to coercion which would impair his freedom to have or to adopt a religion or belief of his choice". Article 18(3) ICCPR allows

---

64 Assuming the concepts of "state" and "territory" have a meaning at all to ETI that would compare to the human idea behind them.

65 See on the wider ramifications of mass surveillance Michael Bohlander, "The Global Panopticon" Mass surveillance and data privacy intrusion as a crime against humanity?, in Martin Böse et al (eds.), *Justice without Borders: Essays in Honour of Wolfgang Schomburg* (Brill | Nijhoff, Leiden Boston, 2018) pp. 73–102; on the self-caused erosion of privacy concerns through the mushrooming use of social networks see Bohlander, Blood Music.

restrictions on these rights only for reasons that "are prescribed by law and are necessary to protect public safety, order, health, or morals or the fundamental rights and freedoms of others". Article 18(4) ICCPR requires the state to respect the liberty of parents or legal guardians to ensure the religious and moral education of their children in conformity with their own convictions". These rights are already being regularly violated by numerous states and regimes on Earth, and they face grave danger from followers of other religions. One of the most glaring examples in present times is political Islamism, which in its extreme, violent Salafist forms does not shrink from the mass murder, and indeed genocide, of persons who are in the view of its followers unbelievers.[66] Article 20(2) ICCPR which requires that "[a]ny advocacy of national, racial or religious hatred that constitutes incitement to discrimination, hostility or violence shall be prohibited by law" is often more honoured in the breach, and those who call for a global jihad would also seem to fall foul of Article 20(1) ICCPR which prohibits propaganda for war. While humanity itself already appears to be unable to eradicate the religious roots of conflict, aggression and violence in its own species, the contact with ETI may add further tension, especially if they are philosophically highly advanced and taking a more sophisticated attitude to the issue of transcendence and what may be called spiritual things. Religion, or better religious faith, is one of the most powerful identifiers, both for individuals and for groups. Having to face an advanced species which either has no religious leanings at all, or one totally different from humans,[67] can give rise to violence out of the fundamental desperation entailed by a perceived loss of identity, even if the network takes a liberal approach to the exercise of

66 See for the Islamist positions, for example, Michael Bohlander, Murder by YouTube – Anti-Islamic Speech and Homicide Liability. 10 *Journal of Islamic State Practices in International Law* (2014) 7–42; *id.*, Political Islam and Non-Muslim Religions – A Lesson from Lessing for the Arab Transition, 25 *Islam and Christian-Muslim Relations* (2014) 27–47; *id.*, "There is no compulsion in religion" – Freedom of religion, responsibility to protect (R2P) and crimes against humanity at the example of the Islamic blasphemy laws of Pakistan. 8 *Journal of Islamic State Practices in International Law* (2012) 36–66.

67 It is difficult to see how any of the great human religions with a claim of exclusivity and their own redemption narrative can survive contact with alien cosmologies unchallenged, or indeed unchanged, especially if these cosmologies are already shared in their essence by a wide interstellar community of ETIs. Fundamentalists of all sides, especially those of revelation based religions, will at the very least struggle with the realisation that their religion is at best restricted to the planet Earth (Mohammed and Christ, for example, are unlikely, to say the least, to have walked on other planets), or at worst that all human religions have, to put it in the words of St. Paul, been looking through a glass, darkly and not recognising much. ("For now we see through a glass, darkly; but then face to face: now I know in part; but then shall I know even as also I am known". – 1 Corinthians 13:12).

religions. Conversely, however, the members of an interspecies network who have in their view overcome or even suppressed religious practices, which they may have experienced as a cause for conflict, may wish to ensure that new candidates for accession do also renounce at the very least the public practice of any religious beliefs, something which is a core element of the current human understanding of religious freedom. The human criteria for restrictions permissible under Article 18(3) may as a corollary to accession to a network have to undergo serious revision. As above, the potential for ultimately unhelpful speculation is obvious but it seems fair to say that this area will be one where the hardest battles will be fought about what is or is not negotiable.

Compared to these issues, those of freedom of opinion, expression and information regulated under Article 19 ICCPR almost pale in significance. There is ample experience in lawful free speech regulation and again a wide array of diverse approaches, so that this area would seem to fall under the negotiable category. The same can be said for the rights to assembly and association under Articles 21 and 22 ICCPR, which are often linked to the other freedoms in this section.

2.2.9 Family and Personal Status; Child Rights

Articles 23 ICCPR states that "[t]he family is the natural and fundamental group unit of society and is entitled to protection by society and the State", tying the founding of the family unit to a union between men and women. Regardless of the human LGBTQ issues around equal marriage, this concept is one which, on the one hand, may not mean anything or at least not the same, to a species which reproduces asexually or through simultaneous spawning of many offspring, and on the other hand, species biology – possibly aided by medical technology – determines the mode of reproduction. There may thus not be much to negotiate in the first place, and as has been the experience from human times of colonisation, family affairs were often among those left to the local population to arrange according to their own customs. Article 24 ICCPR covers the protection of some basic children's rights, which again should be easy, and indeed natural, to arrange as remaining within the respective species' jurisdiction.

2.2.10 Restrictions on Exercise of Rights

Article 4(1) ICCPR allows – on the basis of strict proportionality – for derogations from certain human rights in time of a "public emergency which threatens the life of the nation and the existence of which is officially proclaimed [...] to the extent strictly required by the exigencies of the situation, provided that such measures are not inconsistent with their other obligations under international law and do not involve discrimination solely on the ground of race, colour, sex, language, religion or social origin". Furthermore, "[n]o derogation from articles 6, 7, 8 (paragraphs 1 and 2), 11, 15, 16 and 18" may be made according to Article 4(2) ICCPR. However, the Human Rights Committee has also treated certain aspects of Articles 9, 10 and 14 as non-derogable.[68] By implication, Article 4(2) ICCPR is not derogable itself.[69] The relevance of this is that non-derogable rights would normally seem to be candidates for non-negotiable status for our purposes, too. However, as indicated above, we found that the listed Articles 11 and 15 ICCPR might be susceptible to negotiations, and vice-versa the non-listed rights of Articles 1–3 might not be; Article 4(1) only lists a selection of the criteria from Articles 2 and 3 ICCPR upon which discrimination must not be based. Article 5(1) ICCPR contains an abuse prevention clause to the effect, on the one hand, that the rights set out in the ICCPR cannot be used by anyone to justify imposing any obligations not compliant with the ICCPR or, on the other hand, limiting or destroying the rights under it. Article 5(2) ICCPR clarifies that the ICCPR must not be used to justify reducing rights in domestic frameworks which exceed the requirements of the ICCPR. While Article 5(1) ICCPR seems to be just a matter of logic arising from the fact that the ICCPR is already a fine-tuned balance and compromise between its drafters, Article 5(2) ICCPR may in essence prove to be a moot rule, because "Article 5(2) [does not] require States to be permanently fastened to a higher standard of protection domestically. [...] Article 5(2) does not preclude a State from eliminating from its national bill of rights a right not found in the Covenant, or even from denouncing particular international treaty obligations".[70] The provisions thus do not necessarily aid in our endeavour.

3 Conclusion

We have tried to interrogate the following questions based on the assumption that human rights standards could represent a valid starting point for reflections about which terms and conditions humanity might be willing to accept

68 Taylor, ICCPR, p. 123.

69 *Ibid.*

70 Taylor, ICCPR, p. 135. – This chapter does not address the question of human legal protections for ETI living under human jurisdiction, especially if they go beyond the standards of the respective network which that ETI belongs to. There might be an issue of reciprocity involved and since we do not know anything about what ETI might wish to concede or seek under human law, the matter is too speculative.

as a trade-off for membership of an interstellar network of civilisations: What if the admission to the Galactic Club requires subscription to club rules which are incompatible with human rights as currently interpreted by humans but which humanity might wish to have ring-fenced for its own species? This may be rephrased into the slightly less drastic scenario of what humans would do if adopting the galactic standard was optional but only full adherence would bring full network benefits? As can be expected, the answer is neither easy nor straightforward.

Looking at only one – albeit widely accepted – of the general human rights instruments, the ICCPR, it became clear that certain rights would be relatively uncontested candidates for negotiation while others quite certainly would not. There are, of course, many human rights instruments which cover more specific areas in more detail and are of great importance to the groups protected by them, as well as the development of human rights law in general, and would merit inclusion in an exercise such as this, but as we saw at the beginning, it may be difficult and indeed counter-productive to proceed from a splintered or too individualised base if the negotiation is to be done as one species with other species, and not within our species alone. The network may be rather relaxed in its requirements and loose in its structure (low regulation density), confine itself to general co-operation and non-aggression rules between members but otherwise leave matters in a state of horizontal and voluntary power sharing. Conversely, it may be highly hierarchically organised and require adherence to a large number of rules with direct effect in its member civilisations. The spectrum is very wide and probably could contain structural constellations humans are entirely unfamiliar with and which will in any event become known only once sustained contact occurs.

Humanity may be alone in the galaxy/universe for all practical intents and purposes if the next ETI is so far away that contact will not occur in reasonable time periods or at all – or humanity may just be alone, full stop. That question is still awaiting a solid answer based on incontestable and verifiable evidence. Some may say we will never know, will at best receive a signal from afar and never have direct contact, or will never be in a position to join the club, and that the whole object of this chapter is one of wildly premature speculation and means taking the 25th step before the first in the SETI endeavour. And certainly, there are other issues to be tackled, such as, for example, a proper post-detection protocol to manage the massive risk arising for global society from the public confirmation of an alien signal alone, leave alone direct contact. We may need to consider giving a new meaning to the term “planetary defence” for the possibility that contact might be hostile in nature etc. However, these steps are equally important and in their impact not necessarily sequential but rather overlapping or indeed parallel.

Given the highly complex internal species negotiations for preparing a unified human response to an invitation to join a network of extraterrestrial civilisations will inevitably entail, and that direct contact could, all things being equal, in theory occur at any time, there may not be a lot of time left to take steps 2–24 anymore, depending on the nature of contact. We afford ourselves the financial extravagance of the Breakthrough Programme[71] in the search for ETI. We have been sending out messages into space for decades not knowing who will receive them and what their intentions and reactions will be. We speculate without any reliable foundation about what ETI's philosophy could be and what a cosmic metalaw *erga omnes* would look like. All of this logically means we entertain the possibility that there is something and someone to be found and that one day contact might be made. Yet, we do not want to think about the things we can expound on with some degree of confidence and which precautionary wisdom would counsel we do engage with, one of which is where the moral and ethical pain threshold for us as a species would lie in the relationship with other species. There may be no benefit of hindsight if contact were to find us unprepared, and the present attitude, perhaps born of Seth Shostak's famous "giggle factor",[72] of "could not care less" could well turn out to have been carelessness.

71 https://breakthroughinitiatives.org.

72 Seth Shostak, SETI and the Media, in R P Norris and F H Stootman (eds.) *Bioastronomy 2002: Life Among the Stars– IAU Symposium,* (Astronomical Society of the Pacific, San Francisco, 2004) pp. 540–541.

CHAPTER 8

Conclusion and Outlook

> Look, I really don't think they flew 90 billion light years to come down here and start a fight. Get all rowdy.
>
> CAPTAIN STEVEN HILLER
> Independence Day (1996)

•••

> "I know there is much we can learn from each other, if we can negotiate a truce. We can find a way to coexist. Can there be a peace between us?" – "Peace? No peace". – "What is it you want us to do?" – "Die!"
>
> Conversation between President Whitmore and a captured alien
> Independence Day (1996)

•••

> "I get it", said Noonan. "A roadside picnic". – "Exactly. A picnic by the side of some space road. And you ask me whether they'll come back …". […] – "What, you mean they never even noticed us?" – "Why?" – "Or at least they paid no attention". […] "So-called serious xenologists try to justify interpretations that are much more respectable and flattering to human vanity".
>
> ARKADY STRUGATSKY AND BORIS STRUGATSKY
> Roadside Picnic (Gollancz, London, 2012) 132–133

In this book, we first attempted to build a bridge between the scientific SETI environment, including well-known – but ultimately still unresolved – issues such as the Drake Equation and the Fermi Paradox, anthropocentrism andmorphism, the different methods of SETI, the possible varieties of the nature of contact, and the social science facets of SETI, including the parameters which may determine the risk and impact of first contact on humanity. Problems of

 | DOI:10.1163/9789004677708_009

exolinguistics, exosociology, exophilosophy and exotheology were highlighted, in particular the question of the current usefulness of the concept of a cosmic metalaw and whether the metalaw debate reflects the proper use of legal considerations at the current juncture. We interrogated the relevance of Science Fiction for the real-world endeavours around SETI and the various contact scenarios, with a particular emphasis on interspecies armed conflict and avenues to conflict avoidance.

Building on that, we discussed in detail the problems arising from hostile contact for the underlying principles of the current international and domestic law, especially international and domestic criminal law, and the four international core crimes of genocide, crimes against humanity, war crimes and aggression, with an excursion to the impact of human space exploration for species on other planets. Switching from legal to factual problems, we addressed the means of preparing for hostile contact and the future challenges in areas such as weapons technology, strategy and tactics and the interface between weapons development and deep space strategy, the strategic parameters of deep space warfare, especially distances, speeds, and celestial mechanics, and the relevance of factors such as psychology, logistics, and resources etc. to operating in a deep space combat theatre. We studied the potential for conflict avoidance, such as legal preconditions for peaceful relationships with ETI, including the costs and benefits arising from the highly speculative scenario of a human accession to a "Galactic Club" through the prism of international human rights law as a representative example of our shared global moral values.

The quotes from film and fiction listed above reflect a variety of points of view on the wide spectrum of human attitudes and aspirations related to the question of contact with extraterrestrial civilisations – from the hope for their benevolence to other species, to the fear of annihilation by an unassailable superior alien enemy, to the humiliating realisation that despite our formidable path of development since before the Stone Age, we may not mean that much yet to any other sapient, spacefaring species on an interstellar or even intergalactic scale. After decades of serious SETI research, almost every question is in essence still unresolved, either for lack of hard data or based on an extreme reluctance towards recognizing non-repeatable sources of evidence. The signal from afar has not been received, at least there has been no scientifically satisfactory verification of any of the major candidate signals. Eyewitness accounts of contact with aliens or of UAP sightings, including the highly controversial abduction scenarios, continue to raise academic eyebrows and tend to be explained away, in many cases successfully, in quite a few not so. The remaining confusion was explained in Chapter 1. Any willingness to engage with them, or, as in the case of Stanford professor Garry Nolan, additionally outing oneself as a so-called "experiencer", can still wreck an academic career and reputation.

Against this background, the increasing official acceptance – and as it might after all turn out, possibly precautionary *ex ante* expectation management of revelations to the wider global public – by governments, not least the military, around the world of the legitimacy of scientific UAP research is remarkable and probably nothing short of a paradigm shift.[1] This includes projects laying the groundwork for optical SETI on a new level such as, for example, the Large Synoptic Survey Telescope (LSST) at the Vera C. Rubin Observatory in Chile,[2] which is scheduled to begin operations in late 2023.

While traditional SETI research is increasingly considered as legitimate, we must also be aware of the total lack of a legally binding regulatory framework which controls the scientists who drive that research, and who sometimes seem to have an almost childlike tendency of doing something just because it can be done, and to see what happens – as if the Earth was one gigantic instrumental observation assembly based on the principle of trial and error. One particularly glaring aspect in this context are the supporters of the METI community, whose self-professed aim, as we said earlier, is to bring about a situation which humanity cannot control, as exemplified by the quote from Liu Cixin's *Dark Forest* in Chapter 4 (at 2.5.), or as expressed in less refined words by Robert Charles Wilson in *Blind Lake*:

> People were assholes, and that was what the exocultural theorists always missed […], blind little featherweight optimists. One world full of assholes wasn't enough for them. They wanted more. A whole living universe of assholery.[3]

---

1 Despite the general epistemological caveat and the basic premise of this book not to take final stance on UAP and to maintain scientific caution, we must take note of the persistent officially sanctioned rumours, for example, about alleged cross-domain transmedium travel capacities (i.e., outer space to airspace to underwater movement) of some UAPs observed, with respect to which some members of the US Congress already appear to have conceded that whatever they are, they are not man-made: As far as is publicly known, humanity does not have the technology necessary to develop machines that can operate in all three environments, leave alone at such speeds and rates of acceleration, which is one reason why the Pentagon in July 2022 announced the establishment of an All-domain Anomaly Resolution Office (AARO) with a significant budget attached to it. These investigations need to be accompanied by scientific research.

2 Vera C Rubin Observatory, www.lsst.org.

3 Robert Charles Wilson, *Blind Lake* (TOR Books, New York, 2003) p. 157.

If the current increased public interest in UAP and extraterrestrial life and intelligence in general, as well as the enhanced research effort in all SETI areas are anything to go by, then the next decade might already see evidence come to light that will make the Copernican Revolution look like a faint ripple in human history – for better or for worse. In the latter case, another Latin maxim, "*inter arma silent leges*", may acquire a new meaning. We need to be ready.

Epilogue

We have known for some years that planetary systems are the rule, not the exception, in the universe and that there are countless potentially habitable planets in our galaxy. Statistical analysis based on data from the Kepler mission (2009–2018) concluded that there could be as many as 40 billion Earth-like planets within the Milky Way, in the habitable zones of Sun-like stars and red dwarfs. In addition, it has been known for some time that organic chemical compounds, the basic building blocks of life, are found in abundance in space. Once life has been established, it proves to be highly adaptable and robust. Life on Earth has conquered almost every corner of the planet and exists even where one would never have suspected it: In extreme heat or cold, deep at the bottom of the sea or in sealed caves. There is hardly a place on earth where one would not find traces of life. All of this taken together makes it seem more likely than ever that Earth is not the only inhabited planet, nor is humanity the only intelligent species in the universe. And it raises the question of whether humanity will one day come into contact with an extraterrestrial civilization.

The signal scenario, which still dominates the scientific SETI discussion, is only one of the possibilities of how mankind could come into contact with an extraterrestrial civilization. And there are good reasons to believe that this is not the most likely example. There are a number of conceivable scenarios that must be considered as well – such as the discovery of extraterrestrial artefacts or the discovery of alien space probes in our solar system. Such possibilities should also be considered when thinking about 'first contact' with extraterrestrial civilizations. In recent years, moreover, something has taken place with regard to the UFO topic (in the meantime, the term UAP has become common) that can certainly be called a paradigm shift. The UAP issue has been considered pseudoscience and irrationalism for decades. But now, more than half a century after the end of *Project Blue Book*, there is official UAP research in the US again. UAPs are considered as a potential threat to US national security. Public communication on the subject has turned by 180 degrees and UFOs are becoming more and more established in science as a legitimate and important object of research. Recently, NASA announced its intention to conduct its own research project on UAPs. All this has so far not changed the state of scientific knowledge concerning the UAP phenomenon: There have been and still are cases in which strange objects or phenomena are observed in the sky for which there seems to be no conventional explanation even after examining all the available information. Some of the observed objects appear to be controlled by an intelligence and show flight characteristics that no known human aircraft

 DOI:10.1163/9789004677708_010

can achieve. The association of the UAP phenomenon with extraterrestrials is historical. But of course, alien spaceships are not the only possible explanation for UAPs. There are possible explanations that are much less exotic. However, the extraterrestrial hypothesis cannot be ruled out at this time. To put it bluntly: The increased research activities in this field could indeed lead to hints or even certainty that at least some UAPs have an extraterrestrial origin. This possibility exists and we should be prepared for it.

Certainty about the existence of extraterrestrial civilizations would have profound implications on our view of humanity's place in the cosmos. Moreover, it could have a massive impact on virtually every aspect of human life. This makes a discussion of the question of possible extraterrestrial civilizations, of communication options, and of societal consequences of various contact scenarios not only legitimate, but even urgently necessary. Of course, one can argue that mankind currently has completely different, more important problems to deal with. In the face of climate change, pandemic, war, and famine crises, why deal with *hypothetical* alien contact? In disaster research, the significance of an event is judged by two factors, its probability of occurrence and the extent of its negative consequences. If, in the worst case, contact with an extraterrestrial intelligence could have devastating consequences for humanity, the probability of the first-contact event can become almost arbitrarily small without the overall risk becoming negligible (in futurology, such events are called 'low-probability, high-impact events'). It would be irresponsible not to develop a plan for such events.

No one today knows with certainty whether life has evolved outside the Earth – and certainly not whether other intelligent beings have emerged in the vastness of space. However, there is no scientific reason to exclude this possibility. The more we know about the universe and the more we explore the cosmos through our research activities, the more likely it is that we will be confronted with extraterrestrial civilizations, their signals or artefacts. Preparing ourselves as a global society for this therefore seems imperative.

This book by Michael Bohlander is an important, courageous pioneering work that will hopefully stimulate further studies. The question of which legal principles could play a role in a contact with an intelligent extraterrestrial species may seem absurd to many today. However, if first contact should actually occur one day, such questions are highly relevant and we can all be glad if mankind is not completely unprepared in such a situation. Bohlander's study is interesting for the very reason that, in the face of (so far) hypothetical aliens, it adopts a perspective that looks "from above" at international legal norms. It is a bitter realization that many or even most of the legal frameworks that our species has fought for long and hard, and occasionally with the price of blood, to establish, such as international law or human rights, could quickly lose their validity in the face of confrontation with an extraterrestrial species. As soon as there is the thought that *humanity as a whole* might be threatened, this inevitably undermines the legal conventions within our species. Whether it would come to that, would depend, of course, on the actual behaviour of the extraterrestrials when first contact is made. Just as several hostile first contact scenarios are conceivable, there are also innumerable conceivable variants of a peaceful contact. Here, indeed, the question would arise, on which legal and political foundation we would base our relationship with the extraterrestrial species.

Bohlander's excursion into the world of science fiction is extremely useful and helpful, as it provides clues to the range of possible interactions between humans and aliens – at least within the bounds of human imagination. The reality could, of course, be quite different to all we know from science fiction. The vast majority of aliens in science fiction are hostile to humanity or other intelligent species in general. One may ask: What does this say about us who imagine these fictional aliens in this way? Since we do not know anything about extraterrestrial intelligences, not even about simple extraterrestrial life forms, they are eminently suitable as a projection surface for all kinds of very human fears, wishes and hopes. The fact that the fictional aliens are so often aggressive and hostile certainly refers, on the one hand, to a primal human fear of everything that is strange. On the other hand – and this point seems to me much more important – we encounter our fear of ourselves in the fictitious aliens we create. And exactly this fear could have fatal consequences in case of a real first contact with extraterrestrials, it could even become a kind of *self-fulfilling prophecy*: Fearing that the aliens might be as aggressive and inconsiderate toward us as we are toward our own and other species on Earth, we might react in ways that cause the aliens to act in a hostile manner. This in turn could confirm our fear that the aliens have bad intentions, etc. In this way, a destructive dynamic could quickly develop during a first contact.

This does not mean, of course, that if we have a real encounter with extraterrestrials, we should assume that they will be friendly to us. Bohlander quite rightly points out that such an attitude would be naive or even dangerous. Furthermore, his objection that confronting an extraterrestrial species does not necessarily mean that we are dealing with technology that we would not be able to counter in a conflict situation is very valid.

What are the conclusions to be drawn from these considerations? From my point of view, it would be important to have guidelines or even a binding set of rules in case of a real encounter, which would ask us to exercise *the greatest possible restraint* in the context of a first contact with an extraterrestrial intelligence. Of course, countless scenarios are conceivable in which humanity would be immediately forced to act in the event of an encounter with extraterrestrials, but if this is not the case (and countless scenarios are also conceivable for this), the guiding principle should be to remain as passive as possible. Every action, every rash interpretation of the events could have fatal consequences. This also, and maybe especially so, applies to military action. Any mistake we make here could be our last. In my opinion, there is nothing to be said against at least already thinking intensively about precautions for a planetary defence. I entirely agree with Bohlander on this point. The ability to *potentially* respond defensively as equals to an alien invader could, at best, deter us from radical pre-emptive solutions that could ultimately have catastrophic consequences for our own species. In short: An interstellar fundamental pacifism is ultimately (unfortunately) subject to the same suspicion of naivety as terrestrial fundamental pacifism. The expansion of planetary defence capacities would, however, be accompanied by the very justified fear that we would use this arsenal of weapons against ourselves. For the time being, this risk can rightly be classified as *much greater* than the threat posed by an extraterrestrial species. However, this assessment could change very quickly.

Indeed – and here, too, I fully agree with Bohlander – much will depend on whether humanity will succeed in developing a species consciousness. Regardless of whether or not we will one day encounter an extraterrestrial intelligence, this would be a desirable development because it could be significant in helping us focus more on finding out if extraterrestrial life exists and less on taking each other's lives.

Dr. Andreas Anton
Institut für Grenzgebiete der Psychologie und Psychohygiene e.V.
Freiburg i.Br. / Germany

Annexes

A IAA SETI Permanent Commitee

1 *Declaration of Principles Concerning Activities Following the Detection of Extraterrestrial Intelligence (1989)*

We, the institutions and individuals participating in the search for extraterrestrial intelligence,

Recognizing that the search for extraterrestrial intelligence is an integral part of space exploration and is being undertaken for peaceful purposes and for the common interest of all mankind,

Inspired by the profound significance for mankind of detecting evidence of extraterrestrial intelligence, even though the probability of detection may be low,

Recalling the Treaty on Principles Governing the Activities of States in the Exploration and Use of Outer Space, Including the Moon and Other Celestial Bodies, which commits States Parties to that Treaty "to inform the Secretary General of the United Nations as well as the public and the international scientific community, to the greatest extent feasible and practicable, of the nature, conduct, locations and results" of their space exploration activities (Article XI),

Recognizing that any initial detection may be incomplete or ambiguous and thus require careful examination as well as confirmation, and that it is essential to maintain the highest standards of scientific responsibility and credibility,

Agree to observe the following principles for disseminating information about the detection of extraterrestrial intelligence:

1. Any individual, public or private research institution, or governmental agency that believes it has detected a signal from or other evidence of extraterrestrial intelligence (the discoverer) should seek to verify that the most plausible explanation for the evidence is the existence of extraterrestrial intelligence rather than some other natural phenomenon or anthropogenic phenomenon before making any public announcement. If the evidence cannot be confirmed as indicating the existence of extraterrestrial intelligence, the discoverer may disseminate the information as appropriate to the discovery of any unknown phenomenon.
2. Prior to making a public announcement that evidence of extraterrestrial intelligence has been detected, the discoverer should promptly inform all other observers or research organizations that are parties to this declaration, so that those other parties may seek to confirm the discovery by independent observations at other sites and so that a network can be established to enable continuous monitoring of the signal or phenomenon. Parties to this declaration should not make any public announcement of this information until it is determined whether this information

 | DOI:10.1163/9789004677708_011

is or is not credible evidence of the existence of extraterrestrial intelligence. The discoverer should inform his/her or its relevant national authorities.

3. After concluding that the discovery appears to be credible evidence of extraterrestrial intelligence, and after informing other parties to this declaration, the discoverer should inform observers throughout the world through the Central Bureau for Astronomical Telegrams of the International Astronomical Union, and should inform the Secretary General of the United Nations in accordance with Article XI of the Treaty on Principles Governing the Activities of States in the Exploration and Use of Outer Space, Including the Moon and Other Bodies. Because of their demonstrated interest in and expertise concerning the question of the existence of extraterrestrial intelligence, the discoverer should simultaneously inform the following international institutions of the discovery and should provide them with all pertinent data and recorded information concerning the evidence: the International Telecommunication Union, the Committee on Space Research, of the International Council of Scientific Unions, the International Astronautical Federation, the International Academy of Astronautics, the International Institute of Space Law, Commission 51 of the International Astronomical Union and Commission J of the International Radio Science Union.
4. A confirmed detection of extraterrestrial intelligence should be disseminated promptly, openly, and widely through scientific channels and public media, observing the procedures in this declaration. The discoverer should have the privilege of making the first public announcement.
5. All data necessary for confirmation of detection should be made available to the international scientific community through publications, meetings, conferences, and other appropriate means.
6. The discovery should be confirmed and monitored and any data bearing on the evidence of extraterrestrial intelligence should be recorded and stored permanently to the greatest extent feasible and practicable, in a form that will make it available for further analysis and interpretation. These recordings should be made available to the international institutions listed above and to members of the scientific community for further objective analysis and interpretation.
7. If the evidence of detection is in the form of electromagnetic signals, the parties to this declaration should seek international agreement to protect the appropriate frequencies by exercising procedures available through the International Telecommunication Union. Immediate notice should be sent to the Secretary General of the ITU in Geneva, who may include a request to minimize transmissions on the relevant frequencies in the Weekly Circular. The Secretariat, in conjunction with advice of the Union's Administrative Council, should explore the feasibility and utility of convening an Extraordinary Administrative Radio

Conference to deal with the matter, subject to the opinions of the member Administrations of the ITU.

8. No response to a signal or other evidence of extraterrestrial intelligence should be sent until appropriate international consultations have taken place. The procedures for such consultations will be the subject of a separate agreement, declaration or arrangement.
9. The SETI Committee of the International Academy of Astronautics, in coordination with Commission 51 of the International Astronomical Union, will conduct a continuing review of procedures for the detection of extraterrestrial intelligence and the subsequent handling of the data. Should credible evidence of extraterrestrial intelligence be discovered, an international committee of scientists and other experts should be established to serve as a focal point for continuing analysis of all observational evidence collected in the aftermath of the discovery, and also to provide advice on the release of information to the public. This committee should be constituted from representatives of each of the international institutions listed above and such other members as the committee may deem necessary. To facilitate the convocation of such a committee at some unknown time in the future, the SETI Committee of the International Academy of Astronautics should initiate and maintain a current list of willing representatives from each of the international institutions listed above, as well as other individuals with relevant skills, and should make that list continuously available through the Secretariat of the International Academy of Astronautics. The International Academy of Astronautics will act as the Depository for this declaration and will annually provide a current list of parties to all the parties to this declaration.

Adopted by the International Academy of Astronautics, 1989

II *Declaration of Principles Concerning the Conduct of the Search for Extraterrestrial Intelligence* (2010)

Preamble

The parties to this declaration are individuals and institutions participating in the scientific Search for Extraterrestrial Intelligence (SETI).

The purpose of this document is to declare our commitment to conduct this search in a scientifically valid and transparent manner and to establish uniform procedures for the announcement of a confirmed SETI detection.

This commitment is made in recognition of the profound scientific, social, ethical, legal, philosophical and other implications of a SETI detection. As this enterprise enjoys wide public interest, but engenders uncertainty about how information collected during the search will be handled, the signatories have voluntarily constructed this declaration. It, together with a current list of signatory parties, will be placed on file with the International Academy of Astronautics (IAA).

Principles

1. *Searching*: SETI experiments will be conducted transparently, and its practitioners will be free to present reports on activities and results in public and professional fora. They will also be responsive to news organizations and other public communications media about their work.
2. *Handling candidate evidence*: In the event of a suspected detection of extraterrestrial intelligence, the discoverer will make all efforts to verify the detection, using the resources available to the discoverer and with the collaboration of other investigators, whether or not signatories to this Declaration. Such efforts will include, but not be limited to, observations at more than one facility and/or by more than one organization. There is no obligation to disclose verification efforts while they are underway, and there should be no premature disclosures pending verification. Inquiries from the media and news organizations should be responded to promptly and honestly. Information about candidate signals or other detections should be treated in the same way that any scientist would treat provisional laboratory results. The Rio Scale, or its equivalent, should be used as a guide to the import and significance of candidate discoveries for the benefit of non-specialist audiences.
3. *Confirmed detections*: If the verification process confirms – by the consensus of the other investigators involved and to a degree of certainty judged by the discoverers to be credible – that a signal or other evidence is due to extraterrestrial intelligence, the discoverer shall report this conclusion in a full and complete open manner to the public, the scientific community, and the Secretary General of the United Nations. The confirmation report will include the basic data, the process and results of the verification efforts, any conclusions and interpretations, and any detected information content of the signal itself. A formal report will also be made to the International Astronomical Union (IAU).
4. All data necessary for the confirmation of the detection should be made available to the international scientific community through publications, meetings, conferences, and other appropriate means.
5. The discovery should be monitored. Any data bearing on the evidence of extraterrestrial intelligence should be recorded and stored permanently to the greatest extent feasible and practicable, in a form that will make it available to observers and to the scientific community for further analysis and interpretation.
6. If the evidence of detection is in the form of electromagnetic signals, observers should seek international agreement to protect the appropriate frequencies by exercising the extraordinary procedures established within the World Administrative Radio Council of the International Telecommunication Union.
7. *Post Detection*: A Post-Detection Task Group under the auspices of the IAA SETI Permanent Study Group has been established to assist in matters that may arise in the event of a confirmed signal, and to support the scientific and public analysis by

offering guidance, interpretation, and discussion of the wider implications of the detection.

8. *Response to signals*: In the case of the confirmed detection of a signal, signatories to this declaration will not respond without first seeking guidance and consent of a broadly representative international body, such as the United Nations.

Unanimously adopted by the SETI Permanent Study Group of the International Academy of Astronautics, at its annual meeting in Prague, Czech Republic, on 30 September 2010. These revised and streamlined Protocols are intended to replace the previous document adopted by the International Academy of Astronautics in 1989.

III *Draft Declaration of Principles Concerning Sending Communications with Extraterrestrial Intelligence (1995)*

1. International consultations should be initiated to consider the question of sending communications to extraterrestrial civilizations.
2. Consultations on whether a message should be sent, and its content, should take place within the Committee on the Peaceful Uses of Outer Space of the United Nations and within other governmental and non-governmental organizations, and should accommodate participation by qualified, interested groups that can contribute constructively to these consultations.
3. These consultations should be open to participation by all interested States and should be intended to lead to recommendations reflecting a consensus.
4. The United Nations General Assembly should consider making the decision on whether or not to send a message to extraterrestrial intelligence, and on what the content of that message should be, based on recommendations from the Committee on the Peaceful Uses of Outer Space and from governmental and non-governmental organizations.
5. If a decision is made to send a message to extraterrestrial intelligence, it should be sent on behalf of all Humankind, rather than from individual States.
6. The content of such a message should reflect a careful concern for the broad interests and wellbeing of Humanity, and should be made available to the public in advance of transmission.
7. As the sending of a communication to extraterrestrial intelligence could lead to an exchange of communications separated by many years, consideration should be given to a long-term institutional framework for such communications.
8. No communication to extraterrestrial intelligence should be sent by any State until appropriate international consultations have taken place. States should not cooperate with attempts to communicate with extraterrestrial intelligence that do not conform to the principles of this Declaration.

9. In their deliberations on these questions, States participating in this Declaration and United Nations bodies should draw on the expertise of scientists, scholars, and other persons with relevant knowledge.

Proposed by the SETI Committee of the International Academy of Astronautics, 1995

IV *2015 METI Statement*

Messaging to Extraterrestrial Intelligence (METI), also called Active Searches for Extraterrestrial Intelligence (Active SETI), refers to the act of using high power communications equipment on Earth to transmit various messages to unknown extraterrestrial intelligences.

METI has been conducted sporadically in the past, but recently a surge of individuals and organizations have initiated or suggested new METI programs, both academic and commercial in nature. METI programs carry unknown and potentially enormous implications and consequences. We feel the decision whether or not to transmit must be based upon a worldwide consensus, and not a decision based upon the wishes of a few individuals with access to powerful communications equipment. We strongly encourage vigorous international debate by a broadly representative body prior to engaging further in this activity. We also note the following:

- ETI's reaction to a message from Earth cannot presently be known. We know nothing of ETI's intentions and capabilities, and it is impossible to predict whether ETI will be benign or hostile.
- Because we have just recently (in cosmic terms) attained an interstellar communications capability, it is likely that other communicative civilizations we encounter will be millions of years more advanced than us.
- The Search for Extraterrestrial Intelligence, the scientific effort to determine whether or not other advanced life exists in the universe, is still in its infancy. Even though SETI experiments have been ongoing for more than 50 years, scientists are still decades away from completing a comprehensive search for radio signals similar to those produced by our own technology. As a newly emerging technological species, it is prudent to listen before we shout.
- Although a nearby advanced ETI may have already picked up earth's omnidirectional radio leakage, e.g., early television transmissions, or the presence of industrial wastes in the atmosphere of the earth, such detections are far more difficult than detecting a focused radio or optical signal sent from a large telescope.
- It is not necessary to actually transmit powerful electromagnetic signals in order to study interstellar communication from the perspective of the transmitter, or to develop transmission techniques that might one day be used to respond to a message received from an ETI.

- Opponents of METI would vocally condemn METI transmissions, confusing the public about, and imperiling funding for, bona fide scientific endeavors related to extraterrestrial life.

Intentionally signaling other civilizations in the Milky Way Galaxy raises concerns from all the people of Earth, about both the message and the consequences of contact. A worldwide scientific, political and humanitarian discussion must occur before any message is sent.

Armando Azua-Bustos	George Dyson	Eric J. Korpela	Reinhard Prix
James Benford	William H. Edmondson	Harvey S. Liszt	John D. Rummel
Alan P. Boss	Duncan H. Forgan	Claudio Maccone	Andrew P. V. Siemion
David Brin	John Gertz	Geoffrey W. Marcy	Remington P.S. Stone
Lewis R. Dartnell	Denise L. Herzing	Michael Michaud	Lucianne M. Walkowicz
Paul C.W. Davies	Andrew W. Howard	Elon Musk	Dan Werthimer
Michael M. Davis	Sara Imari Walker	Tim J. O'Brien	Shelley A. Wright

B International Treaties, Agreements and Documents – United Nations [Excerpts]

I *Treaty on Principles Governing the Activities of States in the Exploration and Use of Outer Space, Including the Moon and Other Celestial Bodies [Outer Space Treaty – OST]*

Preamble […]

Recalling resolution 1884 (XVIII), calling upon States to refrain from placing in orbit around the Earth any objects carrying nuclear weapons or any other kinds of weapons of mass destruction or from installing such weapons on celestial bodies, which was adopted unanimously by the United Nations General Assembly on 17 October 1963,

Article II

Outer space, including the Moon and other celestial bodies, is not subject to national appropriation by claim of sovereignty, by means of use or occupation, or by any other means.

Article III

States Parties to the Treaty shall carry on activities in the exploration and use of outer space, including the Moon and other celestial bodies, in accordance with international law, including the Charter of the United Nations, in the interest of maintaining international peace and security and promoting international cooperation and understanding.

Article IV

States Parties to the Treaty undertake not to place in orbit around the Earth any objects carrying nuclear weapons or any other kinds of weapons of mass destruction, install such weapons on celestial bodies, or station such weapons in outer space in any other manner.

The Moon and other celestial bodies shall be used by all States Parties to the Treaty exclusively for peaceful purposes. The establishment of military bases, installations and fortifications, the testing of any type of weapons and the installations and fortifications, the testing of any type of weapons and the conduct of military manoeuvres on celestial bodies shall be forbidden. The use of military personnel for scientific research or for any other peaceful purposes shall not be prohibited. The use of any equipment or facility necessary for shall not be prohibited. The use of any equipment or facility necessary for peaceful exploration of the Moon and other celestial bodies shall also not be prohibited.

Article V

States Parties to the Treaty shall regard astronauts as envoys of mankind in outer space and shall render to them all possible assistance in the event of accident, distress, or emergency landing on the territory of another State Party or on the high seas. When astronauts make such a landing, they shall be safely and promptly returned to the State of registry of their space vehicle.

In carrying on activities in outer space and on celestial bodies, the astronauts of one State Party shall render all possible assistance to the astronauts of other States Parties.

States Parties to the Treaty shall immediately inform the other States Parties to the Treaty or the Secretary-General of the United Nations of any phenomena they discover in outer space, including the Moon and other celestial bodies, which could constitute a danger to the life or health of astronauts.

Article VI

States Parties to the Treaty shall bear international responsibility for national activities in outer space, including the Moon and other celestial bodies, whether such activities are carried on by governmental agencies or by non-governmental entities, and for assuring that national activities are carried out in conformity with the provisions set forth in the present Treaty. The activities of non-governmental entities in outer space, including the Moon and other celestial bodies, shall require authorization and continuing supervision by the appropriate State Party to the Treaty. When activities are carried on in outer space, including the Moon and other celestial bodies, by an international organization, responsibility for compliance with this Treaty shall be borne both by the international organization and by the States Parties to the Treaty participating in such organization.

Article IX

In the exploration and use of outer space, including the Moon and other celestial bodies, States Parties to the Treaty shall be guided by the principle of cooperation and mutual assistance and shall conduct all their activities in outer space, including the Moon and other celestial bodies, with due regard to the corresponding interests of all other States Parties to the Treaty. States Parties to the Treaty shall pursue studies of outer space, including the Moon and other celestial bodies, and conduct exploration of them so as to avoid their harmful contamination and also adverse changes in the environment of the Earth resulting from the introduction of extraterrestrial matter and, where necessary, shall adopt appropriate measures for this purpose. If a State Party to the Treaty has reason to believe that an activity or experiment planned by it or its nationals in outer space, including the Moon and other celestial bodies, would cause potentially harmful interference with activities of other States Parties in the peaceful exploration and use of outer space, including the Moon and other celestial bodies, it shall undertake appropriate international consultations before proceeding with any such activity or experiment. A State Party to the Treaty which has reason to believe that an activity or experiment planned by another State Party in outer space, including the Moon and other celestial bodies, would cause potentially harmful interference with activities in the peaceful exploration and use of outer space, including the Moon and other celestial bodies, may request consultation concerning the activity or experiment.

Article XI

In order to promote international cooperation in the peaceful exploration and use of outer space, States Parties to the Treaty conducting activities in outer space, including the Moon and other celestial bodies, agree to inform the Secretary-General of the United Nations as well as the public and the international scientific community, to the greatest extent feasible and practicable, of the nature, conduct, locations and results of such activities. On receiving the said information, the Secretary-General of the United Nations should be prepared to disseminate it immediately and effectively.

II *Agreement Governing the Activities of States on the Moon and Other Celestial Bodies*

Article 1

1. The provisions of this Agreement relating to the Moon shall also apply to other celestial bodies within the solar system, other than the Earth, except insofar as specific legal norms enter into force with respect to any of these celestial bodies.
2. For the purposes of this Agreement reference to the Moon shall include orbits around or other trajectories to or around it.
3. This Agreement does not apply to extraterrestrial materials which reach the surface of the Earth by natural means.

Article 3

1. The Moon shall be used by all States Parties exclusively for peaceful purposes.
2. Any threat or use of force or any other hostile act or threat of hostile act on the Moon is prohibited. It is likewise prohibited to use the Moon in order to commit any such act or to engage in any such threat in relation to the Earth, the Moon, spacecraft, the personnel of spacecraft or manmade space objects.
3. States Parties shall not place in orbit around or other trajectory to or around the Moon objects carrying nuclear weapons or any other kinds of weapons of mass destruction or place or use such weapons on or in the Moon.
4. The establishment of military bases, installations and fortifications, the testing of any type of weapons and the conduct of military manoeuvres on the Moon shall be forbidden. The use of military personnel for scientific research or for any other peaceful purposes shall not be prohibited. The use of any equipment or facility necessary for peaceful exploration and use of the Moon shall also not be prohibited.

Article 5

[…]

3. In carrying out activities under this Agreement, States Parties shall promptly inform the Secretary-General, as well as the public and the international scientific community, of any phenomena they discover in outer space, including the Moon, which could endanger human life or health, as well as of any indication of organic life.

Article 6

1. There shall be freedom of scientific investigation on the Moon by all States Parties without discrimination of any kind, on the basis of equality and in accordance with international law.
2. In carrying out scientific investigations and in furtherance of the provisions of this Agreement, the States Parties shall have the right to collect on and remove from the Moon samples of its mineral and other substances. Such samples shall

remain at the disposal of those States Parties which caused them to be collected and may be used by them for scientific purposes. States Parties shall have regard to the desirability of making a portion of such samples available to other interested States Parties and the international scientific community for scientific investigation. States Parties may in the course of scientific investigations also use mineral and other substances of the Moon in quantities appropriate for the support of their missions.

[...]

Article 7

1. In exploring and using the Moon, States Parties shall take measures to prevent the disruption of the existing balance of its environment, whether by introducing adverse changes in that environment, by its harmful contamination through the introduction of extra-environmental matter or otherwise. States Parties shall also take measures to avoid harmfully affecting the environment of the Earth through the introduction of extraterrestrial matter or otherwise.

[...]

Article 10

1. States Parties shall adopt all practicable measures to safeguard the life and health of persons on the Moon. For this purpose they shall regard any person on the Moon as an astronaut within the meaning of article V of the Treaty on Principles Governing the Activities of States in the Exploration and Use of Outer Space, including the Moon and Other Celestial Bodies and as part of the personnel of a spacecraft within the meaning of the Agreement on the Rescue of Astronauts, the Return of Astronauts and the Return of Objects Launched into Outer Space.

[...]

Article 11

1. The Moon and its natural resources are the common heritage of mankind, which finds its expression in the provisions of this Agreement, in particular in paragraph 5 of this article.
2. The Moon is not subject to national appropriation by any claim of sovereignty, by means of use or occupation, or by any other means.

[...]

Article 12

1. States Parties shall retain jurisdiction and control over their personnel, vehicles, equipment, facilities, stations and installations on the Moon. The ownership of

space vehicles, equipment, facilities, stations and installations shall not be affected by their presence on the Moon.

2. Vehicles, installations and equipment or their component parts found in places other than their intended location shall be dealt with in accordance with article 5 of the Agreement on the Rescue of Astronauts, the Return of Astronauts and the Return of Objects Launched into Outer Space.
3. In the event of an emergency involving a threat to human life, States Parties may use the equipment, vehicles, installations, facilities or supplies of other States Parties on the Moon. Prompt notification of such use shall be made to the Secretary-General of the United Nations or the State Party concerned.

Article 13

A State Party which learns of the crash landing, forced landing or other unintended landing on the Moon of a space object, or its component parts, that were not launched by it, shall promptly inform the launching State Party and the Secretary-General of the United Nations.

III *Resolution 1721 A and B (XVI) of 20 December 1961 – International Cooperation in the Peaceful Uses of Outer Space*

The General Assembly

Recognizing the common interest of mankind in furthering the peaceful uses of outer space and the urgent need to strengthen international cooperation in this important field,

Believing that the exploration and use of outer space should be only for the betterment of mankind and to the benefit of States irrespective of the stage of their economic or scientific development,

1. *Commends* to States for their guidance in the exploration and use of outer space the following principles:
   (a) International law, including the Charter of the United Nations, applies to outer space and celestial bodies;
   (b) Outer space and celestial bodies are free for exploration and use by all States in conformity with international law and are not subject to national appropriation;
2. *Invites* the Committee on the Peaceful Uses of Outer Space to study and report on the legal problems which may arise from the exploration and use of outer space.

[...]

Bibliography

Treaties, Agreements and Statutes

International

Additional Protocol I to the Geneva Conventions, www.icrc.org/en/doc/assets/files/other/icrc_002_0321.pdf.

African Charter on Human and Peoples' Rights, https://au.int/en/treaties/african-charter-human-and-peoples-rights.

Agreement Governing the Activities of States on the Moon and Other Celestial Bodies (Moon Agreement), https://www.unoosa.org/oosa/en/ourwork/spacelaw/treaties/intromoon-agreement.html.

American Convention on Human Rights, www.cidh.oas.org/basicos/english/basic3.american%20convention.htm.

Arab Charter on Human Rights, http://hrlibrary.umn.edu/instree/loas2005.html.

Asean Human Rights Declaration, https://asean.org/asean-human-rights-declaration/.

Cairo Declaration on Human Rights in Islam, 5 August 1990, (English Translation), http://hrlibrary.umn.edu/instree/cairodeclaration.html.

Charter of Fundamental Rights of the European Union, https://eur-lex.europa.eu/eli/treaty/char_2012/oj.

European Convention on Human Rights, www.echr.coe.int/documents/convention_eng.pdf.

European Council, Solemn Declaration on European Union [1983] *Bulletin of the European Communities* 6-1983, 25–29.

International Covenant on Civil and Political Rights, www.ohchr.org/en/professionalinterest/pages/ccpr.aspx.

International Criminal Court, Core Legal Texts, www.icc-cpi.int/resource-library/Pages/core-legal-texts.aspx.

International Criminal Court, Elements of Crimes, www.icc-cpi.int/Publications/Elements-of-Crimes.pdf.

International Criminal Court, Rome Statute of the International Criminal Court, www.icc-cpi.int/Publications/Rome-Statute.pdf.

Treaty on Principles Governing the Activities of States in the Exploration and Use of Outer Space, including the Moon and Other Celestial Bodies – Outer Space Treaty (OST) United Nations, Treaty Series, vol. 610, No. 8843, www.unoosa.org/oosa/en/ourwork/spacelaw/treaties/outerspacetreaty.html.

Universal Declaration of Human Rights, www.ohchr.org/EN/UDHR/Documents/UDHR_Translations/eng.pdf.

Universal Islamic Declaration of Human Rights. www.alhewar.com/ISLAMDECL.html.

www.ohchr.org/en/instruments-listings.

National

Basic Law for the Federal Republic of Germany, www.gesetze-im-internet.de/englisch_gg/englisch_gg.html#p0019.

Human Rights Act 1998, www.legislation.gov.uk/ukpga/1998/42.

NASA and Breakthrough Starshot Foundation LLC Under Space Act Umbrella Agreement, 2018, www.nasa.gov/saa/domestic/26617_26617_Annex1_Brkthru_Encel_FullyExecuted.pdf.

Case Law

International

Court of Justice of the European Union

Costa v E.N.E.L [1964] ECR 585.

International Court of Justice

Bosnia and Herzegovina v. Yugoslavia (Serbia and Montenegro) (2007) ICJ Reports 43.

Croatia v. Serbia, Application of the Genocide Convention of 3 February 2015, (2015) ICJ Reports 3.

DRC v. Rwanda, Judgment, Armed Activities on the Territory of the Congo (New Application: 2002) Jurisdiction and Admissibility of 3 February 2006, (2006) ICJ Reports 31.

Legality of the Threat or Use of Nuclear Weapons, Advisory Opinion, 8 July 1996, ICJ Reports 1996, 226.

Domestic

England and Wales

R v. Woollin [1999] 1 AC. 82.

Germany

BVerfGE vol. 37, 271 = 2 CMLR (1974) 540.

BVerfGE vol. 73, 339 = 3 CMLR (1987) 225.

BVerfGE vol. 111, 307.

BVerfGE vol. 131, 286.

Books

Akerma K, *Außerirdische – Einleitung in die Philosophie/Extraterrestrische Intelligenz in der Philosophie von Epikur bis Hans Jonas* (Monsenstein und Vannerdat, Münster, 2001).

Ambos K (ed.), *The Rome Statute of the ICC*, 4th edition (Bloomsbury, London, 2021) – Cited by contributor, article and marginal number.

Anderhub W and Müller A, *Phänomen Kornkreise: Forschung zwischen Volksüberlieferung, Grenz-und Naturwissenschaft*, (AT Verlag, Baden/Munich, 2005).

Ascher M, *Ethnomathematics – A Multicultural View of Mathematical Ideas* (Chapman and Hall/CRC, London, 1994).

Ashkenazi M, *What We Know About Extraterrestrial Intelligence – Foundations of Xenology* (Springer, New York, 2016).

Atadjanov R, *Humanness as a Protected Legal Interest of Crimes Against Humanity – Conceptual and Normative Aspects* (Asser Press/Springer, New York, 2019).

Barnes ME, *Linguistics and Language in Science Fiction-Fantasy* (Arno Press, New York, 1975).

Barrow JD et al. (eds.), *Fitness of the Cosmos for Life*, (CUP, Cambridge, 2016).

Baxter S, *The Time Ships*, 1st ed. 1995 (cited after the HarperVoyager, Glasgow, 2016 paperback edition).

Bear G, *Anvil of Stars* (Warner Books, New York, 1992).

Bear G, *The Forge of God*, 1st ed. 1987 (cited after the Gollancz, London, 2010 edition).

Bear G, *Hull Zero Three* (Gollancz, London, 2011).

Bering S, *Solange bis Vergessen – Kritische Analyse der Entwicklung und gegenwärtigen Position der BVerfG-Rechtsprechung zum Verhältnis von EU-Recht und den Grundrechten des Grundgesetzes*, Beiträge zum Europa-und Völkerrecht, vol. 21 (University of Halle-Wittenberg, Halle, 2020), https://tietje.jura.uni-halle.de/sites/default/files/BeitraegeEVR/Heft_21_Bering.pdf.

Bertka CM (ed.), *Exploring the Origin, Extent, and Future of Life* (CUP, Cambridge, 2010).

Blackford R, *Science Fiction and the Moral Imagination – Visions, Minds, Ethics* (Springer, New York, 2017).

Boothby WH (ed.), *New Technologies and the Law in War and Peace* (CUP, Cambridge, 2019).

Böse M et al. (eds.), *Justice without Borders: Essays in Honour of Wolfgang Schomburg* (Brill|Nijhoff, Leiden Boston, 2018).

Boyce TD and Chunnu WM (eds.), *Historicizing Fear: Ignorance, Vilification, and Othering* (University Press of Colorado, Boulder, 2020).

Bracewell RN, *The Galactic Club: Intelligent life in outer space* (San Francisco Book Co., San Francisco, 1976).

Bryan CDB, *Close Encounters of The Fourth Kind: Alien Abduction, UFOs, and the Conference at MIT*. (Knopf, New York, 1995).

Burke S, *Semiosis* (HarperVoyager, Glasgow, 2018).

Burks AW and von Neumann J, *Theory of Self-reproducing Automata* (University of Illinois Press, Illinois, 1967).

Canavan G and Link EC (eds.), *The Cambridge History of Science Fiction* (CUP, Cambridge, 2019).

Card OS, *Ender's Game,* 1st d. 1977 (cited after Author's Definitive Edition, Tor Books, New York, 1994).

Card OS, *Xenocide* (Tor Books, New York, 1992).

Christopher J, *The Tripods Collection – Vol. 1: The White Mountains, vol. 2: The City of Gold and Lead* (hereafter: *City of Gold and Lead*); *vol. 3: The Pool of Fire* (hereafter: *Pool of Fire*); *Prequel: When the Tripods Came* (hereafter: *Prequel*) 1st eds. 1967–1988 (Aladdin Paperback, New York, 2014).

Ćirković MM, *The Astrobiological Landscape* (CUP, Cambridge, 2012).

Ćirković MM, *The Great Silence: Science and Philosophy of Fermi's Paradox* (OUP, Oxford, 2018).

Clancy SA, *Abducted: How People Come to Believe They Were Kidnapped by Aliens* (Harvard University Press, Cambridge, 2005).

Clarke AC, *Childhood's End,* 1st ed. 1953 (cited after the 1990 edition of Del Rey Books, New York, 1990).

Clarke AC, *Rendezvous with Rama* (Gollancz, London, 1973).

Clarke AC, *The Songs of Distant Earth* (Grafton Books. London, 1968).

Clarke AC and Lee G, *Rama II* (Gollancz, London, 1989).

Clarke AC and Lee G, *Rama Revealed* (Orbit Books, London, 1996).

Clarke AC and Lee G, *The Garden of Rama* (Bantam Spectra, New York, 1992).

Cleland CE, *The Quest for a Universal Theory of Life* (CUP, Cambridge, 2019).

Cooper K, *The Contact Paradox – Challenging our Assumptions in the Search for Extraterrestrial Intelligence* (Bloomsbury Sigma/London, 2019).

Correy L, *A Matter of Metalaw* (DAW Books, New York, 1986).

Coulthart R, *In Plain Sight – An investigation into UFOs and impossible science* (Harper Collins, Sydney, 2021).

Crawford K, *Atlas of AI: The Real Worlds of Artificial Intelligence* (Yale University Press, New Haven, 2021).

Csicsery-Ronay, Jr I, *The Seven Beauties of Science Fiction* (Wesleyan University Press, Middletown, 2008).

Damaska M, *The Faces of Justice and State Authority* (Yale University Press, New Haven, 1986).

Dawson L, *War in Space: The Science and Technology Behind Our Next Theater of Conflict* (Springer, New York, 2018).

De Grasse Tysson N and Lang A, *Accessory to War – The unspoken alliance between astrophysics and the military* (Norton, New York, 2019).

Defferard F (ed.), 2017. *Le droit saisi par la science fiction* (Mare Martin, Paris, 2017).

Defferard F, *Le droit selon Star Trek* (Mare Martin, Paris, 2016).

Determann JM, *Islam, Science Fiction and Extraterrestrial Life – The Culture of Astrobiology in the Muslim World* (Bloomsbury, London, 2020).

Deudney D, *Dark skies: space expansionism, planetary geopolitics, and the ends of humanity* (OUP, Oxford, 2020).

Dick BK, *Modern Arabic Science Fiction: Science, Society and Religion in Selected Texts,* 2016, http://etheses.dur.ac.uk/11907/.

Dick SJ (ed.), *Historical studies in the societal impact of spaceflight* (NASA, Washington, 2015), www.nasa.gov/ebooks.

Dick SJ and Lupisella ML (eds.), *Cosmos and Culture: Cultural Evolution in a Cosmic Context* (NASA, Washington, 2009) www.nasa.gov/connect/ebooks/hist_culture_cosmos_detail.html.

Dick SJ and Strick JE, *The Living Universe: NASA and the Development of Astrobiology* (Rutgers University Press, New Brunswick, 2004).

Dick SJ, *Astrobiology, Discovery, and Societal Impact* (CUP, Cambridge, 2018).

Doran PD et al. (eds.), *Life in Antarctic Deserts and other Cold Dry Environments* (CUP, Cambridge, 2010).

Drake F and Sobel D, *Is Anyone Out There? The Scientific Search for Extraterrestrial Intelligence* (Delacorte Press, New York, 1992).

Ekeres RD et al., *SETI 2020: A Roadmap for the Search for Extraterrestrial Intelligence* (SETI PR, San Jose, 2002).

Evans EP, *The criminal prosecution and capital punishment of animals* (Heinemann, London, 1906).

Fasan E, *Relations with Alien Intelligences: The Scientific Basis of Metalaw* (Berlin Verlag, Berlin, 1970 – cited after the version printed in Stearns PM and Tennen L (eds.), *Private Law, Public Law, Metalaw and Public Policy in Space,* Springer, New York, 2016) pp 181–246.

Fasan E, *Weltraumrecht* (Krausskopf-Flugwelt-Verlag, Cologne, 1965).

Fischer J and Spreen D, *Soziologie der Weltraumfahrt* (transcript, Bielefeld, 2014).

Follesdal A and Pogge TW (eds.), *Real World Justice – Grounds, Principles, Human Rights, and Social Institutions,* (Springer, New York, 2005).

Forgan DH, *Solving Fermi's Paradox* (CUP, Cambridge, 2019).

Fournet C, *Genocide and Crimes Against Humanity – Misconceptions and Confusion in French Law and Practice* (Hart, Oxford, 2013).

Freudenthal H, *Lincos – Design of a Language for Cosmic Intercourse, Part 1* (North-Holland Publishing Co., Amsterdam, 1960).

Gargaud M et al. (eds.), *Origins and Evolution of Life* (CUP, Cambridge, 2011).

Gerabek WE et al. (eds.), *Enzyklopädie Medizingeschichte* (Walter de Gruyter, Berlin/New York, 2007).

Gerritzen D, *Erstkontakt* (Kosmos, Stuttgart, 2016).

Godfrey-Smith P, *Other Minds – The Octopus and the Evolution of Intelligent Life* (William Collins, Glasgow, 2016).

Grabenwarter C, *European Convention on Human Rights – Commentary* (CH Beck, Munich, 2014).

Grant JP and Barker JC (eds.), *Encyclopaedic Dictionary of International Law,* 3rd ed. (OUP, Oxford, 2009).

Habermas J, *Moralbewusstsein und kommunikatives Handeln* (Suhrkamp, Berlin, 1983).

Haldeman J, *The Forever War,* 1st ed. 1974 (cited after Gollancz, London, 2010 edition).

Haley AG, *Space Law and Government* (Appleton-Century-Crofts, New York, 1963).

Hassler D and Wilcox C (eds.), *New Boundaries in Political Science Fiction* (University of South Carolina Press, Columbia, 2008).

Hegel GWF, 1820. *Grundlinien der Philosophie des Rechts* (F. Meiner, Leipzig, 1820).

Heinlein RA, *Double Star,* 1st ed. 1956 (cited after Gollancz. London, 2013).

Heinlein RA, *Starship Troopers,* 1st ed. 1959 (cited after Hodder and Stoughton, London, 2005 edition).

Hoerster N, *Ethik und Interesse* (Reclam, Leipzig, 2003).

Hoyle F, *The Black Cloud* (William Heinemann Ltd., Portsmouth, 1957; cited after the Penguin edition, 1960).

Hynek JA and Vallée J (eds.), 1975. *The Edge of Reality: A Progress Report on Unidentified Flying Objects* (Henry Regnery, Chicago, 1975).

James E and Mendlesohn F (eds.), *The Cambridge Companion to Science Fiction* (CUP, Cambridge, 2003).

Johnson-Freese J, *Space Warfare in the 21st Century – Arming the Heavens* (Routledge, Abingdon, 2017).

Jonas H, *Das Prinzip Verantwortung. Versuch einer Ethik für die technologische Zivilisation* (Suhrkamp, Berlin, 1984).

Jones RF, *This Island Earth* (Shasta Publishers, Chicago, 1952).

Joseph F, *Military Encounters with Extraterrestrials – The Real War of the Worlds* (Bear & Company, Rochester, 2018).

Joseph S and Castan M, *The International Covenant on Civil and Political Rights: Cases, Materials, and Commentary,* 3rd ed. (OUP, Oxford, 2013).

Kaikobad K and Bohlander M (eds.), *International Law and Power: Perspectives on Legal Order and Justice – Essays in Honour of Colin Warbrick* (Martinus Nijhoff, Leiden, 2009).

Kant I, *Critique of Pure Reason* (Translated and edited by P Guyer and A W Wood, CUP, Cambridge, 1998).

Kant I, *Grundlegung der Metaphysik der Sitten,* in Gesammelte Schriften, AA IV, 430, https://korpora.zim.uni-duisburg-essen.de/Kant/aa04/430.html.

Kant I, *Prolegomena to Any Future Metaphysics That Will Be Able to Come Forward as Science*, 1783, Revised edition (Trans. Hatfield G, CUP, Cambridge, 2004).

Kaufman M, A History of Astrobiology, NASA, 2022, https://astrobiology.nasa.gov/about/history-of-astrobiology/.

Kaufman M, Life, Here and Beyond. NASA, 2022, https://astrobiology.nasa.gov/about/.

Kean L, 2010. *UFOs – Generals, Pilots and Government Officials Go on the Record* (Three Rivers Press, New York, 2010).

Klahr H and Brandner W (eds.), *Planet Formation: Theory, Observations, and Experiments* (CUP, Cambridge, 2006).

Klein JJ, *Understanding Space Strategy – The Art of War in Space* (Routledge, London/New York, 2019).

Klug J and Leonard S (eds.), *To Boldly Go – Leadership, Strategy and Conflict in the 21st Century and Beyond* (Casemate, Philadelphia, 2021).

Kminek G et al., *The International Planetary Protection Handbook, An online-only supplement to (2019) 205 Space Research Today,* 2019, www.sciencedirect.com/journal/space-research-today/vol/205/suppl/S.

Kramer WM and Bahmer CW, *Fire Officer's Guide to Disaster Control, 2nd ed.* (Pennwell, Tulsa, 1992).

Kreiner A, *Jesus, UFOs, Aliens – Außerirdische Intelligenz als Herausforderung für den christlichen Glauben.* (Herder, Meersburg, 2011).

Kreß C and Barriga S (eds.), *The Crime of Aggression – A Commentary* (CUP, Cambridge, 2017).

Lagodny O, *Zwei Strafrechtswelten – Rechtsvergleichende Betrachtungen und Erfahrungen aus deutscher Sicht in Österreich* (Nomos, Baden-Baden, 2020).

Landfester U et al. (eds.), *Humans in Outer Space – Interdisciplinary Perspectives Studies in Space Policy* (Springer, Vienna, 2011).

Latham R (ed.), *Science Fiction Criticism – An Anthology of Essential Writings* (Bloomsbury and James, London, 2017).

Le Guin UK, *Rocannon's World* (Ace Books, New York, 1966).

Lem S, *Solaris* (Wydawnictwo MON, Warsaw, 1961 – English translation by Bill Johnston, Walker, London, 1970).

Liu C, *The Three-Body Problem* (Head of Zeus. London, 2015).

Liu C, *Death's End* (Head of Zeus, London, 2016).

Liu C, *The Dark Forest* (Head of Zeus, London, 2016).

Loeb A, *Extraterrestrial: The First Sign of Intelligent Life Beyond Earth* (Houghton Mifflin Harcourt, Boston/New York, 2021).

Lupisella M, *Cosmological Theories of Value – Science, Philosophy and Meaning in Cosmic Evolution* (Springer, New York, 2020).

Lyall F and Larsen PB, *Space Law – A Treatise,* 2nd ed. (Routledge, Abingdon, 2018).

Mancuso S, *The revolutionary genius of plants* (Atria Books, London et al, 2018).

Marboe I (ed.), *Soft Law in Outer Space – The Function of Non-binding Norms in International Space Law* (Böhlau Verlag, Vienna, 2012).

Marquard O (ed.) *Einheit und Vielfalt* (Meiner, Hamburg, 1990).

Marx K, *Critique of Hegel's Philosophy of Right* (Translation by Jolin A and O'Malley J, CUP, Cambridge, 1977).

McDevitt J, *The Hercules Text, Revised version* (Ace Books, New York, 2015).

Méheust B, *Science-Fiction et Soucoupes Volantes – Une réalité mytho-physique,* revised ed. (Terre de Brume, Rennes, 1978).

Meltzer M, *When biospheres collide: a history of NASA's planetary protection programs,* 2011 – www.nasa.gov/connect/ebooks/when_biospheres_collide_detail.html.

Michaud MAG, C*ontact with Alien Civilizations – Our Hopes and Fears about Encountering Extraterrestrials* (Copernicus Books, New York, 2010).

Miller R, *Aliens – Past, Present and Future* (Watkins, London, 2017).

Müller A, *Deutschlands UFO-Akten – Über den politischen Umgang mit dem UFO-Phänomen in Deutschland* (Books on Demand, Norderstedt, 2021).

Münkler H (ed.) *Furcht und Faszination – Facetten der Fremdheit* (Akademie, Berlin, 1997).

Myers WE, *Aliens and linguists: language study and science fiction* (University of Georgia Press, Athens, 1980).

Newton I, *Philosophiae Naturalis Principia Mathematica,* 1687.

Niven L and Pournelle J, *The Mote in God's Eye,* 1st ed. 1974 (cited after HarperCollins, New York, 1993 edition).

Niven L and Pournelle J, *The Gripping Hand* (Pocket Books, New York, 1993).

Norris RP and Stootman FH (eds.), *Bioastronomy 2002: Life Among the Stars – IAU Symposium* (Astronomical Society of the Pacific, San Francisco, 2004).

Ollongren A, *Astrolinguistics: Design of a Linguistic System for Interstellar Communication Based on Logic* (Springer, New York, 2012).

Payne K, *I, Warbot: The Dawn of Artificially Intelligent Conflict* (C Hurst & Co., London, 2021).

Peake A, *The Hidden Universe – An investigation into non-human intelligences* (Watkins, London, 2019).

Polchinski J, *String Theory Vol. 1: An Introduction to the Bosonic String* (CUP, New York, 1998).

Polchinski J, *String Theory Vol. 2: Superstring Theory and Beyond* (CUP, New York, 1998).

Powell R et al., *A Forensic Analysis of Navy Carrier Strike Group Eleven's Encounter with an Anomalous Aerial Vehicle,* Scientific Coalition for UAP Studies, www.explore scu.org/post/2004-uss-nimitz-strike-navy-group-incident-report, 2019.

Pritchard A et al. (eds.), *Alien Discussions: Proceedings of the Abduction Study Conference at MIT* (North Cambridge Press, Cambridge, 1994).
Pröschold BM, *Ausserirdische – Das grosse Tabu unseres Zeitalters*, 2nd ed. (Selbstverlag, 2013).
Pudritz P et al. (eds.), *Planetary Systems and the Origins of Life* (CUP, Cambridge, 2007).
Rainey B et al., *Jacobs, White, and Ovey: The European Convention on Human Rights*, 8th ed. (OUP, Oxford, 2021).
Robinson KS, *Aurora* (Orbit, London, 2015).
Rumsfeld D, *Known and Unknown* (Penguin, London, 2011).
Saberhagen F, *Berserker – Collection* (Ballantine Books, New York, 1967).
Sagan C, *Contact.* First Printing edition, (Simon & Schuster Ltd., New York, 1985).
Salkind NJ (ed.) *Encyclopedia of research design* (SAGE Publications, Thousand Oaks, 2010).
Scalzi J, *Old Man's War* (Tor Books, New York, 2007).
Scalzi J, *The Ghost Brigades* (Tor Books, New York, 2007).
Scalzi J, *The Last Colony* (Tor Books, New York, 2008).
Schabas WA, *Nowak's ICCPR Commentary: U.N. International Covenant on Civil and Political Rights*, 3rd ed. (N. P. Engel, Kehl, 2019).
Schabas WA, *The European Convention on Human Rights: A Commentary* (OUP, Oxford, 2015).
Schetsche M and Anton A, Die *Gesellschaft der Außerirdischen – Einführung in die Exosoziologie* (Springer, Wiesbaden, 2019).
Schladebach M, *Weltraumrecht* (Mohr/Siebeck, Tübingen, 2020).
Schmidt N (ed.) *Planetary Defense – Global Collaboration for Defending Earth from Asteroids and Comets* (Springer, New York, 2019).
Schopenhauer A, *On the Basis of Morality.* 2nd rev. ed. (Translation by E.F.J. Payne, Hackett Classics, Indianapolis, 1998).
Schwartz JSJ and Milligan T (eds.), *The Ethics of Space Exploration* (Springer, New York, 2016).
Shostak S, *Sharing the Universe – Perspectives on Extraterrestrial Life* (Berkeley Hills Books, Albany, 1998).
Siddiqi AA, *Beyond Earth – A Chronicle of Deep Space Exploration, 1958–2016.* 2nd ed. (NASA, Washington, 2018) www.nasa.gov/connect/ebooks/beyond_earth_detail.html.
Siegfried T, *The Number of the Heavens – A History of the Multiverse and the Quest to Understand the Cosmos* (Harvard University Press, Cambridge, 2019).
Simmel G, *Soziologie: Untersuchungen über die Formen der Vergesellschaftung,* 4th ed. (Duncker & Humblot, Berlin, 1958).
Singer MG, *Generalization in Ethics* (Macmillan, New York, 1971).

Smith KC and Mariscal C (eds.), *Social and Conceptual Issues in Astrobiology* (OUP, Oxford, 2020).

Springnagel M, *Die Darstellung von außerirdischer Intelligenz im Film* (*Extraterrestrial Intelligence in the Movies*) (Unpublished PhD thesis, 2017) – https://othes.univie.ac.at/49475/.

Stähle K, *Rechtsfragen beim Kontakt mit Extraterrestrischen. Völkerrecht, Wirtschaft und Politik – Ein Gedankenmodell* (Berliner Wissenschafts-Verlag, Berlin, 2023).

Stearns PM and Tennen L (eds.), *Private Law, Public Law, Metalaw and Public Policy in Space* (Springer, New York, 2016).

Steer C and Hersch M (eds.), *War and Peace in Outer Space – Law, Policy, and Ethics* (OUP, Oxford, 2021).

Strugatsky A and Strugatsky B, *Hard to be a God* (Gollancz, London, 2015).

Strugatsky A and Strugatsky B, *Roadside Picnic* (Gollancz, London, 2012).

Taylor PM, *A Commentary on the International Covenant on Civil and Political Rights: The UN Human Rights Committee's Monitoring of ICCPR Rights* (CUP, Cambridge, 2020).

Taylor TS and Boan B, *Alien Invasion – How to Defend Earth* (Baen Books, Wake Forest, 2011).

Tchaikovsky A, *Children of Ruin* (Pan Books, London, 2020).

Tchaikovsky A, *Children of Time* (Pan Books, London, 2016).

Vakoch D (ed.), *Archaeology, anthropology, and interstellar communication* (NASA History Series, 2013), www.nasa.gov/connect/ebooks/archaeology_anthropology_and_interstellar_communication.html.

Vakoch DA (ed). *Extraterrestrial Altruism: Evolution and Ethics in the Cosmos* (Springer, New York, 2014).

Vakoch DA and Dowd MF (eds.), *The Drake Equation* (CUP, Cambridge, 2015).

Vallée J, *Dimensions – A Casebook of Alien Contact* (Anomalist Boks, San Antonio/Charlottesville, 1988).

Vallée J, *Revelations – Alien Contact and Human Deception* (Anomalist Books, Antonio/Charlottesville, 1991/2008).

Vallée J, *Messengers of Deception: UFO Contacts and Cults* (Bantam Books, New York, 1980).

Vallée J, *Passport to Magonia – From Folklore to Flying Saucers* (Daily Grail Publishing, Brisbane, 1969–2014 edition).

Vallée J, *The Invisible College – What a Group of Scientists Has Discovered About UFO Influences on the Human Race* (Anomalist Books, San Antonio/Charlottesville, 2014).

Vallée J, 1990. *Confrontations – A Scientist's Search for Alien Contact* (Anomalist Books, San Antonio, 1990).

Wahlgren Y, *The Universal Translator – Everything you need to know about 139 languages that don't really exist* (The History Press, Cheltenham, 2021).

Walter U, *Astronautics: The Physics of Space Flight*, 3rd ed. (Springer, Cham, 2018).

Watkins E (ed.) *Immanuel Kant – Natural Science* (CUP, Cambridge, 2012).

Watzlawick P, *Wie wirklich ist die Wirklichkeit?* (Piper, Munich, 2012).

Weaver R and McAndrew J, *The Roswell Report: Fact Versus Fiction in the New Mexico Desert*, 1995, https://apps.dtic.mil/sti/pdfs/ADA326148.pdf.

Webb S, *If the Universe Is Teeming with Aliens – Where is Everybody? – Fifty Solutions to the Fermi Paradox and the Problem of Extraterrestrial Life* (Copernicus Books, New York, 2002).

Webb S, *If the Universe Is Teeming with Aliens ... WHERE IS EVERYBODY?: Seventy-Five Solutions to the Fermi Paradox and the Problem of Extraterrestrial Life*, 2nd ed., (Springer, New York, 2015).

Wells HG, *The War of the Worlds* (Harper & Brothers, New York, 1898).

Werber B, *The Empire of the Ants* (*Les Fourmis*). (Trans. Rocques M; Bantam Press. London, 1996).

Werle G and Jeßberger F, *Völkerstrafrecht*, 5th edition (Mohr Siebeck, Tübingen, 2020).

Wilkinson D, *Science, Religion, and the Search for Extraterrestrial Intelligence* (OUP, Oxford, 2013).

Wilson RC, *Blind Lake* (TOR Books, New York, 2003).

Wright JC, 2020. *Deep Space Warfare – Military Strategy Beyond Orbit* (McFarland, Jefferson, 2020).

Wyndham J, 1951. *The Day of the Triffids* (Michael Joseph, London, 1951).

Zwiebach B, *A First Course in String Theory* (CUP, Cambridge, 2009).

Book Chapters

Barrow-Green J, The Three-Body Problem, in Gowers T et al (eds.), *The Princeton Companion to Mathematics* (Princeton University Press, Princeton, 2008), pp. 726–728.

Billingham J, SETI: The Nasa Years, in Vakoch D (ed.), *Archaeology, anthropology, and interstellar communication* (NASA History Series, 2013), pp. 1–22 www.nasa.gov/connect/ebooks/archaeology_anthropology_and_interstellar_communication.html.

Bohlander M, "The Global Panopticon" Mass surveillance and data privacy intrusion as a crime against humanity?, in Böse M et al (eds.), *Justice without Borders: Essays in Honour of Wolfgang Schomburg* (Brill | Nijhoff, Leiden Boston, 2018) pp. 73–102.

Bohlander M, Killing many to save a few? Preliminary Thoughts about Avoiding Collateral Civilian Damage by Assassination of Regime Elites, in Kaikobad K and Bohlander M (eds.), *International Law and Power: Perspectives on Legal Order and Justice – Essays in Honour of Colin Warbrick* (Martinus Nijhoff, Leiden, 2009) pp. 207–234.

Cockell CS, The Ethical Status of Microbial Life on Earth and Elsewhere: In Defence of Intrinsic Value, in Schwartz JSJ and Milligan T (eds.) *The Ethics of Space Exploration* (Springer, New Yor, 2016) pp. 167–180.

De Zwart M, Outer Space, in Boothby WH (ed.). *New Technologies and the Law in War and Peace* (CUP, Cambridge, 2019) pp. 347–349.

Dick SJ, Astrobiology and Society: An Overview, in Smith KC and Mariscal C (eds.) *Social and Conceptual Issues in Astrobiology* (OUP, Oxford, 2020) pp. 9–20.

Finney B and Bentley J, A Tale of Two Analogues Learning at a Distance from the Ancient Greeks and Maya and the Problem of Deciphering Extraterrestrial Radio Transmissions, in Vakoch DA (ed.) *Archaeology, anthropology, and interstellar communication* (NASA, Washington, 2013) pp. 65–78, www.nasa.gov/connect/ebooks/archaeology_anthropology_and_interstellar_communication.html.

Follesdal A, Human Rights and Relativism, in Follesdal A and Pogge TW (eds.), *Real World Justice – Grounds, Principles, Human Rights, and Social Institutions,* (Springer, New York, 2005) pp. 265–283.

Foucault M, 2001. *Des espaces autres in: Dits et écrits, vol. II, 1976–1988* (Gallimard, Paris, 2001) pp. 1571–1581 (English translation: Foucault M, *Of other spaces, 1967,* in Dehaene M & De Cauter L (eds.) *Heterotopia and the City* (Routledge, London/ New York, 2008, pp. 13–30).

Frammartino Wilks A, *Kantian Foundations for a Cosmocentric Ethic,* in Schwartz JSJ and Milligan T (eds.), *The Ethics of Space Exploration* (Springer, New York, 2016), pp. 181–194.

Garber SJ., A Political History of NASA's SETI Program,, in Vakoch D (ed.), *Archaeology, anthropology, and interstellar communication* (NASA History Series, 2013), www.nasa.gov/connect/ebooks/archaeology_anthropology_and_interstellar_communication.html;pp, pp. 23–48.

Harrison AA, Proximity, System Level, and Human Response to Extraterrestrial Life, in: Workshop on the societal implications of astrobiology – Final Report, Ames Research Center, November 16–17, 1999; in NASA, *Workshop on the societal implications of Astrobiology*, 1999, p. 56, www.astrosociology.org/library/pdf/nasa-workshop-report-societal-implications-of-astrobiology.pdf.

Kant I, Universal natural history and theory of the heavens or essay on the constitution and the mechanical origin of the whole universe according to Newtonian principles, 1755, Part Three; in Watkins E (ed.) *Immanuel Kant – Natural Science* (CUP, Cambridge, 2012) pp. 294–306.

Kellermann KI et al., Is Anyone Out There? in Kellermann KI et al., *Open Skies – The National Radio Astronomy Observatory and Its Impact on US Radio Astronomy* (Springer, New York, 2020), pp 229–260.

Korbitz A, Altruism, Metalaw, and Celegistics: An Extraterrestrial Perspective on Universal Law-Making, in Vakoch DA (ed.) *Extraterrestrial Altruism* (Springer, New York, 2014) pp. 231–247.

Maccone C, SETI and the IAA SETI Permanent Committee: Past, Present and Possible Future, in Stearns PM and Tennen L (eds.), *Private Law, Public Law, Metalaw and Public Policy in Space* (Springer, New York, 2016) p. 146.

McConnell BS, *Algorithmic Communication with Extraterrestrial Intelligence*, in Norris RP and Stootman FH (eds.) *Bioastronomy 2002: Life Among the Stars– IAU Symposium* (Astronomical Society of the Pacific, San Francisco, 2004) pp. 445–450.

McMahon S, Do Extraordinary Claims Require Extraordinary Evidence? – The Proper Role of Sagan's Dictum in Astrobiology, in Smith KC and Mariscal C (eds.) *Social and Conceptual Issues in Astrobiology* (OUP, Oxford, 2020) pp. 126–127.

Milligan T, Space Ethics Without Foundations, in Schwartz JSJ and Milligan T (eds.), *The Ethics of Space Exploration* (Springer, New York, 2016) pp. 125–134.

Morrison D, Overview of Active Planetary Defense *Methods*, in Schmidt N (ed.) *Planetary Defense – Global Collaboration for Defending Earth from Asteroids and Comets* (Springer, New York, 2019) pp. 113–121.

Münkler H und Ladwig B, Dimensionen der Fremdheit, in Münkler H (ed.) *Furcht und Faszination – Facetten der Fremdheit* (Akademie, Berlin, 1997) pp. 11–43.

Musso P, Wide Cultural Communications in Interstellar Messages, in Norris RP and Stootman FH (eds.), *Bioastronomy 2002: Life Among the Stars – IAU Symposium* (Astronomical Society of the Pacific, San Francisco, 2004) pp. 511–513.

Newman C, 'The Way to Eden': Environmental Legal and Ethical Values in Interplanetary Spaceflight, in Schwartz JSJ and Milligan T (eds.) *The Ethics of Space Exploration* (Springer, New Yor, 2016) pp. 221–238.

Ollongren A and Vakoch DA, Large-Size Message Construction for ETI: Self-Interpretation in LINCOS, in Norris RP and Stootman FH (eds.) *Bioastronomy 2002: Life Among the Stars– IAU Symposium* (Astronomical Society of the Pacific, San Francisco, 2004) pp. 499–504.

Schetsche MT, Encounters among the stars – exosociological considerations, in Landfester U et al (eds.) *Humans in Outer Space – Interdisciplinary Perspectives. Studies in Space Policy* (Springer, Vienna, 2011) pp. 102–114.

Schwartz JSJ, On the Methodology of Space Ethics, in Schwartz JSJ and Milligan T (eds.), *The Ethics of Space Exploration* (Springer, New York, 2016) pp. 93–107.

Shostak S, SETI and the Media, in Norris RP and Stootman FH (eds.) *Bioastronomy 2002: Life Among the Stars – IAU Symposium,* 2004, p 541.

Simonton D, Heisenberg effect, in Salkind NJ (ed.) *Encyclopedia of research design* (SAGE Publications, Thousand Oaks, 2010), pp. 564–567.

Smith KC, METI or REGRETTI: Ethics, Risk, and Alien Contact, in Smith KC and Mariscal C (eds.) *Social and Conceptual Issues in Astrobiology* (OUP, Oxford, 2020) pp. 209–238.

Smith KC, The Curious Case of the Martian Microbes: Mariomania, Intrinsic Value and the Prime Directive, in Schwartz JSJ and Milligan T (eds.) *The Ethics of Space Exploration* (Springer, New Yor, 2016) pp. 195–208.

Stearns PM and Tennen L, SETI, Metalaw, and Social Media, in Stearns PM and Tennen L (eds.), *Private Law, Public Law, Metalaw and Public Policy in Space* (Springer, New York, 2016) p. 161.

Suvin D, Of Starship Troopers and Refuseniks: War and Militarism in U.S. Science Fiction, Part 1, in Hassler D and Wilcox C (eds.), *New Boundaries in Political Science Fiction* (University of South Carolina Press, Columbia, 2008) pp. 115–144.

Tshisuaka BI, Pocken, in Gerabek WE et al. (eds.), *Enzyklopädie Medizingeschichte* (Walter de Gruyter, Berlin/New York, 2007) p. 1172.

Vincent RJ, *Human Rights and International Relations* (CUP, Cambridge, 2009)

Von der Dunk FG, Shaking the Foundations of the Law: Some Legal Issues Posed by the Detection of Extraterrestrial Life, in Schwartz JSJ and Milligan T (eds.), *The Ethics of Space Exploration* (Springer, New York, 2016) pp. 251–263.

Vossenkuhl W, Jenseits des Vertrauten und Fremden, in Marquard O (ed.) *Einheit und Vielfalt* (Meiner, Hamburg, 1990) p. 109.

Articles

Abney K, Ethics of colonization: Arguments from existential risk, 110 *Futures* (2019) 60–63.

Abou Yehia J and Schrogl KU, European regulation for private human spaceflight in the context of space traffic management, 66 *Acta Astronautica* (2010) 1618–1624.

Ahmed RQ et al., Emerging Trends of Space Weaponization: India's Quest for Space Weapons and Implications for Security in South Asia, 18 *Astropolitics* (2020) 158–169.

Almár I and Race MS, Discovery of extra-terrestrial life: assessment by scales of its importance and associated risks. 369 *Phil. Trans. R. Soc. A* (2011) 679–692.

Almár I, SETI terminology: Do we interpret SETI terms correctly? 68 Acta *Astronautica* (2011) 351–357.

Anderson P and Boucher A, *Starship Troopers: The PITFCS Debate, The Proceedings of the Institute for Twenty-First Century Studies* (PITFCS) No. 133, February 1960, www.panshin.com/critics/PITFCS/pitfcsintro.html.

Anton A and Schetsche M, Anthropozentrische Transterrestrik. Zur Kritik naturwissenschaftlich orientierter SETI-Programme. 15 *Zeitschrift für Anomalistik* (2015) 21–46.

Arnould J, Tele-Reality: How Space Technology Transforms Human Perceptions of Space, Time, and Self, 11 *Astropolitics* (2013) 231–237.

Arnould J, From Quarantine to Exploration: Space Agencies and the Ethical Challenge of Astrobiology, 10 *Astropolitics* (2012) 176–182.

Arun K et al., Alternative standard frequencies for interstellar communication, 18 *International Journal of Astrobiology* (2017) 209–210.

Baack B and Ray E, The Political Economy of the Origins of the Military-Industrial Complex in the United States, 45 *The Journal of Economic History* (1985) 369–375.

Baines P, Non-Offensive Defences: Space Protection Without Space-Based Weapons, 2 *Astropolitics* (2004) 149–174.

Ball J, The Zoo Hypothesis, 19 *Icarus* (1973) 347–349.

Bates H, Farewell to the Master, *Astounding Science Fiction*, October issue (1940) 58–86.

Baum SD, The far future argument for confronting catastrophic threats to humanity: Practical significance and alternatives, 72 *Futures* (2015) 86–96.

Baxter S and Elliott J, A SETI metapolicy: New directions towards comprehensive policies concerning the detection of extraterrestrial intelligence, 78 *Acta Astronautica* (2012) 31–36.

Benford J, A Drake Equation for Alien Artefacts, 21 *Astrobiology* (2021) 757–763.

Bilder RB, Editorial Comment: On the Search for Extraterrestrial Intelligence (SETI), 144 *American Journal of International Law* (2020) 87–95.

Blish J, *Beep, Galaxy* (1954).

Blount PJ, Informed consent v. ITAR: Regulatory conflicts that could constrain commercial human spaceflight, 66 *Acta Astronautica* (2010) 1608–1612.

Bohlander M and Hedayati-Kakhki M, Criminal Justice under Shari'ah in the 21st Century – An Inter-Cultural View, 23 *Arab Law Quarterly* (2009) 417–436.

Bohlander M, Of shipwrecked sailors, unborn children, conjoined twins and hijacked airplanes – Taking human life and the defence of necessity, 70 *Journal of Criminal Law* (2006) 147–161.

Bohlander M, "There is no compulsion in religion" – Freedom of religion, responsibility to protect (R2P) and crimes against humanity at the example of the Islamic blasphemy laws of Pakistan, 8 *Journal of Islamic State Practices in International Law* (2012) 36–66.

Bohlander M, Abandoning Dishonesty – A Brief German Comment on the State of the Law after Ivey, 86 *Journal of Criminal Law* (2022) 170–178.

Bohlander M, Blood Music on Darwin's Radio – Musings on Social Network Data Transparency, Cyborg Technology, Science Fiction and the Future Perception of Human Rights, *The Global Community Yearbook of International Law & Jurisprudence* (2013) 45–64.

Bohlander M, Criminalising LGBT persons under national criminal law and Article 7(1) (h) and (3) of the ICC Statute, *Global Policy* (2014) 401–414.

Bohlander M, In Extremis – Hijacked airplanes, 'collateral damage' and the limits of criminal law, *Criminal Law Review* (2006) 579–592.

Bohlander M, Joining the "Galactic Club": What Price Admission? – A hypothetical case study of the impact of human rights on a future accession of humanity to interstellar civilisation networks, 132 *Futures* (2021) 102801.

Bohlander M, Metalaw – What is it good for? 188 *Acta Astronautica* (2021) 400–404.

Bohlander M, Michael and Dawn L Rothe, "Spock was wrong" – Global Student Views on Head-of-State and Regime Assassination as a Means of Avoiding Collateral Civilian Damage in Armed Conflicts, *The Global Community Yearbook of International Law and Jurisprudence* (2012) 69–127.

Bohlander M, Murder by YouTube – Anti-Islamic Speech and Homicide Liability, 10 *Journal of Islamic State Practices in International Law* (2014) 7–42.

Bohlander M, Of Higher Intentions and Lower Expectations – A report about a failed survey project on using maqāṣid al-shari'ah as a means of comparative governance research, 2 *European Journal of Comparative Law and Governance* (2015) 187–211.

Bohlander M, Political Islam and Non-Muslim Religions – A Lesson from Lessing for the Arab Transition, 25 *Islam and Christian-Muslim Relations* (2014) 27–47.

Bohlander M, Prosecutor v. Dusko Tadic: Waiting to Exhale, 11 *Criminal Law Forum* (2000) 217–248.

Bohlander M, Sisters in Law – Using Maqāṣid al-Shari'ah to Advance the Conversation between Islamic and Secular Legal Thinking, 28 *Arab Law Quarterly* (2014) 257–277.

Bohlmann UM and Bürger MJF, Anthropomorphism in the search for extra-terrestrial intelligence – The limits of cognition? 143 *Acta Astronautica* (2018) 163–168.

Bombardelli C et al., The ion beam shepherd: A new concept for asteroid deflection, 90 *Acta Astronautica* (2013) 98–102.

Borrelli K, Between show-trials and Utopia: A study of the tu quoque defence, 32 *Leiden Journal of International Law* (2019) 315–331.

Brady JB, Justifiability of Hollow-Point Bullets, 2(2) *Criminal Justice Ethics* (1983) 9–18.

Brake M and Griffiths M, Broad horizons – SETI, SF and education, 3 *International Journal of Astrobiology* (2004) 175–181 and erratum at 333.

Brake M and Hook N, Darwin to the double helix: astrobiology in fiction, 6 *International Journal of Astrobiology* (2007) 273–280.

Brin D, A Contrarian Perspective on Altruism: the Dangers of First Contact on the IAASETI Permanent Committee, 2002, http://resources.iaaseti.org/brin.pdf.

Brown T, Revolutionizing Space Warfare: "Power Star" Space Solar Power Concept, 18 *Astropolitics* (2020) 51–72.

Bruck Syal M et al., Limits on the use of nuclear explosives for asteroid deflection, 90 *Acta Astronautica* (2013) 103–111.

Burchell MJ, W(h)ither the Drake equation? 5 *International Journal of Astrobiology* (2006) 243–250.

Caballero A, An approximation to determine the source of the WOW! Signal, 23 *International Journal of Astrobiology* (2022) 129–136.

Calvo P and Trevawas A, Cognition and intelligence of green plants: Information for animal scientists, 564 *Biochemical and Biophysical Research Communications* (2021) 78–85.

Carnelli I, Editorial, Planetary Defence Conference 2011, Bucharest, Romania, 90 *Acta Astronautica* (2013), 1–2.

Carrigan Jr, RA, Is interstellar archaeology possible? 78 *Acta Astronautica* (2012) 121–126.

Carson HL, The Trial of Animals and Insects – A Little Known Chapter of Mediæval Jurisprudence, 56 *Proceedings of the American Philosophical Society* (1917) 410–415.

Chatterjee P, Legality of Anti-Satellites Under the Space Law Regime. 12 *Astropolitics* (2014) 27–45.

Chela-Flores J, Testing evolutionary convergence on Europa, 2 *International Journal of Astrobiology* (2003) 307–312.

Ćirković MM, Astroengineering, Dysonian SETI, and naturalism: A new Catch-22, 152 *Acta Astronautica* (2018) 289–298.

Ćirković MM, Post-postbiological evolution? 99 Futures (2018) 28–35.

Ćirković MM, Space colonization remains the only long-term option for humanity: A reply to Torres, 105 *Futures* (2019) 166–173.

Cockell CS, 'Astrobiology' and the ethics of new science, 26 *Interdisciplinary Science Reviews* (2001) 90–96.

Cohen E, Law, Folklore and Animal Lore, *Past & Present* No. 110 (1986) 6–37.

Coletta D, Space and Deterrence, 7 *Astropolitics* (2009) 171–192.

Collins P and Autino A, What the growth of a space tourism industry could contribute to employment, economic growth, environmental protection, education, culture and world peace, 66 Acta Astronautica (2010) 1553–1562.

Consolmagno GJ, Astronomy, Science Fiction and Popular Culture: 1277 to 2001 (and Beyond), 29 *Leonardo* (1996) 127–132.

Corcos C, Visits to a Small Planet: Rights Talk in Some Science Fiction Film and Television Series from the 1950s to the 1990s, 39 *Stetson Law Review* (2009) 183–246.

Correll JT, The Neutron Bomb, *Air Force Magazine* (2017), www.airforcemag.com/article/the-neutron-bomb/.

Correll R, Military Space Cooperation: Aligning the Balance of Power and Building Common Interest, 2 *Astropolitics* (2004) 133–147.

Cowie C, 2021. The 'Oumuamua Controversy: A Philosophical Perspective, 5 *Nature Astronomy* (2021) 526–527.

Coyle P and Rhinelander J, Space Weapons: Alternatives for Today, 2 *Astropolitics* (2004) 201–213.

Crim BE, "A World That Works": Fascism and Media Globalization in Starship Troopers. 39 *Film & History* (2009) 17–29.

Crim BE, The Intergalactic Final Solution: Nazism and Genocide in Paul Verhoeven's Starship Troopers, 28 *Holocaust and Genocide Cinema* (2010) 104–115.

Davies PCW and Wagner RV, Searching for alien artifacts on the moon, 89 *Acta Astronautica* (2013) 261–265.

De la Torre GG, Toward a new cosmic consciousness: Psychoeducational aspects of contact with extraterrestrial civilizations. 94 *Acta Astronautica* (2014) 577–583.

De Magalhaes JP, A direct communication proposal to test the Zoo Hypothesis, 38 *Space Policy* (2016) 22–26.

De Visscher A, Artificial versus biological intelligence in the Cosmos: clues from a stochastic analysis of the Drake equation, 19 *International Journal of Astrobiology* (2020) 353–359.

De Vladar HP, The game of active search for extra-terrestrial intelligence: breaking the 'Great Silence', 12 *International Journal of Astrobiology* (2013) 53–62.

Defferard F, Star Trek: paradigme juridique et laboratoire du droit, 45 *Revue Générale du Droit* (2015) 613–635.

Delgado López L, Predicting an Arms Race in Space: Problematic Assumptions for Space Arms Control, 10 *Astropolitics* (2012) 49–67.

Deming D, Do Extraordinary Claims Require Extraordinary Evidence? 44 Philosophia (2016) 1319–1331.

Denning K, Unpacking the great transmission debate, 67 *Acta Astronautica* (2010) 1399–1405.

DeVito CL, Getting off planet, 110 *Futures* (2019) 54–55.

DeVito CL, On the Meaning of Fermi's paradox. 106 *Futures* (2019) 21–23.

Dick SJ, Anthropology and the Search for Extraterrestrial Intelligence: An Historical View. 22 (2) *Anthropology Today* (2006) 3–7.

Dinzelbacher P, Animal Trials: A Multidisciplinary Approach, 32 *The Journal of Interdisciplinary History* (2002) 405–421.

Döbler NA, The Concept of Developmental Relativity: Thoughts on the Technological Synchrony of Interstellar Civilizations, 54 *Space Policy* (2020) 101391.

Dominik M and Zarnecki JC, The detection of extra-terrestrial life and the consequences for science and society, 369 *Phil. Trans. R. Soc. A* (2011) 499–507.

Douglas B, Too Attentive to our Duty: The Fundamental Conflict Underlying Human Rights Protection in the UK, 38 *Legal Studies* (2018) 360–378.

Dowd A, Strategic Ignorance and the Search for Extraterrestrial Intelligence: Critiquing the Discursive Segregation of UFOs from Scientific Inquiry, 16 *Astropolitics* (2018) 75–95.

Doyle LR et al., Information theory, animal communication, and the search for extraterrestrial intelligence, 68 Acta Astronautica (2011) 406–417.

Drake F, Reflections on the Equation, 12 *International Journal of Astrobiology* (2013) 173–176.

Drake F, The search for extra-terrestrial intelligence, 369 *Phil. Trans. R. Soc. A* (2011) 633–643.

Einstein A, Zur Elektrodynamik bewegter Körper, 17 *Annalen der Physik* (1905) 891– English translation at www.fourmilab.ch/etexts/einstein/specrel/www/.

Elliott J and Baxter S, The DISC Quotient, 78 *Acta Astronautica* (2012) 20–25.

Elliott J, A human language corpus for interstellar message construction, 68 *Acta Astronautica* (2011) 418–424.

Elliott J, A post-detection decipherment strategy, 68 Acta Astronautica (2011) 441–444.

Elliott J, A semantic 'engine' for universal translation, 68 *Acta Astronautica* (2011) 435–440.

Elliott J, Beyond an anthropomorphic template, 116 *Acta Astronautica* (2015) 403–407.

Elliott J, Constructing the matrix, 78 *Acta Astronautica* (2012) 26–30.

Elliott J, Detecting the signature of intelligent life, 67 *Acta Astronautica* (2010) 1419–1426.

Elliott J, First stage identification of syntactic elements in an extra-terrestrial signal, 68 *Acta Astronautica* (2011) 389–398.

Elliott J, The filtration of inter-galactic objets trouvés and the identification of the lingua ex machina hierarchy, 68 *Acta Astronautica* (2011) 399–405.

Engler JO and von Wehrden H, 'Where is everybody?' An empirical appraisal of occurrence, prevalence and sustainability of technological species in the Universe, 18 *International Journal of Astrobiology* (2019) 495–501.

Fasan E, Discovery of ETI: Terrestrial and Extraterrestrial Legal Implications, 21 *Acta Astronautica* (1990) 131–135.

Fasan E, Legal Consequences of a SETI Detection, 42 *Acta Astronautica* (1998) 677–679.

Fidler DP, The Artemis Accords and the Next Generation of Outer Space Governance, Council on Foreign Relations, 2 June 2020, www.cfr.org/blog/artemis-accords-and next generation-outer-space-governance.

Findlay R and Eßmann O, A space-based mission to characterize the IEO population, 90 *Acta Astronautica* (2013) 33–40.

Forgan DH and Elvis M, Extrasolar asteroid mining as forensic evidence for extraterrestrial intelligence, 10 *International Journal of Astrobiology* (2011) 307–313.

Forgan DH et al., Rebuttal to: 'Deconstructing the Rio Scale: problems of subjectivity and generalization', 18 *International Journal of Astrobiology* (2019) 492–493.

Forgan DH et al., Rio 2.0: revising the Rio scale for SETI detections, 17 *International Journal of Astrobiology* (2019) 336–344.

Forgan DH, A numerical testbed for hypotheses of extraterrestrial life and intelligence, 8 *International Journal of Astrobiology* (2009) 121–131.

Forgan DH, Predator-prey behaviour in self-replicating interstellar probes, 18 *International Journal of Astrobiology* (2019) 552–561.

Forgan DH, Spatio-temporal constraints on the zoo hypothesis, and the breakdown of total hegemony, 10 *International Journal of Astrobiology* (2011) 341–347.

Forgan DH, The Galactic Club or Galactic Cliques? Exploring the limits of interstellar hegemony and the Zoo Hypothesis, 16 *International Journal of Astrobiology* (2017) 349–354.

Foster C et al., Mission concepts and operations for asteroid mitigation, involving multiple gravity tractors, 90 *Acta Astronautica* (2013) 112–118.

Freudenthal H, Logica als methode en als onderwerp, 35 *Euclides* (1960) 241–255.

Galbraith J, United States Creates the U.S. Space Command and the U.S. Space Force to Strengthen Military Capabilities in Space, 114 *American Journal of International Law* (2020) 323–326.

Gale J et al., Will recent advances in AI result in a paradigm shift in Astrobiology and SETI?, 19 *International Journal of Astrobiology* (2020) 295–298.

Garrett MA, SETI reloaded: Next generation radio telescopes, transients and cognitive computing, 113 *Acta Astronautica* (2015) 8–12.

Gartrelle GM, Unknown caller: can we effectively manage the announcement of discovery of extraterrestrial life? 14 *International Journal of Astrobiology* (2015) 577–587.

Genta G, Private space exploration: A new way for starting a spacefaring society? 104 *Acta Astronautica* (2014) 480–486.

Gibbings A et al., Experimental analysis of laser ablated plumes for asteroid deflection and exploitation, 90 *Acta Astronautica* (2013) 85–97.

Gifford J, The Nature of "Federal Service" in Robert A. Heinlein's Starship Troopers, 1996, http://www.nitrosyncretic.com/rah/ftp/fedrlsvc.pdf.

Gindilis LM and Gurvits LI, SETI in Russia, USSR and the post-Soviet space: a century of research, 162 Acta Astronautica (2019) 1–13.

Girgen J, The Historical and Contemporary Prosecution and Punishment of Animals, 9 *Animal Law Review* (2003) 97–133.

Gleeson PK, Perspectives on Space Operations, 5 *Astropolitics* (2007) 145–172.

Gleiser M, From cosmos to intelligent life: the four ages of astrobiology, 11 *International Journal of Astrobiology* (2012) 345–350.

Gödel K, Über formal unentscheidbare Sätze der Principia Mathematica und verwandter Systeme, 38 *Monatshefte für Mathematik und Physik* (1938) 173–174.

Goodman AE, Diplomacy and the search of extraterrestrial intelligence (SETI), 21 Acta Astronautica (1990) 137–141.

Goodman AE, Diplomatic and political problems affecting the formulation and implementation of an international protocol for activities following the detection of a signal from extraterrestrial intelligence, 21 *Acta Astronautica* (1990) 103–108.

Gorove S, On the Threshold of Space: Toward a Cosmic Law, 4 *New York Law Forum* (1958) 305–328.

Gross M, Listen out for life, 25 *Current Biology* (2015) 1151–1153.

Grundmann JT et al., Probes to the inferior planets – A new dawn for NEO and IEO detection technology demonstration from heliocentric orbits interior to the earth's? 90 *Acta Astronautica* (2013) 129–145.

Haley AG, Space Law and Metalaw – A Synoptic View, *Harvard Law Record*, November 8, 1956.

Haqq-Misra J et al., Searching for technosignatures in exoplanetary systems with current and future missions, 198 *Acta Astronautica* (2022) 194–207.

Haqq-Misra J et al., The benefits and harm of transmitting into space, 29 *Space Policy* (2013) 40–48.

Haqq-Misra J, Funding the Search for Extraterrestrial Intelligence with a Lottery Bond, 51 *Space Policy* (2020) 101230.

Harp GR et al., Radio SETI observations of the interstellar object 'OUMUAMUA, 155 *Acta Astronautica* (2019) 51–54 and erratum at 167 *Acta Astronautica* 483.

Harris AW et al., The European Union funded NEOShield project: A global approach to near-Earth object impact threat mitigation, 90 *Acta Astronautica* (2013) 80–84.

Harrison AA, Fear, pandemonium, equanimity and delight: human responses to extra-terrestrial life, 369 *Phil. Trans. R. Soc. A* (2011) 656–668.

Harrison AA, The Search for Extraterrestrial Intelligence: Astrosociology and Cultural Aspects, 9 *Astropolitics* (2011) 63–83.

Hatfield P and Trueblood L, SETI and democracy 190 *Acta Astronautica* (2021) 596–603.

Hearsey CM and Pass J, Astrosociology, 9 *Astropolitics* (2011) 1–5.

Hearsey CM, The Nexus between Law and Astrosociology, 9 *Astropolitics* (2011) 28–38.

Hebert KD, Regulation of Space Weapons: Ensuring Stability and Continued Use of Outer Space, 12 *Astropolitics*: 1–26.

Hegel GFW, Aufsätze aus dem *Kritischen Journal der Philosophie* (1803) 463.

Hein A and Baxter S, Artificial Intelligence for Interstellar Travel, 72 *JBIS* (2019) 125–143.

Heller R, Decryption of messages from extraterrestrial intelligence using the power of social media – The SETI Decrypt Challenge, 18 *International Journal of Astrobiology* (2019) 296–303.

Hendlin YH, Plant Philosophy and Making Sense of Contemporary Plant Intelligence Debates, 31 *Environmental Values* (2022) 253–276.

Herzing DL, SETI meets a social intelligence: Dolphins as a model for real-time interaction and communication with a sentient species, 67 *Acta Astronautica* (2010) 1451–1454.

Hibberd A and Hein AM, Project Lyra: Catching 1I/'Oumuamua–Using Nuclear Thermal Rockets, 179 *Acta Astronautica* (2021) 594–603.

Hickman J, Problems of Interplanetary and Interstellar Trade, 6 *Astropolitics* (2008) 95–104.

Hobe S, The legal regime for private space tourism activities – An overview, 66 *Acta Astronautica* (2010) 1593–1596.

Huskisson D, Protecting the Space Network and the Future of Self-Defense, 5 *Astropolitics* (2007) 123–143.

Jakhu RS and Buzdugan M, Development of the Natural Resources of the Moon and Other Celestial Bodies: Economic and Legal Aspects, 6 *Astropolitics* (2008) 201–250.

Jakhu RS et al., Threats to Peaceful Purposes of Outer Space: Politics and Law, 18 *Astropolitics* (2020) 22–50.

Jebaria K and Olsson-Yaouzis N, A Game of Stars: Active SETI, radical translation and the Hobbesian trap, 101 *Futures* (2018) 46–54.

Ji E, What Does China Think About NASA's Artemis Accords? The Diplomat (2020), https://thediplomat.com/2020/09/what-does-china-think-about-nasas-artemis-accords/.

Jones M, 2015. Reconsidering macro-artefacts in SETI searches, 116 *Acta Astronautica* (2015) 161–165.

Kant I, *On the Supposed Right to Lie From Benevolent Motives*, 1797, Sopha Project Phil Archive, www.sophia-project.org/uploads/1/3/9/5/13955288/kant_lying.pdf.

Kaplinger B et al., Nuclear fragmentation/dispersion modelling and simulation of hazardous near-Earth objects, 90 *Acta Astronautica* (2013) 156–164.

Kayal H, HYPER-SETI – A New Way of Searching for Extraterrestrial Intelligence.–https://www.uni-wuerzburg.de/fileadmin/ifex/2019/IAC-19_A4_1_13_x48686_full_paper.pdf. – Paper given at the 70th International Astronautical Congress (IAC), Washington D.C., United States, 21-25 October 2019.

Kleinberg H, On War in Space, 5 *Astropolitics* (2007) 1–27.

Knuth KH et al., Estimating Flight Characteristics of Anomalous Unidentified Aerial Vehicles, 21 *Entropy* (2019) 939.

Korbitz A, IAC-10-A4.2.10 – Metalaw and the Need for Further Elaboration, 2010 (unpublished paper kindly provided courtesy of the author).

Korbitz A, Toward understanding the active SETI debate: Insights from risk communication and perception, 105 *Acta Astronautica* (2014) 517–520.

Korhonen JM, 2013. MAD with aliens? Interstellar deterrence and its implications, 86 *Acta Astronautica* (2013) 201–210.

Koschny D et al., Asteroid observations at the Optical Ground Station in 2010 – Lessons learnt, 90 *Acta Astronautica* (2013) 49–55.

Leeson PT, Vermin Trials, 56 *The Journal of Law & Economics* (2013) 811–836.

Lempert D, Living in Space: Cultural and Social Dynamics, Opportunities, and Challenges in Permanent Space Habitats, 9 *Astropolitics* (2011) 84–111.

Lempert D, Placing Outer Space: An Earthly Ethnography of Other Worlds, 16 *Astropolitics* (2018) 237–241.

Leonetti C, Space Bandits: The Need for Interstellar Criminal Law, *Kilaw Journal* (2019) 195–271, https://journal.kilaw.edu.kw/wp-content/uploads/2019/10/Carrie-Leonetti-.pdf.

Levin SR and Scott TW, Darwin's aliens, 18 *International Journal of Astrobiology* (2019) 1–9.

Lin P, Viewpoint: Look Before Taking Another Leap for Mankind – Ethical and Social Considerations in Rebuilding Society in Space, 4 *Astropolitics* (2006) 281–294.

Lingam M and Loeb A, What's in a name: the etymology of astrobiology, 19 *International Journal of Astrobiology* (2020) 379–385.

Losch A, Kant's wager – Kant's strong belief in extra-terrestrial life, the history of this question and its challenge for theology today, 15 *International Journal of Astrobiology* (2016) 261–270.

Louis NI and Schulze-Makuch D, The Astrobiology of Alien Worlds: Known and Unknown Forms of Life, 6 (9) *Universe* (2020) 130.

Lubin P, The search for directed intelligence, 1 REACH *Reviews in Human Space Exploration* (2016) 20–45.

Lyall F, Who is an astronaut? The inadequacy of current international law, 66 *Acta Astronautica* (2010) 1613–1617.

Machay M and Pochylá J, European Attitudes Toward Space Exploration and Exploitation, 11 *Astropolitics* (2013) 203–217.

Masson-Zwaan T and Freeland S, Between heaven and earth: The legal challenges of human space travel, 66 *Acta Astronautica* (2010) 1597–1607.

McKay CP, The search for life in our Solar System and the implications for science and society, 369 *Phil. Trans. R. Soc. A* (2011) 594–606.

McVey PJ and Melamed N, Survey of potentially hazardous object threat negation campaign options, 90 *Acta Astronautica* (2013) 22–32.

Michel P, Physical properties of Near-Earth Objects that inform mitigation, 90 *Acta Astronautica* (2013) 6–13.

Mikulak MW, Soviet Philosophic-Cosmological Thought, 25 *Philosophy of Science* (1958) 35 50.

Millera JD and Felton D, The Fermi paradox, Bayes' rule, and existential risk management, 86 *Futures* (2017) 44–57.

Mollin RA, Prime-Producing Quadratics, 104 *American Mathematical Monthly* (1997) 529–544.

Morris SC, Predicting what extra-terrestrials will be like: and preparing for the worst, 369 *Phil. Trans. R. Soc. A* (2011) 555–571.

Moynihan T, Existential risk and human extinction: An intellectual history, 116 *Futures* (2020) 102495.

Musso P, The problem of active SETI: An overview, 78 *Acta Astronautica* (2012) 43–54.

Musso P, A language based on analogy to communicate cultural concepts in SETI, 68 *Acta Astronautica* (2011) 489–499.

Muzyka K, The basic rules for coexistence: The possible applicability of metalaw for human-AGI relations, 11 *Paladyn, J. Behav. Robot* (2020) 104–117.

Nardon L, Cold War Space Policy and Observation Satellites. 5 *Astropolitics* (2007) 29–62.

Narusawa S et al., Which colors would extraterrestrial civilizations use to transmit signals?: The "magic wavelengths" for optical SETI, 60 *New Astronomy* (2018) 61–64.

Nayak M, Fighting a War in Space: The Case for a Space Innovation Force, 16 *Astropolitics* (2018) 157–173.

Neal M, Preparing for extraterrestrial contact, 16 *Risk Management* (2014) 63–87.

O'Brien D, The Artemis Accords: repeating the mistakes of the Age of Exploration, The Space Review (2020), www.thespacereview.com/article/3975/1.

Ollongren A and Vakoch DA, Typing logic contents using Lingua Cosmica, 68 *Acta Astronautica* (2011) 535–538.

Ollongren A, Large-size message construction for ETI: Inductive self-interpretation in LINCOS, 68 *Acta Astronautica* 68 (2011) 539–543.

Ollongren A, On the signature of LINCOS, 67 *Acta Astronautica* (2010) 1440–1442.

Ollongren A, Recursivity in Lingua Cosmica, 68 Acta Astronautica 68 (2011) 544–548.

Osmanov Z, On the interstellar Von Neumann micro self-reproducing probes, 19 *International Journal of Astrobiology* (2020) 220–223.

Othman M, Supra-Earth affairs, 369 *Phil. Trans. R. Soc. A* (2011) 693–699.

Pass J, Astrosociology as the Missing Perspective, 4 *Astropolitics* (2006) 85–99.

Pass J, Examining the Definition of Astrosociology, 9 *Astropolitics* (2011) 6–27.

Pass J, Inaugural Essay: The Definition and Relevance of Astrosociology in the Twenty-First Century, 2004, www.astrosociology.org/Library/Iessay/iessay_p1.pdf.

Pavelec SM, The Inevitability of the Weaponization of Space: Technological Constructivism Versus Determinism, 10 *Astropolitics* (2012) 39–48.

Penny A, Transmitting (and listening) may be good (or bad), 78 *Acta Astronautica* (2012) 69–71.

Peters T, The implications of the discovery of extra-terrestrial life for religion, 369 *Phil. Trans. R. Soc. A* (2011) 644–655.

Petit JL, Communication with aliens, as an opening of the horizon of a scientific Humanity – A philosopher's reflections, 12 *International Journal of Astrobiology* (2013) 263–270.

Pillai Rajagopalan R, The Artemis Accords and Global Lunar Governance, The Diplomat (2021), https://thediplomat.com/2021/06/the-artemis-accords-and-global-lunar-governance/.

Plowes N, 2010. An Introduction to Eusociality, 3(10) *Nature Education Knowledge* (2010) 7, www.nature.com/scitable/knowledge/library/an-introduction-to-eusociality-15788128/.

Prantzos N, A joint analysis of the Drake equation and the Fermi paradox, 12 *International Journal of Astrobiology* (2013) 246–253.

Quast PE, A profile of humanity: the cultural signature of Earth's inhabitants beyond the atmosphere, 20 *International Journal of Astrobiology* (2021) 94–214.

Rathore E and Gupta B, Emergence of Jus Cogens Principles in Outer Space Law, 18 *Astropolitics* (2020) 1–21.

Raulin Cerceau F and Bilodeau B, A comparison between the 19th century early proposals and the 20th–21st centuries realized projects intended to contact other planets, 78 *Acta Astronautica* (2012) 72–79.

Robinson GS, METALAW: From Speculation to Human*kind* Legal Posturing with Extraterrestrial Life, 2 Journal of Space Philosophy (2013) 49–56.

Rollock AE and Klaus DM, Defining and characterizing self-awareness and self-sufficiency for deep space habitats, 198 *Acta Astronautica* (2022) 366–375.

Rossana Deplano, The Artemis Accords: Evolution or Revolution in International Space Law, 70 *International and Comparative Law Quarterly* (2021) 799–819.

Rummela JD and Pugel DE, Planetary protection technologies for planetary science instruments, spacecraft, and missions: Report of the NASA Planetary Protection Technology Definition Team (PPTDT), 23 *Life Sciences in Space Research* 2019, 60–68.

Sadeh E, Viewpoint: The Evolution of Access to Space as an Idea and Technology, 3 *Astropolitics* (2005) 305–318.

Salla ME, Astropolitics and the "Exopolitics" of Unacknowledged Activities in Outer Space, 12 *Astropolitics* (2014) 95–105.

Schmidt N and Bohacek P, First Space Colony: What Political System Could We Expect? 56 *Space Policy* (2021) 101426.

Schwartz JSJ, Myth-Free Space Advocacy Part II: The Myth of the Space Frontier, 15 *Astropolitics* (2017) 167–184.

Seed D, The Course of Empire: A Survey of the Imperial Theme in Early Anglophone Science Fiction, 37 *Science Fiction Studies* (2010) 230–252.

Shapiro JA, All living cells are cognitive, 561 *Biochemical and Biophysical Research Communications* (2021) 134–149.

Shostak S, Are transmissions to space dangerous? 12 *International Journal of Astrobiology* (2013) 17–20.

Shostak S, ETI: the argument for artefact searches, 19 *International Journal of Astrobiology* (2020) 456–461.

Shostak S, Limits on interstellar messages, 68 *Acta Astronautica* (2011) 366–371.

Shoumikhin A, Russian Perspectives on the Military Uses of Outer Space, 1 *Astropolitics* (2003) 95–112.

Slobodian RE, Selling space colonization and immortality: A psychosocial, anthropological critique of the rush to colonize Mars, 113 *Acta Astronautica* (2015) 89–104.

Sommariva A, Motivations Behind Interstellar Exploration and Colonization, 12 *Astropolitics* (2014) 82–94.

Song H, Chinese Science Fiction: A Response to Modernization, 40 *Science Fiction Studies* (2013) 15–21.

Sotos GJ, Biotechnology and the lifetime of technical civilizations, 18 *International Journal of Astrobiology* (2019) 445–454.

Spacy II WL, Assessing the Military Utility of Space-Based Weapons, 1 *Astropolitics* (2003) 1–43.

Stapledon O, Interplanetary Man, 7 *Journal of the British Interplanetary Society* (1948), 213–233.

Stearns P;, SETI and Space Law: Jurisprudential and Philosophical Considerations for Humankind in Relation to Extraterrestrial Life, 46 *Acta Astronautica* (2000) 759–763.

Steinberg A, Weapons in Space: The Need to Protect Space Assets, 10 Astropolitics (2012) 248–267.

Stirn A, Wie die USA das Völkerrecht aushebeln könnten, Spektrum (2020), www.spektrum.de/news/raumfahrt-wie-die-usa-das-voelkerrecht-aushebeln-koennten/1787216.

Straub J, Application of a Maritime Framework to Space: Deep Space Conflict and Warfare Scenario, 13 *Astropolitics* (2015) 65–77.

Strzelczyk F, "Our Future – Our Past: Fascism, Postmodernism, and Starship Troopers (1997)", 15 Modernism/Modernity (2008) 87–99.

Struik PC et al., Plant neurobiology and green plant intelligence: science, metaphors and nonsense, 88 *J Sci Food Agric*, (2008) 363–370.

Suvin D, Part 2, 1975-2001: Post-Fordism, and Some Conclusions, 48 *Extrapolation* (2007) 9–34.

Szocik K and Tachibana K, Research Viewpoint: Human Enhancement and Artificial Intelligence for Space Missions, 17 *Astropolitics* (2019) 208–219.

Tarter J et al., The first SETI observations with the Allen telescope array, 68 *Acta Astronautica* (2011) 340–346.

Taylor ER, If technological intelligent extraterrestrials exist, what biological traits are de rigueur?, 17 *Life Sciences in Space Research* (2018) 15–22.

Taylor R, Coming soon to a field near you, *Physics World* (2011) 1–4.

Teodorani M, A strategic "viewfinder" for SETI research, 105 Acta Astronautica (2014) 512–516.

Teodorani M, Search for high-proper motion objects with infrared excess, 105 Acta Astronautica (2014) 547–552.

Thiemer-Sachse U, Das große Leiden Huey cocoliztli (aztekisch): das große Leiden: Zu den aus Europa eingeschleppten Seuchen, welche die Urbevölkerung Amerikas dezimierten, 2002, www.fu-berlin.de/presse/publikationen/fundiert/archiv/2002_01/02_01_thiemer_sachse/index.html.

Tipler FJ, Intelligent life in cosmology, 2 *International Journal of Astrobiology* (2003) 141–148.

Traphagan JW, Cargo Cults and the Ethics of Active SETI, 46 *Space Policy* (2018) 18–22.

Traphagan JW, Deconstructing the Rio Scale: problems of subjectivity and generalization, 18 *International Journal of Astrobiology* (2019) 463–467.

Traphagan JW, Review of Daniel Deudney, *Dark skies: space expansionism, planetary geopolitics, and the ends of humanity* (OUP, Oxford, 2020) *Space Policy* (2021) 55.

Turchin A and Denkenberger D, Global catastrophic and existential risks communication scale, 102 Futures (2018) 27–38.

Uhran B et al., Updating Planetary Protection Considerations and Policies for Mars Sample Return, 49 *Space Policy* (2019) 101322.

Usikov DA, Information and Communication Technologies (ICT) as keys to the enhancement of public awareness about potential earth impacts, 90 *Acta Astronautica* (2013) 173–179.

Vakoch DA and Matessa M, An algorithmic approach to communicating reciprocal altruism in interstellar messages: Drawing analogies between social and astrophysical phenomena, 68 *Acta Astronautica* (2001) 459–475.

Vakoch DA et al., What should we say to extraterrestrial intelligence?: An analysis of responses to "Earth Speaks", 86 *Acta Astronautica* (2013) 136–148.

Vakoch DA, A narratological approach to interpreting and designing interstellar messages, 68 Acta Astronautica (2011) 520–534.

Vakoch DA, A taxonomic approach to communicating maxims in interstellar messages, 68 Acta Astronautica (2011) 500–511.

Vakoch DA, Responsibility, capability, and Active SETI: Policy, law, ethics, and communication with extraterrestrial intelligence, 68 *Acta Astronautica* (2011) 512–519.

Vakoch DA, The art and science of interstellar message composition: a report on international workshops to encourage multidisciplinary discussion, 68 *Acta Astronautica* (2011) 451–458.

Vedda JA, Challenges to the Sustainability of Space Exploration, 6 *Astropolitics* (2008) 22–49.

Vidal C, Pulsar positioning system: a quest for evidence of extraterrestrial engineering, 18 *International Journal of Astrobiology* (2019) 213–234.

Vidaurri M et al., Absolute Prioritization of Planetary Protection, Safety, and Avoiding Imperialism in All Future Science Missions: A Policy Perspective, 51 *Space Policy* (2020) 101345.

Von der Dunk F, The Artemis Accords and the law: Is the Moon 'back in business'?, The Big Q (2020), www.thebigq.org/2020/06/02/the-artemis-accords-and-the-law-is-the-moon-back-in-business/.

Voros J, On a morphology of contact scenario space, *Technological Forecasting & Social Change* (2018) 126–137.

Weinberger R and Hartl H, A search for `frozen optical messages' from extraterrestrial civilizations, 1 *International Journal of Astrobiology* (2002) 71–73.

Wheeler E, The 'Wow' Signal, Drake Equation and Exoplanet Considerations, 67 *JBIS* (2014) 412–417.

Wie B, Hypervelocity nuclear interceptors for asteroid disruption, 90 *Acta Astronautica* (2013) 146–155.

Wilkinson D, Why Should Theology Take SETI Seriously? 16 *Theology and Science* (2018) 427–438.

Wiltsche HA, The Forever War: understanding, science fiction, and thought experiments, 198 *Synthese* (2019) 3675–3698.

Wolfe AJ, Germs in Space: Joshua Lederberg, Exobiology, and the Public Imagination, 1958–1964, 93 *Isis* (2004) 183–205.

Woodburn Hyde W, The Prosecution and Punishment of Animals and Lifeless Things in the Middle Ages and Modern Times, 64 *University of Pennsylvania Law Review and American Law Register* (1916) 696–730.

Worden PS et al., Breakthrough Listen – A new search for life in the universe, 139 Acta Astronautica (2017) 98–101.

Wortzel LM, The Chinese People's Liberation Army and Space Warfare, 6 *Astropolitics* (2008) 112–137.

Yee S, The Tu Quoque Argument as a Defence to International Crimes, Prosecution or Punishment, 3 *Chinese Journal of International Law* (2004) 87–134.

Yeomansand DK and Chamberlin AB, Comparing the Earth impact flux from comets and near-Earth asteroids, 90 *Acta Astronautica* (2013) 3–5.

Yu C and Liu J, The Dark Forest Rule: One Solution to the Fermi Paradox, 67 *JBIS* (2015) 142–144.

Zaitsev A, Classification of interstellar radio messages, 78 *Acta Astronautica* 78 (2012) 16–19.

News Media

Gorman S, Solar orbiter Ulysses ends mission after 18 years, Reuters Science News, 1 July 2009, www.reuters.com/article/us-space-solar-idINTRE5600A220090701.

Gunter J, Elon Musk: The man who sent his sports car into space, 2018, www.bbc.com/news/science-environment-42992143.

King L, Live, Stephen Hawking's Warning on Space Aliens. 2010, http://transcripts.cnn.com/TRANSCRIPTS/1004/30/lkl.01.html.

Laville S, Met police to use hollow point bullets that killed Jean Charles de Menezes, 2011, www.theguardian.com/uk/2011/may/11/met-police-hollow-bullets-menezes.

Rincon P, Stephen Hawking's warnings: What he predicted for the future, 2018 – www.bbc.com/news/science-environment-43408961.

Sample I, If aliens call, do not hold a referendum on what to do next, say Britons – www.theguardian.com/science/2019/sep/10/aliens-call-vote-referendum-britons.

Youn S, The woman who forced the US government to take UFOs seriously – www.theguardian.com/world/2021/jun/14/leslie-kean-ufo-reporter-us-government-report.

Internet Resources

Ansible, Encyclopedia of Science Fiction, http://sf-encyclopedia.com/entry/ansible.

Ansible, World Wide Words, www.worldwidewords.org/weirdwords/ww-ans1.htm.

Area 51, military installation, Nevada, United States, www.britannica.com/place/Area-51.

Arecibo Message, www.naic.edu/challenge/about-message.html.

Barack Obama Presidential Library, Letter to John Greenewald, https://twitter.com/blackvaultcom/status/1502019931382059016.

Bhathal, R, Signals From Space, www.thelivingmoon.com/43ancients/02files/SETI_LASER_like_Signal_Discovered.html.

Breakthrough Initiatives, https://breakthroughinitiatives.org/.

Breakthrough Listen, https://breakthroughinitiatives.org/initiative/1.

Breakthrough Message, https://breakthroughinitiatives.org/initiative/2.

Breakthrough Starshot, https://breakthroughinitiatives.org/initiative/3.

Breakthrough Watch, https://breakthroughinitiatives.org/initiative/4.

Burns R, *Man was made to Mourn: A Dirge*, 1784, www.robertburns.org/works/55.shtml.

Caldwell J and Kan SR, Japanese Philosophy: Giri 義理, http://kenukan.com/blog/2016/10/12/japanese-philosophy-giri/.

Centre de Données astronomiques de Strasbourg, http://simbad.u-strasbg.fr/simbad/sim-id?Ident=eps+Aur.

Director of National Intelligence, Report, Preliminary Assessment Unidentified Aerial Phenomena, https://documents2.theblackvault.com/documents/odni/DEOM-2021-00006.pdf.

Donald Rumsfeld, press conference of 12 February 2002, www.youtube.com/watch?v=REWeBzGuzCc.

Nolan G, on: Tucker Carlson, Fox News, https://youtu.be/u7cKhIJnTpo.

Dumas S, Catalogue of SETI Publications, www.academia.edu/14895760/Catalogue_of_SETI_Publications.

European Southern Observastory, Part of the Coalsack Nebula, www.eso.org/public/images/eso1539a/.

George W. Bush Presidential Library, letter to John Greenewald, https://twitter.com/blackvaultcom/status/1534242020906045441/photo/1.

IAA SETI Permanent Committee, Rio Scale Calculator, https://iaaseti.org/en/rio-scale-calculator/.

IAA SETI Permanent Committee, Rio Scale, https://iaaseti.org/en/rio-scale/.

IAA SETI Permanent Committee, The San Marino Scale, 2008, https://iaaseti.org/en/san-marino-scale/.

IAA SETI Permanent Committee – Terms of Reference, https://iaaseti.org/en/terms-reference/.

Into the Universe with Stephen Hawking, Series 1, Episode 1: Aliens, 2010, www.imdb.com/title/tt1658579/?ref_=ttep_ep1.

Liberman M, The Four Meanings of an Arabic Word, http://itre.cis.upenn.edu/~myl/languagelog/archives/003264.html.

McGill Manual on International Applicable to Military Uses of Outer Space, www.mcgill.ca/iasl/files/iasl/mcgill_manual_volume_i_-_rules.pdf.

Media in transition, Joe Haldeman (1943-), http://web.mit.edu/m-I-t/science_fiction/profiles/haldeman_index.html.

Müller, A, Auch Russlands Raumfahrtchef Rogozin äußert sich über außerirdisches Leben und UFOs, www.grenzwissenschaft-aktuell.de/russlands-raumfahrt-chef-rogozin-aeussert-sich-ueber-ausserirdisches-leben-und-ufos20220613/ (in German).

NASA Beams Beatles' 'Across the Universe' Into Space, www.nasa.gov/topics/universe/features/across_universe.html.

NASA Breakthrough Propulsion Physics Program, https://ntrs.nasa.gov/citations/19980201240.

NASA Parker Solar Probe, https://blogs.nasa.gov/parkersolarprobe/.

NASA, "Basics of Space Flight", https://solarsystem.nasa.gov/basics/.

NASA, About Astrobiology, https://astrobiology.nasa.gov/about/.

NASA, Analysis Groups (AGs), https://astrobiology.nasa.gov/analysis-groups/.

NASA, Center for Near Earth Object Studies (CNEOS), https://cneos.jpl.nasa.gov/.

NASA, NASA and the Search for Technosignatures – A Report from NASA Technosignatures Workshop, https://arxiv.org/ftp/arxiv/papers/1812/1812.08681.pdf.

NASA, Oort Cloud, https://solarsystem.nasa.gov/solar-system/oort-cloud/overview/.

NASA, The Artemis Accords – Principles for Cooperation in the Civil Exploration and Use of the Moon, Mars, Comets, and Asteroids for Peaceful Purposes, www.nasa.gov/specials/artemis-accords/img/Artemis-Accords-signed-13Oct2020.pdf.

NASA, The Nearest Neighbor Star, https://imagine.gsfc.nasa.gov/features/cosmic/nearest_star_info.html.

NASA, The Science of Star Trek, www.nasa.gov/topics/technology/features/star_trek.html.

NASA, Torino Impact Hazard Scale, https://cneos.jpl.nasa.gov/sentry/torino_scale.html.

NASA, Unidentified Aerial Phenomena Independent Study, https://science.nasa.gov/uap.

NASA, Voyager Mission Status, https://voyager.jpl.nasa.gov/mission/status/.

NASA, What is Pluto?, www.nasa.gov/sites/default/files/thumbnails/image/edu_what_is_pluto_3.png.

National Security Agency, Unidentified Flying Objects (UFOs) and Paranormal Events, www.nsa.gov/Helpful-Links/NSA-FOIA/Frequently-Requested-Information/Unidentified-Flying-Objects-UFOs/.

Natural Resources Ministry, Letter to MP Larry Maguire, www.larrymaguire.com/_files/ugd/ba2ab2_878aa8c5de7749bbb4196435c156271c.pdf.

Nemiroff R and Bonnell J, Astronomy Picture of the Day, 1996. https://apod.nasa.gov/apod/ap960630.html.

New Jersey State Police, Firearms information, Transportation and Use of Hollow Point Ammunition by Sportsmen, www.njsp.org/firearms/transport-hollowpoint.shtml.

Office of the Director of National Intelligence (ODNI), Preliminary Assessment: Unidentified Aerial Phenomena, www.dni.gov/files/ODNI/documents/assessments/Prelimary-Assessment-UAP-20210625.pdf.

Open C3 Subcommittee Hearing on Unidentified Aerial Phenomena, https://youtu.be/aSDweUbGBow.

Pass J, "What is Astrosociology?", www.astrosociology.org.

Pearson B, Where is Starman? Track Elon Musk's Tesla Roadster in Space!, www.whereisroadster.com/.

Report of scientific advisory panel on unidentified flying objects convened by office of scientific intelligence, CIA January 14–18, 1953, (The Durant report of the Robertson Panel proceedings), www.cufon.org/cufon/robert.htm

Robert A Freitas, *Xenology: An Introduction to the Scientific Study of Extraterrestrial Life, Intelligence, and Civilization,* www.xenology.info/Xeno.htm.

Stanford Encyclopedia of Philosophy, *Rights,* https://plato.stanford.edu/entries/rights/.

The Matrix Quotes, www.quotes.net/mquote/60252.

The Matrix: Laurence Fishburne: Morpheus, www.imdb.com/title/tt0133093/characters/nm0000401.

The Woomera Manual, https://law.adelaide.edu.au/woomera/.

UN Office for Outer Space Affairs, Space Law, www.unoosa.org/oosa/en/ourwork/spacelaw/index.html.

United Nations Human Rights Office, Death penalty, www.ohchr.org/EN/Issues/DeathPenalty/Pages/DPIndex.aspx.

United States Space Force, "Why do we need a Space Force?", www.spaceforce.mil/About-Us/FAQs/Whats-the-Space-Force/.

United States Space Force, Space Power, Doctrine for Space Forces, www.schriever.spaceforce.mil/Portals/17/Space%20Capstone%20Publication_10%20Aug%202020.pdf.

United States Space Force, Space-Delta-9, https://www.schriever.spaceforce.mil/About-Us/Units/Space-Delta-9/.

United States Space Force, SPD-4, www.spaceforce.mil/About-Us/SPD-4/.

United States Space Force, www.spaceforce.mil/.

US Dept of Defence, CONPLAN 8888, "Counter Zombie Dominance", US Strategic Command training exercise, 2011, www.stratcom.mil/Portals/8/Documents/FOIA/CONPLAN_8888-11.pdf?ver=2016-10-17-114016-887.

Vera C Rubin Observatory, www.lsst.org.

Weltraumkommando (Space Command), inaugurated on 13 July 2021, www.bundeswehr.de/de/organisation/luftwaffe/aktuelles/das-weltraumkommando-in-uedem-5181718.

Wow!-signal, https://de.wikipedia.org/wiki/Wow!-Signal#/media/Datei:Wow_signal.jpg.

Index

433 Eros 32

abductions 6*n*17, 26, 31*n*88
access to information 7
accession to an interstellar network of civilisations 8
actus reus 118*n*27, 123, 137
advance early warning system 154
African Charter on Human and Peoples' Rights 174*n*49
Aggression 10, 60, 76*n*42, 87, 98, 109, 109*n*5, 111, 125, 130, 143, 160, 183, 186, 189
air space 134–135
alien altruism 1, 54, 59
alien artefact 4, 15
alien decision-making 157
alien hunters 13, 166
alien spaceship 37, 76*n*43
aliens 4*n*7, 7*n*23, 15*n*10, 21*n*43, 21*n*36–39, 25*n*61, 26*n*67, 29*n*78–79, 38*n*4, 47*n*30, 51*n*46, 65, 70, 75*n*39, 76, 78–83, 89*n*86, 96, 99, 110, 117, 120, 124, 134, 166*n*16, 168, 182, 189, 193, 194
altruistic 7, 29, 58, 80, 139
American Convention on Human Rights 174
annexation 148
annihilation 70*n*17, 77, 79, 87, 88, 92, 98, 101, 118–119, 125, 137, 142, 148, 149, 189
ansible device 98
anthropocentrism 8, 21–23, 100
anthropomorphism 21*n*39, 55*n*65
Arab Charter on Human Rights 174
Area 51 237
Arecibo Message 27, 42, 237
armed hostilities 107, 108, 122, 126, 157
Artemis Accords 159*n*67–69
Artemis Programme 159
artificial intelligence (AI) 51, 80*n*60, 122*n*37, 131*n*56
artificially constructed jurisdictions 133
ASEAN Human Rights Declaration 175
Assembly of States Parties 134
asteroids 14, 20, 30, 39, 130*n*55, 145, 159
astrobiological analogs 35
astrobiology 10, 16*n*11–14, 17*n*15, 18*n*21, 23, 20*n*29, 31, 21*n*37–38, 27*n*75, 30*n*85–86, 31*n*88, 34–36, 38*n*4, 40*n*11, 41*n*14, 48*n*36, 51*n*46, 55*n*64, 58*n*74, 60*n*81–82, 67*n*2, 68*n*8, 72*n*32, 80*n*59, 131*n*56, 166*n*16
automated monitor 154
autonomous robots 128

Basic Law (*Grundgesetz*) 171
behavioural and cultural norms 157
benevolent alien hypothesis 162
benevolent aliens 70
benign contact 63
biological contamination 63, 130
biological life forms 60*n*82
biosphere 13, 132, 133
Breakthrough Enceladus 33
Breakthrough Initiatives 32
Breakthrough Listen 32*n*93
Breakthrough Message 32
Breakthrough Starshot 33*n*98, 152*n*42
Breakthrough Watch 32
bridgeheads 128

Cairo Declaration on Human Rights in Islam 174*n*46
celestial bodies 34*n*101, 44, 61, 109, 131*n*56, 158, 197, 203–205
celestial mechanics 11, 151–156, 189
cessation of hostilities 124
chain of suspicion 87
chapeau elements 111, 115
chemical or biological weapons 148
child rights 184
civil liberties 171–172
civilian populations 96, 113–115, 122–123
civilisational 18*n*23, 59, 87, 164*n*13, 170
climate change 11, 59, 146, 193
collateral damage 99, 116, 124, 172*n*34
collective consciousness 94, 98, 164, 165*n*13, 176
collectivist framework 170
colonialist 177
colonisation 13*n*3, 19, 21, 70*n*17, 71, 77, 79, 92, 102–103, 109, 133*n*62, 184
colonise 18, 165*n*14
colony ship 65
combatant 122, 143

commercial gain 133
common destiny 170–171
Communicating with ETI (CETI) 27
communication 5, 6, 10, 14*n*5, 15*n*8, 17, 20*n*29, 21*n*38, 22–23, 23*n*48, 27*n*75, 33, 38*n*4, 42, 45, 47*n*30, 32, 33, 48*n*36, 49, 54, 60*n*81, 61, 69*n*16, 73, 75, 76, 82, 85, 86, 89–96, 99, 100, 124, 132, 136, 147–148, 157, 162, 165*n*13, 166*n*16, 171, 192, 193, 201, 202
communication optimism (*Kommunikationsoptimismus*) 22
compromise 58, 64, 125, 185
conflict avoidance 10–11, 161, 189
conscience of mankind 120
contact narratives 26, 90
contact optimism (*Kontaktoptimismus*) 22
contact scenarios 5, 38, 67–105
contamination 13, 35, 64*n*100, 129–131, 205, 207
corroboration 7
cosmic sociology 86
cosmic species 1, 64, 80, 147, 156, 159, 161, 169
cosmology 18*n*21, 92
crimes against humanity 10, 11, 111, 112–115, 120, 121*n*36, 123–124, 134*n*63, 181, 183*n*66, 189
critical science fiction studies 67
crop circles 26
cross-species settings 179
cruel and degrading treatment 180–181
cultural and human rights relativism 56
customary international law 111

damage control 65, 130
death penalty 180
declaration of incompatibility 173
declarations 10, 39, 41–43, 62, 169
Deconfliction of Space Activities 159
deep space combat environment 149
deep space combat theatre 11, 189
Deep space strategy 11, 148–150, 189
deep space warfare 11, 130*n*52, 146*n*26, 147, 150–157
deep-space stationary setting 150
defence installations 151
defence strategy 5
defensive perimeter 151, 156
dehumanisation 157
dehumanised 101
democracy deficit 62
Denkverbote (intellectual taboos) 106
depersonalised threats 136
derelict space craft 37
dictatorial 91, 177
diplomatic immunity 134
diplomatic negotiations 49
diplomatic relations 124, 162
direct contact 3, 8, 18, 25, 26*n*70, 47*n*31, 49–50, 60, 61, 63, 73–74, 85, 89, 129, 168*n*22, 186–187
DISC quotient 10, 45, 48
discrimination 179, 183, 185, 206
Discriminatory intent 118–119
distant signal detection 25
dolphins 47, 54, 89
domestic jurisdictions 65
Drake Equation 8, 15–21, 30*n*86, 35, 60*n*82, 188
drones 128
due process rights 181–182
Dyson Ships 30
Dyson Spheres 30

ECREE ("extraordinary claims require extraordinary evidence") 3, 31*n*88, 106
Elements of Crimes 111
elitist system of government 101
embodiment of (ultimate) strangeness 24
enemy combatants 122
enforcement mechanisms 171–174
enslavement 57, 65, 77, 113, 114, 128, 137
equality and minority rights 179–180
equivalence to humans 120–122
erga omnes 65, 119, 187
ethical conversations 59
ethnic cleansing 99
ethnomathematics 23
EU Charter of Fundamental Rights 171
European Convention on Human Rights (ECHR) 172, 175*n*53
European Court of Human Rights (ECtHR) 173
European Space Agency (ESA) 61
evidence XII, 3–7, 11, 16, 18, 30*n*86, 31*n*88, 168*n*20
exobiology 34*n*101

exohabitat contamination 35
exolinguistics 10, 23, 45–49, 48*n*37, 189
exophilosophy 10, 49–51, 189
exoplanet XI, 20*n*33, 34*n*104, 70*n*17, 93–95, 133
exosociology 10, 49–51, 189
exotheology 10, 49–51, 189
exploitation 35, 109, 131*n*56, 133*n*62, 159, 178
extermination 58, 65, 91, 96, 102, 113, 114, 118, 119, 123, 129, 132, 149
extinction 38*n*4, 65, 91, 128–130, 137, 166*n*16
extraterrestrial civilisation (ETC) 1, 117
extraterrestrial hypothesis (ETH) 2, 26, 155*n*52, 193
extraterrestrial intelligence (ETI) 163

fair trial guarantees 136, 181
family 176, 182, 184
fascist 177–178
faster-than-light (FTL) 2, 98, 155
Fermi Paradox 8, 15–21, 26–27, 35, 38*n*4, 60*n*81, 80*n*59, 88*n*84, 166*n*16, 188
first contact 10, 25, 37–45, 58*n*73, 59, 61, 67–105, 118, 124, 125, 134, 157, 188, 192–194
fly-by 73, 153*n*45
foo fighters 26
forensic decision-making 3
forms of contact 8, 9
forms of governance 66
forms of impact 9
forms of response 9
forward operating base 128, 150
freedom of assembly 182–184
freedom of association 182–184
freedom of expression 182–184
freedom of movement 182
freedom of religion 182–184
freedom of the will 51
freedom of thought and speech 51
fundamental human ethical and legal values 8

Galactic Club XII, XIV, 8, 11, 18*n*23, 65, 84, 102–103, 163–185
generation ship 70*n*17, 118
generic fundamental rights 175
genocide 10, 65, 71*n*29, 96*n*100, 102, 111, 112, 116–119, 120–128, 132, 137, 149, 178, 183, 189, 210
geo-strategic aims 146
German Federal Constitutional Court (*Bundesverfassungsgericht*) 172
giggle factor 26, 43*n*19, 61, 80, 106, 146, 187
global disruption 140
global human position 163
global society 10, 37–45, 186, 193
Gödel's Incompleteness Theorems 24
Golden Rule 52, 55–58, 119
governmental restrictions 7
gravitational 73, 85*n*76, 99*n*107
Great Filter 162
Green Bank Conference 16
guardian civilisation 133

hardware fatigue 154
Heterotopia 169
higher-order necessities 141
high-risk 63
hive consciousness 98, 100
Hobbesian Trap 28*n*75, 38*n*4, 88, 166*n*16
Hohman Transfer 155
hostile contact 8, 10–11, 23, 63, 72, 107–160, 189
hostile encounters 65, 71
hostile environment 133
human baseline for negotiations 161
human colonial history 128–130, 150*n*34, 170
human dignity (*Menschenwürde*) 171
human ethical parameters 65
human intrusion 132
human narratives 3
human rights *acquis* 177
Human Rights Act 1998 (HRA) 172
human rights law 8, 11, 65, 168–169, 186, 189
human rights protections 163
human space weapons technology 147
humanitarian law 96
humanoid 22*n*40, 91
humans' rights 163–185
human-to-human hostilities 65
HYPER-SETI 33

IAASETI Declarations of Principles 41–43
IAASETI Permanent Committee XIII, 39, 43*n*19, 168*n*21
IAASETI Terms of Reference 43*n*19
imaginative tool 68

impact intensity 41
improper targeting 116
independence from any interplanetary supply lines 154
indifference 6, 73
individual encounter narratives 7
inferior species 156
information technology 90
information-carrying structures 45
Inner Earth Objects (IEO) 14
intent to destroy "in whole or in part" 118
inter-civilisational conversation 87
interdimensional hypothesis (IDH) 26
interhuman XIII, 54, 58, 63, 64, 84, 101*n*113, 108, 115, 125–128, 135, 137, 145, 149
inter-human international and domestic law 10
international and domestic criminal law 10, 189
international armed conflict 124–125
international core crimes 111, 189
International Court of Justice 119, 149*n*31, 210
International Covenant on Civil and Political Rights (ICCPR) 174, 175*n*53
International Criminal Court (ICC) 109–111, 181
international criminal law 8, 10, 65, 96, 109, 110–133
international relations 58, 107, 174*n*42
international tribunal 110
interspecies armed conflict 10, 96–105, 189
interspecies comity 169
interspecies comprehension 10, 89–96
interspecies conflict 10, 63, 68, 118, 124, 129, 137
interspecies environment 11
interstellar civilisational network 170
interstellar colonisation 77
interstellar criminal law 108
interstellar Darwinism 162
interstellar expansion 7
interstellar exploration 71, 81, 131*n*56
interstellar travel 5, 27, 80*n*60, 125, 144, 171
invasion 70, 76, 78, 85, 96, 97, 108, 125, 145
ius cogens 65, 119

joint identity 171
judicial enforcement mechanisms 173

Kant's Categorical Imperative 52, 55
Kuiper Belt 152

lack of preparedness 161
language construction 23
Large Synoptic Survey Telescope (LSST) 190
large-scale commission 116
law of armed conflict 8, 96, 108, 127
layers of meaning 46
legal personhood 178
legal responsibility 136
legitimate target 122
level playing field 79, 108
liability of ETI 10, 134–136
liability of humans 10, 110–134
life support systems 154
lightspeed 1, 40, 83, 153*n*44, 171
Lingua Cosmica (LINCOS) 23*n*48, 47
lingua franca 23, 48, 92
long-distance space operations 148
loss of human knowledge 154
low-probability 63, 146, 193

machine civilisations 193
Manual on International Law Applicable to Military Uses of Outer Space (MILAMOS) 63
Mayan texts 48
means of defence 125–128
membership criteria 65
mens rea 118, 121, 123, 136, 137
message from afar 25, 90
Messaging to ETI (METI) 27
metalaw XIV, 10, 13, 20*n*29, 23, 51, 52–65, 69*n*16, 98, 104, 106, 119, 141, 161, 164*n*11, 168*n*23, 173, 176, 187, 189
METI Statement 28, 88*n*83, 202–203
microorganisms 13
militarisation of near-Earth space 158
militarisation of space 80
military 7, 9, 11, 41, 63, 64, 68, 71, 76*n*42, 79, 82, 85, 88, 89, 96–101, 107*n*1, 108–109, 122, 125–127, 143, 146–159, 190, 195, 204–206
military defensive capability 146
military force 107, 109, 151
military operational planning 64
military space operations 63
military staging area 152

military violence 152
Military-Industrial Complex 100*n*109
minority rights 51, 179, 180
Moon Agreement 44, 158
moral point of departure 59
mutual lack of similarity 157
mutual strangeness 157
mutually assured destruction (MAD) 149

NASA 5*n*14, 14*n*4, 15*n*8, 22*n*39, 25*n*60, 32*n*89, 33*n*97, 34*n*101–104, 41*n*14, 130*n*54, 145*n*2, 147*n*28, 152, 159, 166*n*16, 192, 210
natural science 8, 13, 55*n*65
NEAR Shoemaker probe 32, 167*n*19
Near-Earth-Objects (NEO) 14
near-infinite regression of second-guessing 87
near-relativistic speeds 154
network regulation density 170–171
nomadic civilisation 65, 118
non-human artefact 1
non-militarisation of outer space 135
normative 8, 173
nuclear option 129–130
nullum crimen principle 136

occupation 76, 125, 128, 137, 148, 203, 207
octopuses 47, 54, 89, 95
Octospiders 74, 91, 92
Oort Cloud 152–153
operative independence from Earth 154
optical signal 3, 202
optimum launch windows 155
orbit 1, 9, 14*n*6, 32*n*89, 37, 64*n*100, 65, 73, 78–81, 96, 103, 108, 125, 130*n*52, 135, 144–148, 152, 153*n*43, 155–162, 203, 204, 206
orbital plane 151–156
osmosis effect 65
othered 101
Oumuamua 4, 31*n*87, 37, 68
Outer Space Treaty 44, 134, 158–159, 203–205

peaceful relations 125, 161
peaceful relationships with ETI 11, 161–187
peaceful use of outer space 158–160
Pentagon 139, 190*n*1
personal freedom 170, 177
personal status 184
Phaistos Disc 49
Philosophy 9, 10, 16*n*12, 23*n*46, 35, 50*n*43, 51*n*46, 52*n*51, 55*n*67, 56, 90, 94*n*95, 164*n*11, 173, 174*n*41, 175*n*54, 187
planetary defence 14*n*5, 63, 89, 145, 146, 147, 158, 186, 195
planetary gravity assist manoeuvres 153
planetary protection 14*n*4, 35, 95, 109, 130*n*54, 132*n*60
political activity 177, 178–179
political decision-makers 62, 64, 146
post-biological 58
post-detection protocols 61
power disparity 157
power politics 54, 64, 176
practical ethics 56
precautionary rules 106
pre-emptive 60, 84, 87, 88, 97, 92, 102, 108, 119, 122, 132, 149, 150, 195
pre-emptive annihilation 88, 98, 149
pre-emptive solutions 108, 195
Prime Directive 7*n*22, 11, 13, 103, 132, 156, 161*n*1
prisoners of war (POWs) 116, 126
privacy 165, 179, 182–184
prohibited weapons 116
proportionality 99, 184
propulsion technology 1, 156
protected characteristics 118
protected group 116–117
psychological aspects 156–157
psychological factors 11
public peace and safety 136
pulsar 72

radio or optical astronomy 4
radio signal 37, 45
rapid dominance 125
rational actors 58
realpolitik 54
reasonable creatures 121–122
recognition as a person before the law 177–178
regulatory spectrum 110
Reine Rechtslehre (Pure Theory of Law) 56
reliability 7, 46
Reply Protocols 42
resource exploitation 35
resource mining 132

restrictions on exercise of rights 184–185
retaliatory action 125
Richter Scale 39
right to liberty 181–182
right to life 180–181
rights hierarchies 171–174
rights-based 173, 176
Rio Scale 39, 40*n*11, 45, 200*n*2
Rio Scale Calculator 39*n*10, 40
risk and disaster management 37, 41
risk management 10, 38*n*4, 166*n*16
Roswell 26
rules of engagement 96, 137
ruse of war 140

San Marino Scale 41
Sapience 120, 122
sapient plants 93
satellites 20, 125, 135, 143, 144, 150
Science Fiction (SF) 10, 22, 51*n*46, 67–105, 145, 148, 164*n*13, 189, 194
scientific 13–36
search for extraterrestrial artefacts (SETA) 30, 167
search for extraterrestrial intelligence (SETI) XIII, 13*n*1, 42, 50*n*43, 197, 199–201
self-determination 53, 58, 178–179
self-explanatory system 24
self-replicating probes 71, 81
semantic complexity 46
semantic content 45
sentient life 94
SETI Permanent Study Group of the International Academy of Astronautics 42, 201
SETI Protocol I 41
SETI Protocol II 42
shared moral values 11
Shariah 117, 180
signal
  signal decipherability 45
  signal decipherment 10
significance of impact 45
slavery 180–181
slingshot effect 153
social constructs 117, 169
social sciences 3, 36, 50
social structure 117
soft law 62
software deterioration 154
space
  space exploration 10, 13*n*3, 15*n*8, 18*n*20, 25*n*59, 35, 50*n*43, 59, 61, 69, 95, 109, 130, 131*n*56, 132, 145, 189, 197
  space fleet 86, 95, 150
  space habitats 153
  Space law 13, 15, 50*n*43, 55, 67, 159*n*68, 198
  space opera 70, 147
  Space Policy Directive 143
  space travellers 130
  spacefaring capacities 41
  space-usable armaments 145
  special theory of relativity 156
species
  species cleansing 101
  species consciousness 1, 195
  species dominance 125
  species equality rights 179
  species identity 1, 95, 159, 177
  species memory 157
  species preservation 124, 129, 134
  species protection 133
  species-related defences 136
Star Trek 7, 13, 22, 67, 76, 81, 89*n*85, 103, 161*n*1
Star Wars 22
state or organizational policy 114, 115
state-of-nature 88
stellar engineering 105
strategic options 148
strategic parameters 11, 150–157, 189
strategy 147–157
structural understanding 45
supremacist 177
surgical warfare 108
surrender 125, 142, 148–149

tactical and operational necessities 102
tactics 147–157
technological artefact 37
technological disruption 10
technological singularity 10
terraforming 77, 79, 94, 130
territorial criminal jurisdiction 110

territorial disagreements 157
territorial sovereignty 135
theatre of combat 108
thermoethics 58
Thucydides trap 157
Torino Scale 39
Torture 142, 180–181
trained military personnel 7
transfer orbit 155
transmission pattern 45
transspecies 51
treaty enforcement 162
tu quoque 119

UFO literature 6
UFOlogists 13, 167
ultimate weapon 108
UN Charta 109
UN General Assembly 62
UN Security Council (UNSC) 109, 160, 175*n*52
Unidentified Aerial Phenomena (UAP) 26*n*63, 139*n*1
Unidentified Flying Object (UFO) 1–7
unified legal human response framework 23
unified world government 163
unilateral human response 54
United Nations 175*n*52, 202, 203–205
United Nations Office for Outer Space Affairs (UNOOSA) 14*n*6, 62
Universal Declaration of Human Rights (UDHR) 174
Universal Islamic Declaration of Human Rights 174
universal jurisdiction 135
Universal Natural History 55
unmanned probes 130
US Space Force (USSF) 142
usque ad coelum 134
USS Nimitz 4

Vera C. Rubin Observatory 190
vertical territorial expanse 134
virus 60, 141
von Neumann machines 80–81
Voynich manuscript 49

Wager 55
war crimes 10, 111, 115–116
war in space 100, 107*n*1, 126*n*48, 144*n*16
weapons development 11, 125, 144, 148–150, 189
weapons of mass destruction 99, 148, 158, 203, 204, 206
weapons technology 11, 144–147, 189
widespread or systematic attack 113, 115, 120
Woomera Manual 63, 107
world ship 68
Wow! Signal 1, 20*n*31

Xenocide 96*n*100, 119
Xenophilism 157
Xenophobism 157

www.ingramcontent.com/pod-product-compliance
Lightning Source LLC
Chambersburg PA
CBHW071226230926
51849CB00001B/43